Michael Schmidt set himself a formidable undertaking in surveying six crowded centuries of British [poetry] but his experience as poe[t,] publisher, and critic fitt[ed him for the] task. He has extended to [the whole] tradition of English poetr[y the] perceptiveness which he br[ought to] bear upon the twentieth cen[tury in] *Fifty Modern British Poets*, also in this series.

The selection is personal but not eccentric. The reader will find a predictable 'top thirty' — poets of the rank of Chaucer, Milton, or Blake. Where inclusion is less automatic, Michael Schmidt applies the criteria of intrinsic merit and importance in forming or being important within a tradition. Where a minor figure does not have an individual essay devoted to him, he may often be found, through use of the index, in another essay — Dunbar and Douglas in that on Henryson, and Carew and Suckling in that on Lovelace.

While not designed as a systematic history of poetry, the book provides many associational links which together build up a sense of the tradition: Gower and Chaucer; Raleigh and Spenser; Pope, Gay, and Swift; Wordsworth and Coleridge. Schmidt points to 'imaginative relationships' such as Keats's with his masters Shakespeare, Spenser, and Milton.

The book is further strengthened
by frequent references to critics,
themselves leading poets of their
day — notably Johnson, Coleridge,
Arnold, and T. S. Eliot. Like Eliot,
Schmidt does not hide his sense of a
cultural decline affecting all but the
peaks of poetic achievement after
about 1650.

Like other books in this series, *Fifty
British Poets 1300-1900* provides an
accessible but substantial introduction
to its subject, especially appropriate
for the basic needs of the student and
the interests of the general reader.

The Author

Michael Schmidt is the Editorial
Director of Carcanet Press, one of
the leading British poetry publishing
houses. He is also the founder editor
of *PN Review*, a magazine of new
poetry, criticism, interviews and
features and is editor of *Fifty Modern
British Poets*, also published in this
series. Michael Schmidt is Special
Lecturer in Poetry at the University
of Manchester.

A Reader's Guide to
Fifty British Poets 1300–1900

Reader's Guide Series
General Editor: Andrew Mylett

A Reader's Guide to

Fifty British Poets 1300–1900

by Michael Schmidt

Heinemann – London
Barnes & Noble – Totowa, New Jersey

Heinemann Educational Books Ltd

LONDON EDINBURGH MELBOURNE AUCKLAND HONG KONG
SINGAPORE KUALA LUMPUR NEW DELHI IBADAN NAIROBI
JOHANNESBURG KINGSTON PORT OF SPAIN

First published 1980 by Pan Books as
An Introduction to Fifty British Poets 1300–1900
in the Pan Literature Guides Series
First published in this casebound edition 1980

British Library CIP Data
Schmidt, Michael
    A reader's guide to fifty British poets,
    1300–1900. – (Reader's guide series).
    1. English poetry – History and criticism
    I. Title   II. Series
    821'.009   PR502

    ISBN 0–435–18811–9

    ISBN (USA) 0–389–20137–5

Published in Great Britain by
Heinemann Educational Books Ltd
22 Bedford Square, London WC1B 3HH
Published in the U.S.A. 1980 by
Barnes & Noble Books

Printed and bound in Great Britain by
Richard Clay (The Chaucer Press) Ltd,
Bungay, Suffolk

for Peter Jones

I should like to thank C. H. Sisson and Fraser Steel for reading a draft of this book and offering corrections and criticisms. Such errors as remain are the author's.

Contents

Introduction

General histories of poetry are more common than books such as this. I provide here a brief guide to the work of fifty poets in the period 1300 to 1900. My aim is to point general readers in the direction of the poems, giving them a few useful, I trust, tools for their own expeditions. I have tried to provide sufficient biographical detail to indicate each writer's orientation. To this I have added brief general descriptions of the work, observations on specific poems, and a selection of critical views. The views of other poets are generally the most illuminating, reflecting as they do both on the critic and the poet criticized, and contributing to that texture of relationships – enthusiasms, friendships, rivalries and polemical antipathies – which constitute a tradition. This survey is restricted to non-dramatic verse (the drama being the subject of another Guide in this series). Hence the accounts of Chapman, Marlowe, Jonson, Dryden, Gay and others are necessarily partial.

Some of these brief essays are distorted by personal preference, others by a temperamental dislike or critical distance from the poet in question. It is impossible for me to remain cool in recommending the poetry of Marlowe, Jonson, Herbert or Arnold; nor can I summon much warmth in discussing Thomson, Browning or Swinburne. Where my antipathy is strongest, I have tended to present the views of other writers to provide a corrective to my distaste.

I have in many cases attempted to give a notion of the social and religious allegiances of the poets concerned. Such allegiances had a bearing on their conception of the art of poetry itself and often were fraught with personal consequences.

Over the years, the guides I have most valued in my own reading of poetry have been Dr Johnson, Coleridge, Arnold and Eliot, men whose criticism has a civic dimension, and who were among the best poets of their age. A stimulating guide to the fourteenth and fifteenth centuries is Thomas Warton, whose *History of English Poetry* I was fortunate to acquire in the original eighteenth-century edition. Yvor Winters is a useful lamp to carry through the sixteenth and early seventeenth centuries, though one cannot entirely trust his light. There are of course many others: Dryden, De Quincey, Keats and Hopkins among them. I value too – against the current of fashion – the not always accurate but usually in a deep way *true* critical enthusiasms and revulsions of Ford Madox Ford. Among the recent poet-critics I have attended to the work of Edgell Rickword, C. H. Sisson, Donald Davie, and a number of others.

From this book emerges no theory of English poetry over six centuries, no definition of 'English' or 'British' as consistent terms; no strict pattern of trends and movements. Instead the book is – I trust – pervaded by a sense of particular voices, particular worlds, and those formative relationships between contemporaries which determine the development of a tradition: Gower and Chaucer; Raleigh and Spenser; Jonson and his 'Sons'; Pope, Gay and Swift; Johnson and Goldsmith; Wordsworth and Coleridge; Tennyson and Arthur Hallam; Hopkins and Robert Bridges. There are, too, the imaginative relationships, for example between Keats and his masters Shakespeare, Spenser and Milton; or Milton and Spenser and Chaucer. Whenever it seemed useful to do so, I have discussed the work of different poets by contrast and comparison, indicating affinities as my ear detected them. Thus the index of this volume is useful for any reader eager to pursue a poet beyond the bounds of his chapter. Chaucer, for example, is discussed with Gower in the first essay. To complete the account of Marlowe there are passages in the essays on Chapman, Donne and Rochester. Spenser and Milton refused to remain confined: they turn up everywhere, with Shakespeare, whose poems are dealt with in another Pan Literature Guide but who is inevitably a presiding figure in this volume.

The choice of the first thirty poets was easy. Many readers, however, will take exception to some of the others. Why did I choose Lovelace over Carew or Suckling? I have tried to make that clear in the essay on Lovelace. Where are the Gawain poet, the balladeers, Thomas Nashe, Arthur Golding, Michael Drayton, Fulke Greville? Where is Crashaw? Where is Clough? These are fair questions. For my part I regret the absence of Golding, Greville and Clough. I am uneasy about omitting the Gawain poet and the balladeers. I regret the necessary inclusion of Thomson, and of Swinburne and other nineteenth-century imperatives. But I chose, after the first thirty, fifteen whose work has intrinsic merit and who are important within the tradition; and five whose individual achievement may be debatable but whose importance to their successors was significant.

Anyone who asks for Dunbar and Douglas will find them dealt with at some length in the essay on Henryson. Hardy, Kipling and Housman are considered in *An Introduction to Fifty Modern British Poets*, a sequel to this volume, though written before it.

The reader will discern soon enough my partiality for the pre- and anti-Romantic poets. In reading chronologically through English poetry from the fourteenth century, I could not help sensing again a decline in poetic intelligence, in culture, beginning in the mid-seventeenth century. There are, of course, remarkable, and a few great, poets after that time, but only a very few of them have the thematic scope and stylistic balance, the natural passion and taste, which even minor poets in the earlier period possessed, once the language had been prepared.

Michael Schmidt
Manchester 1979

John Gower 1330?–1408

But wolde god that now were on
An other such as Arion,
Which hadde an harpe of such temprure,
And therto of so good mesure
He song, that he the bestes wilde
Made of his note tame and milde ...

John Gower's *Confessio Amantis* was the first English
poem to be translated into the languages of the Continent.
Long before Caxton printed it in 1483, Spanish and
Portuguese versions existed. The poem is as much a part
of the international literature of the 'clerks', with its
Latin and French affinities, as of English. Gower approached the English language tentatively, having written
his first major poem in French, his second in Latin. He
deploys English with the precision of a prose-writer, intent on his matter. He is neither formally nor thematically
inventive: he is efficient, a great virtue in a moral writer.
His work illuminates the mind and temper of his age, but
only occasionally the social reality that lent substance to
them.

Were it not for the pre-eminence of his friend Chaucer,
Gower might be regarded almost as a great poet. As it is,
he is normally dismissed as an 'also-ran'. The native rusticity of Langland and the alliterative verve of *Sir Gawain
and the Green Knight*, the formal perfection of *Pearl* and
shorter allegorical and devotional romances, assure their
place in popular esteem. Chaucer's shadow does not obscure them. But Gower is obscured, and unjustly so, for

though he lacks a native originality he – even as Langland does – tills a different ground from Chaucer's. The similarities are obvious; so too should be the thematic and technical differences. Gower's excellence is notable not in the whole *oeuvre* but in specific parts. Academic critics make a case for the aesthetic wholeness of the *Confessio Amantis*, but it is an academic, not a poetic case. The reader turns to particular stories in the poem, to 'Deianira and Nessus', 'Constantine and Sylvester', 'Pygmalion', 'Demephon and Phyllis', 'Ceix and Alceone', 'Jason and Medea', and a score or so of others, and to some of the direct statements which link story to story, as well as to the 'Prologue' and 'Epilogue', in which he sees something of the turbulent fourteenth-century England Gower sought to instruct.

A gaudily restored tomb commemorates Gower in the north aisle of the Cathedral Church of St Saviour and St Mary Overie in Southwark, near where the poet spent the last thirty years of his life. Under a stone canopy he reclines, overlooked by three allegorical angel muses, his feet resting on a benign lion, his head propped awkwardly on his three principal works: the French *Mirour de l'homme* (*Speculum Meditantis*, 1376–9), the Latin *Vox Clamantis* (*c.* 1382) and the English *Confessio Amantis* (first recension 1390, third recension 1393). The effigy portrays a tall, bearded man. He wears a long red gown embroidered with gold foliage, as though he were himself a figure out of allegory.

It is a fitting monument for a man of such imaginative and material substance. Gower came of a prominent family with estates in Yorkshire, Suffolk, Norfolk and Kent. He was born, probably in Kent, around 1330. He had the advantages that landed wealth afforded: security, leisure, and education 'liberal and uncircumscribed', as Thomas Warton says. He grew learned. Little is known of his early years. He may have received training for legal or civil office. He was certainly more than the 'burel clerk' (common clerk) he claims to be in the *Confessio*. He bought and sold estates and may have divided his time between rural and urban abodes until, in 1377, he took up residence at St Mary Overie's Priory beside the Thames, where he wrote most of his poetry. He probably helped to finance the restoration and improvement of the Priory, and he had a scriptorium where he supervised the copying of his poems.

In 1378 his friendship with Chaucer was already established, for Chaucer left him power of attorney in his affairs when he travelled abroad that year. William Warburton suggests that Gower instructed Chaucer in the new visionary philosophy of Roger Bacon. It may be that Chaucer encouraged Gower to try his hand at English verse. In 1385 Chaucer dedicated *Troilus and Criseyde* to 'moral Gower' and 'philosophic Strode'. Gower returned the compliment by dedicating the first recension of the *Confessio* to Richard II and Chaucer; but when the second and third recensions appeared, these dedications had been removed. Gower had become disaffected as regards Richard. Some critics suggest he had become estranged from Chaucer as well and identify passages in the *Canterbury Tales* which seem critical of some of Gower's moral beliefs.

Originally, the prologue of the *Confessio* told of a meeting on the river between poet and King. The King asked the poet to write 'some newe thing' for him. Despite ill-health, the poet promised to oblige 'for king Richardes sake', to provide 'wisdome to the wise/And pley to hem that lust to pleye'. But in the second recension Henry of Lancaster is mentioned, and the third recension is dedicated to the future King, who rewarded Gower with an ornamental collar. When Henry was crowned, he awarded Gower two pipes of Gascony wine per annum, and Gower's later Latin poems and French *ballades* were for the delight of the strong king, whose laureate the old poet became. He deserted Richard because Richard proved an ineffectual monarch.

Gower's recorded marriage in 1398, when he was well

into his sixties and perhaps suffering from failing eye-sight, may have been a second marriage. He died in 1408.

For three centuries he had his champions among poets and critics. Skelton said his 'matter was worth gold' – praising, as Gower would have wished, the content of his work. He appears as the moralizing chorus in Shake-speare's *Pericles*, and Shakespeare used him in shaping some of his plots. Ben Jonson in his *English Grammar* cites Gower more often than any other writer as a model of correctness. But gradually his hold on readers weak-ened. He is now sadly confined for the most part to students of Middle English. He should be given back to a wider audience.

Coleridge describes nicely the state of the English language when, at the age of sixty, Gower began the *Confessio*: 'In the days of Chaucer and Gower our language might ... be compared to a wilderness of vocal reeds, from which the favourites only of Pan and Apollo could construct even a rude Syrinx; and from this the con-structors alone could elicit strains of music.' Gower re-jected the native accentual and alliterative verse, preferring (as Chaucer before him) metrical composition. The *Confessio* is composed entirely in iambic tetrameter couplets. What makes Gower's art compelling is the free-dom with which he handles so narrow and potentially tedious a measure. Take these lines from 'Pyramus and Thisbe':

The pomel of his swerd to grounde
He sette, and thurgh his herte a wounde
He made up to the bare hilte:
And in this wise himself he spilte
With his folhaste and deth he nam;
For sche withinne a while cam,
Wher he lai ded upon his knif.
So wofull yet was never lif
As Tisbee was, whan sche him sih:
Sche mihte noght o word on hih

Speke oute, for hir herte schette,
That of hir lif no pris sche sette,
Bot ded swounende doun sche fell.

The couplet is capable of great flexibility. In this passage
it forces the reader on: the ear requires that rhyme and
rhythm be resolved, while the mind requires syntactical
resolution. When the ear is satisfied, the need to complete
the sense compels us forward; and when sense is complete, the ear insists that we continue and complete the
metrical phrase. The enjambements are managed to
dramatic effect.

Gower's French *Speculum Meditantis* is in octosyllabics
arranged in eight-line stanzas which produce a calculated
symmetry over 32,000 lines. It is an allegory which, in
Warton's words, illustrates the 'general nature of virtue
and vice, enumerates the felicity of conjugal fidelity ...
and describes the path which the reprobate ought to pursue for the recovery of divine grace'. It includes a gene-
alogy of sin and a catalogue of vices and virtues, pre-
figuring the *Confessio* in metre and in structural elements. The Latin *Vox Clamantis* which Gower wrote next
was less deliberate and literary in conception, composed
under the pressure of social circumstance, among other
events the Peasants' Revolt, and it is more impassioned
and historical in character. It is a dream fable, like the
Confessio. In its seven books of elegiacs it sets out to
illustrate how irresponsible action at every level leads to
social apocalypse.

From these poems emerges a politics and morality no
less compelling for being traditional. Sisam curtly summarizes Gower's famous moral matter: to avoid the seven
deadly sins in their five subsidiary classifications and to
'keep your degree without presuming'. There is more to
it than that. Gower was a descriptive moralist, not an
innovator (except in his leniency over incest). He believed
as others believed and his poems took shape around the
facts of his beliefs. His task was to deepen, not to alter,

moral attitudes. He recognized that individual identity depended upon religious belief and on a structured and secure society. His identity was threatened when church and state were threatened. For the good of England he advocates a strong monarchy and an honest church. In Richard he renounces not monarchy but a brittle monarch.

As a poet he seeks illumination from precedent, as a lawyer might do. Men were once candid: 'Of mannes herte the corage/Was shewed thanne in the visage.' Language was close then to its meanings, not inflated or distorted by metaphor and hyperbole. 'The word was lich to the conceite/Withoute semblant of deceite.' Today, even the church is at fault: 'For if men loke at holy cherche,/Betwen the word and that thei werche/Ther is a full gret difference'; and elsewhere, 'For now aday is many on/Which spekth of Peter and of John/And then-keth Judas in his herte.' Gower seems to propose an aesthetic here to which he adheres in his plain, even style that draws aside from the age in which 'stant the crop under the rote'.

The convention of the poem is courtly love, the theme civic love and order, conceived hierarchically: 'For alle resoun wolde this,/That unto him which the heved is/The membres buxom scholden bowe.' In the failure of love and order the church is again implicated: 'In to the swerd the cherche keie/Is torned, and the holy bede/Into cursinge.' Man is responsible for this fallen state, hence moral instruction is necessary: 'the man is overal/His oghne cause of wel and wo.' It is a remarkably uncompromised intelligence which can write, 'who that lawe hath upon hande,/And spareth for to do justice/For merci, doth noght his office.' The wheel of fortune is a figure Gower uses with somewhat mechanical gusto.

The *Confessio* drew on Gower's French and Latin work and on the traditions that had nourished them. As a poetic convention, the confession had a long history, with its perennial source in the *Consolation of Philosophy* in which Boethius, condemned to death, confesses to and is consoled by Philosophy, in verse and prose. Chaucer translated this work as *Boece*. Gower and Chaucer both used (and Chaucer in part translated) the *Romance of the Rose*, the French poem which established and ironically qualified the courtly love conventions. It is a large and disorderly masterpiece, composed by two men with contrasting temperaments. As a formal model, it is disastrous.

The direct and courtly tone of the *Confessio* is due in part to the fact that the poem was intended for reading aloud. The poem aims to entertain and inform. The encyclopaedic pretensions of this as of other mediaeval romances (particularly the *Romance of the Rose*) mean that there is considerable extraneous matter, inert chunks of lore and information which retard the confession and diffuse the concentration – such as it is – that the poem achieves.

The 'Prologue' is a telling comment on the age, passing in review state, church and commons. From this turbulent world we retreat to Book One. Since the poet cannot put the world to rights, he declares, he will speak of love. The convention is introduced. It is May. Amans (the speaker) tells us his condition: 'For I was further fro my love / Than Erthe is fro the hevene above.' Falling asleep, he sees Venus, complains to her, and she summons her priest Genius to hear his confession. Thus the framework for the eight books of tales and lore which follow is established. Amans confesses, Genius questions him closely and with his tales illustrates the categories of sin, asking Amans to declare his guilt or innocence. At the end of eight books comes the 'Epilogue', delivering us back to England and the 1390s.

The *Confessio* has meanings on many levels. It has a literal, didactic and allegorical design. The melancholy irony at the heart of the poem is that Amans has been virtuous by default. He is old. C. S. Lewis reads the poem as 'Love cured by Age', 'Passion at war with Time'; but since the Love is not very credible nor the Passion very violent, perhaps we should see it as Will controlled by

Resoun, the essential civic theme in all Gower's poetry.

Amans has a voice as well as an unhappiness. He delivers much of the best verse, speaking with melancholy directness. For example, he remembers taking his lady into chapel on his arm:

Thanne is noght al mi weie in vein,
Somdiel I mai the betre fare,
When I, that mai noght fiele hir bare,
Mai lede hir clothed in myn arm:
Bot afterward it doth me harm
Of pure ymaginacioun;
For thanne this collacioun
I make unto miselven ofte,
And seie, 'Ha lord, hou sche is softe,
Hou sche is round, hou sche is smal!
Now wolde god I hadde hire al
Withoute danger at mi wille!'

C. S. Lewis justly calls Gower 'our first formidable master of the plain style' – but unlike the Augustans, 'noble rather than urbane'.

For all his virtues Gower has a vice which sets him far below Chaucer. He works out the overall form of his poem mechanically, not imaginatively. It is finally a collection of good and dull fragments awkwardly linked by the confessional material. Even within the tales there is a lack of formal tact. The morals are often not contained in the narrative but appended at the end, in the conventional manner, and many of the morals hardly suit the tales they conclude.

At its best, Gower's is an art which, as Lewis says, does not presume to more knowledge than it has. More than once he says of a character, 'He thoghte more than he seide.' Gower can be thrifty, trusting to transitive verbs, to movement and action rather than description. The focus on observable fact is the essence of a moral art. There is little imagery or decoration.

Gower's and Chaucer's difference of approach is illustrated by a comparison between Gower's 'Tale of Florent' and Chaucer's 'Wife of Bath's Tale', both of which recount the same story: Florent's imposed task of discovering 'What alle wommen most desire'. Chaucer's tale is told in 407 rhymed pentameters, Gower's in 455 rhymed tetrameters. Chaucer's tale is more complex in the telling: it emanates from the Wife and reflects her character and meanings, not Chaucer's. She weaves Arthurian motifs into her tale, giving it colour and visual substance. For her, Florent's sin against love is rape. How different is the moral Florent Gower presents, a man who has slain his foe and been taken prisoner by his foe's relations: for Gower Florent is no sinner but an exemplum of honour tried. Gower does not linger over any but morally significant detail – for instance the physical ugliness of the crone Florent must marry in order to learn the answer to his appointed question and save his honour and his neck. His is a drama of motive, conscience and action. The Wife of Bath's version is primarily an entertainment, and hardly a moral one. Gower's tale is psychologically more credible, morally sounder, and more dramatic than the Wife of Bath's, though less appealing on the surface. Chaucer's artistic superiority is exemplified in the Wife's interweaving of plots which Gower treats separately. Yet in the 'Tale of Florent' Gower gives rein to his verses with stark, impressive effect. When Florent at last beds his hideous wife, before she turns into a beautiful young woman, the moment is rendered in two lines worthy of Shakespeare: ' "For now," sche seith, "we ben both on." / And he lay stille as any ston.'

With Chaucer, allegorical personification gives way to characterization. With Gower there is only a tendency in this direction, for his art is not able readily to engage the world in which the poet lives: it is tentative, cautious, abstract; even as he had been cautious in composing in the language of his country. But the 'Prologue' and

'Epilogue' relate to his actual world, and there is audible – inevitably in the work of so humane an intelligence – in the best tales and in the words of Amans the tones of some of the finer voices of his time.

William Langland 1331?–1399?

'Bi Cryste,' quod Conscience tho, 'I will bicome a pilgryme,
And walken as wyde as al the worlde lasteth,
To seke Piers the Plowman ...'

Piers Plowman, one of the most popular poems of its
time, surviving in over forty manuscripts from the fifteenth century, was lost from sight in the late sixteenth
and re-emerged only in the late eighteenth century.
Warton helped to restore it to the conscious tradition in
the 1770s. It has not lacked readers since.

William Langland himself is almost an anonymous
poet. His name may not have been William. Warton calls
him *Robert* Longlande, following Robert Crowley who
first printed the poem in 1550. His name may not have
been Langland, either. He may have been born about
1331, possibly out of wedlock, in Cleobury Mortimer,
Shropshire, or in Shipton-under-Wychwood, Oxfordshire,
or in Somerset, Dorset or Devon, where Langland connections exist. Chambers constructs a plausible hypothetical biography, diverging from Skeat's equally credible
hypotheses. The poet tells us he was 'put to school' and
received a clerical education, possibly at Malvern Priory,
where he was made a clerk or scholar. This theory nicely
accommodates the Malvern references in the poem. He
was certainly a *poeta doctus*, and his great poem is littered
with scholastic digressions and embellishments.

The first (A) text of the poem dates from about 1362.
Shortly afterwards the poet settled in London, in

Cornhill, with – he tells us – his wife Kitte and daughter Calote. In 1376 the second (B) text was begun. It is generally held to be poetically the best. The third (C) text was composed between 1392 and 1398. If all three texts were by the same man, the poem was virtually the work of a lifetime. Langland may have composed 'Richard the Redeles' in 1399. Thereafter he disappears.

In the poem we meet a tall poet – 'Lange Wille' he was nicknamed (as George Gascoyne was called 'Long George'). He probably took minor orders but because of his marriage failed to ascend in the church hierarchy. He may have suffered great poverty, earning his keep by – in Coghill's words – 'saying prayers for people richer than himself', and perhaps copying legal documents. The poem attests to his close knowledge of courts, lawyers and legal procedures. Suitably proud, he shows himself reluctant to defer to lords, ladies and other social superiors unless he thinks they merit his deference. His 'I' is vigorous and masculine – one might say 'modern' – in comparison with Gower's and Chaucer's *personae*.

In *Piers Plowman* – its full title is *The Vision of William about Piers the Plowman and the Vision of the Same about Do-Wel, Do-better, and Do-Best* – we must picture the poet as striding in threadbare garb through the streets of London (for London is the principal setting), with his eyes wide open and his conscience constantly stung and amazed by what he sees. He is the first of our reformer poets, a visionary but not a revolutionary. Skeat quotes Marsh's admirable description of the poem in *Origin and History of the English Language* (1862): 'It was a calm, allegorical exposition of the corruption of state, of the church, and of social life, designed, not to rouse the people to violent resistance or bloody vengeance, but to reveal to them the true causes of the evils under which they were suffering, and to secure the reformation of those grievous abuses.' It was then – and it is now – fashionable to convert Langland into another sort of radical. But he was as disgusted as most of his contemporaries at the Wat Tyler uprising; he was a devout Catholic and a royalist. Those poets who learned from him – for example the anonymous author of 'Piers Plowman's Crede' – were decidedly Wycliffite in conviction, and John Ball in his famous letter (1381) appears to be referring to the poem when he incites the people of Essex to insurrection. The poem was put to use – but not exactly the use Langland intended.

Coghill's description of Langland's form underlines this point: 'The form of the poem is a series of visions of the Kingdom of England and the Kingdom of Heaven, and how to reach the one from the other.' The visions are various but the purpose is single. In the metamorphosis of Piers himself the single purpose is revealed. He first appears, well into the poem, as a plowman, representing the common laity; then as a priest; and finally as a Bishop – with St Peter and his papal successors. '*Petrus, id est Christus.*' Piers is exemplary, and in his developing example we read an indictment of those who fail to follow him.

The three texts of the poem differ widely one from another. The A Text is a rough and vigorous 2,500 lines. The B Text runs to three times that length, with many more Latin quotations, less urgency and more detail. The chief additions are a lament upon the death of the Black Prince, the events of 1377 (the last year of Edward III's reign) and the Commons' dissatisfaction with the Duke of Lancaster. Like a sermonizer, Langland takes his text and develops it. He chooses a verse from Ecclesiasticus, '*Vae terrae ubi rex puer est.*' The fable of the Belling of the Cat (represented, incidentally, on one of the misericords at Malvern Priory) is first included here. The C Text is digressive and diffuse and much longer than A and B. Divided into chapters called Passus, there are ten devoted to Piers the Plowman, seven to Do-Wel, four to Do-Better, and two to Do-Best – twenty-three in all. It was this text which was printed in 1550.

Ford Madox Ford's impression of the poem is partial but illuminating. It has, he says, 'the air of having been written in a place of public assembly. As if, while he wrote, individuals came up and whispered into his hooded ear: "Don't forget the poor cooks," or: "Remember the hostelers," or: "Whatever you do, don't forget to expose the scandalous living of the lousy friars."' And no one is forgotten: 'Kokes and her knaves crieden, "hote pyes, hote!/Good goos and grys go we dyne, gowe!"' One can hear similar demotic strains in Swift and Gay, each vocation acknowledged in its own idiom. In part the public tone is due to Langland's didactic method, with its affinities with the sermon tradition, explaining the unfamiliar through the familiar. Chaucer has tales, Gower has legends, and Langland has homilies.

Verse form sets Langland apart from Chaucer and Gower. So too does the directness of his didacticism. His detail is more literally drawn, but his characterization is more typical, than Chaucer's. For him more than for Chaucer social conduct is a dimension of spiritual conduct. Langland uses the dream convention to pass into a real world from the partial, semblant secular world; to pass into truth – a passage which is beautifully symbolized in the 'Prologue' where, by the stream, he first falls asleep:

And as I lay and lened and loked in the wateres,
I slombred in a slepyng, it sweyued so merye.
    Thanne gan I to meten a merueilouse sweuene,
That I was in a wildernesse wist I neuer where;
As I bihelde in-to the est an hiegh to the sonne,
I seigh a toure on a toft trielich ymaked;
A depe dale binethe, a dongeon there-inne,
With depe dyches & derke and dredful of sight.
A faire felde ful of folke fonde I there bytwene,
Of alle maner of men, the mene and the riche,
Worchying and wandryng as the worlde asketh ...

Langland's poem allegorizes from the outset. Men in the fair field of the world make their way either to the tower of truth or to the dungeon. His vision includes the social, moral and spiritual world.

A pull of opposites coordinates the poem: between the tower and the dungeon, Christ and Anti-Christ, good and bad shepherd. Langland wrote in a tradition characterized by structural expansiveness, digression and inconclusiveness. This is the poem's virtue and its vice, for it includes *longueurs* as well as fascinating detail.

Langland allegorizes. Allegory presents various levels of meaning at one time and requires intuitive and analytical comprehension. It is the quintessential mediaeval Christian form, resting in a belief that the Creator can be perceived through his creation, that every created thing signifies in relation to the Creator and to the created things about it. The poet's task is to witness beyond the particulars of his experience to what underlies them, their significance in a wider scheme. C. S. Lewis describes this as 'rendering imaginable what was before only intelligible'. Chaucer's secular allegory works on three levels: a literal; a 'parable-sense' (Coghill's phrase), transferring meaning to the present world; and a moral sense. In Langland there is a fourth level, the anagogical, which (Coghill again) 'adumbrated the spiritual world of being'. A consistent allegorical interpretation – if not experience – of the whole poem should be possible.

Taking the B Text as our poem, *Piers Plowman* is in four parts. First we witness the world of human transactions and meet Piers. Debates and trials are enacted, involving among others Holy Church and Lady Meed, supported by lesser allegorical figures, especially the Seven Deadly Sins. Here is Avarice:

He was bitelbrowed and baberlipped also,
With two blered eyghen as a blynde hagge;
And as a lethern purs lolled his chekes,
Well sydder than his chyn thei chiveled for elde;
And as a bondman of his bacoun his berde was bidraveled.

With a hode on his hed, a lousi hatte above,
And in a tawny tabarde of twelve wynter age,
Al totorne and baudy and ful of lys crepynge ...

Appropriately we focus on mouth and eyes: we see them
and we see what they mean. Avarice is not a seductive sin:
he is like an old hoarding hag, cheeks like a purse, beard
like a bondman. Visual and moral detail are conveyed
simultaneously.

The first part ends with a general decision to make a
pilgrimage to St Truth, and Piers, a ploughman, offers to
serve as guide, provided the pilgrims first help him to
finish harrowing his land. After further complications,
the poet wakes up. In the second part of the poem he reflects on his vision. Piers returns in the third part, and
gradually the poem builds beyond its theological to its
spiritual climax, the evocation of God as man in the
Incarnation, Crucifixion and descent into Hell. The final
part tells of Christ's triumph over sin and death, and our
possible triumph through Christ and his authority vested
in Peter (now Piers). The poem resolves not in triumph
but in a determination to seek the exalted Piers, after
Holy Church has been besieged by Anti-Christ. The unresolved dialectic can be solved only by individual conscience and effort.

What at once attracts and repels Warton and other
readers is Langland's verse form and language, his refusal
to avail himself 'of the rising and rapid improvements of
the English language'. He adapts the unrhymed alliterative versification of the older tradition, 'a capricious sort
of metre', Warton calls it. 'But this imposed the constraint
of seeking identical initials, and the affectation of obsolete English, by demanding a constant and necessary departure from the natural and obvious forms of expression,
while it circumscribed the powers of our author's genius,
contributed also to render his manner extremely perplexed, and to disgust the reader with obscurities.' Critic-
ally, Warton is right, but he may err in his philology, since

Langland uses a vocabulary every bit as riddled with Norman French and 'new words' as Chaucer's. This indicates what wide currency that vocabulary had, and how little Chaucer was the inventor of our language.

Despite its apparent freedom, the verse form is constricting. Gower wrung a variety of paces and syntactical licences from his metrical couplets. In the accentual alliterative line of Langland, with its varying number of syllables but constant number of stresses, a strong caesura is required at mid-line; there is seldom a run-on rhythm or cadence, the syntax is repetitive in its constructions. It is a bunched poetry, even when used with such freedom as Langland's. There are compensating advantages, chiefly the accentual poet's ability to vary the language register abruptly, and to excellent effect. One fascination of Langland's verse is the number of voices it accommodates, from the cries of street-vendors and the exclamations of the poor to the honeyed words of Lady Meed and the eloquence of moral lawyers. The Latin tags add a further register: ' "What lorde artow?" quod Lucifer, "quis est iste?"/"Rex Glorie" the lighte sone seide.' Langland further elaborates the texture of his poem with repeated words, internal assonance and rhyme, and other verbal devices which contribute to the rhetorical effect. Despite an apparent homeliness, this most English of poems is in no sense a crude production.

Like Gower, Langland is a moralist who would have us study his matter, not his manner. He seeks to portray not only the world, but the truth as well. Today, with Gower, he seems to have subsided and become a subject for academic study. But he is a man speaking not only to professors but to men. His poem is only secondarily a 'literary text'. Its primary purpose is to teach, and it has much beyond its morality to make known. It reveals its *milieu* and age even in the terms in which it addresses it.

Geoffrey Chaucer 1340?–1400

... kis the steppes, where as thou seest pace
Virgile, Ovide, Omer, Lucan, and Stace.

'The English Tityrus', 'the well of English undefiled',
Spenser called him; 'O reverend Chaucer, rose of rethoris
all', was Dunbar's tribute; and Skelton's:

Chaucer, that famous clerk
His termes were not dark,
But pleasant, easy, and plain;
No word he wrote in vain.

Matthew Arnold missed in him the very highest poetic
seriousness, but knew the value of 'his large, free, simple,
clear yet kindly view of human life'; also, 'He gained the
power to survey the world from a central, a truly human
point of view.' Of course there are dissenting voices, among
them Abraham Cowley's. He described Chaucer as 'a dry,
old-fashioned wit, not worth reviving'.

Better poets continued to disagree. Dryden 'modernized' Chaucer and wrote one of the first great English
essays in literary criticism in large part about him. Wordsworth, too, 'modernized' him. Few English poets before
the First World War were entirely free of a debt to him.
As Dryden says, 'he is the father of English poetry', whom
he venerated as the Greeks did Homer. 'Spenser more than
once insinuates, that the soul of Chaucer was transfused
into his body; and that he was begotten of him two

hundred years after his decease. Milton has acknowledged to me, that Spenser was his original.' Thus Dryden establishes Chaucer's place as a patriarch.

Geoffrey Chaucer was born in London around 1340. His father was one of a prosperous line of vintners. Well placed as the Chaucers were with regard to the court, they remained a merchant family, and despite aristocratic patronage Geoffrey Chaucer was never assimilated into courtly life, nor did he – as Gower tended to do – stand aloof from his world.

He may have been educated at St Paul's cathedral school. It is unlikely that he attended university, though he was a member of the Inns of Court, and as a young man was probably fined two shillings for beating a Franciscan friar in Fleet Street. At the age of nineteen he served with the English army in France. He was captured near Rheims and later ransomed. Some critics believe that, during his captivity, he translated part of the *Romance of the Rose*, his *Romaunt of the Rose*. Chaucer's version, perhaps only in part his, runs to 7,700 lines as compared with the more than 22,000 lines of Guillaume de Lorris's and Jean de Meung's composite original. It embodies the lore and many of the literary conventions of courtly romance: the dream, the allegorical garden, the cardboard personifications. The latter part of the original includes satire on women, the church and the established order. Such satire struck a responsive chord in Chaucer.

In 1367 Edward III granted him – *dilectus vallectus noster* – a pension of twenty marks a year, which was later increased. Around this time he married Philippa, and it is thought to have been an ideal match. He undertook various embassies for the King. Most important for his poetry were those of 1372 and 1378 to Italy, where he acquainted himself at first hand with Italian literature and met some of the leading writers, among them (perhaps) Boccaccio and Petrarch. He also took Dante's poetry to heart.

He was made Controller of Customs and Subsidy of

Wools, Skins and Hides in the Port of London in 1374. Evidently he was a man of trust who generally seems to have served well. After 1378 most of his public services were performed in England. He lived for a time in Kent where around 1386 he began seriously planning his *Canterbury Tales.*

He served as Clerk of the King's Works in 1389 and was more than once beaten and robbed in the London streets. He left Works for Forestry – he was appointed deputy forester of a royal forest in Somerset – in 1391, an appointment renewed in 1398, possibly as a sinecure. His patron during these years was Henry, Earl of Derby, later Henry IV, whose patronage may have been desultory, for there is some evidence in the poems – 'Envoy to Scogan' and 'Complaint to his Purse' – that Chaucer may have suffered poverty in his later years. Henry did give him a purple robe trimmed with fur. In 1400 Chaucer died and was buried in Westminster Abbey.

'The ideal career for a writer was that of Chaucer,' Ford Madox Ford wrote. 'As a young man he was a fighter and, as that, taken prisoner in battle, and so occupied himself in his cell with the translation of a world masterpiece. By birth he was a vintner and thus knew, not as a newspaper reporter, but as a practitioner, how trade went. Then he is a diplomat engaged in the delicate negotiation of marrying kings' sons to princesses; then a place-man in such an office that its duties could be performed by deputies. So he had leisure to write, out of the fullness of his real human contacts, things to please.' It is a fair, if not perfectly accurate, account of how Chaucer, without Langland's religious fervour or Gower's courtly didacticism, came to develop his humane, inclusive poetry. 'Through all the words of Chaucer there reigns a cheerfulness, a manly hilarity, which makes it almost impossible to doubt a correspondent habit of feeling in the author himself,' wrote Coleridge. Chaucer was undisturbed by religious zeal, happily sceptical of the refinements of court.

Critics tend to place Chaucer's work in three periods,

the French, the Italian, and the mature. The French period includes the *Romaunt of the Rose* (pre-1373) and the *Book of the Duchess* (1369), a consolatory romance for John of Gaunt on the death of Blanche, his first wife. It develops techniques and figures adapted from the *Romaunt*. Its octosyllabic couplets resemble Gower's; but Chaucer's poem keeps close to a single subject. Indeed the poem illustrates a crucial difference between Chaucer and Gower. Gower is consciously encyclopaedic, inclusive by design; Chaucer is inclusive by nature. His verse is more integrated than Gower's because the human and poetic context of his poems admits more *more* economically and naturally. Allusion and illustration were a poetic means, not a poetic end. So too his morality is more often implicit in his poems than appended to them. The *Book of the Duchess* foreshadows much that is to come, even as it adapts French conventions: the dream framework, the garden, personification, confession, allegory, May mornings and the hunt. What makes it distinctly Chaucerian is the genuine human grief and sympathy expressed at the end, acknowledging the impotence of consolation. The expression of this grief depends upon the creation of two credible human figures, the poet and the mourner. ' "She ys ded!" "Nay!" "Yis, by my trouthe!"/"Is that youre los? Be God, hyt ys routhe!" '

In the same poetic form Chaucer wrote his ambitious *House of Fame* (*c.* 1380). The poem is more controlled in pace, with a new eloquence borrowed in part from Dante, passages of whose *Divine Comedy* are translated and adapted. The Italian poem may have suggested the general direction of Chaucer's unfinished or truncated poem. It belongs to the second or 'Italian' period. A love-vision, it incorporates a number of love stories, much French material, an abridgement of the *Aeneid*, and other matter – too much, in truth, to add up to a whole. It has a touch of the eclecticism of Gower, but its manner is humorous, and the unity it does possess is of tone. From love his attention turns to fame. There may be a measure of autobiography in the narrator's boredom with his routine 'reckonings', his mundane job. There is a vivid portrait of the bookish poet who goes home after work, ignores his neighbours and 'domb as any stoon/Thou sittest at another book/Tyl fully daswed ys thy look'. The talking eagle who snatches the poet away to the House of Fame is a charming creation.

Chaucer began experimenting with the pentameter probably in *Anelida and Arcite*, a short unfinished poem which is also his first in stanza form. In *The Parliament of Fowls* we meet the mature Chaucer, employing the stanza he deployed so expertly in *Troilus and Criseyde*: seven pentameter lines rhymed ababbcc. *The Parliament*, like the earlier long poems, is a love-vision. It is also a bird and beast fable, pointing towards the 'Nun's Priest's Tale' from the *Canterbury Tales*. The poet reads, falls asleep and has his vision with all the conventional appurtenances. Unlike the earlier poems, this one has no established source. It fuses elements from Latin, French and Italian works into an original whole. It includes more direct social satire than Chaucer had practised hitherto, allegorical satire rising out of the conflict between the 'gentil' birds and the 'cherles', or common birds.

The opening lines are among the best-known in Chaucer's work. The craft he speaks of in the first line is not poetry, as some who quote it out of context assume, but love:

> The lyf so short, the craft so long to lerne,
> Th'assay so hard, so sharp the conquerynge,
> The dredful joye, alwey the slit so yerne:
> Al this mene I by love, that my felynge
> Astonyeth with his wonderful werkynge
> So sore, iwis, that whan I on hym thynke,
> Nat wot I wel wher that I flete or synke.

> For al be that I knowe nat love in dede ...

His professed ignorance of love-craft and his desire to

learn from books and dreams rather than from action in the field contribute to the humour of this and other poems by Chaucer. The volume he read before this particular dream was the apocryphal Ciceronian *Somnium Scipionis*, that classic which is neglected today but which had an importance for mediaeval writers almost as great as Boethius's *Consolation of Philosophy*.

In *The Parliament* Chaucer again reveals his power to *visualize*, something given only at rare moments to his contemporaries, who can evoke detail but not context. He would attribute this power to his reading of past classics. He always stresses the derivative nature of his work. He is a re-teller of tales: 'out of olde bokes, in good feyth/Cometh al this new science that men lere.' He is, of course, not merely a regurgitator. He assimilates and re-tails past knowledge in present terms. Selection and collection are preliminary acts to creation. In *The Legend of Good Women* he makes the point the other way round: 'And if that olde bokes weren aweye,/Yloren were of remembraunce the keye.' Translation and creation go hand in hand. He chooses, participates in the text, adapts, prunes and patches it.

Troilus and Criseyde, written between 1380 and 1385, is Chaucer's greatest finished poem, the outstanding verse narrative in the English language. Boccaccio's *Il Filostrato* suggested the story, and Chaucer's telling of it in five books improved upon the plot and characterization of his original, providing it with philosophical and dramatic coherence and a fully visualized setting. The Chaucerian theme of predestination has important aesthetic consequences. If the poem began as allegory, however, it soon outgrew its beginnings. Here the woodenness of Chaucer's earlier presentation of figures has softened into a kind of realism which we do not find again in English poetry before Marlowe. The characters may be to some extent representative, but they are not stylized.

In *Troilus and Criseyde* the plot has few surprises. The poet tells us the outcome in the opening passages: 'The double sorwe of Troilus', 'Fro wo to wele, and after out of joie', and as early as line 55 we are prepared for Criseyde's bad faith: 'the double sorwes here/Of Troilus in lovynge of Criseyde,/And how that she forsook him ere she deyde.' It is not the working of the plot but the philosophical process of predestination and the motive and development of character we are to watch. In the fifth book the poet insistently intervenes, to hold our sympathies at bay so that we can judge his characters fairly. They have grown too big for the moral clarity he seeks. Criseyde is too plausible, too beguiling. And yet we do keep a certain distance. The poet uses various devices to make sure we do.

He insists, even as he makes Troy visible before us, that it is remote in history, a different world altogether. In book two he labours the point. It is not he, the poet, who recommends courtly morality. It is his original. But just as languages change, so customs do, and 'sondry ben usages' in love. The poet presents not a morality but a philosophy.

The time element is treated in such a way as to enforce a critical distance from the action and to illustrate the philosophical theme. The facts of the story are foreknown and static. The narration is not linear but descriptive, turning back on itself, allowing lacunae in sequence. Thus Chaucer exemplifies the theme in the very presentation of factual detail. The poet stops and starts the action, accelerates and brakes, lingers when we would have him hurry and hurries when we would have him stay. This is a technique Chaucer uses in 'The Knight's Tale' as well, leaving Palamon and Arcite 'ankle deep' in blood while he visits another part of the story. Our perspective becomes inclusive, as Troilus's does when his 'lighte goost' escapes from his body and ascends to the seventh sphere, from which cold altitude he regards the vanity of earth.

There are two time schemes. One is plainly chronological, the other seasonal. It is April in the first book, May (appropriately) in the second and third; book four takes place three years later, and it is autumn; book five passes in a cold season. This poetic chronology provides imagery and a satisfying cycle, an additional unity. With autumn the tone of the narration begins to change.

The philosophical theme is proven by certain facts in the narrative. Dreams never lie: Troilus's dream of the boar and Criseyde's of the eagle are symbolically true. Pandarus who, like Criseyde's turncoat father, is an astrologer, foresees what is to be and catalyses it. His foreknowledge is great. At one point the poet tells us, 'But God and Pandarus wist al what this ment.' Only the lovers lack foreknowledge.

Criseyde, when she falls in love, wonders 'Who yaf me drynce?' She is natural and passionate, her virtue pragmatic. We learn little of her past except that she has been widowed. Her father's treachery has made her presence in Troy precarious. Pandarus advises her to love Troilus in part to protect herself. All these facts tend a little to exculpate her.

If Criseyde is natural and active once she has been aroused, Troilus the knight and warrior, in matters of love proves phlegmatic and philosophical. Just when we expect his heart to break, he launches into Boethian lectures on predestination: 'For al that comth, comth by necessitee;/Thus to ben lorn, it is my destinee.' When he first falls in love his response is not virile and eager but passive and reflective.

The word 'think' is associated almost exclusively with Criseyde. Talking is the prerogative of Troilus. Action characterizes Pandarus. These are, despite the particularity of characterization, their generalized modes of being. To this extent Chaucer's characters are clauses in a thematic argument.

It is the narrator (not to be confused with 'Chaucer himself') who changes most during the course of the poem. Criseyde's infidelity is well prepared. But the narrator, who at the outset is merely an innocent servant of the servants of Venus – a sort of Pandarus himself – is overcome by his story. He tries to draw positive morals from it; it defeats him. He interrupts the story to pre-empt our objections. In the end, with the same pity Dante evinces for Francesca, he lets Criseyde go. His moral condemnation is reluctantly absolute. He admits pathetically, 'Men seyn, – I not, – that she yaf hym hire herte.' 'Hym' is of course Diomede. At the end of the last book the embittered narrator stands before us as moralist, pointing young people towards heaven. All his efforts to keep us at a moral distance from the story have snared him in it.

Chaucer's scenes are visualized; but he can make emotions and abstractions accessible to the senses as well by a skilful use of metaphor, usually homely in origin. When Troilus loves, his heart like a loaf of bread begins to 'sprede and ryse', suggesting nourishment, leavening. Better still is Criseyde's memory of Troy, which Chaucer compares to a knotless thread drawn through her heart painlessly – she has forgotten.

The language is fully transitive. Characters fight, touch, kiss, embrace. The dialogue is colloquial and dramatic. Pandarus reports to his niece from the battlefield: 'There nas but Grekes blood, – and Troilus.' The pause is masterly, providing the most effective hyperbole in the poem.

Chaucer develops an overall symmetry or architecture in the poem, balancing scene against scene and linking, by a deft reiteration, passages in different books. This patterning begins in the very stanza form. Normally the pivot of the stanza is in the fourth line, the centre. The language builds up to it, then changes tone or direction into the final couplet. The pivot can be the whole line, a word, or a subject and verb carefully prepared for. In book two, we read Pandarus's subtle exhortation:

Now, nece myn, the kynges deere sone,
The goode, wise, worti, fressche, and free,
Which alwey for to do wel is his wone,
The noble Troilus, so loveth the,

That, but ye helpe, it wol his bane be.
Lo, here is al! What sholde I moore seye?
Do what your lest, to make hym lyve or deye.

There at the stanza's heart is 'Troilus, so loveth,' preceded by his virtues and followed by his desires. The language climbs smoothly to subject and verb, then stutters down in short, uneven, tentative phrases that are all insinuation and instigation. It is the same organization as in the opening stanza of *The Parliament of Fowls* quoted above.

There is, further, Chaucer's mastery of the enjambement. One example must suffice, Troilus's declaration:

But fro my soule shal Criseydes darte
Out nevere mo ...

Is 'darte' a noun? 'Out' comes at the head of the line with the emphasis of a verb. It becomes a preposition only in retrospect. It is 'darte out', no talk of darts but of mingled souls; yet the suggestion of the dart remains.

After *Troilus and Criseyde*, Chaucer's next production, *The Legend of Good Women* (c. 1385) looks more minor than it is. It is Chaucer's penance, exacted by the God of Love, for his defamation of women in *Troilus and Criseyde*: he must write of 'Cupid's saints'. It is another love vision, most original and interesting in its Prologue, where the daisy undergoes her memorable metamorphosis into that most faithful of Trojan women, Alceste.

Apart from minor and miscellaneous work, Chaucer's last great poem, from what critics call his third or 'mature' period, is the *Canterbury Tales*. I cannot do better than transcribe some of Dryden's comments in his great Preface to *Fables Ancient and Modern*. He set out to translate 'some of the *Canterbury Tales* into our language as it is now refined'. 'Chaucer, I confess, is a rough diamond, and must first be polished ere he shines.' Dryden's polish is less effective than his Preface.

Chaucer respected the 'dignity of the subject', adopting

the right register of language for each speaker, high and low, especially in the Prologue and the linking passages. Dryden praises the vividness of the portrayals: 'All the pilgrims in the *Canterbury Tales,* their humours, their features, and the very dress, [I see] as distinctly as if I'd supped with them at the Tabard in Southwark.' The breadth of Chaucer's direct knowledge and observation is formidable. 'He is a perpetual fountain of good sense; learned in all sciences; and therefore speaks properly on all subjects. As he knew what to say, so he knows also when to leave off; a continence which is practised by few writers.' The accuracy of literal detail impressed Dryden too. 'Chaucer followed nature everywhere; but was never so bold to go beyond her.' In their scope the *Tales* reveal 'a most wonderful comprehensive nature', a breadth of learning and social vision, despite what the Roman Catholic Dryden sees as a slight Wycliffite blemish in his thought – revealed perhaps in the 'Parson's Tale', though certainly not stridently.

The *Canterbury Tales* is an anthology of narrations of various kinds set in the broader framework of a pilgrimage. The tales are told by specific characters, to pass the time on their journey from Southwark to Canterbury. Our first interest is in the pilgrims, introduced in the 'Prologue', one of Chaucer's most original pieces, evoking first a season, then a place, then a motive for the gathering of pilgrims, and then the pilgrims themselves, in order of social eminence. The range is wide: a knight at the top, a ploughman at the bottom, and in between representatives of the church in its various manifestations, a shipman, a cook, a franklin, a widow, and so on. The host at the Tabard, where they congregate, becomes their master of ceremonies and accompanies them on the journey.

Since the work is incomplete, the sequence of tales, which was to include four by each pilgrim, exists only in extended fragments. Nonetheless, rivalries and friendships develop; surrounding the drama of each tale is the larger drama of the story-tellers, who reveal themselves in their prologues, and whose tales as often as not provide a window onto their enthusiasms and hostilities. Thus 'The Knight's Tale' (one of Chaucer's earlier compositions, placed in the mouth of the gentle knight) is obliquely answered by the Miller's obscene but delightful tale, which in turn gives offence to the Reeve and provokes from him a further low tale.

'The Knight's Tale' introduces most of the themes that come to dominate the rest of the tales: love, marriage, justice, predestination, and others. It is the courtly, civic and philosophical opening of the pilgrimage which is crowned with the tedious theological didacticism of 'The Parson's Tale', and ends in Chaucer's recantation of all but his moral works: the translation of Boethius, the legends of saints, homilies, moralities and devotions. Between Knight's and Parson's stretch the other tales, twenty-four in all, but not all complete.

Chaucer's women are among his best creations. Criseyde, his most complete and complex woman, is his chief triumph. But in the *Tales* there are others. The Prioress is one, a woman who faints at the sight of blood, but mothers her puppies and feeds them meat and swoons if one of them dies. She combines courtliness with her easy religious vocation: *amor vincit omnia* is her motto. She suffers from a frustrated desire to be a mother. Hence her dogs and her tale about the murder of a child. Chaucer realizes her physically and psychologically. Her charming hypocrisies endear her to us.

More deeply realized is the Wife of Bath. Her Prologue, for which no source has been traced, and her Tale express rather than reflect her character. Her syntax, her face, her clothes, her stars, her past, all particularize her. Her dress is out of fashion: it is the fashion of her youth, her better years. She introduces her five husbands. Her vitality makes us forgive her numerous sins. Opposite to her, and hostile to her, is the repugnant Pardoner; she, the insatiable, throbbing but sterile woman faces in him the impotent sterile man.

Chaucer is 'the father of English poetry' for two reasons. The first is technical: he adapted continental forms and evolved a relaxed and comprehensive style distinctly English despite its pedigree; he enriched the vocabulary of poetry; and he introduced through translation and adaptation the great Latin, Italian and French poets into English. The second reason relates to the first. In his powerful and original – but not eccentric – style Chaucer provided not only a formal model but a thematic one as well. He brought England into the new English poetry. Langland had portrayed London, but his was a highly moralized metropolis, presented in the spirit of didactic documentary. Chaucer introduced the diversity of English character and language, of English society at large. He had themes rather than polemics. His eyes were mild and unclouded. Gower wrote from books. Chaucer started writing from books, but the world took over his verse.

Robert Henryson ?–1508?
and the 'Scottish Chaucerians'

To cut the winter nicht and mak it schort,
I tuik an quair, and left all uther sport,
Written be worthie Chaucer glorious,
Of fair Creisseid, and worthie Troylus.

The Scottish poet William Dunbar pays tribute to
Chaucer, Gower and Lydgate in 'The Golden Terge':

Your angel mouthis most mellifluate
Our rude langage has clere illumynate,
    And fair ourgilt oure speche, that imperfyte
    Stude, or your golden pennis schupe to wryte:
This ile before was bare and desolate
    Off rethorike or lusty fresch endyte.

Robert Henryson and, less generously, Gavin Douglas
acknowledge a similar debt. They have been called 'Scottish Chaucerians'. It is a title they invited and to some
extent deserve. A number of Scottish critics overstress, for
nationalistic reasons, the Scottishness of phrasing in
Henryson and Dunbar. Though their very different
languages admit dialect elements, neither poet consistently adopts an historical, spoken Scottish idiom. Each
employs 'an artificial, created, "literary" language, used,
for almost a century, by writers of very different locality
and degree, with an astonishing measure of uniformity',
as H. Harvey Wood stresses. The debt to Chaucer is
crucial, especially for Henryson. Only Douglas finds it

necessary to call the language he uses 'Scots', to distinguish it from the tongue of the 'Inglis natioun'. Before his time, 'Scots' was used with reference to the Celtic language of the Highlands.

Henryson's fame rests, first of all, on his *Testament of Cresseid*, which 'completes' Chaucer's *Troilus and Criseyde* and is one of the great moral romances of the fifteenth century. Sir Francis Kinaston in 1640 gave a sour account of Henryson's purpose: 'he learnedly takes upon him in a fine poetical way to express the punishment and end due to a false unconstant whore.' The poem is more humane and moral than this suggests. Henryson wrote other poems as well, notably the *Moral Fables* which set him among the few major fabulists in our literature.

Little is known of Henryson's life, less even than of Langland's. Kinaston says he was 'sometime chief school-master in Dunfermling' and adds that he was 'a learned and witty man'. He further records the only anecdote we have about the poet: 'being very old he died of a diarrhoea or flux', to which he appends a 'merry' if 'un-savoury' tale. When the physician despaired of his patient's life, an old witch came to the bedside and asked Henryson if he would be cured. She indicated a 'whikey tree' in his orchard and instructed him to walk about it three times, repeating the words: 'whikey tree whikey tree take away this flux from me.' Henryson was too weak to go so far. Pointing to an oak table in his room, he asked her, 'gude dame I pray ye tell me, if it would not be as well if I repeated thrice theis words oken burd oken burd garre me shit a hard turd.' The woman departed in a rage and in 'half a quarter of an hour' Henryson was dead.

H. Harvey Wood prepared the 1933 edition of Henryson's *Poems and Fables*. He claims his poet to be the greatest of the Scottish *makars*. It is a judgement I share. Henryson is not so startling a technician as Dunbar, though he is expert within his range. He lacks Dunbar's eccentricity. What he possesses is a humane imagination well beyond Dunbar's reach, and a wealth of particular observations of detail and human conduct greater than Dunbar's. Dunbar is 'a poet', always anxious to prove it; Henryson is a moralist who writes poems. Dunbar is *literary*; and he has a following among poets. Henryson is an illustrator of common truths and a story-teller using verse as his medium, and appeals to a wider audience. Dunbar is a poet of abrupt changes of tone. Henryson can manage such changes, but is capable of subtler modulations as well.

Modulations take various forms in his work. In the *Testament*, they are emotional: the progress of Cresseid, of her father Calchas, and of Troilus himself, correspond to changes in the moral argument which rhythm and diction substantiate. A clearer example is to be found in the fable entitled 'The Preaching of the Swallow'. The seasonal stanzas move from a Spring of lush, latinate and aureate diction to a thoroughly native diction, bristling with consonants, as the year moves into the harshnesses of Winter. Henryson is closer to the alliterative tradition than is sometimes acknowledged. In descriptive passages as well as in passages of action he sometimes employs the 'rim ram ruf' with gusto and authority, normally in such instances adapting a monosyllabic vocabulary almost without Latinisms. Hence to his Chaucerian techniques he adds resources from the older alliterative tradition. Chaucer was the principal resource for his verse, but not an invariable model.

The tradition of allegory remained vital in fifteenth-century Scotland. Henryson is a better moral allegorist than Gower because, though he appends a moral to his fables and other poems, the poetry substantiates and embodies the moral drawn. One feels again and again the informing presence of Dante in Henryson's verse. Sometimes the echo is so unmistakably Dantescan that one wishes Henryson had done with the *Commedia* what Gavin Douglas did with the *Aeneid*. Take, for example, the prologue to the fable of 'The Lion and the Mouse'.

The poet in sleep is visited by his master Aesop. He is at once inquisitive and respectful:

'Displease you not, my gude maister, thocht I
Demand your birth, your facultye, and name,
Quhy ye come heir, or quhair ye dwell at hame?'

'My sone' (said he), 'I am off gentil blude,
My native land is Rome ...'

The clarity of the exchange is exemplary. Also, like Dante, Henryson selects his metaphors exactly, and his diction is often subtly mimetic, as in 'The Harrowis hoppand in the saweris trace'. This is in the same spirit as the language of William Barnes.

We cannot but think of Dante in 'Orpheus and Eurydice', in which Henryson sends Orpheus to an underworld not pagan but very like Hell. Orpheus allows himself (as we sometimes wish Dante could) certain merciful liberties with the damned. He plays his instrument so that the waters are still and Tantalus can drink; briefly Tityrus is relieved of agony. Though it is a Hell in which all are dying 'and nevirmoir sall de', Orpheus cannot resist brief acts of charity. It is the same pitying charity which Henryson evinces in the *Testament* both for Cresseid and for Troilus.

The *Testament* grows out of Chaucer's poem, an extraordinary fact since *Troilus and Criseyde* is so complete and so Chaucerian that it seems immutable. Henryson's poem is different in temper, but the gap is only a little greater than that between Marlowe's and Chapman's passages in *Hero and Leander*. In the midst of winter Henryson, who presents himself as an old man, takes down Chaucer's poem to while away the night. Both the seasonal setting and the narrator's age are appropriate to the poem's theme. What happened to Cresseid? he asks himself. He answers the question: Diomede cast her off, she went home to her father Calchas who received her with love as a returning prodigal. She visited Venus's temple to pray, but in her prayer she railed against Cupid and Venus. She fell asleep and dreamed that those gods summoned their peers to try her. Saturn, the judge, an old and repellent figure, found her guilty and Cynthia, the moon, struck her with a leprosy. Waking, Cresseid found the dream to be true. She departed, disfigured and lamenting (in nine-line stanzas which contrast with the Chaucerian seven-line stanzas of the rest of the poem), drawing a partial moral:

Nocht is your fairnes bot ane faiding flour,
Nocht is your famous laud and hie honour
Bot wind inflat in uther mennis eiris.
Your roising reid to rotting sall retour.

In the sequel she learns a fuller moral lesson. Urged by a leper lady to 'mak vertew of ane neid' (make virtue of necessity), 'To leir to clap thy clapper to and fro,/And leir efter the Law of Lipper Leid', she goes begging by the roadside. Troilus passes that way,

And with a blenk it come into his thocht,
That he sumtime hir face befoir had sene.
Bot scho was in sic plye he knew hir nocht.

He recalls but does not recognize her, feels the spark of love, and empties his purse into her lap. Cresseid does not recognize him either, but another leper announces the good knight's name. Cresseid swoons, recovers, and comes to a full recognition of her guilty infidelity. She writes her testament and dies; the ruby ring Troilus had given her is returned to him. Henryson suggests that he may have built her a marble monument. The poet rounds off the poem with a moral for the women in his audience.

On the strength of this poem alone Henryson would have a place well above the tree-line on Parnassus. But there is more: the eclogue 'Robene and Makyne', and 'The Garmont of Gud Ladeis', 'The Bludy Serk', 'Orpheus and Eurydice', and especially the *Moral Fables*, all of which contribute to our sense of the breadth as well as the depth of Henryson's genius. The breadth includes allegorical satire, for the animals in the fables are representatives of classes and types of men, and the fable form liberates them from a merely local *milieu* into a general significance.

There are thirteen fables. Henryson pretends they are all translations of Aesop, though the best – 'The Country Mouse and the Town Mouse' – is from Horace, and the others are not all attributable. With further modesty, the poet claims to be ignorant of rhetoric and promises to write 'In hamelie language and in termes rude'. Though the low style prevails, the rhetoric is impeccable.

The fable of the country and the town mouse – 'The Taill of the Uponlandis Mous, and the Burges Mous' – is the most fully achieved, vivid in visual detail, corresponding closely to social types, and full of good humour and good sense. Henryson's narrative is dramatic as well. The town mouse sets out to seek her sister:

Bairfute, allone, with pykestaf in hir hand,
As pure pylgryme scho passit out off town,
To seik hir sister baith oure daill and down.

Speech – mouse-speech married to common speech – is rendered. When in town the mice are first surprised at their dinner, by a servant, the country mouse flees and swoons. Her sister calls, 'How faire ye, sister? cry peip, quhair ever ye be.' Most vividly observed and dramatic is the arrival of 'Gib hunter, our Jolie Cat' (Gilbert – a common name for cats well into the sixteenth century) who catches the country mouse:

Fra fute to fute he kest hir to and ffra,
Quhylis up, quhylis doun, als cant as ony kid;
Quhylis wald he lat hir rin under the stra,
Quhylis wald he wink, and play with hir buk heid.
Thus to the selie Mous grit pane he did,
Quhill at the last, throw fortune and gude hap,
Betwix ane burde and the wall scho crap.

As in the *Testament*, so in the *Fables* the trial and confession motifs are used, adding to the Chaucerian tone.
Patrick Crutwell, comparing Henryson and Chaucer,
comments that Henryson's 'picturesque detail owes its
effectiveness to the solidity and seriousness of what it
grows from'. There emerges from the *Fables* – by analogy
– a more or less complete human world, judged in moral
terms. The animals exist as animals and as types of man.

Gavin Douglas (1475?–1522) acknowledged a debt to
Henryson. In reading his *Eneados*, the translation of
Virgil's *Aeneid*, we sense the nature of that debt in
Douglas's subtle control of his couplets and his skill at
writing with complete directness, especially in his original
Prologues.

Douglas was the third son of 'Bell-the-Cat', fifth Earl
of Angus. After a good education he was caught up in the
political struggles of the day on the 'other side' (the
victorious side) in the Battle of Flodden and its aftermath. He entered St Andrews University in 1490, took
his Masters Degree in 1494, and in 1501 was Provost of
St Giles, Edinburgh. He probably studied in Paris as
well. He took orders and ultimately, after much con-
troversy, became Bishop of Dunkeld (1515). He died, out
of favour, of the plague in London in 1522. But by 1513
his poetic labours had come to an end. When he completed the *Eneados* he wrote, 'Thus up my pen and in-
strumentis full yor/On Virgillis post I fix for evirmore ...'
He would wait 'solitar, as doith the byrd in cage', his
youth now past.

It took him about eighteen months to translate Virgil.
The *Eneados* is the first important translation into
English of a major classical poem. Caxton had produced
a pedestrian version, in criticizing which, Saintsbury says,
Douglas proved himself a considerable negative critic.
His other works include the 'Palice of Honour', a substantially original dream allegory. Some of his poems and
translations, notably his version of Ovid's *Art of Love*,
have not survived.

Douglas's working text of Virgil was hardly a perfect one; and it had appended to it a full commentary. His method was to translate keeping close to the original but interpolating into his version matter from the commentary. He also included Mapheus Vegius's apocryphal thirteenth book (1428). His poem is almost twice as long as Virgil's, and yet close to it in spirit. The Renaissance humanists in their passion for pure Latinity divorced the poem from its wider audience by academicizing it.

Ezra Pound declared, 'Gavin Douglas re-created us Virgil, or rather, we forget Virgil in reading Gavin's *Aeneids* and know only the tempest, Acheron, and the eternal elements that Virgil for most men glazes over.' This tribute to Douglas's directness reflects upon Pound's own sense – which many readers share – that the Virgil we read is defracted through centuries of scholarship and exegesis, so that we can hardly look the poem in the face. But Douglas could, and in reading Douglas's version we experience Aeneas's adventures afresh.

Reflecting on the work of Chaucer, Gower, Henryson and Douglas, we can understand what Dryden meant when he wrote of Chaucer, 'the genius of our countrymen in general' is 'rather to improve an invention, than to invent themselves; as is evident not only in our poetry, but in many of our manufactures'. Translation nourished the native literature. 'Improvement' is too strong a word to apply to Douglas's Virgil; but his transposition of the poem into the courtly idiom, with a peculiarly Scottish flavour, is characteristic of the writings of the age. It is remarkable that Douglas achieved so much, having few models to work from. His modesty remains genuine, however: 'Not as I suld, I wrait, but as I couth.'

He used roughly one couplet per Latin hexameter – twenty syllables for sixteen. He had recourse to numerous poetical auxiliaries and doublets to plump out his measure, giving a roughness to its rightness. Douglas is most himself in the 'Prologues' to the various books. There he allows himself an experiment in alliterative verse (book eight). There he states his mind. Warton praised particularly the prologue to book twelve: the lines 'are effusions of a mind not overlaid by the descriptions of other poets but operating, by its own force and bias, in the delineation of a vernal landscape, on such objects as really occurred.' Douglas loved to write (the excesses of 'The Palice of Honour' attest to this), and he was remarkably clear in his mind about style and genre. This he reveals in the prologue of book nine:

The ryall style, clepyt heroycall,
Full of wirschip and nobilnes our all,
Suldbe compilit but thewhes or voyd word,
Kepand honest wys sportis quhar thai bourd,
All lowus langage and lychtnes lattand be,
Observand bewte, sentens and gravyte.
The sayar eik suld weil considir thys,
Hys mater, and quhamto it entitilit is:
Eftir myne authoris wordis, we aucht tak tent
That baith accord, and ben convenient,
The man, the sentens, and the knychtlyke stile,
Sen we mon carp of vassalage a quhile.

He briefly develops principles of poetic decorum entirely functional and by no means as restricting as those the Renaissance humanists were promoting.

Douglas is modest again when he says, 'Guf ocht be weill, thank Virgil and nocht me.' He takes credit for the flaws, being unequal to his original's 'ornat fresch endyte'. If he has 'pervert' Virgil, he has also caught the movement and spirit of the *Aeneid*, and woven into the poem his prologues which might be taken as northern eclogues.

More famous than Henryson and Douglas is Dunbar. His credit this century has risen thanks to Hugh MacDiarmid's attempt to 'recreate' a distinctively Scottish literature with the cry (1927), 'Not Burns – Dunbar!' The masculinity of Dunbar's verse, its formal accomplishment and verve, its effective malice, set him apart from his contemporaries. He is the least obviously Chaucerian of them, marrying the moribund but still useful alliterative tradition to the French syllabic tradition. There is none of Henryson's transparency of language or Douglas's directness. The sound surface of Dunbar's poems calls attention to itself: we are required to admire the technique.

William Dunbar (1460?–1520?) was a *makar* in the courtly tradition, a friar and a courtier in one, busy about other people's lives and secrets. James IV was his patron. His verse was part of the brief flowering of an aristocratic culture which ended with the Scottish defeat at Flodden. James IV was a responsive patron, though perhaps less responsive than he has been portrayed. He was certainly among the last great princes of chivalry. His death proved that. Learned, an accomplished linguist in as many as eight tongues, he cultivated the arts and sciences in his court and in his country. All this Dunbar celebrated, but he also showed a dark side.

His love for ceremony and pomp is reflected in several poems, even in the particular organization of imagery, much of which has an heraldic colouring, disposition and stiffness, especially in 'The Thistle and the Rose' and 'The Golden Terge'. The aureation which he learned from Chaucer contributes to the rich surface of his verse, but he can also use the coarse colloquial diction of his day. His style is an amalgam between a literary English and a demotic, mingling registers, passing from the sublime to the grotesque in a single sentence. He is a master of parody.

Rhyme-royal, short stanzas, couplets, alliterative forms: the technical variety is great; and he is at home in many modes: allegory, dream vision, hymn, prayer, elegy, panegyric, lyric, comic narrative, satire and flyting. Edwin Morgan writes, 'His first mark is a certain effectual brilliance that may commend him more keenly to the practising poet than to the ordinary reader – an agility, a virtuosity in tempo and momentum, a command of rhythm.'

One cannot help feeling that Warton is disappointed in Dunbar. 'I am of opinion, that the imagination of Dunbar is not less suited to satirical than to sublime allegory: and that he is the first poet who has appeared with any degree of spirit in the way of writing since *Piers Plowman*.' It is sad that Warton did not have access to the work of Henryson. On Dunbar, he continues: 'The natural complexion of his genius is of the moral and didactic cast.' And yet he has not Langland's social scope or conscience, nor Chaucer's bemused humanity. A vitiating ungenerosity of spirit mars many of the poems; it disappears only in the elegies and the religious poems. He flays his foes, his greatest pleasure is in the flyting, the bawdy, the grotesque. His longest poem, and one of his best, 'The Tretis of the Tua Mariit Wemen and the Wedo', combines in a single unrhymed alliterative parody of the romantic mode bawdy satire and moral censure.

His is a poetry without intimacy – in that respect like Langland's – and with feelings, when it has them, which attach more to the subject and the chosen form than to the poet's intimate emotion. He seems emotionally implicated only in his elegies. His religious poems, C. S. Lewis writes, are 'public and liturgical' rather than devotional. He brings an equal lucidity and professional polish to his flytings and to his elegies. One does not always sense psychological or philosophical depth, or perceptual accuracy, beneath the polish. It is as though for all his courtliness, his political and diplomatic activity, and the potency of his technical arsenal, he were a poet local to a time and place: James IV's court. There is no wide world, though the narrow world is entertaining.

Dunbar's fancy is fertile. In 'Dregy of Dunbar' he parodies the liturgical form, presenting the King's stay in Stirling as purgatory, his return to Edinburgh as a return to heaven. The interweaving of Latin among other language registers can be parodic or, in the sombre poems, add ritualistic emphasis. He appears to have been born a technician: there is an even excellence of composition and we cannot detect development or establish chronology with any ease. Throughout the comedy tends towards the grotesque, the nightmare. Primary colours, little shading, nothing overheard: Edwin Morgan points to Dunbar's 'startling indifference to theme in poetry'. He is a poet one cannot but admire; yet it is hard to do more than admire his dazzling artifice.

John Skelton 1464?–1529

> The Indy sapphire blue
> Her veines doth ennew,
> The orient pearl so clear
> The whiteness of her leer ...

No Englishman more relished the Scottish defeat at
Flodden than John Skelton. He gloated over it in his
indecently chauvinistic poem 'Against the Scots'. He
played for a time in the Tudor court a role comparable
to Dunbar's in the court of James IV. Like Dunbar he
was a man of the cloth and a courtier undertaking responsible duties. He was tutor to the Duke of York, later
Henry VIII. He commented wryly on the pleasures and
vices of that *milieu*. With Dunbar he shared a certain
public heartlessness; but he was never very convincing as
a courtier. He kept getting in trouble. He wasn't particularly convincing as a priest, either, though he was for
some years rector of Diss, Norfolk, where his diocesan
bishop, Nykke, punished him for 'having been guilty *of
certain crimes* AS MOST POETS ARE'.

Skelton is not formally competent the way Dunbar is;
instead of a diverse skill he possesses a distinctive style
with certain affectations: those aggressive rhymes, a continual refusal to stay still before his subject. His poetry is
directly in touch with the spoken language of the day. He
is not, of course, merely a reporter of court or gutter
speech, but his natural language partakes of the language
he heard from highly-placed and humble people alike.

His experience at Diss took him among wool-merchants, farmers and clerics; the new religious notions were flowing in at the port.

He is capable like Dunbar of the most savage flytings, and he spares no foe. But his best work is compassionate and moral in a new manner. In his time allegory was no longer an entirely viable mode. The new humanism found it crudely scholastic. Skelton drew upon it to exaggerate and satirize, driving it to the extreme by his individual idiosyncrasy.

Skelton was born in the 1460s, possibly in Cumberland. He was first known to the world as a great humanist. He translated Diodorus Siculus's *History of the World* (*c.* 1485) and the *Epistles* of Tully (Cicero). In 1489 he was laureate of Oxford and Louvain and a scholar of international reputation. Erasmus called him *Britannicarum literarum decus et lumen*. He compiled *A New English Grammar*, now lost with much of his other work. In 1439 he was admitted laureate of Cambridge. In 1498 he took religious orders and wrote his bitter satire, 'The Bouge of Court'. The next year he was tutoring the future King: 'I gave him drink of the sugared well/Of Helicon's waters crystaline.' His Latin verses gained much praise, even from Warton, who found little enough to praise in the rest of his work.

In 1504, upon his removal to Diss, his vernacular poetry came into its own. There is no record of the effect his fresh and extremely 'low' verses had on his humanist colleagues. 'Philip Sparrow', which includes the first mention in English poetry of some seventy species of bird, 'The Tunning of Elinour Rumming', and other pieces did his reputation as a serious modern scholar no good. His conduct as rector did him no credit either. He was said to keep 'a fair wench in his house'. When the bishop instructed him to expel her through the door, Skelton obeyed, only to receive her back again through the window. Or so the legend has it. His Christianity was orthodox, however unorthodox his character as a rector.

By 1509 he was back at court, where the King pardoned him for an unrecorded offence. In 1512 he was appointed King's Orator and allowed to wear a green and white robe embroidered 'Caliope'. In 1516 he wrote *Magnificence*, his only surviving interlude and a not negligible contribution to the development of the secular drama. By 1519, living in a house within the sanctuary of Westminster, he launched his campaign against Cardinal Wolsey in 'Colin Clout' and other works. 'Speak Parrot' was composed in 1521. The next year, 'Why Come Ye Not to Court' brought the conflict with Wolsey to a head. The King could no longer protect his Orator. Skelton was abandoned to the Cardinal who sent him to prison. He earned his liberty by a penance and a jest. Kneeling before Wolsey, he suffered a long lecture, and at last said, 'I pray your Grace to let me lie down and wallow, for I can kneel no longer.'

He enjoyed the patronage of the Howards in Yorkshire, wrote his self-staged apotheosis in *The Garland of Laurel*, and returned to London where he now flattered Wolsey in the hope of receiving a prebend. It was not granted. He died in 1529, the year before Wolsey fell, leaving several children by a marriage he confessed to upon his deathbed. He was buried at St Margaret's, Westminster.

There is a long-standing case against Skelton. Pope dismissed him as 'beastly Skelton'. Long before, Puttenham had called him 'but a rude railing rhymer, and all his doings ridiculous; he used both short distances and short measures, pleasing only the popular care'. Meres branded him 'buffoon'. Warton states the case most fully: 'Skelton would have been a writer without decorum at any period.' His humour is 'capricious and grotesque. If his whimsical extravagances ever move our laughter, at the same time they shock our sensibility.' Not only his subjects but his manner Warton finds objectionable: 'he sometimes debases his matter by his versification. On the whole, his genius seems better suited to low burlesque, than to liberal and manly satire.' But Caxton had claimed that

Skelton improved the language. How could this be so, asks Warton, for Skelton 'sometimes adopts the most familiar phraseology of the common people'.

About the style he is emphatic: 'his petty measure: which is made still more disgusting by the repetition of the rhymes' is an 'anomalous and motley form of versifica-tion'. 'Motley': there we have Skelton the buffoon and jester once again.

Warton's is a fair description; but the judgements we make are different from his. In this century there is a contrary prejudice in favour of 'the most familiar phrase-ology of the common people', the language men actually speak. Not that anyone ever *spoke* Skeltonics, but Skel-ton's language bears a direct relation to the demotic of various classes of men. Warton does not mention, how-ever, the large number of invented and obscure words in the poems, a literariness in some of them which derives from Skelton's master Lydgate and from Chaucer. Suf-ficient evidence of Skelton's deliberate artistry exists to make us trust even his most apparently off-the-cuff verses. Robert Graves and W. H. Auden have found in him the English poet of the transition between the Middle Ages and the Renaissance.

The taproots of Skelton's English work go deep into the fourteenth century and beyond. The rhyming Goliardic tradition of mediaeval Latin verse affected him. He called his poems 'trifles of honest mirth', which aligns him with the Goliardic, though he preferred accentual to syllabic prosody. If his Latin elegiacs were free of monastic phrase-ology, as Warton tells us, his English verses often include monastic Latin tags, developing into the macaronic style which had been practised in English for centuries, usually in carols, hymns and other religious compositions, seldom in so light-hearted and witty a fashion, except by Dunbar.

Skelton can be seen as a renegade humanist who realized – having contributed substantially to the move-ment – the spiritual and linguistic impoverishment im-plicit in extreme Renaissance humanism. He came to appreciate the very elements in literary language which humanism sought to extirpate in its passion to purify Latin and, in a different sense, English.

His first English poem is an elegy on the death of Edward IV. It is generically less an elegy than a meditative monologue spoken by the King, reflecting on ephemerality, fortune (with 'sugared lips'), and 'mutability'. The complex verse form includes Latin refrains and an effective use of the *ubi sunt* motif, celebrating deeds even as it acknowledges their vanity. The poem is wooden, but suggestive. The accentual verse, with a marked caesura, seems to fall into two short, phrased lines. Though not systematically alliterative, it has the pondered emphasis of alliterative verse, with short syntactic phrases.

In his second poem, also an elegy, he asks Clio to help him 'expel' his 'homely rudeness and dryness'. 'My words unpolished be, naked and plain,/Of aureat poems they want illumining.' But nakedness and an individual plainness were to be his hallmarks.

'Woefully Arrayed', a monologue spoken by Christ, takes its idiom from mediaeval verse. Alliteration and inner rhyme give the poem a considered, solemn pace. It is Skelton's first notable achievement, marred only by a lack of progression. It advances by iteration and variation, re-working the same point. The refrain which opens and closes the poem is in proto-Skeltonics:

Woefully array'd,
  My blood, man,
  For thee ran,
It may not be nay'd:
  My body blo and wan,
Woefully array'd.

Skelton still had some way to go before he achieved his technique. Along the way came some pleasing poems, including 'My Darling Dear, My Daisy Flower' and 'Mannerly Margery Milk and Ale'. With the satiric

'Bouge at Court' he came of age. 'Bouge' (bouche) means 'rewards'. The poem is a secular allegory in which a dreamer takes ship and experiences the comradeship of courtly Disdain, Riot, Dissimulation and other personified perils. Boarding in innocence, he is reduced to paranoid dread. Chaucer is Skelton's master here: the stanza form is that of *Troilus and Criseyde*, and when the language is most achieved, we feel Chaucer in the very movement of the verse. Riot is described in these terms:

His cote was checkerd with patches rede and blewe,
Of Kirkbye Kendall was his short demye;
And aye he sang *in fayth decon thou crewe*:
His elbowe bare, he ware his gere so nye:
His nose droppinge, his lippes were full drye:
And by his syde his whynarde, and his pouche,
The devyll myght dance therin for any crouche.

As he entered his forties, living in the provinces, perhaps intellectually uncompanioned, driven back upon himself, Skelton's style of life and of writing changed. The eccentric poet, implied in the earlier poems, came into his own in 'Philip Sparrow'. The first line reads *'Pla ce bo'*, the first word of the Office of the Dead, divided into three mock-solemn stressed syllables which set the rhythmic pattern: short-lined, three-stressed. The first part of the poem is spoken by Jane, lamenting her pet sparrow 'Whom Gib, our cat, hath slain'. The elegy develops at great length to wide-ranging parody and satire. The famous catalogue of birds is not just a list: it evokes some of Philip Sparrow's cousins, 'The lark with his long toe', 'And also the mad coot,/With balde face to toot', and many more. An erotic sub-text gives the poem its force: Jane laments her sparrow as a lover:

  It had a velvet cap,
And would sit upon my lap,
And seek after small wormes,
And sometime white bread-crumbes;

And many time and oft
Between my breastes soft
It would lie and rest;
It was proper and prest.

Sometimes he would gasp
When he saw a wasp;
A fly or a gnat,
He would fly at that;
And prettily he would pant
When he saw an ant.

Jane pleads her simplicity and ignorance, then entertains with a show of erudition and an enormous reading list. Finally Skelton takes the poem over and praises her. She loved the bird, the poet loved her. The syndrome is Catullan, but the poem is very English.

'The Tunning of Elinour Rumming' is certainly not charming: a poem in seven 'Fits', it owes some debts to *Sir Gawain and the Green Knight*. Elinour's obnoxious 'tunning' or alcoholic brew, luridly described in its vat, attracts fallen women of all sorts. Elinour herself, apparently based on an actual 'publican' who lived near Leatherhead, Surrey, is Skelton's most repulsive creation. Her face was 'Like a roast pig's ear,/Bristled with hair'. He evokes a wide cross-section of English womanhood. The poem is the quintessence of Skelton's 'motley' verse, which he describes in 'Colin Clout':

For though my rhyme be ragged,
Tattered and jagged,
Rudely rain-beaten,
Rusty and moth-eaten,
If ye take well therewith,
It hath in it some pith.

The 'pith' is that of satirical moralist. In the poems against Wolsey he satirizes with equal verve ecclesiastical corruption and the faithless laity. He appears a man of

the establishment opposed to those who would use rather
than serve it. Skeltonics, a helter-skelter measure bordering on doggerel, suits the helter-skelter social world Skelton satirized.

When, late in his career, he chose to use a long line, a
more relaxed syntax followed and a greater real, as opposed to surface, brilliance. 'Speak Parrot' is – even in the
corrupt texts we have – the masterpiece of his maturity.
The years of learnedness laugh at themselves in his obscure references and allusions. His attention has shifted
from immediate effects to a more integrated poetic
language that reflects a mind which, to begin with, seems
abandoned to eloquent mania. The parrot who speaks is
a polyglot, stuffed with knowledge, all of which seems –
given the situation of the bird, a pet and a captive, caged
– garbled and useless.

My lady mistress, Dame Philology,
  Gave me a gifte, in my nest when I lay,
To learn all language ...

'Speak Parrot' celebrates language and, as it were in the
same breath, acknowledges its impotence in the world of
action. The poem gradually slides away from mock-
allegory, rhetorical and linguistic jollity, until we are left
with a final bold, unmasked indictment of the state of
learning, morality, the church, the judiciary.

In Skelton's later work there is a constant pull towards
dramatic form. The poems employ dialogue and idiomatic speech and develop character. In this as in other
ways Skelton is a poet of transition, still dignified with the
authority of the Middle Ages, yet expert in the new
learning and the new forms. In *The Garland of Laurel*
occur those lyrics – 'With marjoram gentle', 'By Saint
Mary, my lady', 'Merry Margaret' and others – which
crown the mediaeval lyric tradition and are among the
finest celebratory lyrics of the early Renaissance.

Sir Thomas Wyatt 1503–1542

But here I am in Kent and Christendom,
  Among the Muses where I read and rhyme.

Almost all Wyatt's lyrics are dramatic. The reader is plunged *in medias res,* usually into a complaint against an unregarding or unattainable lady. They can be located on a map of passion. They are thrifty poems, with little detail and a minimum of physical evocation. Like other poems in the song tradition, their imagery is conventional.

The verse forms Wyatt employed or invented – over seventy different stanza forms in the lyrics alone – tax him often beyond his technical skills. In recent decades critics have debated about Wyatt's metres: are his irregularities poetic flaws, manifestations of a peculiar genius, or proof that his language was still in a state of accentual transition? Metre apart, one cannot argue against the *rhythm* of the best poems, the variations – less numerous than is normally thought – on a static metrical pattern. Those variations ensure Wyatt's poetic superiority to Surrey and even to Sidney, whose metrical smoothness can be cloying. Breaches of metrical decorum answer – or seem to answer – to the modulations of specific emotions.

Sir Thomas Wyatt busied himself in the King's affairs more than Skelton ever did. He was born at Allington Castle, beside the Medway in Kent, in 1503. His father was devoted to the Tudors and presented his son at court when he was thirteen. He attended St John's College,

Cambridge. When he was seventeen he married Lord Cobham's daughter. She bore him a son and a daughter, then proved unfaithful, and Wyatt refused to have her under his roof.

When he was twenty-three he began actively to serve his King. He accompanied an embassy to France, and the next year another to the Pope. Captured by Spanish troops, he managed to escape. In 1528 he became Marshal of Calais, a post he held for four years. When he returned to England he held prominent posts in Essex and was Chief Ewer (in his father's place) at the coronation of Anne Boleyn.

Did he have relations with Anne Boleyn? It is likely, and that his confession to the King prior to the royal marriage saved him his head when the Queen lost hers. His imprisonment in the Tower in 1536 resulted from a quarrel with the Duke of Suffolk and had none of the sinister overtones that papist propagandists and romantic critics have suggested.

Wyatt was soon back in favour. He became Sheriff of Kent and in 1537 Ambassador to Spain. He left Spain in 1539, on his father's death.

Tagus, farewell, that westward with thy streams
    Turns up the grains of gold already tried:
With spur and sail for I go seek the Thames
    Gainward the sun that sheweth her wealthy pride
And to the town which Brutus sought by dreams
    Like bended moon doth lend her lusty side.
My King, my Country alone for whom I live,
Of mighty love the wings for this me give.

These lines speak his honest zeal on the King's behalf. He had detractors at home, and a trial at which he was acquitted of charges of treason and immorality. He returned to his post at Calais, later served as MP for Kent and then as Vice-Admiral of a new fleet under construction. He died suddenly, in 1542, of a fever in Sherborne, on his way to accompany a Spanish envoy from Falmouth to London.

Wyatt's poems were first published in *Tottel's Miscellany* (1557). Tottel regularized their metre by doctoring the language, and Wyatt was thus misprinted for many years. Even now his work presents serious textual difficulties. What we have was collected largely by G. F. Nott (1816) and revised and improved by A. K. Foxwell (1913).

Some verse forms Wyatt invented, others he imported. From Italy he brought *terza rima*, *ottava rima* and the sonnet. Though he was the first great English sonneteer, the sonnets he translated and composed had little effect on his smooth-mannered successors, who went to the fountainhead in Petrarch rather than to Wyatt's sometimes awkward efforts. He failed to domesticate *terza rima*, which he used with mixed effects in his three satires. They tend towards blank verse, with enjambements so frequent that the rhymes appear to be accidents rather than elements of form, except in a few passages. One is the opening of the first satire, on court life:

Mine own John Poins, since ye delight to know
  The cause why that homeward I me draw,
  And flee the press of courts whereso they go,
Rather than to live thrall, under the awe
  Of lordly looks, wrapped within my cloak,
  To will and lust learning to set a lawe ...

The theme is familiar from Skelton; but the added note of personal seriousness in the sixth line is an important development. The tone is more intimate than public, the image 'wrapped within my cloak' quick and vivid, part of the subject and not decorative.

On the strength of the satires, one of which evokes the Horatian mice Henryson translated in his *Fables*, Warton called Wyatt 'the first polished English satirist' and suggested he mistook his talent when he became a sonneteer.

The poet's genius 'was of the moral and didactic species; and his poems abound more in good sense, satire, and observations on life, than in pathos and imagination'. That eighteenth-century perspective few today would share.

If Wyatt sometimes failed to acclimatize his imported forms, he did add to the resources of English poetry. His immediate legacy to his successors was 'poulter's measure', an alexandrine followed by a rhyming fourteener. C. S. Lewis finds it hard to forgive him this invention, though Surrey, Turberville and Gascoigne, among others, used it with a kind of authority.

Wyatt and Henry Howard, Earl of Surrey, are normally bracketed together as the fathers of English Petrarchanism. Puttenham saw them as 'the two chief lanterns of light to all others that have since employed their pens upon English poesy: their conceits were lofty, their styles stately, their conveyance clear, their terms proper, their metre sweet and well-proportioned, in all imitating very naturally and studiously their master Francis Petrarcha'. This is more true of Surrey than of Wyatt. Puttenham no doubt read him in Tottel's 'polished' text. Certainly Wyatt's imitations of Petrarch are neither studious nor merely Petrarchan.

The introduction of Petrarchanism into English poetry was not an unalloyed good. It taught two lessons, one of form and one of subject. The formal lesson provided dangers for native syntax and diction, requiring adjustments and mannerisms against the grain of the language. The thematic lesson had perils for lesser talents: Petrarchan love conventions recast courtly conventions in a new age, and their chief novelty for English poetry depended on a certain disregard for elements latent in the native tradition. Petrarchan conventions required not so much translation as transposition into English culture. This Wyatt achieved with some mastery. Those who followed him were less successful.

The refined, spiritual love of Petrarch Wyatt found uncongenial. His most un-Platonic sonnets and poems, expressing a carnal passion, are his best. He avoids the aureate style which later Petrarchans developed. By contrast, his poetry is forthright, clear in outline, colloquial, undecorated. Shakespeare was able to use Wyatt's poems familiarly in, for example, *Hamlet* and *Twelfth Night*.

In Petrarch's sonnets the octave normally establishes the experience – a thing perceived, an emotion sensed. The sestet generalizes a meaning. Wyatt saw Petrarch's skill at structuring an idea, a structuring more allusive and concise than the procedure of allegory, but related to it. His own poems structure emotions: the generalizations that emerge relate to physical passion and hardly seek to transcend it. Surrey and Sidney established an orthodox Petrarchanism in England; Wyatt was not so deliberate in his writing as they: the energy of the old tradition, even when mediated through imported models, is active.

The best illustration of Wyatt's freedom with Petrarch is his imitation of '*Una candida cerva*' (*Canzoniere* cxc), which he renders in 'Whoso list to hunt'. Petrarch's sonnet is conventional. The poet sees a doe and follows her, coveting her as a miser covets gold. Around her neck he notices a diamond and topaz collar which says, '*Nessun mi tocchi*'. She is Caesar's. He follows half a day and falls exhausted. She disappears. Wyatt takes the poem and rearranges the halves of the sestet. '*Nessun mi tocchi*' he translates with superb blasphemy into Christ's words, '*Noli me tangere*'. He does away with the miser image and from the outset presents the lover as a tired hunter. He heightens the hunting image – not in Petrarch at all – with the words, 'Yet may I by no means my wearied mind/Draw from the deer' – suggesting an arrow (a Cupid's arrow, too) that has hit its mark and stuck without slaying it. Wyatt imparts a dramatic unity, with a fitting climax in the last three lines. The poem has the authority of personal statement. It lacks Petrarch's intellectual clarity, but it has been transmuted into Wyatt's more manly, less reflective idiom. The deer is, in all likelihood, Anne Boleyn.

Most of his poems and songs develop a single theme. Statements of feeling are tight-lipped and masculine, neither overstated nor ironized. He uses rhetorical devices with restraint: they are means of expression, not ends in themselves. His economy renders some poems easily memorable, either in whole or in part. Yvor Winters characterizes Wyatt's poetry as 'not striking nor original as to subject, but merely true and universal'.

An earlier English tradition survives in Wyatt, despite the Petrarchan debts, and it helps to explain his prosody. He combines metrical with the older accentual verse. Unless we read him with a metronomic ear, we must expect to hear at times a regular iambic pentameter line followed by a line straight from the accentual tradition, with a marked caesura and probably two strong stresses (and perhaps a secondary stress) in each half line. His best known poem, with verbs and adjectives suggesting animal passion, reflects this:

They flee from me that sometime did me seek
   With naked foot stalking in my chamber.
I have seen them gentle, tame and meek
   That now are wild and do not remember
   That sometime they put themself in danger
To take bread at my hand ...

It includes the most prosodically contested of Wyatt's lines, 'But all is turned thorough my gentilness/Into a straunge fashion of forsaking', which Tottel amended for regularity, as he did the first passage. It is a waste of effort to force Wyatt to scan, as, for example, by voicing the 'e' in 'straunge'. Yet, without that, the two accented syllables, 'stránge fáshion', lacking an unstressed syllable between them, force a brief pause not substantiated by syntax or metre, an irregularity with a subtle dramatic rightness.

Are Wyatt's poems better or worse for not scanning

consistently? Only a metronome would answer 'worse', for the variations and 'faults' often answer to a voice, articulating an experience with consequences for the heart. To suggest a latent accentual tradition underlying the a-metrical lines is merely a way of saying that Wyatt wrote the way he had to, pursuing a subject rather than following a norm. In his best poems he heard with both ears. Of course there are bad patches. Some of the poems we have are probably only unfinished drafts.

Imagery is spare but effectively deployed, whether suggested or stated. 'O goodly hand' depends entirely on conventional imagery. In the first two stanzas the poet praises the beauty of the hands which are engaged in removing the lover's heart. The contrast between the hands' beauty – cold and emotionless – and the passionate wound develops; in the third and fourth stanzas the poet begs the beloved to replace the heart or, if not, in the fifth stanza he begs her to wring it to death: mercy or death. The poem is not one of Wyatt's best, but it reveals his sense of dramatic progression and concentration.

The persona of the unhappy lover, like a glum Hilliard miniature against a background of flame, becomes repetitive and tiresome. There are few celebrations. Occasionally he uses a female *persona*, but the effect is not striking. The poems vary greatly in quality, from the twenty or so masterpieces – among the best lyrics in English – to the merely conventional works in which word-play, so cherished by sixteenth-century poets, displaces thought and experience, or where a poem develops by accretion rather than progression.

Much ill has been spoken of Wyatt's *Penitential Psalms*. One critic suggests that the real penance is to read them at all. Yet they are among the first and certainly among the better of the early metrical versions of psalms. A comparison between Wyatt's uneven efforts and those of Sternhold and Hopkins, or Archbishop Parker, proves that, though they do not crown his achievement, they do him no dishonour.

He is the first of a *type* – the noblest type – of poet in English literature: a man of action, servant to King and muse, like Surrey, Raleigh, Sidney, Fulke Greville, Lovelace and others. Surrey defines the type in his elegies to Wyatt. The elegies fall short of Wyatt's own achievement but have the merit of sincerity. After praising the verse 'That reft Chaucer the glory of his wit', he continues:

A tongue that served in foreign realms the king;
Whose courteous talk to virtue did inflame
Each noble heart; a worthy guide to bring
Our English youth by travail unto fame.

Henry Howard, Earl of Surrey
1517–1547

I call to mind the navy great
That the Greeks brought to Troye town,
And how the boisterous winds did beat
Their ships, and rent their sails adown,
Till Agamemnon's daughter's blood
Appeased the gods that them withstood.

Henry Howard, Earl of Surrey, long regarded as Wyatt's
superior, is now in eclipse. His very virtues tell against
him: his prosodic skill, his formal competence. He contributed more to the development of poetry in his century
than Wyatt did. Not only did he develop blank verse; his
sonnets, too, were influential, while Wyatt's were only
admired. He was a more thoroughgoing Petrarchan than
Wyatt. He may be a literary stepping-stone from Wyatt
to Sidney, but that is no mean fate.

He was born in Kenninghall Palace, Norfolk, in 1517,
into an illustrious family. His father was the third Duke
of Norfolk. From the outset he had advantages. The
learned and widely-travelled tutor John Clerke took his
education in hand and made him an exemplary linguist.
He mastered Latin, Italian, French and Spanish. As a boy
he was a close friend of the young Duke of Richmond,
illegitimate son of Henry VIII, and stayed with him at
Windsor. He recalled this happy period later in life, after
Richmond's death and during his detention in the castle,

Where each sweet place returns a taste full sour,
The large green courts, where we were wont to hove,
With eyes cast up unto the maiden's tower,
And easy sighs such as folk draw in love ...

He recalls the ladies, the dances, the tales, games, tournaments and confidences:

The secret thoughts imparted with such trust,
The wanton talk, the divers change of play;
The friendship sworn, each promise kept so just,
Wherewith we past the winter night away ...

In a sonnet he recalls those years with uncharacteristic physical particularity, more like Gascoigne than Surrey in its realization: 'When Windsor walls sustain'd my wearied arm,/My hand my chin, to ease my restless head.'

In 1532 Surrey married the Earl of Oxford's daughter, enhancing his position. He progressed as courtier and warrior, fighting on land and at sea. From time to time he got in trouble for quarrels, but generally he served the King well. In 1545 he was given command of Boulogne, but the next year he was arrested and charged with high treason: conspiring against the succession of Edward VI. Henry resented the popularity of his knight – a man ostentatious and ambitious, though not for the crown. He was a blood-relation of Catherine Howard, and this too the King held against him. In January 1547 Surrey was beheaded at the Tower.

He passed into legend, on a slightly lower plain than Sidney was to do. Thomas Nashe fictionalized him, much exaggerating his qualities, in *The Unfortunate Traveller*. One speech Nashe attributes to Surrey is certainly in character: 'Upon a time I was determined to travel, the fame of Italy, and an especial affection I had unto poetry my second mistress' – the first being Elizabeth Fitzgerald, the Geraldine of the sonnets, who had doubtful Italian origins – 'for which it was so famous, had wholy ravished me unto it'.

Geraldine was to Surrey what Laura was to Petrarch, an incarnate muse, a pretext for poems, an ideal. Warton calls her 'a mistress perhaps as beautiful as Laura', and describes Surrey's achievement in Petrarchan terms: 'at least with Petrarch's passion if not his taste, Surrey led a way to great improvements in English poetry, by a happy imitation of Petrarch and other Italian poets.' Certainly he was more imitative, even in love, than Wyatt, and most of his poems concentrate on the 'anxieties of love'. He returned from his first journey to Italy, Warton tells us, 'the most elegant traveller, the most polite lover, the most learned nobleman, and the most accomplished gentleman, of his age'. He would have seemed a bit out of place at Hampton Court. Excess of accomplishment contributed to his undoing. It was rumoured that he had designs to wed Princess Mary.

A not altogether native grace characterizes his lyrics. There is little of the suggestive awkwardness of Wyatt but instead an acquired facility. The poems please rather than move the reader. Warton approved: 'Surrey, for justness of thought, correctness of style, and purity of expression, may justly be pronounced the first English classical poet. He unquestionably is the first polite writer of love-verses in our language.' Correct, pure, classical, polite: unfortunately, a little dull as well.

The poems have at times a metronomic regularity. They tend towards cadence rather than short phrasing. From Wyatt he learned poulter's measure and wrote well in it occasionally:

I know to seek the track of my desiréd foe,
And fear to find that I do seek. But chiefly this I know:
That lovers must transform into the thing beloved,
And live (alas, who could believe?) with sprite from life
    removed.

Poulter's measure is best used for serious statements, where the fourteener bears a strong caesura, or for burlesque. It can betray the serious statement when its strict demands undermine the tone of a sober poem: 'And when I felt the air so pleasant round about,/Lord, to myself how glad I was that I had gotten out!' The lighter tone comes only to mar with a human warmth an otherwise chilly poem. His triumph in poulter's measure, 'In winter's just return', is a triumph *over* rather than *with* a form which only Gascoigne, and Arthur Golding in his translations of Ovid, fully mastered.

Surrey developed what came to be known as the Shakespearean sonnet and – most importantly – attempted blank verse in his translations of books two and four of Virgil's *Aeneid*. Only grudging respect has been paid this work, yet it is subtly conceived and executed with exemplary plainness, a verse direct and transparent, displaying its matter rather than its manner. Roger Ascham approved Surrey's attempt to write without what Warton called the 'gothic ornament' of rhyme. It was part of the humanist strategy. In the hands of Surrey's successors, it proved to be much more.

A passage from Surrey's version of book two illustrates the virtues of his blank verse. The Greek fleet withdraws behind Tenedos.

There stands in sight an isle, hight Tenedon,
Rich, and of fame, while Priam's kingdom stood;
Now but a bay, and road unsure for ship,
Hither them secretly the Greeks withdrew,
Shrouding themselves under the desert shore.
And, weening we they had been fled and gone
And with that wind had fet the land of Greece,
Troyè discharged her long continued dole.
The gates cast up, we issued out to play,
The Greekish camp desirous to behold,
The places void, and the forsaken coasts ...

Though rhyme has gone, the sound structure within each line, and between consecutive lines, is tight; assonance and alliteration, inner rhyme and half-rhyme, tauten the verse. The varied placement of the caesura reveals a subtle prosody uncommon elsewhere in Surrey's work. The verse lacks the verve of Gavin Douglas's translation of Virgil, but it is direct and faithful to the spirit of the original. It moves at a pace at once dignified and speakable. Surrey's attempt was to approximate Virgil's means as well as his meaning, and in this he revealed himself the first English poet thoroughly within the humanist tradition as espoused in England by such scholars as Ascham and Sir John Cheke. We may say that by following rather than leading Virgil into English Surrey extended English verse technique. By contrast, Douglas, who was after the meat of his original, served it up according to a mediaeval recipe.

Surrey's work, like Wyatt's, was first published in *Tottel's Miscellany* in 1557. Forty of his poems appeared there. Though a decade had passed since his death, Surrey's reputation was still fresh. He was the only poet named on Tottel's title-page.

It is difficult to summon up enthusiasm for the lyrics. 'The soote season, that bud and bloom forth brings' recalls the spirit of Langland in phrase and alliteration, and in the not entirely conventional particularity of its images:

The hart hath hung his old head on the pale;
The buck in break his winter coat he flings;
The fishes flete with new repairéd scale;
The adder all her slough away she slings . . .

But in a poem with preponderantly end-stopped lines and only two rhymes, the effect is of accretion, not progression. This is a common vice in Surrey: his poems draw on conventional tropes but do not integrate them into the statement. 'Brittle beauty' and even 'Set me whereas the sun', each poem in its way memorable, are assortments of image and allusion, not coordinated structures.

'Alas, so all things now do hold their peace', 'When raging love', 'O happy dancer', 'Laid in my quiet bed', 'Epitaph on Thomas Clere' and 'Sardanapalus' possess as poems some of the virtues of his blank verse, but in rhymed forms, with integrated structures of thought and image which place them amongst the best work of their period. Some are clearly records of personal experience, and they are often the most memorable. And Surrey can be memorable. Thomas Hardy may have recalled lines of Surrey such as 'Now he comes! will he come? alas, no, no!', and who can deny that the poet who wrote 'I Look into my Glass' did not have deep in memory Surrey's lines, 'Thus thoughtful as I lay, I saw my wither'd skin,/How it doth show my dinted jaws, the flesh was worn so thin'?

Surrey's debt to Wyatt is occasionally apparent in style and image. 'Wrapt in my careless cloak' recalls Wyatt's first satire; the poem with the extended chess conceit has a Wyatt-like lightness of touch; there are poems with mere wordplay, too; and memorable verses spoken by women characters. But Surrey's four elegies for Wyatt witness to the fact that the older poet was for Surrey an inspiration rather than a model. Surrey was a more ambitious and sophisticated man than Wyatt, and though a fine poet, certainly a lesser one.

George Gascoigne 1530–1577

My worthy Lord, I pray you wonder not
To see your woodman shoot so oft awry,
Nor that he stands amazéd like a sot
And lets the harmless deer, unhurt, go by.

George Gascoigne has been branded by literary historians
a 'transitional poet'. He tends to fall between two stools:
between 'silver' and 'golden' poets, plain and decorated
or, simply chronologically, between the first and second
half of the sixteenth century, Wyatt and Spenser. It is an
unfair categorization, but it has stuck, and Gascoigne
until recent years has been more a property of scholars
than of critics and readers.

One critic, Yvor Winters, took Gascoigne seriously.
Winters loves 'sentence' in poetry, the concise, sometimes
aphoristic expression of general truths. At times he ap-
plauds the merely sententious, but when he writes, 'Gascoigne is, I believe, one of the great masters of the short
poem in the century', it is an observation worth attending
to. The best poems are extraordinarily good. It is no wonder he was among Raleigh's favourite writers, that Ben
Jonson admired him, that even Shakespeare was touched
by him. Gascoigne successfully took up the original qualities of Wyatt – and his vices, especially facile wordplay and
the poulter's measure, which he sometimes put to good
use. He added to what Winters calls the 'native tradition',
ungilded by Italian influences.

Gascoigne was born in 1530 in Cardington, Bedfordshire, a descendant of Sir William Gascoigne, Henry IV's chief justice. His father, Sir John, was a man of substance. George studied at Trinity College, Cambridge, and in 1555 entered Gray's Inn, London. There he produced two plays. One, out of Ariosto, Warton calls our first English prose comedy. It provided Shakespeare with the sub-plot of *The Taming of the Shrew*. The other was a translation of an Italian version of Euripides. It was the first classical Greek play to appear on the English stage.

Because of his prodigality, Gascoigne was disinherited. To mend his finances, and perhaps for love, he married in 1561 Elizabeth Breton, a widow and the mother of the poet Nicholas Breton. Debt continued to pursue him. He fled from his creditors to Holland, where he served the Prince of Orange (1572-4), was imprisoned by the Spanish and released. On his return to England he discovered that some of his poems had been issued in unauthorized versions. He published authorized versions in *An Hundred Sundrie Floures bound up in one Poesie*. This included the first linked sonnet sequence in English (see, for example, 'Gascoigne's Memories IV') and the prose narrative *The Adventures of Master F. J.* which, if not translated from an Italian original, has claims to being the first English 'novel' or *roman à clef*. In 1575 he published *The Posies*, in which he scored another first by including 'Certain Notes of Instruction', a treatise on the writing of English verse derived from Ronsard's 1565 treatise. James I based his *Reulis and Cautelis of Scottish Poesie* on it.

The next year he produced *The Glass of Government* and *The Steele Glass*, the first use of blank verse for non-dramatic original composition. His *Complaint of Philomene*, also in 1576, set the pattern of Ovidian narrative verse Shakespeare was to follow in *Venus and Adonis* and *The Rape of Lucrece*. When he died in 1577, he had been an MP, a courtier, a soldier, a farmer, a writer and friend of writers, including Spenser. On his own account, especially in 'Gascoigne's Woodmanship' and 'The Green

Knight's Farewell to Fancy', he had failed in all he attempted.

As a writer, even in his own time, he was not a failure. Indeed he was the best-known writer of his day. *The Steele Glass*, a satire on the debasing effect of Italian manners in England, provoked Raleigh's first surviving poem. The plain-spokenness of his style had wide appeal. Winters calls it 'almost an affectation of plainness, even of brusqueness'. Gascoigne's 'I' speaks with the authority of a person, is not refined, polite, or pure like the 'I' of more literary writers. Gascoigne makes no secret in his verse of his personal circumstances, his incompetence and failure, which he in fact plays upon and exaggerates in order to generalize it. There is a witty candour and self-consciousness in his confessions.

One advantage of so plain a style is that the good poems immediately stand out from the bad, no figured veil obscures his faults. And from the weak poems good ones float free with the force of aphorism:

If so thy wife be too, too fair of face,
It draws one guest too many to thine inn;
If she be foul, and foiléd with disgrace,
In other pillows prickst thou many a pin.

The thought is commonplace; but tone, diction, and conciseness bring the commonplace to life. What is good in Gascoigne, and there is considerable and varied good, has positive verbal impact, abrupt clarity.

An elegiac tone pervades much that he wrote. The poet memorializes his failures and losses not in a tone of self-pity but of wry resignation. A rich sense of the physical reality and desirability of what he has lost or failed in is captured in the strongly accentual and alliterative lines of his 'native' poems and in the taut expression of his metrical compositions. His most delicate achievement is in his humour, a bitter-sweetness without irony or burlesque, without loss of poetic seriousness.

In 'Certain Notes of Instruction' Gascoigne stressed the

importance of poetic 'invention', the finding of the right word or phrase of illustration and amplification; and he urged the avoidance of *'trita et obvia'*, the merely conventional and familiar. Verbal discovery and surprise: he rejuvenates convention in new structures, or with new metaphors.

The emphatic alliteration that binds many of his poems together produces, not an archaic effect as we might expect, but a strongly colloquial tone, a sense of unrefinement. In the passages relating to failure his mastery is clearest. 'The Lullaby of a Lover', who puts his youth, his eyes, his will, his sex, to sleep, is in metrical verse, but alliteration and assonance heighten the effect. In this stanza he sings his youth to sleep:

First lullaby my youthful years;
It is now time to go to bed,
For crooked age and hoary hairs
Have won the haven within my head.
With lullaby, then, youth be still;
With lullaby content thy will;
Since courage quails and comes behind,
Go sleep, and so beguile thy mind.

This poem progresses from image to image naturally. Other poems, for instance the religious 'Gascoigne's Good Morrow', are accumulations of imagery, thematically repetitive, not integrated poetic statements.

In 'Gascoigne's Memories III' the failure he celebrates is spiritual and material:

The common speech is, spend and God will send;
But what sends he? A bottle and a bag,
A staff, a wallet, and a woeful end
For such as list in bravery to brag.

This has tones of Thomas Tusser at court, with all the good advice he could not follow himself. One can hear, not fancifully I think, the tones of the Ben Jonson of

Timber and suggestions of the colloquial Shakespeare.

In 'Gascoigne's Woodmanship' he confesses to his lord: he has failed in hunting, philosophy, and everything else. He is luckless, ill-starred. A quiet but persistent line of satire accompanies his personal confession: he is not himself the sole object of his ridicule. 'The Green Knight's Farewell to Fancy' shows him at his most accomplished. Another account of his failures, it is his most witty production in prosody, in concentrated detail, and in tone. Here he gardens:

To plant strange country fruits, to sow such seeds likewise,
To dig and delve for new found roots, where old might well
    suffice;
To prune the water-boughs, to pick the mossy trees –
Oh, how it pleased my fancy once! to kneel upon my knees,
To graft a pippin stock when sap begins to swell;
But since the gains scarce quite the cost, Fancy (quoth he),
    farewell.

The 'Green Knight' is Gascoigne: his visor does not hide him. His only hope is divine grace, for on earth he is doomed, in each vocation, to fail. If one comes to Gascoigne after reading Surrey, one has the sensation of stepping out of the library into the world: a thoroughly English world.

Edmund Spenser 1552–1599

For of the soul the body form doth take;
For soul is form, and doth the body make.

Queen Elizabeth I valued, though she did not like, the
'little man with little hands and little cuffs', Edmund
Spenser. His allegorical epic *The Faerie Queene* celebrates her; she features in idealized forms elsewhere in his
work. Spenser was a poet of the established order: the
monarchy, the court, the English church, those powers
that sustained and rewarded him. His was not a critical
but a celebratory commitment.

Keats, who pays him the tribute of imitation in his
early work, called him the 'elfin poet'. Coleridge valued
him: 'In Spenser ... we trace a mind constitutionally
tender, delicate and ... I had almost said effeminate.'
Milton regarded him as a great poet and moral teacher,
and his work is full of direct debts to Spenser's early poems.
Blake, Wordsworth and Thomas Hardy imitated him at
the outset of their careers. His formal influence can be
felt in the early long poems of Byron and, pre-eminently,
in James Thomson's *The Castle of Indolence*. Up to the
end of the nineteenth century, poet after poet pays
Spenser high tribute. Landor was the tartest dissident; he
wrote to Wordsworth, 'Thee gentle Spenser fondly led,/
But me he mostly sent to bed.'

Spenser himself claims poetic descent from Chaucer, a
claim it is hard to credit unless we consider his archaizing
style to be Chaucerian. The contrast between Chaucer

and Spenser is more striking than the similarity. Chaucer's language 'made it new'; Spenser's deliberately antiquates. Chaucer's poetry develops from allegory towards a world peopled with characters rather than personifications. Spenser's moves backwards into allegory, deserting the ground Chaucer had himself helped prepare, in which Marlowe, Shakespeare and other major writers of the time were at work. Chaucer developed towards the literal world, Spenser towards the figurative and ideal. They share, however, a sensuous imagination. Chaucer makes the world visible and tangible, while Spenser exploits the senses to make ideas imaginable.

Born in London in 1552, Spenser was the son of a gentleman who was also a journeyman in the art of cloth-making. Later in life the poet claimed a not impossible kinship with the noble Spencers of Northampton. Some of his childhood he spent in Burnley, Lancashire, where he probably experienced the unrequited love that 'Colin' laments in *The Shepheardes Calender*. He was educated at the Merchant Taylors' School under the headmaster-ship of Richard Mulcaster, a humanist deeply interested in the English language. At that time Spenser was already at work as a poet, translating the sonnets of Du Bellay and probably studying the Platonic philosophers who were to direct his philosophical imagination.

He went up to Pembroke College, Cambridge, in 1569. Lancelot Andrewes was his contemporary, but Spenser took up instead with Gabriel Harvey, a young Fellow of the college who advocated all the modish humanist and Puritan prejudices of the day, and whose dogmatic re-vulsion from the mediaeval made him hostile to Spenser's eventual plans for *The Faerie Queene*.

Harvey secured a place for Spenser in the Earl of Leicester's household. There the poet met Sidney, Dyer and other writers. There he lived when *The Shepheardes Calender*, dedicated to Sidney, was published in 1579, and there he may have begun work on his epic romance that same year. By the time the first part of the epic was published in 1590, the Earl of Essex had succeeded the late Earl of Leicester as Spenser's patron.

In 1580 he was appointed secretary to the new Lord Deputy of Ireland. He travelled to Ireland, perhaps saw action during the Desmond Rebellion, and in 1586 was awarded – as one of the 'undertakers' – an estate which included the ruined castle of Kilcoman. Raleigh visited him and encouraged him to return to England and publish the first three books of *The Faerie Queene*. Spenser followed his friend's advice, returning only reluctantly to Ireland, where he dedicated to Raleigh the allegorical account of his trip, *Colin Clouts Come Home Againe* (1591, published 1595).

His courtship and marriage (1594) are the likely pretext for the eighty-eight sonnets in the *Amoretti* and the great 'Epithalamion' (1595). Two years later books four to six of *The Faerie Queene* were published in London. It is possible that Spenser completed, or nearly completed, the last six books of his epic. If he did, then the manuscript went up in the flames that consumed Kilcomman when the Irish drove him out. He returned to England penniless and died the next year in London. At the Earl of Essex's expense he was buried near Chaucer in Westminster Abbey.

Spenser started with eclogues and proceeded to patriotic and moral epic. This was the ideal course, established by the example of Virgil. *The Shepheards Calender*, Spenser's first notable poem, is twelve eclogues which exploit thirteen different metres and forms. Colin Clout, a figure for Spenser himself, speaks the first and last eclogues, laments of frustrated pastoral love. The other ten are dialogues with some recognizable characters. Hobbinol, for example, is Harvey. One poem celebrates Eliza, the Queen. Four are about love, four are religious and moral allegory in pastoral disguise, one is an elegiac lament, and one, October, is devoted to a perennial theme of poets: the low regard and reward for the art. The swain called Cuddie exclaims:

They han the pleasure, I a slender price;
I beat the bush, the birds to them do fly:
What good thereof to Cuddie can arise?

His friend Piers consoles him: 'Cuddie, the praise is better
than the price.'
    Two elements of Spenser's mature style are visible here:
he tends to archaize his diction, and he chooses vividly
typical metaphor. Though in a 'low style', the eclogues
have only a remote sense of being spoken. The rusticity is
in their homely truths:

To kirk the nar, from God more far,
    Has been an old-said saw,
And he, that strives to touch a star
    Oft stumbles at a straw.

Such commonplace wisdom he may have gleaned from
his days in Burnley. He has passages of realized natural
observation: 'Keeping your beasts in the budded broom'
is a line Keats must have valued, or this:

See'st how brag yond bullock bears,
So smirk, so smooth, his prickéd ears?
His horns bene as broad as rainbow bent,
His dewlap as lithe as lass of Kent.

In *The Faerie Queene* these qualities are translated into
the 'high style' and acquire an allegorical dimension.
They retain a sensuous directness, for instance in the catalogue of trees in the first canto of book one, especially:

The Eugh, obedient to the bender's will;
The Birch for shaftes; the Sallow for the mill;
The Mirrhe sweete-bleeding in the bitter wound.

    Sir Philip Sidney's death prompted Spenser's best elegy,
'Astrophel' (1586) with its circular rhetoric and repetitions, and 'The Ruins of Time' (1591), a much less
achieved work in the measure of Chaucer's *Troilus
and Criseyde*. *Mother Hubberd's Tale* (1590), a beast

fable, recalls Chaucer and Henryson but does not rival them. In 1591 the success of the first three books of Spenser's epic led his publisher to issue his minor poems and juvenilia. They add little to the *oeuvre*.

Beside the sonnets of Sidney and Shakespeare, Spenser's *Amoretti* appear, for all their accomplishment, thin and uninspired. The best is sonnet lxxv, 'One day I wrote her name upon the strand'. But the praise of marriage and the courtly sentiment seldom rise above the conventional. These themes are best developed in *The Faerie Queene* itself. One sonnet admits a personal note, referring to his epic and the poet's genuine exhaustion:

After so long a race as I have run
Through faeryland, which these six books compile,
Give leave to rest me being half foredone,
And gather to myself new breath awhile.

The great 'Epithalamion' is far superior in conception and execution to the *Amoretti*. Following in the tradition of classical marriage odes, it displays in the purest form that idealized sensuality which animates parts of *The Faerie Queene*. Eager for the bridal night, he exclaims:

How slowly does sad Time his feathers move!
Haste thee, O fairest planet, to thy home,
Within the western foam.

When in book four of his epic he came to adapt Lucretius's invocation to Venus from *De Rerum Natura*, it was with this refined passion that his chorus of lovers is made to exclaim:

Great God of men and women, queen of th' ayre,
Mother of laughter, and welspring of blisse,
O graunt that of my love at last I may not misse!

The 'Prothalamion' (1596), written for the marriage of others, is less intense. But its refrain, 'Sweet Thames! run softly, till I end my song', and the control of rhythm over long sentences in a complex stanza form, make it memorable for its superb virtuosity.

The first three books of *The Faerie Queene* were prefaced with an explanatory letter to Raleigh. Of the projected twelve books, we have the first six and fragments of the seventh, the 'Mutability Cantos' from the Legend of Constance.

Spenser states in his prefatory letter to Raleigh that his purpose in the poem was moral: 'to fashion a gentleman or noble person in virtuous and noble discipline.' Nineteenth-century admirers lost sight of the moral aim, disregarded the system of allegory and appreciated the poem's 'beauty'. Milton presented Spenser as a great moral teacher in the *Areopagitica*; but Coleridge, in his day, read the poet differently: 'Spite of the licentiousness with which Spenser compels the orthography of his words into a subservience to his rhymes, the whole *Faerie Queene* is an almost continued instance of beauty.' This is true, but incomplete. It became the general view, and the poem was emancipated from its purpose. The morality appeared archaic, the allegory obscure, and the poem survived for the quality of its images, techniques and incidents, not for its more serious aims.

Borrowing from Tasso's discourses on epic poetry and from the example of Ariosto, Spenser distinguishes in his prefatory letter between the historian's and the poet's perspectives: 'an historiographer discourseth of affairs orderly as they were done, accounting as well the times as the actions; but a poet thrusteth into the midst, even where it most concerneth him, and there recoursing to the things forepast, and divining the things to come, maketh a pleasing analysis of all.

'The beginning therefore of my history, if it were to be told by an historiographer should be by the twelfth book, which is the last; where I devise that the Faery Queene kept her annual feast twelve days; upon which twelve several days, the occasions of the twelve several adventures happened, which, being undertaken by the twelve several knights, are in these twelve books severally handled and discovered.' There follows a description of how the completed poem would have worked. The description does not quite fit the poem we have.

'A gentle Knight was pricking on the plain,' the first book opens. This book belongs to the Red Cross Knight who defends Una from Archimago and Duessa or, in the allegory, Anglicanism defends truth. Sir Guyon, Temperance, destroys the Bower of Bliss in book two. Book three is dominated by Britomart and Belphoebe (Chastity); in book four Triamond and Cambell exemplify Friendship, and we encounter Scudamour and Amoret. Artegall, Knight of Justice, appears in book five, and Spenser devotes much of his allegory to events in recent English history. Sir Calidore, in book six, embodies Courtesy.

The projected twelve books would have contained twelve cantos each, presenting twelve virtues and twelve exemplary knights. Prince Arthur, who symbolizes Magnificence, the perfection of all the virtues, after a vision sets out to seek the Fairie Queene (Elizabeth, variously figured in the poem by Belphoebe, Gloriana, Mercilla and others). Arthur was to seek her for twelve days, encountering each day one of her knights and assisting each to triumph. The poem would have ended in Arthur's marriage to Gloriana (Glory). Spenser hoped by the device of Arthur to give the poem an overall unity, without forfeiting the freedom to develop each romantic book separately, as a largely self-contained unit.

So mechanical a conception of the form and the allegory, arbitrarily conceived rather than rising out of any integrating action, accounts for many of the difficulties of the poem. In part the allegory derives from legend and convention, in part it is fabricated by Spenser to shadow his own ideas. It works like a code, while traditional allegory functions at best as an accessible common language. Spenser, with a humanist education, returned to the Middle Ages for his material, but he took only part of what he found there, leaving behind much of the necessary substance. Similarly, he only partly archaized his language, giving it an antique patina. His allegory is over-charged with moral, literary and conventional elements. Britomart is not only Chastity: she stands for aspects of the Queen, for the religious figure of St Catherine. She even recalls Camilla. Artegall recalls Achilles in action and dress, if not in temperament. Arthur contains some of Aeneas, Guyon some of Odysseus. These literary dimensions have an appositeness, but they complicate rather than clarify the figures who lose rather than gain expressive value when they come to act.

Spenser modelled his figures in part on those of Thomas Sackville in the 'Induction' to the *Mirror for Magistrates*. Sackville, C. S. Lewis says, 'greatly enlarged the former narrow bounds of our ideal imagery'. Yet it was the narrower bounds that ensured clear definition and therefore lucid communication. Spenser 'characterizes' his allegorical figures in varying degrees. There are those purely made of cardboard, such as 'Despair'. Then there are slightly more particularized figures, often with emblematic names – 'Sansfoy' and his brothers, for example – who act, but in a limited area. Amoret belongs to a still more differentiated category, a type more than a figure, with recognizable flesh on stylized bones. Central to the poem are the vital actors who represent virtues but are developed as characters whose virtues are vulnerable.

When such almost-real figures move among the more static figures of allegory, dramatic interest is seldom high. The moments of tension in the poem are not when a dragon appears or a battle is fought, but the seductions in which human motive and action are recognizable. One moment is especially well-achieved: when Paridell woos the miser's wife with his eyes, speaking not a word. Spenser's condensed history of the British kings in book two is expository verse of a high order. Thus he moralizes the story of king Leyr (Lear) even as he tells it:

But true it is that, when the oyle is spent,
The light goes out, the weeke is throwne away:
So, when he had resign'd his regiment,
His daughter gan despise his drouping day,
And wearie wax of his continuall stay.

For his poem Spenser invented the 'Spenserian Stanza', comprising eight iambic pentameter lines and a final hexameter, rhyming ababbcbcc. It is slow-moving, the hexameter giving a finality to each stanza. Compared with the natural expressive flow of Chaucer's stanzas in *Troilus and Criseyde*, with its central climax, Spenser's dignified, rather ceremonial measure can retard the narrative. It works most effectively in descriptive passages or where the poet expresses motion rather than action. A characteristically rich passage occurs in the fourth canto of book three, where Cymoënt speeds over the sea to the side of wounded Marinell:

Great Neptune stoode amazéd at their sight,
Whiles on his broad rownd back they softly slid,
And eke him selfe mournd at their mournful plight,
Yet wist not what their wailing ment; yet did,
For great compassion of their sorrow, bid
His mighty waters to them buxome bee:
Eftesoones the roaring billowes still abid,
And all the griesly Monsters of the See
Stood gaping at their gate, and wondered them to see.

A teme of Dolphins raungéd in aray
Drew the smooth charett of sad Cymoënt:
They were all taught by Triton to obay
To the long raynes at her commaundement:
As swifte as swallowes on the waves they went,
That their brode flaggy finnes no fome did reare,
No bubling rowndell they behinde them sent.
The rest, of other fishes drawen weare,
Which with their finny oars the swelling sea did sheare.

By contrast, *action* in this form seems to be magnified and slowed down, impressive rather than exciting.

We miss in Spenser's mature work 'human interest'. There is also a sense in which the poetry works by extension rather than concentration. One must read *The Faerie Queene* in large passages, for the impact is cumulative. The best effects are so much a part of the overall verbal context that they do not detach themselves as aphorisms or vivid images.

Despite his importance to the development of what one might call a Spenserian tradition which includes Milton, Keats, Byron, Tennyson and others, Spenser does not today command the audience he did even forty years ago. He has often been called a 'poets' poet'. In the latter half of this century he has become more a 'scholars' poet'. His work does not merit such a fate. For the ease and lucidity of his language over long stretches of narrative he has no superior but Chaucer. Ignorance of Spenser's work is ignorance of one of the fountainheads of English poetry.

Sir Walter Raleigh 1552?–1618

To seek new worlds for gold, for praise, for glory,
To try desire, to try love sever'd far,
When I was gone, she sent her memory,
More strong than were ten thousand ships of war,

To call me back ...

Shakespeare's Antony and Sir Walter Raleigh have much
in common: great gifts, a passionate disposition, impul-
siveness, influence, great friends and great foes. Each is
undone in service of a queen. Writing poetry was only a
small part of Raleigh's activity. Judging by how little care
he took to preserve his work and how fragmentary the
surviving poems are, it was not of central concern to him.
His principal literary undertaking was to write the
History of the World during his detention in the Tower,
but the prose he lives by is that of his letters and miscellaneous works.

Outside prison, his was an exemplary life of service and
action. He brought to the composition of his best poems
an imagination matured in the wide world: his most acute
experiences were ambition, love and disappointment. By
strenuous efforts he had climbed into the Queen's favour;
then by his action he had fallen. Two lines from his
earliest surviving poem, 'In Commendation of George
Gascoigne's Steel Glass', may have come back to him
during his trials and imprisonment: 'For whoso reaps

renoun above the rest,/With heaps of hate shall surely be opprest.'

Gascoigne was one of his poetic mentors. Where Gascoigne's poetry tended to literalize conventional material, planting Petrarchan flowers in actual English soil, Raleigh's poetry, initially by logic and later by the passion of disappointment, reduced the conventional to the absurd, as in the reply to Marlowe's 'Passionate Shepherd'; or distorted and personalized it. His verse, usually fragmentary or formally flawed, bears the impress of a mind more tortured and with much more powerful imagination than Gascoigne's. Gascoigne accepted failure with moderately good grace. Raleigh had to swallow disappointment after success, and the slow punishment of two monarchs. He may have no distinctive style: now he resembles Surrey, now Gascoigne, now Sidney or Spenser; but he has a more distinctive voice than any of them. He often succeeds on their terms. He has no poetic terms of his own.

Among the early poems are tributes to Spenser's epic, for Raleigh was the dedicatee of the first three books. In 'Methought I saw the grave where Laura lay', Raleigh asserts the superiority of Spenser over Petrarch. Spenser had complimented Raleigh as well, calling him 'the summer's Nightingale'; and in *Colin Clouts Come Home Againe* he evokes Raleigh fallen from royal grace:

His song was all a lamentable lay,
Of great unkindness, and of usage hard,
Of Cynthia the lady of the sea,
Which from her presence faultless him debarr'd.

'A lamentable lay' describes the best poems. They reflect on fortune, ephemerality and fate. When resignation comes, they meditate the pilgrimage through death towards judgement. 'Give me my scallop-shell of quiet', said to have been written by Raleigh (though it may not all be by him) while he was awaiting execution in the

Tower, is a remarkable statement of religious hope for a man so wedded to this world. 'Go, Soul, the body's guest', is not so resigned. From the point of death it turns back and regards the world, delivering a cumulative, incantatory indictment of what it sees. It is not an argument but an envenomed series of specific condemnations, with a deftly modulated refrain: a poem after experience, not merely after thought.

Born in East Budleigh, Devon, around 1552, Sir Walter Raleigh was the son of a not particularly distinguished gentleman. He grew up in Devon and perhaps retained a Devon accent throughout his life. In his mid-teens he went up to Oriel College, Oxford, and from there to the Middle Temple. Anthony à Wood reports that he was 'worthily esteemed' there, and we know that Francis Bacon, his friend, walked arm in arm with him around the gardens of Gray's Inn.

His life as a soldier included service with the Huguenots in the French Wars of Religion. He was active in Ireland, and his name is associated particularly with Smerwick and Youghal and the suppression of Irish resistance. By 1576 he was writing verse. By 1580 he was in the Queen's confidence. For a dozen years he was a real power in the land, in and out of favour. He became a Knight in 1584, was appointed Captain of the Guard in 1587, and received other preferments. In particular the Queen granted him a monopoly in connection with wine trading and gave him a patent to conquer and colonize in her name. He wore his favours ostentatiously and did not prepare for, though he prepared, his fall.

In 1592 he married secretly one of the Queen's maids of honour. After a spell in the Tower he was released to live in Sherborne, Dorset. He served the Queen again in naval action against Spain and later in his unsuccessful voyage of exploration to Guiana. The Queen died in 1603. James I's accession did not improve Raleigh's lot. James had him tried, condemned to death, reprieved and detained in the Tower for thirteen years. In 1616 the King released him unpardoned to pursue the royal interest in further exploration of Guiana, but under impossible conditions. Raleigh lost his son on the expedition, returned to England, and was executed in 1618.

His longest and most ambitious poem, 'Oceanus to Cynthia' ('The 11th: and last Book of the Ocean to Scinthia') is a fragment of what may have been an essentially autobiographical epic romance. The manuscript was lost until 1860, when it turned up among the Cecil Papers at Hatfield House. It was not published until 1870. Apart from this large, uneven fragment, fifty-odd other poems survive, about a dozen more doubtfully attributed, and some sixty metrical translations of passages from Latin and Greek authors scattered through the *History*. More may yet be discovered. Raleigh's work, like Wyatt's, was in no useful sense available until the latter half of the nineteenth century.

His tribute to Gascoigne's satire *The Steele Glass* reveals Raleigh's early preference for the plain style and for brusque, masculine utterance. His reply to Marlowe's 'Passionate Shepherd' is conventional, but like Marvell's 'To his Coy Mistress', speaks with the commonplace wisdom of the flesh:

If all the world and love were young,
And truth in every shepherd's tongue,
These pretty pleasures might me move
To live with thee and be thy love.

But Time drives flocks from field to fold,
When rivers rage and rocks grow cold ...

That last image, releasing literal weather on Marlowe's idealized landscape, shows the cast of Raleigh's imagination. There is a sense in which he wrote not out of a habit of versifying but when he had to. Satire, parody, elegy, lament and lyric seem to be the product of occasions or experiences which demanded expression. He speaks for and as himself. At his trial in 1603 he declared he was 'wholly gentleman, wholly soldier'. This man wrote the poems.

They fall into two categories. There are the aphoristic poems, pithy and spare; and the elaborated poems, rich in verbal texture and in metaphor – metaphor extended sometimes to 'metaphysical' lengths. Besides the formal flaws and fragmentariness of the longer poems, they are weakened by the mixing of various conflicting styles and, like the short poems, by the lack of progression.

His first notable work was the 'Epitaph on Sir Philip Sidney', an elegy in rhymed pentameter quatrains, each end-stopped, so that each stanza has force and finality. The poem follows roughly the chronology of Sidney's life and thus informs, celebrates and laments all at the same time. It is superior to Surrey's elegies to Wyatt which, equally sincere, lacked the courage to particularize.

Raleigh's sonnet 'Farewell to Court' prefigures in its three quatrains the verse form and the tone of 'Oceanus to Cynthia'. This poem must have been especially important to him since in the later 'Conceit Begotten of the Eyes' he alludes back to it, and he quotes it outright in 'Oceanus to Cynthia'. The original passage is among his best.

As in a country strange without companion,
I only wail the wrong of death's delays,
Whose sweet spring spent, whose summer well nigh done;
Of all which past, the sorrow only stays.

In 'Oceanus to Cynthia' he recalls:

Twelve years entire I wasted in this war;
Twelve years of my most happy younger days;
But I in them, and they, now wasted are:
'Of all which past, the sorrow only stays' –

So wrote I once, and my mishap foretold,
My mind still feeling sorrowful success,
Even as before a storm the marble cold
Doth by moist tears tempestuous times express.

The presence of a transcending, spiritual love even in the frustration of worldly love raises some of Raleigh's complaints to the level of devotional poetry. The 'true love' is not 'white nor brown'; she is a form, angel and nymph. 'As you came from the holy land/Of Walsinghame', almost certainly by Raleigh about the Queen of England, seems to include the Queen of Heaven. The human queen 'likes not the falling fruit/From the withered tree'. The pilgrim has seen her, the ageing poet's true love:

Such an one did I meet, good Sir,
    Such an angelic face,
Who like a queen, like a nymph, did appear
    By her gait, by her grace.

The poise of the last line, effecting a semantic surprise prepared by the repetitive construction Raleigh favours, places him not as C. S. Lewis contends, in an archaic school, but in the company of his metaphysical successors. When in another poem he writes, 'She is gone, she is lost, she is found, she is ever fair', the extra four syllables in his line are necessary: the requisites of experience override the prescriptions of form.

Raleigh occasionally binds his poems together by a specious seeming-logic, using 'Or' and 'But' to suggest connection. The underlying principle is contrast or juxtaposition. The discontinuity is only intellectual, since imagery develops with a lucid consistency. By sequential discontinuity he sometimes defeats his great foe, time, gaining freedom within memory. But memory itself embitters the present, and history offers little consolation: 'On Sestus' shore, Leander's late resort,/ Hero hath left no lamp to guide her love.'

Sir Philip Sidney 1554–1586

Reason, look to thyself! I serve a goddess.

Sir Philip Sidney is the first major English poet-critic, the model of correctness, clarity and measure. A man with enviable social advantages, he put them to full use and excelled in all he did. He is the most unambiguously attractive English writer, a renaissance *uomo universale* without Surrey's ambition or Raleigh's *hubris*. He was all of a piece, somewhat brittle, with a carefully acquired polish, but noble and consistent in thought and action. Fulke Greville – his lifelong friend and his first biographer – called him 'the wonder of our age' in his great 'Epitaph', which ends with the lines:

Now rhyme, the son of rage, which art no kin to skill,
And endless grief, which deads my life, yet knows not how to
  kill,
Go, seek that hapless tomb, which if ye hap to find,
Salute the stones, that keep the limbs, that held so good a mind.

Sidney, the hope and the patron of English poetry, died at the age of thirty-two, in 1586, of wounds received at Zutphen in the Netherlands campaign.

Most of his contemporaries elegized him. Raleigh's verses trace the life:

A king gave thee thy name; a kingly mind,
That God thee gave, who found it now too dear
For this base world, and hath resumed it near,
To sit in skies, and sort with powers divine.

Kent thy birth-days, Oxford held thy youth;
The heavens made haste, and stay'd nor years nor time,
The fruits of age grew ripe in thy first prime;
Thy will, thy words; thy words the seals of truth.

Great gifts and wisdom rare employ'd thee thence,
To treat from kings with those more great than kings ...

Raleigh's final stanza calls Sidney 'Scipio, Cicero, and Petrarch of our time'.

Sidney was born in 1554 at Penshurst Place, Kent, an estate Ben Jonson celebrated in 'On Penshurst'. The king who gave Sidney his name was Philip of Spain, his godfather. He came of the best aristocratic stock. He entered Shrewsbury School, Shropshire, on the same day as Fulke Greville. From there he went up to Christ Church, Oxford, but left on account of the plague. He spent time at Queen Elizabeth's court, writing a masque in her honour in 1578, and going on missions for her to the Continent. He spent time as well with his sister, later Countess of Pembroke, in Wiltshire. She is said to have suggested that he write *Arcadia*.

His travels began early. At the age of eighteen he was in Paris during the Massacre of St Bartholomew. From Paris he travelled to Germany and to Italy, where at Padua his portrait was painted by Veronese. He also visited Ireland and Wales with his father, Deputy of Ireland and President of Wales, and ably defended his conduct of Irish policy. He received from Spenser the dedication of *The Shepheards Calender*, and from Hakluyt the dedication of the *Voyages*.

In 1580 he forfeited the Queen's favour by opposing her proposed marriage to the Duke of Anjou. That cloud past, he served as an MP, was knighted in 1582, and in 1583 married the daughter of Sir Francis Walsingham. He made preparations to accompany Raleigh and Drake to the West Indies in 1585, but he was sent instead to the Netherlands and his death the next year.

Another book dedicated to Sidney was Gosson's famous attack on writers, *The School of Abuse, Containing a Pleasant Invective against Poets, Pipers, Players, Jesters, and such like Caterpillers of a Commonwealth* (1579). The young poet did not find it 'pleasant' and in reply composed his *Apology for* (later *Defence of*) *Poesy* (probably 1581, published 1595). Sidney does not adopt Gosson's invective but writes an urbane and reasoned argument which, without originality of thought but with great clarity, distils the literary criticism of the Italian Renaissance. In the words of Spingarn, 'so thoroughly is it imbued with this spirit, that no other work, Italian, French, or English, can be said to give so complete and so noble a conception of the temper and principles of Renaissance criticism.' Sidney's original sources were the critical treatises of Minturno and Scaliger. What his essay lacks in novelty it makes up for in conviction, unity of feeling, and elegance of style.

For Sidney poetry is the first art, the light-bearer. Following Aristotle (as mediated through his disciples) he defines art as imitation, *mimesis*: poetry is 'a speaking picture' whose end is 'to teach and delight'. Sidney's aesthetic is inseparable from his general view of life. The idea of imitation was crucial. The artist is a second creator producing a second nature. He imitates the ideal, showing what may or should be rather than merely copying what is. C. S. Lewis calls in Plotinus to clarify the neo-Platonic notion of imitation or invention. 'If anyone disparages the arts on the ground that they imitate Nature, we must remind him that natural objects are themselves only imitations, and that the arts do not simply imitate what they see but re-ascend to those principles from which Nature herself is derived ... Pheidias used no visible model for his Zeus.'

This moral art frees the will from the trammels of nature, draws it to virtue. The philosopher teaches by precept and the historian by example. The poet marries precept and example. Philosopher and historian address the learned; the poet addresses all men.

The *Defence* remains a living text today. It states a case no longer frequently heard, and the more interesting for that reason. Sidney is conscious of the uniqueness of the poetic art and its limitations. All vocations, he says, *follow* nature, except poetry. 'Only the poet, disdaining to be tied to any such subjection, lifted up with the vigour of his own invention, doth grow in effect another nature, in making things either better than nature, as the Heroes, Demigods, Cyclops, Chimeras, Furies, and such like; so as he goeth hand in hand with nature, not enclosed within the narrow warrant of her gifts, but freely ranging only within the zodiac of his own wit.' Nature's 'world is brazen, the poet only delivers a golden'. So in *Astrophel and Stella*, when the Muse – echoing Petrarch – says, 'Look in thy heart and write', or when Sidney criticizes in other poets 'a want of inward touch', he is not after an indulged sincerity or a freedom from convention, but a creative power which animates an imaginative world, different from this world but consistent with it and, in that specialized Platonic sense, 'real'. After all, 'what we call Cupid's dart/An image is, which for ourselves we carve.'

The nobility of Sidney's conception of poetry emerges in passage after passage, but chiefly when he reflects on the purpose of the art: 'this purifying of wit – this enriching of memory, enabling of judgement, and enlarging of conceit – which commonly we call learning ... the final end is to draw us to as high a perfection as our degenerate souls, made worse by their clayey lodgings, can be capable of.' The poet is 'the least liar' among writers: 'he nothing affirms, and therefore never lieth. For, as I take it, to lie is to affirm that to be true which is false.' The poet has thus a boundless freedom to invent and the sanction of inspiration. He is restrained only by his moral purpose, to inculcate virtue.

Astrophel and Stella (1582), the first major sonnet

sequence in English; the poems from *Arcadia*; and a few additional pieces constitute Sidney's poetic *oeuvre*. Within so small a body of work, Sidney proves himself formally and metrically more inventive than Spenser and other contemporaries. The sonnets have a linguistic and intellectual thriftiness and an emotional control that place them in a class of their own. *Astrophel and Stella* is his poetic masterpiece.

The sequence is Petrarchan in manner, but with an overall unity of theme and imagery and, though it has no plot, a progression of feeling. Astrophel is lover, Stella the beloved. The names themselves ('lover of stars' and 'star') correspond nicely to the theme. When a time setting is suggested in a sonnet, it is normally night. The imagery of light and darkness provides a recurrent reminder of the underlying relationship. In the sequence the poet labours first to express his love, then to win its object. He gets her at last, then circumstances part him from her. There are 108 sonnets and nine other poems in the sequence. Diversity of tone from poem to poem requires of the reader a continual readjustment of expectation, restraining him from direct involvement. He witnesses, does not participate in, the emotion.

Many of the individual sonnets have a dramatic structure. 'What, have I thus betray'd my liberty?', deriving from Catullus's '*Miser Catulle, desinas ineptire*' (viii), declares his liberty of Stella – and his thraldom:

I may, I must, I can, I will, I do
Leave following that which it is gain to miss.
Let her go! Soft, but here she comes ...

Another sort of drama develops in 'Be your words made, good Sir, of Indian ware', in which he demands of his interlocutor 'whether she did sit or walk;/How cloth'd; how waited on; sigh'd she or smil'd'. One is put in mind of Cleopatra demanding news of Octavia. Elsewhere Sidney addresses his Heart, Desire or Absence. Sometimes he debates against the sage whose wisdom is powerless against love. The poems develop logically, but often the last line or couplet refutes logic by a simple statement of emotional fact. In more than one sonnet he debates with himself:

Come, let me write. And to what end? To ease
A burthened heart. How can words ease, which are
The glasses of thy daily-vexing care?
Oft cruel fights well pictured-forth do please.
Art not ashamed to publish thy disease?
Nay...

Variety of form complements the variety of address. The rhyme schemes vary, and a few of the sonnets are in alexandrines. Sidney is endlessly resourceful in the matter of syntax, diction and diverse clarity: 'Come, Sleep, O Sleep, the certain knot of peace' made its impact on Shakespeare; 'As good to write, as for to lie and groan./ O Stella dear'; 'I am not I: /pity the tale of me'; and Herbert's line, 'Let me not love thee if I love thee not', has a source in Sidney's 'That I love not without I leave to love'; and Herbert may have been touched by the line, 'But ah, Desire still cries: "Give me some food!"' The spell is often achieved by simple repetition: 'Do thou then – for thou canst – do thou complain/For my poor soul.' The sequence runs the gamut of love. The non-sonnets at the end of the sequence, though not of a piece with what precedes them, have the merit of smoothness.

Sidney began his *Arcadia* in 1587. The first version was an 'idle work' composed for his sister's entertainment. He revised it radically, and we have three versions, the last of which appeared in the 1593 folio edition of his work and was in five books. In this version *Arcadia* enjoyed considerable popularity and influenced poets and prose writers, including Shakespeare and Milton. The first version was novelistic, while in revised form it is more in the spirit of Spenser, or Ovid's *Metamorphoses*. Sannazaro instructed Sidney in romance: from him he learned to alternate prose and verse. Prose supplies a context – plot and setting – for the verse. Despite pastoral trappings, *Arcadia* is an heroic romance.

Among the most striking poems in *Arcadia* are the experiments in classical metres, especially the Sapphics and Asclepiads ('If mine eyes can speak to do hearty errand' and 'O sweet woods'). Critics have generally damned with faint praise Elizabethan experiments in classical metres, with some reason since the humanists never established how a quantitative verse could be consistently developed in English, and even Spenser in his debate with Gabriel Harvey failed to resolve the problem. Despite the absence of a convincing theory, and despite the many bad pseudo-classical poems produced, Sidney with his faultless prosodic tact managed to achieve something new which amply rewards the attentive ear. 'O sweet woods, the delight of solitariness/O how much I do like your solitariness!' And there is the line, 'What man grafts in a tree dissimulation?' The prosody of Ezra Pound has made these poems more audible to us.

Much of the metrical verse in *Arcadia* is smooth, or over-smooth, verse narrative, the impulse diffused, the content thin. There are a few fine lyrics on age and love, including 'My sheep are thoughts, which I both guide and serve'. One senses here and in the sonnets the presence of a religious intelligence which might have written more than the one great devotional poem 'Leave me, O love, which reachest but to dust', a fitting resolution of carnal in metaphysical desire, of human in divine love.

Among the *Arcadia* poems there are lapses of taste. 'The lively clusters of her breasts' recalls the sonnet where Sidney promises in future to kiss, rather than bite, Stella's nipples. But there are triumphs, too: 'Reason tell me thy mind, if there be reason', 'Phoebus, farewell', 'My true love hath my heart', and the long and inventive 'The lad Philisedes'.

Sidney's brand of integrity is not fashionable today. Nor does his verse appeal as widely as it has in the past.

'So good a mind,' Greville said, and so it is. Sidney's verse, like his prose, like his life, is exemplary, like a statue: handsome, evocative of an age, an intelligence, even if the stone is cold.

George Chapman 1559?–1634

Kneel then with me, fall worm-like on the ground,
And from th' infectious dung hill of this round,
From men's brass wits and golden foolery,
Weep, weep your souls, into felicity.

Swinburne, who loved Chapman's verse, complained of
its obscurity. Chapman in his early work confuses obscurity with profundity. It is only in his translations of
Homer and in the four Sestiads he wrote to complete
Marlowe's *Hero and Leander* that his gifts are seen to
full advantage, as it were following in the wake of precedent clarities.

In the dedicatory letter to *Ovid's Banquet* (1595) he
writes, after Horace, 'The profane multitude I hate.' He
will consecrate his 'strange poems to those searching
spirits, whom learning hath made noble, and nobility
sacred'. If he wrote plainly it would 'make the ass run
proud of his ears'. That 'clearness of representation, required in absolute poems, is not the perspicuous delivery
of low invention; but high, and hearty invention expressed in most significant, and unaffected phrase'. The
terms are like, but subtly different from, those of Sidney,
for here is the Platonic view conceived, the poems prove
this, as a form of licence, not as the highest form of responsibility. As against Sidney's classical, aristocratic
clarity, we have a self-indulgent mind at work. Ideas become vaporous. *Ovid's Banquet*, at moments vivid, at
moments metaphysically elaborated (as in stanza 99),

suffers from a mechanical progression. It adds up to little. Decoration passes for development of thought. The poem is intellectually complicated rather than poetically complex.

The vice was not peculiar to Chapman. There was, centred largely on Raleigh, a 'School of Atheism' (as its detractors called it) or a 'School of Night', perhaps the subject of direct ridicule in Shakespeare's *Love's Labours Lost*. It included Marlowe and a few notable scientists and thinkers as well. The School of Night might have taken as its anthem Chapman's lines:

Sweet Peace's richest crown is made of stars,
Most certain guides of honoured mariners;
No pen can anything eternal write
That is not steeped in humour of the Night.

George Chapman was born of gentleman-farmer stock in or near Hitchin, Hertfordshire, around 1559. Little is known of his early life. He may have attended Oxford, though by his own account he was self-taught. He may have seen service in the Netherlands. His first published poems were 'The Shadow of Night' and a companion piece (1594) in both of which he developed a theory of false and true dreams. The poem is a mixture of eloquence (see the epigraph of this essay), wilful obscurity, and dull comprehensibility. The matter was not so deep as he thought. Chapman grew away from, but never outgrew, this clouding aesthetic.

In 1595 his first play was produced. Soon he had a reputation and was admired by Spenser, Samuel Daniel, Shakespeare and others. There is a theory that associates him with the 'rival poet' in Shakespeare's *Sonnets*, 'Was it the proud full sail of his great verse,/Bound for the prize of all too precious you.' Chapman became a sonneteer with the elegant 'Coronet for his Mistress' appended to *Ovid's Banquet*. In 1596 he wrote *De Guiana,* supporting Raleigh who had fallen from the Queen's favour. The poem, which did not influence Elizabeth, includes a fine

evocation of Chapman's figure of the Hero, a figure often
encountered in his plays, a man of intellect and passion:

But you patrician spirits that refine
Your flesh to fire, and issue like a flame
On brave endeavours, knowing that in them
The tract of heaven in morn-like glory opens ...
You know that death lives, where power lives unus'd,
Joying to shine in waves that bury you,
And so make way for life e'en through your graves.

De Guiana, his only poem in blank verse, is a *carmen
epicum* without narrative, an oration addressed to the
Queen, almost dramatic in its eloquence.

In 1598 he completed *Hero and Leander* and began to
publish his translations of Homer. In 1609 *Euthymiae
Raptus*, a philosophical poem subtitled 'The Tears of
Peace', was published. In it Homer, as guide, reveals to
the poet Peace in tears. The poem was dedicated to Prince
Henry, a patron of his translation work who died two
years later. Chapman composed the 'Epicede on Prince
Henry'. The loss of a noble patron was disastrous to him
and his purse. Chapman was impecunious: he was first
arrested for debt in 1599 and the last ten years of his life
were plagued by creditors.

He saw prison, too, after the accession of James I,
when with his then friends Ben Jonson and John Marston
he was locked up for having staged with them the comedy
Westward Hoe, which included some ill-timed jests at the
expense of the Scots. Chapman grew hostile to Jonson,
resenting his arrogance and his success. In 1634 Chapman
died in poverty and probably in bitterness. He was buried
in St Giles-in-the-Fields, London, and Inigo Jones provided a monument.

It is now almost *de rigueur* to criticize Chapman's four
sestiads of *Hero and Leander*. Warton long ago commented on the 'striking inequality' between Marlowe's
and Chapman's parts of the poem. Edward Thomas wrote
Chapman off: 'Marlowe died, and Chapman knew not

the incantation.' Yet the tide against Chapman should turn. Edgell Rickword, in an important essay in 1921, pointed to the crucial line in the transition to the third sestiad. 'Love's edge is taken off' – the moral must follow. Marlowe enacted the consummation; Chapman, more temperamentally suited to the task, had to enact the consequences. Rickword writes that Chapman 'does not understand more profoundly than Marlowe, but his thought processes are nearer the surface, and interfere with its crystallization, first into imagery and then into formal expression.' In his original writing this was Chapman's perennial difficulty: he was by nature a thinker, his verse at times decorates or clouds ideas. Some of his best writing is directly expository – and so is some of his worst.

He is clear from the outset about the nature of his task in *Hero and Leander*. 'New light gives new direction, fortunes new.' The poem finds a new register and a different intensity. There are moments of Marlovian physicality. Of Leander he says: 'Now (with warm baths and odours comforted)/When he lay down he kindly kiss'd his bed.' Hero behaves similarly to her bed. Throughout Chapman's sestiads there are small transformations, metamorphoses, preparing for the culminating transformation of the lovers into birds. Chapman has a sense of the whole poem. The parallelisms are not mechanically but dramatically right, the characters develop; there is nothing static in their recognition of the consequences of their action.

The lovers have sinned against Ceremony, furtively committing an act for which they should have sought public sanction. Leander is visited by Thesme, goddess of Ceremony. She appears

> with a crown
> Of all the stars, and heaven with her descended,
> Her flaming hair and her bright feet extended,
> By which hung all the bench of deities;
> And in a chain, compact of ears and eyes,

She led Religion; all her body was
Clear and transparent as the purest glass:
For she was all presented to the sense;
Devotion, Order, State, and Reverence
Her shadows were; Society, Memory;
All which her sight made live; her absence die.

The poetry contains a political and social vision. C. S. Lewis regards it as the classic evocation of the Elizabethan world order. To Chapman Ceremony is what Concord is to Spenser and Degree to Shakespeare: the ordained proportion that provides actions with significance and institutions with permanence and authority. Ceremony is nothing less than that culture which draws a human and divine meaning from mere nature. To offend against Ceremony is to offend against her shadows, Devotion, Order, State and Reverence. It is to deny society's *mores*, ignore memory, usurp authority. Ceremony admonishes Leander. She

Told him how poor was substance without rites,
Like bills unsign'd, desires without delights;
Like meats unseason'd; like rank corn that grows
On cottages, that none or reaps or sows ...

The drama of two lovers broadens out into an interpretation of social experience at large. Hero is compared with a city surprised and pillaged: thoughts are the invading troops. So far-fetched a simile would seem absurd in another context. Chapman makes it work. The development of their reactions – Leander's decision to act, Hero's to accept – is realized with psychological aptness which cannot but recall Chaucer's *Troilus and Criseyde*.

Chapman's name is best known because of Keats's sonnet 'On First Looking into Chapman's Homer'. Keats was right: Chapman made Homer an integral part of English literature. His *Iliad* in fourteeners and his *Odyssey* in decasyllabic couplets are – with Golding's *Metamorphoses* of Ovid – major neglected masterpieces of our poetry.

C. S. Lewis contrasts Gavin Douglas's translation of Virgil with Chapman's of Homer. Both read their own philosophy into their originals. Both embodied practical ideals in their borrowed heroes. Chapman's notion of the 'great man' hardly squared with the Homeric heroes, and the poet distorts them to some extent. Since for him Homer is 'learning's sire', he makes him didactic: he seeks a deep sense in each phrase and action, interpolates, moralizes. Douglas finds Virgil fresh and eloquent, Chapman finds Homer sage. Douglas roughens Virgil while Chapman civilizes Homer. In a way, it is sad that Douglas didn't tackle Homer and Chapman Virgil.

Prefacing the *Iliad*, Chapman wrote, 'it is the part of every knowing and judicious interpreter, not to follow the number and order of words, but the material things themselves, and sentences to weigh diligently.' Sentences are 'meanings'. The prescription is thoroughly Horatian. It accounts for the virtues and the flaws of Chapman's versions. Warton was critical: Chapman had forfeited dignity and simplicity, had written redundantly, had impoverished where he could not 'feel and express'. Warton, with some justice, criticizes the fourteeners used in the *Iliad* as 'awkward, inharmonious, and unheroic'. Pope, himself a translator of Homer, was not so dismissive. Warton possessed Pope's copy of Chapman's Homer and comments on Pope's annotations. Chapman, Pope had noted, covers his defects 'by a daring fiery spirit that animates his translation, which is something like what one might imagine Homer himself to have writ before he arrived at years of discretion'.

Homer was Chapman's destiny – 'angel to me, star and fate'. He completed the *Iliad* in 1611, the *Odyssey* in 1616, and the *Hymns* in 1624. 'The work that I was born to do, is done,' he says. And for all its manifest flaws it is a triumph. It can be appreciated only *in extenso*. I offer one brief example, the death of Hector from the *Iliad*:

> Then all the Greeks ran to him,
> To see his person; and admired his terror-stirring limb:
> Yet none stood by, that gave no wound, to his so goodly form;
> When each to other said: O Jove, he is not in the storm
> He came to fleet in, with his fire; he handles now more soft ...

The verse is plain, the syntax loose but clear and dramatically phrased to the climax, and the choice of words
unexpected and right.

Chapman was a prolific writer. He did not suffer academic critics gladly, especially when they attacked his
Homer. His purpose had been 'With poesy, to open poesy'.
Certainly in translating Homer he became a form of his
own notion of the hero. There are four hundred pages of
his poetry and about a thousand of his translations.

Possibly it was from Homer that he learned the plain
style which surfaces occasionally in the otherwise dull
'Eugenia', an elegy:

> the large bon'd oxen look'd
> Oft on broad heaven, and the soft air suck'd,
> Smelling it in; their reeking nostrils still
> Sucking the clear dew from the daffodil:
> Bow'd to their sides their broad heads, and their hair
> Lick'd smooth at all parts; lov'd their night-tide lair:
> And late in night, did bellow from the stall,
> As thence the tempest would his blasts exhale.

Christopher Marlowe 1564–1593

In summer heat, and mid-time of the day,
To rest my limbs upon a bed I lay;
One window shut, the other open stood,
Which gave such light as twinkles in a wood,
Like twilight glimpse at setting of the sun,
Or night being past, and yet not day begun.

Christopher Marlowe the poet achieves quite different
effects from Christopher Marlowe the playwright. The
playwright explores ambition and power, but the poet is
a younger man, creating or translating a world of balance
and proportion. The poems lack the exaggeration of
language and action, the grandiloquence of the 'mighty
line'. Puttenham dispraised Marlowe's hyperbolic dramatic style: 'the over reacher, otherwise called the loud
liar': and Nashe commented on 'the specious volubility
of a drumming decasillabon'. The poems are not implicated in these strictures. They neither over-reach nor
drum. They are not voluble nor specious but economical
of language and serious in content, even when the tone is
light-hearted.

Marlowe was born in Canterbury in 1564. His father
was a shoemaker. Christopher became a scholar at the
King's School, Canterbury, and afterwards at Corpus
Christi College, Cambridge. He took his BA in 1584 and
his MA in 1587, by which time he had probably completed *Tamburlaine*. He was the first of the university
wits to employ blank verse. It is generally thought that

most if not all of Marlowe's small surviving body of non-dramatic verse, *Hero and Leander*, 'The Passionate Shepherd', and the Ovid and Lucan translations, were executed in his years at University, the work of youth and relative leisure. The six years that elapsed between his taking his MA and his death at the hand of Ingram Frizer in a Deptford tavern in 1593 were busy ones. He wrote his plays, was regularly attacked for his 'atheism', associated with Chapman and Raleigh in the 'School of Night', and lodged with Thomas Kyd (author of *The Spanish Tragedy*) who later brought charges of blasphemy against him. These he had to answer at Privy Council in 1593 – the very Council which secretly employed him as a spy. It is remarkable that he achieved so much, given the variety of his activities.

Hero and Leander, his fragment of an epyllion or miniature epic, a form common in the sixteenth century, was popular: it went through ten editions in the forty years after its first appearance. Poets other than Chapman attempted to 'complete' it. Henry Petowe was one: 'I being but a slender Atlas to uphold and undergo so large a burden.' His happy ending turned the lovers into pine trees. Had Chapman not brought the poem to a competent end, it is likely we would consider Marlowe's two completed sestiads a whole poem. In a sense we would be right. If it was work done at Cambridge, he had time left to complete it himself, had he wished.

The epyllion derives from Theocritus, Catullus and Ovid. Marlowe certainly knew his Ovid, and his poem is Ovidian mythological-erotic verse of a high order. Indeed, it is one of the great poems of the language. Edgell Rickword has written: 'Putting aside *Paradise Lost*, it would seem impossible to find a later rival to *Hero and Leander*' as a narrative poem. No other has 'so perfect and consistent a balance maintained between the natural world and the world of poetic imagination. It is the most classical of English love poems, if classic means that the emotions are represented in their natural proportions, their significance revealed by selection, not by elaboration, and the whole human spectacle worked out against a background of destiny which the reader is brought to realize by purely aesthetic means.' Rickword in his justifiable enthusiasm may have lost sight of Chaucer's *Troilus and Criseyde*. But that poem is Marlowe's only serious rival.

Hero and Leander provides a sharp contrast with Shakespeare's efforts in the same genre, *Venus and Adonis* and *The Rape of Lucrece*. Shakespeare's poems begin in action. In the earlier poem, 'rose cheek'd Adonis' is at chase by line three, laughing love to scorn in line four, and being loved in line five. *The Rape of Lucrece* similarly begins *in medias res*, the lustful Tarquin off hotfoot, 'Borne by the trustless wings of hot desire'. Both poems are conventionally dramatic. They accommodate only with difficulty the reflective laments which, excellent in themselves, interrupt the established dramatic pace.

It may be that Marlowe is fortunate in that we cannot judge him as a tragic poet in *Hero and Leander*. He portrays a consummation, and *desunt nonnulla* leads into Chapman, who had the task of judgement. It is not, however, the lack of tragedy that makes Marlowe's poem superior to Shakespeare's: it is the difference of procedure and tone. Shakespeare's six-line pentameter stanzas distort his natural pace and seem to conflict with narrative continuity, much as the sonnet form sometimes distorts thought and weakens emphasis in his great sequence. The stanzas have a finality about their ababcc rhyme scheme which gives a tonal sententiousness or resolution just when a more fluid movement is required. Marlowe chose pentameter couplets which have a swiftness of movement when they must, and can be used for reflection and description as well. Moreover, they carry his voice, with its passions and its ironies, effortlessly, modulating from one register to another.

Marlowe is careful to avoid, or to deflate, the heroic exaggerations that vitiate other epyllions. He does not caricature but humanizes his protagonists in the process. They are, in the end, girl and boy. The strategy of the poem seems to be to get them to this natural end. When Hero first appears in the temple, she wears a gaudy veil of artificial flowers and leaves that covers her from head to foot. She looks rather like a pot of ivy. In seeming to praise her, Marlowe defines the unnatural conventions that overlie the natural girl. He praises her chastity, but does not condemn her for letting drop her fan. Only her eyes and hands are plainly visible. He thwarts idealization by ironizing the ideal elements or by simple satire. The truth he presents boldly: 'Love is not full of pity, as men say,/But deaf and cruel where he means to prey.' The word 'prey' suggests the animal imagery which runs throughout the poem: it is animal desire and not some courtly refinement that drives the action. The animal imagery is presented as natural, not in a spirit of censure. Love is stripped of its mystique. Hero is finally naked. Leander's argument against chastity is not convincing, but his desire is. He speaks 'like a bold sharp sophister' with borrowed arguments, for he is (like Hero, but in a different sense) 'a novice'. 'My words shall be as spotless as my youth,/Full of simplicity and naked truth.' The core of his argument is charming: I shall be as faithful to you as you are more beautiful than Venus. With such logic Satan prevailed upon Eve. The indictment of virginity, 'Of that which hath no being do not boast,/Things that are not at all are never lost', can be extended as an indictment of all metaphysical belief, an expression of Marlowe's famous atheism. The poem is thoroughly wedded to the physical world. The imagery effects metamorphoses which always tend to make the poem more sensually vivid. Hero has 'swallowed Cupid's golden hook/The more she striv'd, the deeper was she strook'. When Neptune enters, he touches Leander's swimming body, making it in the most evocative passage in the poem exquisitely real. The gods too are creaturely.

The love of Hero and Leander is not consummated in

the Temple. Hero will not let Leander so much as touch her sacred garments. There is no element of consecration apart from desire itself. She bids him 'Come thither' to her turret set squarely in the natural world:

Upon a rock, and underneath a hill,
Far from the town, where all is whist and still
Save that the sea, playing on yellow sand,
Sends forth a rattling murmur to the land,
Whose sound allures the golden Morpheus
In silence of the night to visit us,
My turret stands ...

The suspended subject and verb and the dramatic unpleating of the syntax demonstrate the flexibility of the form and Marlowe's subtlety in handling it. The drama is in the language and the characters, not in the action. This is a measure of what Rickword calls its 'classical' success.

The process of metamorphosis is at the heart of the poem, and Hero's own change is richly Ovidian. She is the first and last character we see, and her transformation is subtly effected. At the outset she is the antithesis to Leander. Her wreath and veil entirely 'shrub her in', her costume and scent are hyperbolically described, yet she exists only as a figure. Leander, by contrast, is 'beautiful and young'. 'His body was as straight as Circe's wand.' It was with her wand that Circe transformed men into beasts. Marlowe does not let the suggestion pass.

These very different characters encounter one another in Venus's temple, among portrayals of 'heady riots, incests, rapes', the loves of the gods, and especially those in which they became animals; bulls or swans. In this place Hero sacrificed turtle-doves. The mythological portrayals are humorous as well as affective: by his tone, Marlowe has indicated that we are not to take them too seriously, yet he expresses them in such vivid terms that they are full of suggestion, even if their emblematic significance is ironic.

Hero's metamorphosis is complete at last:

Thus near the bed she blushing stood upright,
And from her countenance behold ye might
A kind of twilight break, which through her hair,
As from an orient cloud, glims here and there.

In the very completeness of his two sestiads, Marlowe
suggests there are no lessons to be drawn from love, only
about it.

Chief among his other poems are his translations of
Ovid's *Elegies* (the *Amores*). For his contemporaries,
Drayton and Daniel in particular, his translation of
Lucan may have seemed more important. For us that
labour has lost much of its interest. But the Ovid remains
brisk and accurate verse, with an expressive range almost
as wide as that of *Hero and Leander*. Jonson, Donne and
other poets owe him a debt for the *Elegies*.

'Elegy' was originally the generic term for a song of
mourning in a metre which alternated hexameters and
pentameters. But the elegiac metre was later adopted for
the expression of personal feelings, as distinct from narrative or lyric. For Ovid, as later for Jonson, Donne,
Marvell, Carew and others, it was a language of reflection,
exhortation, tribute, wide in subject-matter and tone, and
often amorous.

Marlowe condensed Ovid's *Amores* from five into three
books. This exercise may have taught him his prosodic
skill with the couplet and the Ovidian manner. There are
direct echoes of *Hero and Leander* or, if the *Elegies* came
first, in *Hero and Leander*: a similar variety of tone,
emotion and allusion. In the translations we find the
familiar arguments against chastity. The quest for
pleasure as an end, and the 'atheism' ('God is a name, no
substance, fear'd in vain') are met here. One critic sees
the *Elegies* as the Marlovian equivalent of Shakespeare's
Sonnets. That dignifies them above their real excellence.

'The Passionate Shepherd', Marlowe's best-known
poem, was made the more memorable by the number of

replies it occasioned, among them Raleigh's and, perhaps indirectly, Marvell's 'To his Coy Mistress'. Taking Marlowe's poems and translations together, it is a small body of work, and yet in a quieter way than the plays it was influential. The dramatist may have given up writing poems at the age of twenty-three. But the Marlowe lamented in Shakespeare's *As You Like It* is the poet of *Hero and Leander*, 'The Passionate Shepherd' and the *Elegies*.

Thomas Campion 1567–1620

See how the morning smiles
On her bright eastern hills
And with soft steps beguiles
Them that lie slumb'ring still.
The music-loving birds are come
    From cliffs and rocks unknown,
To see the trees and briars bloom
    That late were overflown.

Little information survives about Thomas Campion's
life. He was born probably in London (possibly in
Essex) in 1567. His father, a clerk of the court of chancery
and owner of property in Essex, died when the boy was
nine. His mother remarried, but died when he was thirteen. His stepfather sent him to Peterhouse, Cambridge,
which he left at the age of seventeen without taking a
degree. He entered Gray's Inn, London, in 1586. There
is no evidence that he ever practised law, and in his verse
he occasionally expresses a strong distaste for the pro-
fession. How he earned a living before 1605 is unknown.
In that year he qualified in medicine at the University of
Caen and thereafter practised as a physician. With several
other writers patronized by the Howards or their re-
tainers, he was implicated in the notorious case of the
murder of Sir Thomas Overbury in the Tower. He remained faithful to Thomas Monson, who took much of
the blame on the Howards' behalf, attending him during
his imprisonment and dedicating a book to him on his

release. Campion died in 1620, leaving all he had to his close friend the lutenist Philip Rosseter, with whom he had composed many of his songs and ayres. His estate was valued at £22.

Campion first appeared in public as the figure of 'Melancholy' in a masque in 1588. But 'Content' was the pseudonym under which his first poems were published in Thomas Newman's 1591 edition of Sidney's *Astrophel and Stella*. His poems at that time were in the manner of Sidney. The first work to appear under his own name was *Poemata* (1595), including a minor epic about the defeat of the Armada, elegies, epigrams and Ovidian fragments, all in Latin. In 1601, with Philip Rosseter, he published the first *Book of Ayres*, those 'superfluous blossoms', in English, of his 'deeper studies'.

An 'ayre' is a poem sung by solo voice with, in Campion's case, a harmonized accompaniment. He likened the ayre in music to the epigram in poetry, 'Skilfully framed, and naturally expressed'. Unlike other writers of ayres, Campion often composed the words *and* the music, achieving remarkable correspondences between the two mediums. The ayre conventions were as strict as those for madrigal. The poems, taken apart from the music, appeal most to what Campion's editor W. R. Davis calls the 'auditory imagination'. There is little vital imagery. No English poet – not even Herrick – had a nicer sense of vowel values or the force of the monosyllable.

As a Latin epigrammatist second only, the critics say, to Sir Thomas More, Campion naturally turned his attention to classical metres and their possible use in English. He believed them to be more 'ayreable' than accentual metres. Sidney's example may have inspired his *Observations of the Art of English Poesie* (1602) and his experiments in classical metres. The *Observations* are elliptical and sometimes obscure and they cover ground first explored by Roger Ascham and Thomas Watson in the previous century, and by Drant, who influenced Spenser and Harvey. The argument against rhyme, towards an alien prosody, was almost exhausted by Campion's time. He revived it as argument, practising it only in a few illustrations to his argument. His dimeters have some authority:

> Yet not all the glebe
> His tough hands manured
> Now one turf affords
> His poor funeral.
> Thus still needy lives,
> Thus still needy dies
> Th' unknown multitude.

His contribution to the debate was to identify quantity with accent, at the same time positioning the accent according to classical rules. He sought a rationale for his system in English itself. He discarded hexameter and dactyl as thoroughly foreign to our language. 'We must esteem our syllables as we speak, not as we write, for the sound of them in verse is to be valued, and not their letters.'

Samuel Daniel's *Defense of Rhyme* answers Campion on patriotic grounds, but makes also the valid point that Campion frequently dresses up the iambic, so natural to English, in new names and pretends it is something rich and strange. The virtues of the *Observations* are local: the system is useless. There are occasional definitions of perfect clarity. The caesura is 'the natural breathing place' in the line. Campion *hears* rather than reads poetry. His case against rhyme is worth attending to even now. Rhyme *distorts* the work of many poets: 'it enforceth a man oftentimes to abjure his matter, and extend a short conceit beyond all bounds of art.'

1613 saw the publication of Campion's 'Songs of Mourning' for the death of Prince Henry, and *Two Books of Ayres*, the first of *Divine and Moral Songs*, the second *Light Conceits of Lovers*. In 1614 appeared his treatise on music. He expended much effort on writing masques, and the imagery in his verse has some of the brittle sharpness of masque properties. Many of the poems include little physical evocation. Their effect depends almost entirely on their prosodic virtuosity. Few poets can have used a greater variety of stanza forms, to such diverse effect, given the narrow range of diction, allusion and theme. One is inclined to class Campion as a miniaturist, a Nicholas Hilliard of poetry, an artist who requires close attention, whose work disappears if you stand at any distance from it. Anyone reading Campion should try to hear at least some of the ayres.

In his Latin poems he acknowledges a debt to Chaucer. More tangible debts are to Wyatt, Surrey and Sidney; and to the Latin poets. The poems fall into four rough categories: amorous laments (and occasional, but rare, celebrations of love); wanton and witty fancies; devotional poems; and frank declarations of love.

Campion's natural world is not the world of nature: it is Arcadia, a masque setting with nymphs and shepherds. This must be accepted: it is the context of the poems. Yet there is an indubitable personal note, and sometimes there are glimpses of a very solid reality. There is much invention in the sound, the balanced syllables, the manipulation of rhythm and rhyme, the attempt to give vowels 'convenient liberty', and the juxtaposition of stanzas with similar syntactical and rhythmic progression but contrasting emotional content. It is striking how many lines have an odd number of syllables and begin with a stress, an effect which may have been required by the music.

The enjambement serves so meticulous a craftsman well. Yvor Winters singled out one example to illustrate a general point:

Now winter nights enlarge
    The number of their hours,
And clouds their storms discharge
    Upon the ayrie towers ...

The suspended syntax at the end of the first and third

lines suggests two possible directions for the meaning. The following line takes up one meaning, but the second meaning remains active in our mind and in the poet's mind. He takes it up later. 'Enlarge' can mean increase in number or increase in space. It is number the poet means, but space that is implied and taken up in the last stanza. These are the subtle effects that give the poems their aural and intellectual power. It is all on a small scale, but carried out with the assurance of a fine craftsman, in some respects the most brilliant in the language.

At the opening of the *Fourth Book of Ayres* (1617), Campion writes, 'The apothecaries have books of gold, whose leaves being opened are so light as that they are subject to be shaken with the least breath and yet rightly handled, they serve both for ornament and use; such are light ayres.' It is a fair description of the art Campion mastered. It would be hard to name poems more formally perfect than 'When to her lute Corinna sings', 'Follow thy fair sun', 'The man of life upright', 'To music bent is my retired mind', 'Fire, fire, fire, fire!', 'There is a garden in her face', and many others – with or without their music. Even in its own day Campion's work must have seemed a little archaic and over-refined. Marlowe, Jonson and Donne were near contemporaries. Their world was beyond his grasp – or beyond his interest. But within his field Campion is an incomparable master.

Ben Jonson 1572–1637

And since our dainty age
   Cannot endure reproof,
  Make not thyself a Page,
To that strumpet the Stage,
   But sing high and aloof
Safe from the wolf's black jaw, and the dull
   Ass's hoof.

History set Jonson adjacent to Shakespeare. In the drama, this proximity does not help Jonson's reputation, though the two poets write plays so different as to seem distinct in kind. A part of that difference can be seen in Jonson's artistic deliberateness: he knew what he wanted to say and he had the means of saying it. The effect of his work is more of conclusion and finality than discovery and surprise. Jonson speaks for the age, while Shakespeare speaks for himself. Jonson's art is normative, Shakespeare's radical and exploratory. In Jonson there is structure and gauged variegation, in Shakespeare there is movement and warmth. Such, at least, is the common case against Jonson. Coleridge disliked the 'rankness' of his realism, the absence of 'goodness of heart'. He condemned the 'absurd rant and ventriloquism' in the tragedy *Sejanus*. At times Jonson's words, unlike Shakespeare's, tend to separate and stand single rather than coalesce.

There is some truth in all this. Jonson's attitude to the very sound of language seems to have been casual. Except in some of the songs from the plays (for instance, 'Queen, and huntress, chaste and fair') and isolated lyrics, the words are chosen first for their meaning and accent, only secondarily for their sound value. There are many clumps of consonants and an often indiscriminate collocation of vowels. Swinburne called him 'one of the singers who could not sing', and Eliot said, 'his poetry is of the surface'. Dryden pilloried him as 'not only a professed imitator of Horace, but a learned plagiary of all others; you track him everywhere in their snow.' This is over-harsh. If he could not sing, he could speak, an art which Swinburne never learned. If his poetry was 'of the surface', it must be said he chose his surfaces sometimes with amazing care and effect. If he borrowed from classical literature, he was no different in that from any of his contemporaries, except that he had a deeper knowledge than most of them of what he was quarrying. He translated Horace's *Ars Poetica*. Many of his poems borrow lines, but he integrates them into his verse. And he is of a stature with Martial and Juvenal, so that one feels that collaboration rather than plagiarism is the proper term for his action. As Eliot said, Jonson and Chapman 'incorporated their erudition into their sensibility'.

Dryden's criticism is telling at one point: Jonson 'weaved' the language 'too closely and laboriously' and he 'did a little too much Romanize our tongue, leaving the words he translated almost as much Latin as he found them'. Dryden ends with the inevitable verdict: 'I admire him, but I love Shakespeare.'

The one part of Jonson's *oeuvre* across which the shadow of Shakespeare does not fall is the non-dramatic verse, verse which was an example to a generation of writers following and which includes poems so distinctively Jonsonian in kind that we could confuse them with the work of no other master. Most notable among these are the 'country house' poems, the elegies and the epigrams.

Originally, 'epigram' referred to the inscription on a tombstone, usually in elegiac verse. But like the term 'elegy' itself, 'epigram' became detached from its original usage. For Jonson it described a genre that included the short and not so short occasional poem with a single mood or idea, sometimes satirical, at other times amatory, dedicatory, or elegiac. He and the 'Sons of Ben' – those younger poets who learned their craft from his example – developed it to a high perfection. Even Jonson's long poems tend to epigram. Couplets and longer passages detach themselves and catch in the mind, even when their contexts are forgotten.

If not a master of the 'music' of verse, Jonson is a master of stress. His poems are regular, with the authority of speech. The clarity of expression is matched by a moral clarity. His aesthetic is expressed in an aphorism: 'Language most shows a man. Speak that I may see thee.' In the poems we often hear and see the man himself. He speaks of a wide variety of topics, with an equal variety of feelings. He does not reserve poetry for moments of crisis or climax. It is a natural language, for him, that answers to occasion. Edmund Bolton writing in his *Hypercritica* in 1722 commented, 'I never tasted English more to my liking, nor more smart, and put to the height of use in poetry, than in the vital, judicious, and most practicable language of Benjamin Jonson's poems.' Those are useful adjectives: smart, vital, judicious, practicable. Jonson wrote with feeling, tempering thought and wit, in a language close to that he actually spoke. His is a comprehensive colloquial diction.

Jonson's omnicompetence as a writer, his ability to catch the tone of every situation, class and calling, was due in part to his background. He was born in London in 1572, probably a month after his father's death. His mother remarried, and he spent his youth with her and his stepfather, a bricklayer. He was educated under William Camden at Westminster School. It is worth reflecting on how many writers from the less privileged classes made their way through the Grammar Schools of the time. In 1588 he left school and began work as a bricklayer, a trade with which his later detractors used to stigmatize him. After military service in Flanders he married in 1594. He had two children, both of whom died and were lamented in notable elegies: 'Here lies to each her parents ruth' and 'Farewell, thou son of my right hand, and joy'.

In 1597 he was acting. His first work for the stage may have been additional scenes for Kyd's *Spanish Tragedy*. In the same year he was imprisoned for his part in *The Isle of Dogs*, a play of which he was probably part author. In 1598 he killed a fellow actor with a rapier and narrowly escaped hanging. He made progress as a playwright and was soon established as a leading tragic and comic dramatist.

In 1612–13 he completed the first book of *Epigrams*. The next year he travelled abroad with Raleigh's son and wrote a commendatory poem for Raleigh's *History*. In 1616, the year of Shakespeare's death, Jonson's 'first folio' was published – the only first folio to have been seen through press by its author. It was a crucial book, preparing by its success the way for Shakespeare's first folio, in which Jonson had a financial interest and for which he composed his famous elegy for Shakespeare in 1623.

After 1616 began what Dryden called Jonson's 'dotages', a string of unsuccessful plays. But Jonson was hardly in his dotage. He made his legendary journey on foot to Scotland to visit William Drummond of Hawthornden, with whom he stayed for three weeks until Drummond's cellar was drunk dry. Drummond gave an account of his conversations with Jonson and, since he as a *poeta doctus* was vain of his achievements, he took pleasure in commenting on Jonson's ignorance. In effect, he says that Jonson had little French and less Italian. Certainly Jonson was not in the contemporary European mainstream. He took his bearings from the Latin classics.

In later years Jonson may have been a deputy professor of rhetoric at Gresham College, London. Such an appointment would be one explanation of the pedagogic relations he had with the 'Sons of Ben', but he seems to

have won respect as a technical master, as Pound did. He
was venerated by the younger poets, those who knew him
and those who knew his work – notably Herrick, Carew,
Lovelace and Suckling.

He had worked in masques, and some of his imagery
draws on the masque, especially in his elegies that end in
staged apotheoses. He made a friend of Inigo Jones,
though as Jones grew more puffed up with self-import-
ance, and more successful, Jonson rounded on him. He
resented the superior success of his friends and juniors.
His later years, in which he suffered from palsy and
paralysis, were especially trying. He had been neglected
by King Charles upon his accession (James had showed
him some attentions). Six petitions of debt were filed
against him. Charles eventually recognized his value and
he gained new aristocratic patronage so that he did not
die, as Chapman did, in want. He was buried in 1637 in
Westminster Abbey.

Two modern poets have assiduously championed
Jonson: Yvor Winters and Thom Gunn. Winters places
Jonson at the centre of what he calls the 'native tradition',
exemplified by the plain-spoken poems of Wyatt, Gascoigne, Greville and others. Jonson's poems are 'expository in structure' but 'they engage in very little
figurative excursion ... and very little illustrative repetition.' From Marlowe Jonson had learned that verse is
the more effective for having integrated imagery rather
than decorative imagery. This lesson is evident in the best
plays and also in the poems. Further, he had learned a
control of rhetoric and a complexity of tone. He is expository rather than suasive. He has, in Winter's term, a
specific morality, and the poems apply this morality to the
social world: relations between people and people,
people and God.

Gunn's feeling for Jonson is deeper than Winters's. He
suggests that Jonson chose classical models for their
balance, to counteract his personal tendency towards extremes of response and action – a credible reading, given

what we know of the life and what we sense in the controlled vehemence of some of the satirical epigrams, and also the black world of the comedies. There is also, Gunn believes, a problem of 'willed feeling' which the modern reader dislikes. This is especially the case in the poems of flattery which continually protest that they are not flattering their subjects. There are several poems to King James, King Charles, their relations, and noblemen of various sorts which are laboriously fulsome and repetitive. 'How, best of Kings, do'st thou a sceptre bear!' Jonson's flattery comes off best when it is indirect, as in 'To Penshurst' and 'To Sir Robert Wroth', his finest extended poems, in which he praises his patrons by celebrating their estates or their manner of life. There are, too, the sincere tributes to Camden, Shakespeare, Donne, Drayton and others, which are in a different class of seriousness.

The poems tend to be occasional, responses to external events. But as Thom Gunn argues, all poetry is, even if remotely, occasional, and good poems retain a truth to their occasion, which is to say their subject. An occasion can be the death of a prince, or of a boy actor ('Weep with me all ye that read'), it can be a moment of anger at social affectation, or a thank-you letter, or a desire to translate a classical poem ('Drink to me only, with thine eyes', 'Come, my Celia', 'Follow a shadow').

It can be a large-scale social indictment ('On the Famous Voyage'), or the publication of a book, or a sickness, or a journey. Such poems are 'works of a diverse nature', united by a voice and sensibility to some extent typical of the best of its age. The religious verse has its occasions: 'A Hymn to God the Father' is utterly chaste and precise:

Who more can crave
  Than thou hast done:
  That gav'st a Son,
To free a slave?

Only in the sequences of love poetry does Jonson descend to the commonplace, but even there has a command which makes the poems readable. Best are the elegies in which an old man addresses his young mistress:

Alas, I ha' lost my heat, my blood, my prime,
Winter is come a quarter ere his time,
My health will leave me; and when you depart,
How shall I do, sweet mistress, for my heart?

In the elegy which begins 'Let me be what I am' there is less resignation. We see the face of the speaker in such poems.

In the moralizing poems, moral qualities gain a certain solidity from their context and generalize their significance as it were from a specific point. In 'To John Donne' he writes:

Those that for claps do write
Let pui'ness, porters, players praise delight,
And, till they burst, their backs, like asses, load:
A man should seek great glory, and not broad.

Or, in another poem, 'He that departs with his own honesty/For vulgar praise, doth it too dearly buy.' 'The verse movement,' Gunn says, 'has a variety within firmness that conducts the reader with great ease through the descriptive passages, giving each description the liveliness of comment.'

Jonson is above all a moral critic – of literature and society. Even the personal poems, the elegies on his children, the 'Execration upon Vulcan' (after a fire destroyed his manuscripts and library), the 'Ode to Himself', have general point and reference, they do not exist simply for themselves. Poetry is occasional and *applied* writing. Few poets equal the range of his work, and his greatness is in large part due to this range. The development in Jonson is moral rather than formal, we follow from work to work a mind which sometimes runs deep. The work should be read *in extenso*, taking the *Epigrams, The*

Forest, The Underwood and the *Miscellany* whole, prose aphorisms along with verse. The best poems have a tone of *just* approval or censure, and this justice is a product of his formal control, the sense of balance and conclusion, of considered wisdom. 'Rare poems ask rare friends', 'A good poet's made, as well as born', 'In small proportions, we just beauties see;/And in short measures, life may perfect be'. Such pithy rightness is Jonson's hallmark. He is our greatest epigrammatist.

'To Penshurst' and 'To Sir Robert Wroth', one in pentameter couplets, the other in pentameter/tetrameter couplets, develop with epigrammatic precision, a tidy conclusiveness of progression, each descriptive detail discretely moralized and adding to the development of broader themes of order, proportion and natural hierarchy. 'To Penshurst' is one of the great 'country house' poems celebrating a place associated with Sir Philip Sidney. Jonson first praises its lack of affectation and studied grandeur, its healthy naturalness. In classical terms he evokes the park and generalizes its qualities by a subtle use of the definite article and the possessive pronoun with collective and plural nouns:

The lower land, that to the river bends,
Thy sheep, thy bullocks, kine and claves do feed:
The middle ground thy mares, and horses breed.
Each bank doth yield thee coneys; and the tops,
Fertile of wood, Ashore, and Sydney's copse,
To crown thy open table, doth provide
The purpled pheasant, with the speckled side:
The painted partridge lies in every field,
And, for thy mess, is willing to be killed.

The participles 'painted' and 'purpled' suggest the hand of the maker. The word 'open' unostentatiously moralizes upon the hospitality of the place. Jonson presents not an artificial but a cultivated landscape, a distinction worth bearing in mind. It is Pope, in 'Windsor Forest', who artificializes. 'To Penshurst' celebrates cultivated order, responsible hierarchy, social and natural proportion. It is more like praise justly rendered, than grateful flattery.

'To Sir Robert Wroth', with its diminishing couplet, a diminution accented by the strong caesura in many of the tetrameters, has a similar tone of just praise. Sir Robert is the natural squire, a hunter and a farmer, with fields, livestock and fruit-trees. The natural cycle is contained in a simple pair of lines: 'The trees cut out in log; and those boughs made/A fire now, that lent a shade!' Jonson evokes a golden age, cultivating the landscape with classical tools, but avoiding excessive pastoral idealization. 'Strive, Wroth, to live long innocent,' he urges. Others can be soldiers, merchants, usurers, profiting from their victims' distress, or courtiers who abase themselves. Wroth leads a life of service: he serves God, his country and his neighbours.

John Donne 1572–1631

These miracles we did; but now alas,
All measure, and all language, I should pass,
Should I tell what a miracle she was.

Only a little more than a decade separates Marlowe's
Elegies and Donne's love poems. And yet the differences
are startling. Set Marlowe's thirteenth elegy from book
one beside Donne's 'The Sun Rising', for example. Both
are in the same genre, draw on the same conventions.
This is Marlowe:

Now o'er the sea from her old love comes she
That draws the day from heaven's cold axle-tree.
Aurora, whither slidest thou? down again,
And birds for Memnon yearly shall be slain.
Now in her tender arms I sweetly bide,
If ever, now well lies she by my side.
The air is cold, and sleep is sweetest now,
And birds send forth shrill notes from every bough:
Whither runn'st thou, that men and women love not?
Hold in thy rosy horses that they move not.

Donne, by contrast, must have seemed raw and new in his
time:

 Busy old fool, unruly Sun,
  Why dost thou thus,
Through windows and through curtains call on us?

Must to thy motions lovers' seasons run?
   Saucy pedantic wretch, go chide
   Late schoolboys, and sour prentices,
  Go tell court huntsmen, that the King will ride,
  Call country ants to harvest offices;
Love, all alike, no season knows, nor clime,
Nor hours, days, months, which are the rags of time.

The second stanza of 'The Good Morrow', or 'Break of
Day', would have done as well. Between Donne and Marlowe there are, first, formal differences, and consequently
radical contrasts between the cadenced couplets of Marlowe and the harsh, phrased, spoken lines of Donne.
Marlowe's language of convention (no less expressive for
its conventionality) has been replaced by an 'unpoetic'
and dramatic handling of the conventions themselves.
The chief difference is conceptual. Marlowe's elegy, with
the tenderness of lines five to seven, creates with each
image a specific scene of love. Donne, by line four, is dealing with generalities. His attention has been distracted
from his beloved onto the image of the sun, and thence to
the street and the world. We lose sight of the ostensible
subject in a poetry of extension, until the third stanza
when the poet's mind returns to bed, and his relationship,
a microcosm, swells to the proportions of a macrocosm.
'She is all states, and all princes, I,/Nothing else is.'
Donne's attitude to the sun changes from rancour to
charitable pity. Yet one remains unenlightened about the
relationship which has occasioned such superb arrogance.
Donne's poem has great wit, but one is undecided whether
it has a subject or is merely a pretext for poetic conceit.

Donne, who was not widely appreciated in the nineteenth century, has been passionately championed in the
twentieth. T. S. Eliot's advocacy of the poet was the most
effective. But Eliot himself suggested that, while Donne
spoke directly to readers in the first half of this century,
he might prove less audible later on. The case against

Donne and other 'Metaphysical' poets is of long standing, and it is worth remembering the terms in which it was made.

Jonson, who admired Donne above most of his contemporaries, said that 'for not keeping number' he deserved hanging. Donne attempted to animate his metres with the energy of speech, and his phrased verse is usually effective, though at times we must agree with Yvor Winters that there are examples 'more of rhythmic violence than subtlety'. His satires consciously roughen the surface and defy scansion. Take, for example, the passage on plagiarists from the first satire:

> But he is worst, who (beggarly) doth chaw
> Others' wits' fruits, and in his ravenous maw
> Rankly digested, doth those things out-spew,
> As his own things; and they are his own, 'tis true,
> For if one eat my meat, though it be known
> The meat was mine, th' excrement is his own.

In this manner he spoke after Juvenal, harshly, departing from metre without completely forfeiting the norm.

Dryden's case against him was more telling. He notes how, even in the amorous poems, Donne is 'metaphysical'; he 'perplexes the minds of the fair sex with nice speculations of philosophy, when he should engage their hearts.' For Dryden, he is a great wit but not a great poet. The force of this accusation will be felt by those who, in the manifest brilliance of Donne's word-play, his spinning out of startling analogies and conceits, find at work a deliberate intelligence rather than an imagination, a talent of the surface rather than the depths, for whom the fascination of language is greater than the fascination of experience. Donne at times seems intent to move us by surprise rather than by truth. Marvell and Herbert deliver us the core of experience, while Donne might seem to be delivering us a husk that held experience. We tend to focus on the speaker rather than upon his subject, and the poems are dramatic not only in structure but in enactment: we are aware of an actor in various roles delivering the poems. Coleridge sensed this when he wrote, 'The vividness of the descriptions or declamations in Donne, or Dryden, is as much and as often derived from the forced fervour of the describer as from the reflections, forms or incidents which constitute their subject and materials. The wheels take fire from the mere rapidity of their motion.' Coleridge penned an amusing epigram on Donne:

With Donne, whose muse on dromedary trots,
Wreathes iron pokers into true-love knots;
Rhyme's sturdy cripple, fancy's maze and clue,
Wit's forge and fire-blast, meaning's press and screw.

The epithet 'self-impassioned' rises to Coleridge's lips. The famous 'Valediction Forbidding Mourning' justifies Coleridge's criticism. Metaphors and conceits develop by association of ideas or semantic nuances, not by appositeness of physical form. The image of the dying man suggests the lovers' separation. Stoically, the poet urges that it be without tempests (tears); tempests suggest the sky and moving earth, an image detailed without reference to the precedent images. Astronomy follows naturally and is developed until, on the word 'refined', Donne's mind turns to metals and perhaps alchemy: gold is the next image. The expansion of hammered gold suggests attachment in separation, and in come the famous compasses. Double meaning or intellectual association leads from stanza to stanza. A powerful pseudo-argument is developed, convincing because of the *sense* of logic, and the spell holds for the duration of the poem. As Winters says, the 'rational structure' in Donne is used to 'irrational ends'. Elaboration and decoration develop at the expense of theme, sometimes to such a degree that they displace it altogether. 'A Valediction: of Weeping' works in the same way.

The most influential case against Donne was made by Dr Johnson in his *Life of Cowley*. 'Who but Donne,' he

asks, 'would have thought a good man was a telescope?'
Borrowing Dryden's word 'metaphysical' to describe
Donne and other poets of his time, he characterizes them
as 'men of learning' whose 'whole endeavour' was 'to
show their learning'. They wrote verse rather than poetry,
'and very often such verses as stood the trial of the finger
better than the ear'. Dryden, according to Dr Johnson,
falls below Donne in wit but surpasses him in poetry. For
Pope, wit had meant 'what oft was thought, but ne'er so
well expressed'. Poets of Donne's type have not that
quality of wit, for they endeavoured to be 'singular in
their thought, and were careless of their diction'. For
Johnson wit is what is 'at once natural and new', not
obvious but 'upon its first production, acknowledged to be
just', so we wonder how we ever missed it. In Donne the
thought is new, but seldom natural; it is not obvious but
neither is it just. Yet if we define wit as *discordia concors*,
sensed similarity in things dissimilar, then Donne and his
fellow Metaphysicals have that – at a certain cost: 'Their
courtship is void of fondness, and their lamentation of
sorrow.' They are neither sublime nor pathetic, they
evince none of 'that comprehension and expanse of
thought which at once fills the whole mind'. They replace
the sublime with hyperbole, 'combinations of confused
magnificence, that not only could not be credited, but
could not be imagined'. A fine example is 'Twickenham
Garden':

> Blasted with sighs, and surrounded with tears,
> Hither I come to seek the spring,
> And at mine eyes, and at my ears,
> Receive such balms, as else cure every thing;
> But O, self traitor, I do bring
> The spider love, which transubstantiates all,
> And can convert Manna to gall,
> And that this place may thoroughly be thought
> True Paradise, I have the serpent brought.

What have we here? – a storm-tossed wandering lover – a

self-traitor, an alchemist, a god and an Adam. We have a serpent and a spider. We have various levels of experience and metaphor woven in a resonant, affective, but meaningless stanza, or meaningful to the exegete, who teases out the sacramental themes, and recognizes the dramatic reversal of religious imagery, in the service of secular passion.

Johnson does not seek to dismiss but to characterize the Metaphysicals. Herbert and Marvell are not mentioned. Johnson believes Donne's kind of poetry to be inferior to other kinds. For him, the best poems are true from any angle of approach, and Donne's are true only from one angle. Each word is restricted by context to a single significance. Joan Bennett makes this into a virtue in her account of Donne: he impresses words and images into service in a specific way, they appear clean of conventional associations. They are made new and singular.

The most powerful of Johnson's criticisms is that Donne's allusive strategy is to point always outward, away from the experience of the poem, not to refer inward and concentrate. Thus the reader is required to bring various pieces of information to his reading, where ideally 'every piece ought to contain in itself whatever is necessary to make it intelligible'.

Many of the thematic preoccupations and radical poetic procedures in the *Songs and Sonets* and in the religious poems express a personality as complex and controversial as the verse itself. Donne was born in London in 1572. He was a city creature and when he had to reside outside the metropolis for a time he complained bitterly. He has in his heart no place for the pastoral.

Donne's father was a prosperous ironmonger. The poet often resorted for imagery to metallurgy and alchemy: it had a special significance for him. His mother was the daughter of John Heywood, poet and playwright, and a descendant of the family of Sir Thomas More. Donne received a Catholic education and was reared as a recusant. For a decade from 1584 he studied at Oxford, Cambridge and the Inns of Court. Before 1596 he had travelled widely on the Continent and his Catholicism lapsed. He developed an interest in other churches.

He did naval service and in 1598 was appointed secretary to Sir Thomas Egerton, Lord Keeper. He seemed bound for secular preferment. By this time he had composed the *Satires* (1593–8), the majority of the *Elegies* and many of the *Songs and Sonets*. In 1601 the course of his career altered. He completed *The Progress of the Soul*, became a Member of Parliament, and contracted a secret marriage with Anne More, a niece of Lady Egerton. Thus he sacrificed the goodwill of his patron and any chance of preferment. He was briefly imprisoned. Forced to live off the generosity of friends, he pursued his study of canon and civil law to provide himself with a livelihood. His depressions of mind were acute, and he may have contemplated suicide. He wrote *Biathanatos*, a partial justification of suicide, in 1606.

In that year he removed with his growing family to Mitcham, retaining for himself lodgings in the Strand. He made a number of valuable friends, among them Mrs Magdalen Herbert, mother of George Herbert and of Lord Herbert of Cherbury; the Countess of Pembroke; and the Countess of Huntingdon, and several of them received tributes of verse.

By 1609, drawn by Dean Morton's anti-Jesuit pamphleteering, he contributed to the debate his *Pseudo-Martyr*, an incitement to papists to take the oath of loyalty to the Crown. This and other pamphlets attracted the King's attention. In the next two years the King urged him against his secular ambitions into the church. During the period of his resistance to the King's prompting he wrote the *Holy Sonnets* (1609–11), an expression of his faith and of his doubt of vocation. He continued to resist through 1614, when he was able briefly to return to Parliament. In 1615, after a final attempt at secular preferment, he took orders. In that year he completed his *Epicede and Obsequies*, probably begun in 1601. They were Donne at his most fantastic and 'public'. The bulk of his religious verse was by then completed as well.

Having taken orders, he was made a royal chaplain, preaching to King and court, and his talent for sermons was such that a few of them are still read today. He dealt too (a form of secular work no doubt to his taste) with diplomatic correspondence. He travelled. In 1621 he was appointed Dean of St Paul's. It was between 1619 and 1623 that he wrote his three Hymns; and in 1623, as a result of serious illness (he expected death), he composed the *Devotions*. But he survived another eight years. In 1630 he began to weaken. In 1631 he preached the sermon he knew would be his last, and died.

During his life, his verse had circulated widely – it is hard to determine how widely – in manuscript. It was not till two years after his death that the poems were published. They ran through six editions before 1670. The Dean's great fame recommended the poems.

As a man, Donne appeals to many modern critics. Allen Tate speaks of feeling him as 'a contemporary', and proceeds to misread him in this light. With Donne, if one misunderstands the man one tends to misread the poems. T. S. Eliot wanted to draw Donne back into the mainstream of English verse, and his attempt involved a little critical distortion. But he did not misread the man. Donne's scepticism is unlike our own. His religious struggle was due to an uncertainty about the terms, not the fundamentals, of faith. His problem was to believe *rightly*, not to believe *at all*. It is a misunderstanding of this radical fact that has led some to traduce Donne into 'our contemporary'. We do Donne no honour by loading him with our doubts; nor does he (as Herbert does) offer us help against doubt. His struggle in the secular poems was to determine and resist the finitude of man's nature; in the religious poems to establish the finite man's relations with the infinite God manifested in the Incarnation and celebrated in the Mass.

'Determine' is perhaps too narrow a term to describe

the process of Donne's imagination. The poems seem logical, but they work by association as often as not. Mario Praz reflects on the baroque nature of the verse. Donne's 'sole preoccupation is with the whole effect'. It is not so much a quest for truth as a quest for effectiveness. The poems are dramas, enactments, rather than arguments or explorations. The imagery is illustrative, imported rather than implicit in situation. There are analogies with some modern techniques, but those poets who claim kinship with Donne do not as a rule pursue his formal ends or share the philosophical and theological verities that underlie his work. 'A thought to Donne was an experience; it modified his sensibility,' Eliot wrote. This is true, but Donne had a consistent sensibility secured by a consistent faith which provided him with, however tormented, an *identity*. The difference between his sensibility and the sensibilities of many modern poets who pretend to learn from him (Eliot and Edgell Rickword excepted) is the difference between a poet turning an idea into poetry and a poet ruminating poetically on an idea. Donne's poems generate ideas, do not merely decorate them. They are concentrated, dramatic and realized.

Donne is inevitably the dramatic centre of his poems – the actor or the acted upon. This requires detachment on his part in order to dramatize the self. Even in the religious poems he presents him*self* struggling, and regards the personal drama from an impersonal remove, so that at times we are justified in doubting the actual – as opposed to the dramatic – intensity of the struggle. We can see it, with Rickword, as Donne's 'intense preoccupation with the individual at the extreme tension of consciousness', or less charitably as a form of fruitful posturing. The technique would favour the latter conclusion, given Donne's general inability to focus long on an actual subject. His wit continually hops off at a tangent, he cannot resist the grandiloquent phrase or its suggestions, the peripheral drama or sub-plot. It is often the tangents that are most memorable.

Rickword brings us closest to Donne the poet, as he continues to be vital for us today. If one labours the case against Donne, it is because his actual achievement has been obscured by critics who praise his faults, paint him as a contemporary, and thus deprive him of his true authority, a rich, even an alien *otherness*. Even Ford Madox Ford can say, 'His note is, indeed, singularly that of modernity', and claim that his 'bad taste' appeals to an age of bad taste. Rickword sees him, rather as he sees Swift, not as a proto-contemporary 'one of us' but in his general, timeless significance. He places Donne perhaps too high, but places him there in terms of actual instead of hypothetical virtues.

'The faculty which distinguishes the noblest poets from the interesting majority of writers and artists,' Rickword writes, 'is the gift of perceiving the universe, not through the disparate evidence of the senses or through the conceptual entities of the intelligence, but as a unity in which all the dualisms are extinguished. But once the evidence for the possession of this gift has been received we are not to demand that the poet shall testify incessantly to a unity.' With the clarity attained from this wholeness of vision 'he descends to illuminate the dualistic world in which we pass our time'. This is John Donne, the lover and the divine. He apprehends the ambivalence within himself, fastens it to objects outside himself, keeping his love but forfeiting the object of his love until he finds the greater object, and in it finds self-doubt. How is this dualism manifest? In the physical world he experiences now ecstasy and now disgust. The ecstasy is as intense as the disgust; a love of the timeless pleasure in one poem becomes in another a bitterness for the ephemeral nature of all attachments. On the spiritual plane he experiences both exalted joy and a deep sense of unworthiness. There is, as it were, an idealism always checked by realism or by spiritual pessimism. The city, love affairs, longing for secular preferment and later for religious certainty produce in him a profoundly ambiguous poetry, the final ambiguity being between idealism and Christianity. Such a perplexity occasions that 'forcing of congruities' which is responsible for his best and worst work. Where the Augustans solved the perplexity in one way and the Romantics in another, Donne, like Crashaw, Vaughan and Herbert, left it unresolved, placing it with a reluctant confidence on the altar of a living faith. Donne wrestles with idea and reality at once, and cannot lie still in bed with his beloved as Marlowe can in his 'Elegy'.

The *Songs and Sonets* and the *Divine Poems* contrast principally in the form of drama they take. The persistent wooer becomes the penitent object of wooing. As a lover Donne can be passionate and sometimes cruel, but seldom tender. In the *Divine Poems* he experiences such treatment from his God. In 'The Jeat Ring' he writes, 'Circle this finger top, which didst her thomb', at once revealing how small her hand was, how large his own: a relative power in the relationship. In the first of the 'Holy Sonnets' he writes,

Despair behind, and death before doth cast
Such terror, and my feeble flesh doth waste
By sin in it, which it toward hell doth weigh ...

giving us a vision of a man hemmed in before and behind, and like Faust weighed downward by his own sin. 'Only thou art above' – with leave he looks. God is a magnet drawing him to heaven. As in the love poems, emotion – in this case fear born of a sense of unworthiness – is a stimulant to thought and not a pleasing drug to the senses. Emotion accentuates his egotism: there is no broad typicality about his struggle, as about Herbert's. It is too extreme. This is its dramatic virtue and its poetic bound, a bound he sometimes transcends, as in the meditative ninth Elegy, 'The Autumnal', so infused with affection and regard that it is rapt, adjusting in a tone of appreciative banter its bizarre elements into a series of statements with aphoristic precision. It is also transcended in the best religious sonnets and poems, especially in 'Thou hast made me', 'I am a little world', 'This is my play's last scene' (with the first person singular acquiring a sort of typicality), and in the Hymns. It is found more rarely in the *Songs and Sonets*.

Robert Herrick 1591–1674

The bed is ready, and the maze of love
Looks for the treaders; everywhere is wove
  Wit and new mystery; read, and
  Put in practice, to understand
    And know each wile,
Each hieroglyphic of a kiss or smile,
  And do it to the full; reach
High in your own conceit, and some way teach
    Nature and art one more
  Play than they ever knew before.

Robert Herrick's antecedents can be traced in large part
to 'rare arch-poet Jonson', but his verse has a complete
polish we seldom find in Jonson's. He concentrates not
so much on argument as elaboration. Swinburne, who had
been hard on Jonson, called Herrick the 'greatest song-
writer ever born of English race'. Coming from Swinburne, this should alert us to certain verbal qualities in
Herrick: a concentration on the sound of his poems,
even at the expense of sense.

  Figurative language, delightful conceit, revived conventions: these are part of Herrick's small, intimate
world, far from the urban commotion that informed
Jonson's verse. Even Herrick's epigrams seem leisurely.
The poet expects us, after hearing his poem, not to judge
or to act, but to reflect and savour. His is a benign world,
with something of the charm of Marvell's, though only a
little of its latent violence and lacking its intellectual

quality. For Herrick, the natural order was rural. He was not compelled to seek aristocratic patrons who drew writers such as Marvell inevitably into politics and the violence of the day. History broke in on Herrick's life with the Rebellion, and like his fellow Cavaliers he felt deeply the loss of his King, but as a poet he was relatively remote from affairs: a pastoral poet in every sense.

Herrick was born in London in 1591. His father was a goldsmith and banker from Leicestershire, his mother a mercer's daughter. The year after his birth, his father died, leaving a sizeable estate of £5,068. In 1607 Robert was apprenticed goldsmith to his uncle. After six years of this he went up to St John's College and later Trinity Hall, Cambridge, where he secured an MA in 1620. Three years later he was ordained along with his college friend John Wickes, to whom (under the name of Posthumus) he dedicated 'His Age', a fine long poem based on Horace. His formal mastery is nowhere clearer than in the fourth stanza, on his favourite theme of ephemerality. The fifth and sixth lines contain the essential quality of Herrick's art:

But on we must, and thither tend,
Where Anchus and rich Tellus blend
    Their sacred seed;
Thus has infernal Jove decreed;
    We must be made,
Ere long, a song, ere long, a shade.
Why, then, since life is so short,
Let's make it full up by our sport.

The last couplet offers a feeble consolation in this context.

Herrick's first recognition as a poet came in 1625 with his verses on the death of James I. He may have started writing much earlier, probably two or three years before he went up to Cambridge. But he was a perfectionist, something of a goldsmith even in his verse, and revised, compressed and rendered smooth his verses with great dedication. Some of his epigrams are in bad taste, but very few are flawed in execution.

In 1627 he accompanied the Duke of Buckingham, as chaplain, on his expedition to the Isle of Rhé. The next year he was given the living of Dean Prior, Devon, though he did not settle there until 1630, and perhaps then with some reluctance. In a few poems he expressed dislike for the place:

> More discontents I never had
>   Since I was born than here,
> Where I have been and still am sad,
>   In this dull Devonshire.

This may have been merely classical imitation of dissatisfaction, for he wrote poems of contentment as well. Most notable of these is 'A Country Life: To his Brother', which in form, theme and moral resembles Jonson's 'To Sir Robert Wroth'. The difference is one of class. Wroth was an aristocrat, Herrick's brother a lesser being. Herrick calls him to a life of paternity and good husbandry. 'A Panegyric to Sir Lewis Pemberton' follows Jonson's poem more closely still, and to good effect.

Herrick was ejected from his living in 1647 by the Parliamentarians. After some years in London, where in 1648 he published his *Hesperides* and *Noble Numbers*, without much success, he was reinstated at the Restoration and held his living from 1662 to his death in 1674. Most of his surviving poetry was written before 1649. The body of work is large: over a thousand poems.

His politics were Cavalier. The execution of Charles I was for him the end of natural social order. His best poem on the subject speaks through convention with a profound personal conviction:

> Dull to myself, and almost dead to these
> My many fresh and fragrant mistresses;
> Lost to all music now, since every thing
> Puts on the semblance here of sorrowing.

Sick is the land to th' heart, and doth endure
More dangerous faintings by her desperate cure.
But if that Golden Age would come again,
And Charles here rule as he before did reign;
If smooth and unperplexed the seasons were
As when the sweet Maria livéd here,
I would delight to have my curls half drowned
In Tyrian dews, and head with roses crowned;
And once more yet, ere I am laid out dead,
Knock at a star with my exalted head.

The note is again Horatian, the feeling intense and heightened by the technical skill. Herrick does not judge. Perhaps, he suggests, the state was sick, but the 'cure' was 'desperate' and destroyed as much as it set out to cure. Little work survives from the years after the death of the 'brave Prince of Cavaliers'. Perhaps Herrick, in losing his England, lost his voice as well.

Like the other Cavalier poets, Herrick is essentially an 'agreeable' writer, 'consciously urbane, mature, and civilized' as Leavis says. He owed debts to Donne as well as Jonson, but primarily to the classics. Leavis overstates 'the idiomatic quality of the Caroline lyric, its close relation to the spoken language'. Herrick's language bears little relation to the English spoken in his Devon parish, or to the language of the London merchant class from which he came. His was the language of the wits, somewhat old-fashioned even at the time he used it. It is *clear*, but that is not to say that it is close to the language of speech.

Herrick's language is rich in transitive verbs. His is a poetry of movement, if not action, and he rejects the Spenserian manner *tout court*. He rejects too the Arcadian landscape. A literal experience underlies his pastoral. One might regard it more properly as rural rather than pastoral, for the nymphs and shepherds are replaced with figures very like his parishioners. It is England, and Devon, he writes of.

At the opening of *Hesperides* he lists his subjects:

I sing of brooks, of blossoms, birds, and bowers;
Of April, May, of June, and July flowers.
I sing of Maypoles, hock-carts, wassails, wakes;
Of bridegrooms, brides, and of their bridal-cakes.

Youth, love, 'cleanly wantonness', weather, luxuries, ephemerality, myth, fairyland, dreamland, heaven and hell:
'The Argument of his Book' accurately advertises its con-
tents. Generally the poems address a single or an imagined
hearer. Sometimes he talks with himself, or with 'Prew'
(Prudence Baldwin, his housekeeper, who died during his
first incumbency). His words emerge from a shared solitude, as though to fill the rural silence. There is no public
authority about them.

His lived pastoral, enhanced with classical allusion, includes a good deal of practical wisdom and close observation. The earthy influence of Thomas Tusser's versified
advice to farmers is felt at times in Herrick, but Herrick
keeps his hands clean and his prosody under close control.

Herrick was a clergyman. It is therefore striking that
his poetry is almost totally innocent of the Fall. He is
classical to such a degree that most of his poems are
virtually pagan in the attitudes they suggest. There are
his 'many fresh and fragrant mistresses', pre-eminently
Julia, but also Anthea, Perilla, Sappho, Electra, Lucia,
Corinna, Amarillis and others. The poems are erotically
frank and joyful. When he celebrates a wedding, as in the
epigraph, it is with a persuasion to enjoy the lawful bliss.
The bed itself he animates enthusiastically:

And to your more bewitching, see the proud
Plump bed bear up, and swelling like a cloud,
    Tempting the two too modest; can
    Ye see it brustle like a swan,
        And you be cold
To meet it when it woos and seems to fold
    The arms to hug you? Throw, throw
Yourselves into the mighty overflow

> Of that white pride, and drown
> The night with you in floods of down.

Herrick always urges consummation, his recurrent theme is *carpe diem*. The frankness within so refined and conventional a style gives it authority. He is seldom solemn, always the wooer or the sad (though never bitter) elegist of happiness. In his 'Farewell' and 'Welcome' to Sack he speaks with his whole voice, as to a wife or mistress.

Normally he suggests, with a few paradoxical adjectives, an actual passion or disruption underlying the formalized statement. The poems are perfect, but they celebrate the conscious or unconscious imperfections or relaxations of rule that beguile the heart. 'A sweet disorder in the dress', 'an erring lace', 'bewitch' him more than 'when art/Is too precise in every part'. He is delighted with the way Julia's petticoat errs and transgresses. Phrases such as 'harmless folly' in 'Corinna Going a Maying' provide the key. Or in 'Upon Julia's Clothes' – his most famous poem – the unstated, underlying image of the fish and the hook adds vividness to a brittle conceit. And in 'To Music', 'the civil wilderness' – a phrase met with elsewhere in his poetry – is one of those expressions bordering in effect on the oxymoron. Some of the elegies, for example the one written on the death of Endymion Porter's brother, or on his own dying brother, and poems such as 'To Live Merrily, and to Trust to Good Verses', address themselves directly to the dark realm of passion and the ephemeral. But usually the bright surface is not broken. There are implicit hints, sufficient to recommend the present pleasure. 'Gather ye rosebuds while ye may', 'Fair daffodils, we weep to see ...' – such poems are suasive and in no sense morbid.

So generous, so pagan a poet at Dean Prior, with his cure of souls, made little impression on the poetry of his time. He was an anachronism, the last Cavalier. In the nineteenth century his poems were revived. In this century, his work and that of the other Cavaliers has been overshadowed by the Metaphysicals. Herrick is as beguiling as Marvell, though he lacks Marvell's intelligence; technically the equal of Donne, though without his scope. He speaks in a variety of voices about a wide range of human experiences. He is free of Arcadia and free too of those extremes of attitude, those posturings, which mar much metaphysical verse. He does not display his learning: he uses it. His work is not, in Johnson's phrase, 'singular'; it is general in application and normative in effect – a 'moral' art, like Jonson's, only gentler, more temperate, more pagan, and perhaps as durable.

George Herbert 1593–1633

The stars have us to bed;
Night draws the curtain, which the sun withdraws;
  Music and light attend our head.
  All things unto our *flesh* are kind
In their *descent* and *being*; to our *mind*
  In their *ascent* and *cause*.

George Herbert was born in 1593 in Montgomery, Wales, fifth son of Richard Herbert of Montgomery, scion of a distinguished Anglo-Welsh family, and Magdalen Herbert, a woman of parts and a patroness of Donne. Richard Herbert died in 1593; Magdalen influenced her youngest son until her own death in 1627. After just over a decade of widowhood she married Sir John Danvers, a man twenty years her junior.

George Herbert's eldest brother, Lord Herbert of Cherbury, a noted poet and philosopher, was urbane, worldly, and abandoned religion. George Herbert went in another direction, moving from secular ambition to divine vocation, intensifying and particularizing his language as he went. From the outset his idiom was figurative. A figure contains and, in its development, extends meaning. By contrast, an ornament merely glosses meaning, while a conceit tends to displace it. Herbert's figures – often adaptations of familiar religious material – not only carry the argument; to a large degree they *are* the argument, proceeding with an inherent logic and resisting abstraction.

From the age of twelve to sixteen, Herbert attended

Westminster School. He studied music, among his other disciplines, and became proficient especially as a lutanist. The poems allude to music with the sanction of the poet's love for an art which could relieve him of depression and set him among the angels. From 1609 to 1612 he was at Trinity College, Cambridge, where he took his BA and wrote among other things two Latin elegies on the death of Prince Henry and a new-year letter to his mother reproving 'the vanity of those many love-poems, that are daily writ and consecrated to Venus', and lamenting 'that so few are writ, that look towards God and Heaven'. He enclosed two sonnets consecrating 'my poor abilities in poetry' to 'God's glory'. Walton in his *Lives* gives us the poems. One of them foreshadows Herbert's superb declaration of his aesthetic in 'Jordan (1)'. At sixteen he approximated to his adult vision:

My God, where is that ancient heat towards thee,
   Wherewith whole shoals of martyrs once did burn,
   Besides their other flames? Doth Poetry
Wear Venus' livery? Only serve her turn?
Why are not sonnets made of thee? and lays
   Upon thine altar burnt? Cannot thy love
   Heighten a spirit to sound out thy praise
As well as any she? Cannot thy Dove
Outstrip their Cupid easily in flight?

He wrote those lines as much to please his mother as his God. Yet it is remarkable that all of Herbert's surviving English poems are devotional, given his secular ambitions and his reluctance – like Donne's – to take religious orders.

Despite delicacy of health, Herbert took his MA and a fellowship in 1615–16. He was required to take orders within seven years, which he failed to do. At this time he was friendly with Donne, who had just taken orders himself.

The first major step towards a secular career he took in 1618 when he became Reader in Rhetoric. The next step came in 1620 when he was appointed Public Orator of the University. His friendship with Bacon, whose *Advancement of Learning* he helped translate into Latin, and with Lancelot Andrewes, developed. In 1624–5 he served as MP for Montgomery. But in 1626 a sudden change occurred: he took deacon's orders and thus debarred himself from further secular preferment. The deaths of friends and patrons or perhaps the influence of Donne, Andrewes and Nicholas Ferrar, may have sobered him. Many of the poems of discontent and uncertainty date from this period. His mother's death the next year was a further blow. In 1628 he resigned his Oratorship. He married Jane Danvers, a relation of his step-father, and in 1630 became rector of Bemerton, near Salisbury. His last three years were marked by exemplary devotion and unostentatious charity. In 1633 he died of a consumption. Shortly before his death he sent a manuscript of his poems, *The Temple*, to his friend Ferrar at Little Gidding, urging him to publish or burn the book. Ferrar published it. Before the end of the year two editions had appeared.

At Bemerton Herbert had revised the poems and composed more than half *The Temple*. The collection begins with 'The Church Porch', an extended moral and stylistic preparation for the poems that follow. The short poems he described as 'a picture of the many spiritual conflicts that have passed betwixt God and my soul'. There is throughout the book a continuity of tone, yet each poem represents a unique experience.

His tone and phrasing deeply influenced Vaughan and, to a lesser extent, Crashaw. Herbert had many near-contemporary imitators, but in the late seventeenth century he went out of fashion. Addison pilloried him as a 'false wit'. The error of his early champions – good men of faith – had been to sell their poet on the strength of his piety rather than his poetry. Even the advertisement to the first edition attests to this. Herbert's form of piety became unfashionable.

Yet his piety contributed to his re-emergence. John

Wesley, in the eighteenth century, adapted several of the poems as hymns, altering them to suit hymn form, and published a selection without alteration. It remained for Coleridge, in his *Biographia Literaria*, to revalue Herbert's poetry. In a letter Coleridge confessed that at one time he had read Herbert to chuckle over quaint and obscure passages with extraordinarily indecorous diction. The mature Coleridge saw the matter differently: he praises the 'style where the scholar and the poet supplies the material, but the perfect well-bred gentleman the expression and arrangements'. Here he perceives complex and fantastic thought expressed in a language of the utmost clarity and plainness. With this he contrasts those later poets whose fantastic and complex language conveys trivial thoughts. 'The latter is a riddle of words; the former an enigma of thoughts.'

Eliot developed this argument, indicating how Herbert's simple diction is deployed in very complex sentence structures. It is primarily in the development of syntax that Herbert resembles Donne. Otherwise, they have less in common than is normally supposed. Donne fills the canvas with himself and his own drama; Herbert keeps proportion and retains in all his poems a sense of the context of his experience. The context can be natural or temporal. Herbert looks through or beyond manifest nature towards God. His eye never stops at detail itself. In this sense he is the most metaphysically transitive of the Metaphysical poets, passing from the finite and particular to the infinite and eternal, or recording a failure to do so. He had what Charles Cotton (1675) described as 'a soul composed of harmonies'. The imagery is at times far-fetched, but it is almost always suitable. It is such qualities – the transitive nature of prayer, the surprising appositeness of imagery and diction – that appealed to the imprisoned Charles I, and to Cowper in his early depressions. The typicality of his spiritual struggles is part of the universality of his utterance.

A superficial similarity with Donne's work is the

dramatic cast which Herbert gives his poems. Many of them begin *in medias res*, addressing, cajoling, lamenting. But they have not Donne's histrionic stance. The logic of their development is often correct, not Donne's pseudo-logic but Sidney's strict logic. A mediaeval quality, unlike Donne's scholasticism, enhances Herbert's work. His allusions, his direct use of scripture and traditional imagery, his natural reversion to parable and allegory, imply that the Anglican devotional poet cannot but return to these time-proven processes of thought and response. His dependence on scripture takes the brittleness from his erudition. His poems address a common source of wisdom in a common language. The esoteric he introduces either to make it familiar or to debunk it. Critics attend sometimes too closely to the personal nature of his spiritual struggle, overlooking or undervaluing the impersonal and very effective didactic element of poems spoken from faith and by a priest – a priest who is not above direct, almost sermonic, didacticism from time to time.

Herbert is a master of form. The shapes of his stanzas often visually corroborate the meaning or process. There are the obvious picture-stanzas, 'The Altar' in the shape of a classical altar and 'Easter Wings' in the shape of wings. In a more subtle sense, in a poem such as 'Mortification', the stanza contracts and expands, a process which depends on syllabic length and indentation:

> When man grows staid and wise,
> Getting a house and home, where he may move
> Within the circle of his breath,
> Schooling his eyes;
> That dumb enclosure maketh love
> Unto the coffin, that attends his death.

The trimeter moves into a wide, secure pentameter, full of confidence. Then a tetrameter erodes it, and it dwindles to a dimeter. By the time the expansion to tetrameter and pentameter again is complete, the tone is changed. Each stanza enacts a rhythmic and visual process in this fashion.

The shape is an emblem of mortification and finally of grace. The poem has an appropriate dwelling, an architecture, in this case further heightened by the repeated 'breath' and 'death' rhyme in each stanza. 'Denial', 'The Star' and 'Frailty' are among the poems in which the form itself is an object of meditation.

Another subtle form of integration can be observed in 'Love bade me welcome'. As Christopher Ricks has pointed out, we sense an unstated, underlying pun on the word 'host' as the poem unfolds: God is the soul's host at the table; he is also the consecrated host of which the sinner is to partake. Similarly, in 'The Temper (1)', the word 'temper' takes on its full complement of meanings, including the tempering of steel.

The colloquial tone of the best poems is sustained by an undecorated diction. 'Jordan (1)' asserts an aesthetic of plainness, though in itself it is so complex a poem that it seems to be at variance with its statement. In general Herbert rejects the style of verses that 'burnish, sprout and swell,/Curling with metaphors'. His imagery includes stars, trees, food, wine – images with a symbolic value but a firm literal meaning. All objects exist first as themselves, though they cast a shadow beyond themselves, tracing the pattern of grace. Herbert works from small clauses and word-clusters, advancing an idea or an emotion by degrees, coordinating the nuances of his words in order to achieve a consistent metaphorical as well as a consistent literal meaning. 'Prayer (2)' begins:

Of what an easy quick access,
My blessed Lord, art thou! how suddenly
May our requests thine ear invade!

The words are simple and simply arranged. Yet 'quick' means 'speedy' and 'vital'; 'access' and 'invade' carry the same military overtone. These suggestions collaborate the literal meaning without distorting or displacing it. 'Thou can'st no more not hear, than thou can'st die.' God is all-powerful, yet powerless to be inaccessible or to cease. The paradox is perfectly contained:

> Of what supreme almighty power
> Is thy great arm, which spans the east and west,
> And tacks the centre to the sphere!

Yet even at the height of cadence, Herbert contrives to bring God's action to simple comprehensibility by the verb 'tack'. That engages the imagination and makes solid the vast motion of God. It is a minimal verb which magnifies the agent and the action. Often, when he develops a rhetorical description, he magnifies the effect by reducing the terms of action.

Herbert can be as autobiographical as Donne in some of his best poems, yet we focus not on him but on the experience he evokes. 'Affliction (1)' is most directly autobiographical. But it presents a type, even despite references to his university career, illness, incumbency, private frustrations: a type for the development of faith. It is grief that instructs him: 'grief did tell me roundly, that I lived.' His learning is of little use:

> Now I am here, what thou wilt do with me
> None of my books will show:
> I read, and sigh, and wish I were a tree;
> For sure then I should grow
> To fruit or shade: at least some bird would trust
> Her household to me, and I should be just.

The afflicted man longs for clear purpose, the tree's purpose to give fruit and shade; and for sure foundation, for roots. Were he a tree, he would stand in the same relationship to the bird as God stands to him; only (by implication), unlike God the tree would be just to its tenant. Such an oblique blasphemy heightens a contrast in the following stanza and highlights the poet's longing for a *sign*, even a negative sign of proof. The colloquial diction builds to a metaphysical paradox suggested by Sidney's love poems, but here used with an urgency beyond Sidney's scope. Each monosyllable calls for a stress; the line is effectively spondaic: 'Let me not love thee, if I love thee not.'

When the poet speaks as Christ, it is often with a reversed affliction: Christ unable to comprehend the conduct of man, just as man is perplexed by God's conduct to him. Herbert's Christ is also, however, the Christ in the garden.

Herbert's language can be typified by its verbs. They are usually transitive. A catalogue of the verbs in any of the better poems proves Herbert to be a poet of moral action or enactment rather than gesture. There is movement even when the thought is static. This is a quality one relishes the more when one comes to the more assured and elegant work of Dryden and the brittle century for which his refinements paved the way. The simple drama of Herbert's sonnet 'Redemption' is unequalled in English poetry before or since. It is a new parable, worthy of the old:

Having been tenant long to a rich Lord,
 Not thriving, I resolved to be bold,
 And make a suit unto him, to afford
A new small-rented lease, and cancel th' old.
In heaven at his manor I him sought:
 They told me there, that he was lately gone
 About some land, which he had dearly bought
Long since on earth, to take possession.
I straight return'd, and knowing his great birth,
 Sought him accordingly in great resorts;
 In cities, theatres, gardens, parks, and courts:
At length I heard a ragged noise and mirth
 Of thieves and murderers: there I him espied,
 Who straight, *Your suit is granted*, said, and died.

John Milton 1608–1674

All is best, though we oft doubt
What th' unsearchable dispose
Of highest wisdom brings about,
And ever best be found in the close.

John Milton was born in London in 1608. His father was a well-to-do scrivener and money-lender who had attended Oxford, rebelled against his father's Roman Catholicism, and been disinherited. From his father, Milton picked up a taste for music and received encouragement and support in his ambition to be a writer. Aubrey tells us that by the age of ten Milton was already a poet.

At St Paul's School, under the guidance of the excellent Alexander Gill, Milton began his formal studies. Gill used English poetry in his teaching. Milton learned Latin, Greek and Hebrew and wrote Latin verses. When he went to Christ's College, Cambridge, in 1625, he found the place disappointing, the curriculum dry and narrow. He craved a broader and more liberal education than was offered. He composed Latin poems in the manner of Ovid and Horace, epigrams, a Latin mock-epic on the Gun-powder Plot, Italian sonnets, English paraphrases of the Psalms, and the eleven stanzas 'On the Death of a Fair Infant Dying of a Cough'. His Latin elegies are in some respects his most personal utterances, including details of his life and thought not elsewhere recorded. He was at this time as much at home in Latin as in English verse.

'Upon an Infant', for a nineteen-year-old poet, is a remarkable production, Elizabethan in manner, full of

conceits which attest to Milton's mastery of English conventions. It is notable for its finish, not its feeling. In the
seventh stanza there is a rumour of things to come:

Wert thou some star which from the ruined roof
Of shaked Olympus by mischance didst fall;
Which careful Jove in nature's true behoof
Took up, and in fit place did reinstall?
Or did of late Earth's sons besiege the wall
  Of sheeny heav'n, and thou some goddess fled
Amongst us here below to hide thy nectared head?

The images of falling, rebellion, and the pagan gods are
here with some of the delicacy (marred by archness) of
the poet of *Comus*: accomplishment in wait for a subject.

Milton stayed on at Cambridge after taking his BA in
1629. That was the period of his three religious poems,
'On the Morning of Christ's Nativity', and the incomplete
'The Passion' and 'Upon the Circumcision'. The Nativity
ode is his first important English poem, celebrating the
birth as an event without losing sight of the theological
and cultural consequences. The central paradox is crucial
to all Milton's poems: the human child and the Son of
God. The poet, like one of the Magi, follows to the
manger. Four introductory stanzas are followed by the
hymn. He evokes the cold weather, but neither Mary nor
Joseph. Nature is humbled and bared before the swaddled
infant. Nature seems to displace the Virgin – a pagan
nature, accustomed to 'wanton with the sun, her lusty
paramour'. Those who expected an imperious Messiah
stand in awe of the helpless infant who becomes the focal
point of the whole natural world. The image of music
and harmony acquires great force. It is not, however, the
Millennium:

    ... wisest Fate says no,
This must not yet be so;
    The Babe lies yet in smiling infancy,
That on the bitter cross
Must redeem our loss ...

The presentation in these lines is so elliptical that the image is of the *Babe* crucified. Into the hymn of joy flows reflection, and the sombre truth that the Dragon is not dead, and that the delightful pagan world has been superseded. The pagan gods depart, and we lament them: this Babe is a Puritan. In the last stanza Babe and Virgin are left together, one asleep, the other watching, protected by angels.

Milton took his MA in 1632. By then his career was well begun. Not only the great sonnet 'On Shakespeare' (1630) but 'L'Allegro' and 'Il Penseroso' had been completed (1631). The latter productions are delicate and clear, using the tetrameter couplet with complete assurance and achieving, by means of sound organization and syntax as well as diction, a remarkable distinction of *tone* between the voices of the happy and the thoughtful man. The thoughtful man lingers in our company longer (176 lines) than the happy man (152). Both poems refer to the same conventionally visualized world, rather as Blake's 'Innocence' and 'Experience' offer two perspectives upon the same material. Milton reveals two distinct temperaments or humours, 'L'Allegro' pastoral in mode, 'Il Penseroso' elegiac. 'Il Penseroso', with his passion to know the secrets of the dark and his concern with death, is a little absurd, with the gentle self-mockery we hear in Chaucer. Chaucer is directly referred to in lines 109–120 and echoed in lines 8–9. 'Il Penseroso' is a little scholastic, while 'L'Allegro' is a less reflective renaissance sort. Milton was young enough to encompass both moods within himself. History had yet to instruct him in the sober facts of political life, and his religious faith, though firm, was not yet hard.

Leaving Cambridge, Milton retired for six years to his father's estate in Buckinghamshire in order to complete his deliberate preparations for the poetic calling. 'I take it to be my portion in this life, joined with a strong propensity of nature, to leave something so written to after-times, as they should not willingly let it die.' He prepared himself more thoroughly and systematically than any other English writer: he would know all that a man could know. He wrote three major works at this time: *Arcades*, the result of his musical interests, which brought him in touch with the composer Henry Lawes; *Comus* (1634), his great masque; and 'Lycidas'. Other work included the sonnets on time and the flight of youth, the tardiness of achievement, and the poem 'At a Solemn Music'.

Arcades shows Milton able to command essentially Elizabethan idioms and to address an aristocratic audience. Henry Lawes came back to Milton with a commission to write *Comus*, to celebrate the inauguration of the Earl of Bridgewater as Lord President of Wales. It was performed at Ludlow Castle, Shropshire. Milton, it is conjectured, may have played the part of Comus, that seductive prototype for Satan.

Comus is not dramatic but ceremonial, the characters are clauses in a moral argument. Here, as in the earlier work, we sense a fusion between Milton's Platonic and Christian thought. The theme of chastity brought both into play. The Lady rejects Comus's advances and is freed into a universal love of the good. The allegory is simple: the Lady begins lost in a wild wood, is tested, and in the end is found, and found virtuous. The Earl of Bridgewater's three children were shown off to advantage and themselves received instruction from the masque: on the first night they played the Lady and her two brothers.

There is a *mélange* of styles in *Comus*, which is a transitional work, the fruit of Milton's retired studies in philosophy, theology and poetry. Some of the writing is richly Elizabethan; some cannot but remind us of Dryden. Spenser and Shakespeare echo in the wings. Matthew Arnold speaks of Milton as at the 'close' of Elizabethan poetry. If this is so, then *Comus* must be the last great Elizabethan poem, already something of an anachronism when it was performed. It resists the excesses of metaphysical wit, and yet opens out, beyond that, to the drier regions of the late seventeenth and early eighteenth centuries, when language began to hover above its subject and to regard itself; when, in Arnold's phrase, expression took precedence over action.

The character of Comus himself is the triumph of the masque. He not only tempts but embodies the temptation he promotes, a corrupt corrupter who exclaims when he hears the Lady sing, of her vocal ravishments:

> How sweetly did they float upon the wings
> Of silence, through the empty-vaulted night,
> At every fall smoothing the raven down
> Of darkness till it smiled.

The word 'wing', though it belongs to silence, prepares the way for 'down'; silence and darkness are smooth-feathered birds. These overlaid images establish expectations both of texture and of movement which *Comus*'s later poetry bears out in the verbs of flight and in specific phrases: 'the winged air darked with plumes' and 'smooth-haired silk' which 'spinning worms' weave 'in their green workshops'.

The voice of the poet of *Paradise Lost* is audible too:

> ... he that hides a dark soul and foul thoughts
> Benighted walks under the mid-day sun;
> Himself his own dungeon.

These lines belong to the Elder Brother, a stiff, slightly priggish character. Milton was not successful with his protagonists. His Christ, God and Samson repel the reader in different ways, so that what they represent becomes repugnant. His antagonists, by contrast, can be admirable. They are entrusted, too, with some of the best verse. Comus and Satan are attractive villains. Blake could claim Milton as 'of the Devil's party' and John Middleton Murry could brand him a 'bad man' on these grounds. Their errors were tactical. There was an explanation for Milton's unequal skill in moral characterization. For him goodness and virtue were qualities which could not be particularized without limiting their significance. His virtues are flimsy because they tend towards abstraction in seeking comprehensiveness. Evil, however, could be – indeed, had to be – particularized. Fallen men exemplified it. Hence the abstract qualities of evil act in a fallen world of recognizable characters. We are prepared to recognize the characters but not the qualities. The devil has the best, because the most familiar and audible, tunes. The marriage between virtues and characters, between pure qualities and mundane objects, was beyond the poet's ability. He was too rigorous a philosopher to poeticize and make imaginable absolute truths.

'Lycidas' was an occasional poem, composed for a collection of elegies dedicated to Edward King, a fellow undergraduate of Milton's at Cambridge, who was drowned. King was not intimate with Milton, but the poet knew him to have been a Latin versifier and a candidate for holy orders. The conventional pastoral-elegiac mode, lamenting a fellow 'shepherd-poet', seemed appropriate. King's intended vocation, pastoral in another sense, provided a pretext for introducing the theme of the Church; and the manner of his death, by water, supplied a wealth of classical reference suitable to the chosen idiom and a variety of water imagery.

Spenser's *Shepheards Calendar* was valuable to Milton in composing his poem. There are verbal echoes and borrowed motifs, but 'Lycidas' is immeasurably superior as a poem. Johnson condemned it for its diction, rhymes and prosody, but he disliked the pastoral mode itself and found extremely distasteful the introduction of criticisms of the Church in such a context. He also comments that 'Where there is leisure for fiction there is little grief.' The conventional grief in the poem is no more or less real than that of other pastoral elegists. The poem is not a lament but an elegy in the wider sense, like Milton's Latin elegies. King's death provoked in the no-longer-so-young Milton (he was 29) reflections on his own mortality, his achievements, and the Church for which he himself had been destined. He is embittered by the loss of so promising a life, and he asks why the just and good should suffer.

Every element in the poem belongs to the Christianized tradition of pastoral elegy. The procession of mourners, the catalogue of flowers, the lament to nature, were given, conventional forms for receiving content. It is what the poet makes of the conventions, how he combines them, what he puts into them, that is important. They are part of an accepted framework.

That Dr Johnson should have been deaf to the deep feelings that inform and unite the poem, which moves from a sad apprehension of death, through regret, passionate questioning, rage, sorrow and acceptance, is surprising. The feelings begin in a low key but move on to the large questions of divine justice and human accountability. As poet and mourners question, the poem moves to its climax, the blistering attack on the clergy, the 'shepherds' corrupted by self-interest. Beside this passage is set the catalogue of flowers, a superb tonal contrast. No hearse draws by to place the flowers upon, for Lycidas was drowned. Milton describes the body afloat in the sea. Beside this image of nature's impersonal force he places the affirmation of resurrection. Order is restored to the pastoral world ('Tomorrow to fresh woods, and pastures new'). The final harmony is established by a stanza of *ottava rima*, tight and orderly after the preceding verse paragraphs which develop on a modified *canzone* pattern, with varied line lengths that bring about expressive enjambements and vary pace to suggest gradations of feeling. In a sense, 'Lycidas' justifies God's ways. It is the finest elegy in the language.

It was the last poem of Milton's 'youth'. In 1638 he travelled to Italy. He was away from England for fifteen months and was recalled only upon the outbreak of the Civil War. On his return he memorialized in his best Latin elegy, the 'Epitaphium Damonis', his only intimate friend, Charles Diodati. He became a private tutor and began to plan an epic poem. It was to be an Arthurian epic celebrating the English nation.

The Civil War drew him into political activity. He began pamphleteering. If he wrote his prose with his 'left hand' and verse with his right, the left hand produced four fifths of the surviving *opus*. His whole endeavour was to see the Reformation through. He felt it had been arrested.

His marriage in 1642 to a sixteen-year-old papist girl was a disaster. It prompted him to write his pamphlet on divorce. The pamphlet was censored. Censorship provoked his best-known prose work, the *Areopagitica* (1644), an attack on official censorship. In 1646 his first volume of *Poems* appeared. It included Latin, Greek, Italian and English writing. In 1649, the year of the execution of Charles I, Milton waded deep into politics, defending the regicides in print. He was appointed Secretary for Foreign Tongues to Cromwell's Council of State, a post he held for ten years. He had no say in policy matters but was required to compose official propaganda. This he did with skill and conviction. Blindness overtook him in 1652. He wrote his famous sonnet, 'When I consider how my light is spent'; but he did not stint in his secretarial labours. During this period he suffered another loss. In 1656 he had married a second time, happily, but his new wife died in 1658. For her he wrote his last and possibly his best sonnet, 'Methought I saw my late espoused saint'. He was to marry once again in 1662. His third wife survived him.

The Restoration put an end to his pamphleteering for a time. It seemed that he might be punished. But several of his friends, among them Andrew Marvell, secured his safety, though he was briefly imprisoned. The period of the Commonwealth had extracted from him, by way of finished verse, sonnets of personal moment; impassioned invectives in sonnet form; and celebratory sonnets to Lawes, Sir Thomas Fairfax, and to 'Cromwell, our chief of men' – a Shakespearean sonnet (rare for Milton, who preferred the Petrarchan form) ending on an authoritative couplet asking Cromwell to 'save free conscience from the paw' of Cromwell's own extremist followers, 'hireling wolves whose gospel is their maw'.

In his remaining years he completed three major works upon which he had been engaged before: *Paradise Lost* (1667 in ten books, revised 1674 in twelve), *Paradise Regained* (1671) and *Samson Agonistes* (1671). His revised *Poems* appeared in 1673. In his later years he was internationally known, plagued with visitors, invited abroad. But he stayed at home, fulfilling his vocation. In 1674 he died.

'My mind,' wrote Coleridge of the later Milton, 'is not capable of forming a more august conception than arises from the contemplation of this greatest man in his latter days: poor, sick, old, blind, slandered, persecuted: "Darkness before and danger's voice behind", in an age in which he was as little understood by the party for whom, as by that against whom, he had contended, and among men before whom he strode so far as to dwarf himself by the distance; yet still listening to the music of his own thoughts, or, if additionally cheered, yet cheered only by the prophetic faith of two or three solitary individuals, he did nevertheless

> argue not
> Against Heaven's hand or will, nor bate a jot
> Of heart or hope; but still bore up and steer'd
> Right onward.

It was once assumed that the sequence of publication of the three last great works reflected the sequence of composition. However, in recent years a different chronology has emerged. W. R. Parker suggests that *Samson Agonistes* was begun in the late 1640s and continued in the 1650s. By 1655 Milton had probably written the dialogues of *Paradise Regained* – about three quarters of the poem. This places *Paradise Lost* at the end rather than the beginning of the last period. Poetically, this makes sense. *Samson Agonistes* is the thinnest poem in terms of texture. Images are introduced and then dropped: they do not inter-qualify and build. The intellectual and moral aridity; the uncompromising and obnoxious 'moral' suggested in the lines of Samson's father, upon hearing of the destruction of the theatre and the foe (as well as his son), 'Come, come; no time for lamentation now'; the strong echoes of Shakespeare; and the intensity of the lament over blindness which suggests that Milton had contracted the disability recently (for later he grew to accept it calmly enough): these factors seem to point to a work not of final resolution but of transition towards the primarily dialogue-form of *Paradise Regained*. *Samson Agonistes*'s magnificent passages are well known: the description of Delilah, the lament on his blindness, and so on. But the tragedy is generally found, as a whole, intolerable. It is a political, not a moral poem.

Paradise Regained of course refers *back* to *Paradise Lost* in its opening lines, but this need not reflect chronology of composition. It is in conception more modest than *Paradise Lost*, and the poetry has neither the grand style nor the lushness of imagery we experience in the epic. Spenser, in the manner of Virgil, proceeded from pastoral eclogue to epic. Is it unlikely that Milton followed the same prescribed route? E. M. W. Tillyard, and later Louis Martz, have indicated the similarities between *Paradise Regained* and Virgil's *Georgics*. If one prefers to argue for *Paradise Regained* as a dramatic poem, one must apologize for its shortcomings in every aspect, from characterization to dialogue and action, for it is a conflict in the mind of Christ. It deals exclusively with his temptations in the wilderness. We do not observe that mind's processes, but in the stylized temptations by Satan 'the effect', as Northrop Frye suggests, 'is that of a negative clarification of Christ's own thought'. There is a continuous parallel between Old Testament history and Christ's development. It is not an epic in style or manner:

it sings not actions but inactions, refusals of temptation which are actions only on a moral plane. It is illuminating to read it as a Puritan Georgic, converting, as Martz says, 'the modes of classical poetry into the service of Christianity': the Georgic as a poem about the cultivation of the spirit, not the soil. Simplicity of phrasing, lack of decoration, a general plainness, set it well apart from *Paradise Lost*. One need only compare the diction and style of the closing passages of each poem to register the radical difference. In *Paradise Regained* 'characters' exist only as clauses in Christ's self-discovery.

Paradise Lost deals with the fall from which Christ redeems us. By the middle of the Commonwealth Milton's social optimism and his desire to celebrate England in Arthurian epic had faded. The Christian epic was the highest form he could attempt. Its scope was cosmic and timeless, its moral purpose clear. Other forms of poetry were trivial by comparison.

He began the poem in 1658 and finished it around 1663. He defended his choice of blank verse on aesthetic and political grounds. He claimed the authority of Homer and Virgil and advanced the usual arguments against 'trivial' rhyme. 'True musical delight,' he says, 'consists only in apt numbers, fit quantity of syllables, and the sense variously drawn out from one verse to another.' Milton is most expert at this drawing out, spreading his meanings, as Spenser had done, sometimes over more than a dozen lines. Each sentence has a number of functions to perform on the literal and moral level. The latinate syntax and diction are of great use, allowing him considerable flexibility and through echo or etymology creating complex harmonies inaccessible to a simpler style. In using blank verse Milton claimed he was recovering an 'ancient liberty' for English, long confined to the bondage of rhyme. Arnold praised Milton above all for this style, the poet's 'perfect sureness of hand': nothing could be changed without violence to the prosodic or intellectual context.

Along with latinate syntax and diction comes the whole panoply of classical (and Biblical) allusion. The use of specific geographical names gives the poem enormous scope in space. The forward narration of the angels makes it possible for Milton to include all historical time, and in portraying the godhead he manages to incorporate eternity as well. The poem bristles with Milton's great learning. It is deliberate in plan, development and decoration. The fortunate irony is that, despite this deliberateness, the poetry rises well above the level of conception, the characters stand out and speak with some independence from their creator. They have their idioms: each fallen angel who joins the great debate in Hell speaks with a different inflection; and Satan has many voices and forms. The poet, who speaks in the first person at several junctures, establishes a voice and an orientation, so that we can attribute the narrative to a speaker. The autobiographical matter adds considerable power to the poem.

There is too the matter of perspective. Scenes are normally presented through the eyes of particular characters, so that we see not only what they see but *as* they see. Satan's vision of paradise is more vivid than an 'objective' vision could have been, for it is seen with the eyes of jealousy and resentment.

Milton integrates various levels of meaning convincingly. There is the literal story, the moral drama, the political overtones. Imagery of natural processes substantiates the action or figures the movement of the poem, most poignantly in book nine when nightfall and the human fall are developed side by side. 'Earth felt the wound' of the fall: it was an act which changed not only the human condition but nature itself.

The twelve books move from the defeat of the rebel angels and their expulsion and fall to the Fall of man and the expulsion from the garden. There is 'architecture' in the careful parallelism of scenes, and in the development of clusters of imagery connected with the several themes.

Johnson was not alone in objecting to the 'want of human interest' in the poem. Adam and Eve – apart from the Archangel Michael's prophecies – are the only people in the poem, and they are remote in their innocence and in their guilt. We observe without involvement. Coleridge's distinction between the epic and the dramatic imaginations is useful here. Both discover unity in variety, but the epic discovers unity by throwing its subject into the past, regarding it from a distance, while the dramatic brings it up close. It is a fair distinction, casting light both on the failure of *Samson Agonistes* and on the success of *Paradise Lost*. Our human access to *Paradise Lost* is, initially, through the realized character of Satan. Milton diminishes him, through animal imagery and transformations, until he is the serpent. Thereafter we stand aside and follow the sensuous argument, the symbolic enactment of our fall. The weakness of the poem, whose action is so simple and whose telling so majestic and gradual, is in the long conversations of Adam with Raphael and Michael. Here one feels the expression exceeds the matter. We may come to agree, but only briefly, with Yvor Winters's criticism of the 'pompous redundancy' of the verse, the rhetoric working as it were in spite of and away from the subject, 'a dependence on literary stereotypes'. But whole books of the poem, notably the first, second, fourth and ninth, survive such criticism, and none of the books is without fine passages.

The case against Milton is in large part a case against his influence in the eighteenth and nineteenth centuries. This influence was widespread and by no means all to the good. Milton is strictly inimitable. The most forceful assaults have come in this century. T. S. Eliot delivered a few glancing blows, some of them against the moral content which were sensible and telling. The poem's moral purpose, like that of *The Faerie Queen*, has become muted to remoteness. We read it for reasons other than moral edification.

It fell to F. R. Leavis to square his shoulders before the seventeenth-century master and try to knock him down. Leavis attacks first *Paradise Lost* and the grand style. He finds it predictable, 'routine gesture', 'heavy fall', 'monotony'. He speaks of Milton's 'sensuous poverty' – the language is self-regarding, not turned to 'perceptions, sensations, or things'. Moreover the grand style 'compels an attitude to itself, that is incompatible with sharp, concrete realization'. Elevation, remoteness, impoverish rather than enrich our experience. Milton is 'cut off from speech . . . that belongs to the emotional and sensory texture of actual living and is in resonance with the nervous system; it could only confirm an impoverishment of sensibility'. 'Milton's Grand Style had renounced the English language' and thus Milton 'forfeits all possibility of subtle or delicate life in his verse'. Having finished with *Paradise Lost,* he goes on to the other poems and makes short work of them. In 'Lycidas' there is 'no pressure behind the words'. Milton 'offers as ultimate for our worship mere brute assertive will'.

The vehemence of the attack tells against the case. Many of Leavis's charges are in part true. There is sometimes monotony; the grand style does compel an attitude in the reader, the language is cut off from speech. But these facts need not be incriminating. The poem itself eloquently answers the more serious charges. It is certainly far from 'sensuous poverty'. It is richly imagined and in part richly realized, imaginable, enriching. There is subtle and delicate life in the verse, and a variety both of subtleties and delicacies. In dismissing Milton so absolutely Leavis assaults a wide area of English poetry which Milton in fact affected; and his effect is still felt, either directly or defracted through his disciples, the last of whom in this volume is Gerard Manley Hopkins, a poet very popular among the anti-Miltonists. The prejudice of our age, as much an unwritten rule of our age as the rules of decorum were in the eighteenth century, is contained in Leavis's declaration that Milton's language is 'cut off from speech'. Milton's sin is his language. Yet for two and a half centuries – even for a 'speaker' like Wordsworth – Milton's virtue was his language, which engaged and developed subjects difficult to combine, moral verities and the created world. The language of speech is not the only language of poetry. To criticize the work in terms that are strictly irrelevant to it is a labour of limited value: a critical act of 'brute assertive will', or a prejudice so ingrained as to be indistinguishable, for the uncritical reader, from truth itself. With the decline of literacy Milton becomes more difficult and apparently remote from the 'common reader'. And yet so do Chaucer and Shakespeare, the only poets in the tradition who are Milton's superiors.

Richard Lovelace 1618–1657

So you but with a touch of your fair hand
　　Turn all to saraband.

Andrew Marvell's royalist poem commending Richard
Lovelace's *Lucasta* (1649) predicts a harsh reception for
the thirty-one-year-old Cavalier's first book of poems:

The barbed censurers begin to look
Like the grim consistory on thy book;
And on each line cast a reforming eye,
Severer than the young Presbytery.

Marvell looks back to the happier age of Charles I, when
the poems were composed by a favourite of the King, the
court and the wits. Now, 'Our Civil Wars have lost the
civic crown./He highest builds who with most art destroys'. *Lucasta* appeared in the year the King was executed. The book belongs to the fallen order.

　　Marvell's predictions were not far off the mark. *Lucasta*
achieved no great success then. Lovelace is remembered
now chiefly for 'To Althea, from Prison' ('Stone walls do
not a prison make,/Nor iron bars a cage') and 'To
Lucasta, Going to the Wars' ('I could not love thee, dear,
so much,/Loved I not Honour more'). Yet he has a
diverse and achieved body of work to his credit. It was
unfortunate that he should appear in print in the very
year his case was lost. Also unfortunate was his choice of
styles and modes which demand continual intellectual

and prosodic control, conscious devising. Some poems are marred by a preciosity which in Herrick would appear charming, but in Lovelace indicates a failure of tact. Formal and prosodic lapses, gaps in argument, a lack at times of imaginative energy, weaken many poems. Yet there are fewer flaws than are normally supposed. The best of Lovelace – perhaps thirty poems – is fully accomplished work.

Richard Lovelace, eldest son of a Kentish gentleman, was born either in Holland or in Kent in 1618. His poetry clearly attests to his rural roots in the famous creature poems – for example 'The Grasshopper', an invitation to the elder Charles Cotton to carouse:

Up with the day, the sun thou welcom'st then,
    Sport'st in the gilt-plats of his beams,
And all these merry days mak'st merry men,
    Thyself, and melancholy streams.

But ah, the sickle! Golden ears are cropped;
    Ceres and Bacchus bid good night;
Sharp frosty fingers all your flowers have topped,
    And what scythes spared, winds shave off quite.

Poor verdant fool! and now green ice! Thy joys,
    Large and as lasting as thy perch of grass,
Bid us lay in gainst winter, rain, and poise
    Their floods with an o'erflowing glass.

The moral is as rural as the emblematic creature. 'The Ant' and 'The Snail' are less familiar than 'The Grasshopper', but almost as good.

Lovelace's father was not only a gentleman. He was a soldier, killed at the siege of Groll when the boy was nine. Lovelace became his mother's ward. In 1629 he was admitted to Charterhouse, possibly on the King's nomination, at the same time as Richard Crashaw. In 1631 the King made him Gentleman Waiter Extraordinary.

Anthony à Wood describes the sixteen-year-old poet:

he was 'accounted the most amiable and beautiful person that ever eye beheld, a person also of innate modesty, virtue and courtly deportment' – and a great success with the ladies. His adolescent comedy *The Scholars* was played 'with applause'. His accomplishments are a shadow of Sidney's. As Charles Cotton wrote in his memorial verses:

Thy youth, an abstract of the world's best parts,
Enured to arms, and exercised in arts;
Which with the vigour of a man became
Thine, and thy country's pyramids of flame;
Two glorious lights to guide our hopeful youth
Into the paths of honour, and of truth.

Among his other deeds, he was the first literal translator of Catullus into English.

In 1636, at Gloucester Hall, Oxford, he was made an honorary MA on the occasion of a visit by the King and Queen. The next year he received a Cambridge MA and went to court. When the King's serious troubles began, Lovelace served him, first as an ensign in the Bishops' Wars (1639–40), along with Suckling and Carew. During 1640 he wrote *The Soldier*, a tragedy now lost. In 1642 he was arrested and committed to the Gatehouse at Westminster for presenting to the House of Commons the Kentish petition, asking for the retention of Bishops and the Prayer Book. During this captivity he is said to have written 'To Althea, from Prison'. He was released on condition that he cease actively supporting the royalist cause. From that time began his lavish spending on the King's campaign, leading to his eventual poverty.

He was with Charles in Oxford in 1645, then travelled abroad, and was arrested on his return. The execution of his King changed everything for him. He was a man whose cause was lost, who had no clear future in Cromwell's England. He survived for eight years, writing still, but with a different tone and purpose. In 1656 he composed 'The Triumph of Philamore and Amoret' for the marriage of Charles Cotton the younger – the poet who memorialized him. It was his last outstanding poem. Probably in 1657 he died in reduced circumstances. *Lucasta, Postume Poems* was assembled and published in 1659 by his youngest brother.

Donne and Jonson were the Cavalier poets' chief models. Carew leaned more to Jonson, who leaves the younger poet at times stiff and wooden. Lovelace followed Donne more closely, and the flaws in his work might have been repaired had he attended more to Jonson. But he preferred brilliance and surprise to clarity. Thus in 'Ellinda's Glove' he wrote:

Thou snowy farm with thy five tenements!
  Tell thy white mistress here was one
  That called to pay his daily rents;
But she a-gathering flowers and hearts is gone ...

Pure conceit, carried to extremes: the opening surprises and charms, but the charm goes on too long.

Donne is directly echoed in several poems, notably in 'The Scrutiny' and 'Night'. This is not the spirit in which Vaughan echoes Herbert, but less subtle, for Lovelace is a Metaphysical only by design, not by nature, and only on occasion. 'Gratiana Dancing and Singing' is wildly implausible: when she ceases dancing, 'The floor lay paved with broken hearts', a line which delights but diminishes in force on each re-reading. We hear in Lovelace continental echoes, too, of those writers who were to be important to the Restoration poets, especially Rochester.

Just over a hundred poems by Lovelace survive. Even in so small a body of work, the formal variety is enormous. There are poems connected with war and prison; complaints and love and anti-love conceits; poems about creatures; poems on painting, for Lovelace, a friend of Peter Lely, was learned in the art; occasional poems including elegies, epithalamia and anniversary celebrations; pastorals such as 'Aramantha' and 'Amyntor's Grove'; a formal satire; meditations, dialogues and others.

Such range is wider than Herrick's, though the final achievement is not so great.

Lovelace's poetry evolves in a way that illustrates the general trends of change in English poetry at the time. His early poetry has intimacy and privacy of concern. It was written for a friend or a circle of friends, wits and courtiers. When that world was destroyed his address became more general and public. The change reflects the poet's circumstances: the favoured courtier was now outcast and fugitive.

Sir John Suckling's poetry shows a wry cynicism on the surface, a bitter wit. In Lovelace when there is cynicism it is thematic, and the irony in his poetry is not a technical device but a thematic verity. He is not so accomplished a writer as Thomas Carew, but he is perhaps more memorable and his development more interesting for its typicality. He survived a great loss and endured the aftermath.

> I would love a Parliament
> As a main prop from heaven sent;
> But ah! who's he that would be wedded
> To th' fairest body that's beheaded?

It is an awkward stanza, but the awkwardness proceeds from and mirrors feeling.

The best Restoration poets resemble Lovelace. Yet even a casual reading shows how coarse their work is by comparison with his, how keen they are to be satisfied with the mere present. They lack whole registers of feeling, their view of poetry is at once more precise and more narrow. Though courtiers, they were not like Cavaliers. The ideals of devotion and service were a thing of the past. Lovelace epitomizes the Cavalier virtues: he was an *uomo universale*, a courtier, scholar, soldier, lover, musician, connoisseur of painting, a latter-day Sidney, devoted to his king, his mistress and his art. 'To Althea, from Prison' is the quintessential Cavalier statement, passionate and *lived*. He is the last of the knightly poets, whose death in poverty rather than in service proved that the age of Wyatt, Surrey, Raleigh, Sidney and others of their stamp was over.

Andrew Marvell 1621–1678

And now to the abyss I pass
Of that unfathomable grass,
Where men like grasshoppers appear,
But grasshoppers are giants there:
They, in their squeaking laugh, contemn
Us, as we walk more low than them:
And, from the precipices tall
Of the green spires, to us do call.

Andrew Marvell's father was a low-church clergyman –
'facetious, yet Calvinistical' – in Hull. Marvell was born
in 1621. The town boasted a good grammar school which
he attended. Then he went up to Trinity College, Cambridge, at the age of twelve, during the poetic ascendancy
of Cowley and Crashaw. He received his BA in 1638–9
and was briefly a convert to Papism. He left the university
in 1641, without taking a further degree. Nonetheless, he
was well-versed in languages. He composed his earliest
verses, in Greek and Latin, on the death of Princess Anne.

When the Civil War came he was noncommittal. He
went abroad for four of the seven years between 1642 and
1649, spending two years in Rome. He may have travelled
as a tutor in preparation for his later posts. In 1649 he
was probably keeping royalist company. He contributed
to Lovelace's *Lucasta* and wrote verses on the death of
Lord Hastings:

Go, stand betwixt the morning and the flowers;
And, ere they fall, arrest the early showers.
Hastings is dead ...

Already the garden image is there. In a poem full of Donne and generalization, the authentic Marvell is stirring.

His royalist sympathies had certainly not faded in 1650 when he composed his 'Horatian Ode upon Cromwell's Return from Ireland'. It is the most complex, and certainly the best, directly political poem in the language. It retains an effectively subversive political balance – an Horatian virtue – in the terms of its celebration, notably in the lines on Charles I on his 'tragic scaffold'. He

... nothing common did or mean
Upon that memorable scene:
   But with his keener eye
   The axe's edge did try;
Nor call'd the Gods with vulgar spite
To vindicate his helpless right,
   But bow'd his comely head
   Down as upon a bed.
This was the memorable hour
That first assur'd the forced pow'r.

Cromwell, the 'forced pow'r', is by contrast all movement, agitation. He has an 'active star', seeks glory and adventure – adventure in more than one sense. The poem lives because of Marvell's finally unresolved attitude. Charles embodies right. Marvell respects him, while he admires Cromwell. Cromwell's forced victory was 'To ruin the great work of time':

Though justice against fate complain,
And plead the ancient right in vain:
   But those do hold or break
   As men are strong or weak.

Might prevailed, and Marvell, though in practical terms

never cured of his royalism, at one moment came to look forward to a dynasty of Cromwells. That was not to be.

Still, he found favour with the moderate elements of Cromwell's party and became tutor to Mary, daughter of Lord Fairfax, a retired general in the Parliamentarian cause who had wished – but not quite dared – to save the life of the King, and to whom Milton dedicated a fine sonnet. Marvell spent two years at Nunappleton, Yorkshire, in Fairfax's household. Poetically they were his most fruitful years. He wrote to praise and please his patron, celebrating Appleton House and the park and creating those poems whose charms are as strong as they are hard to define.

In 1653 Milton recommended Marvell for the post of assistant Latin Secretary. It was a post eventually awarded him in 1657. Meanwhile, residing at Eton, he tutored a ward of Cromwell's and became more fervently a supporter of the Commonwealth. He was intent above all to serve his country and the government it had *de facto*. In 1655 he published anonymously 'The First Anniversary of the Government under O.C.'.

He was elected MP for Hull in 1660 and held the seat until his death. He supported the Restoration and seems to have been accepted as a man whose loyalty (unlike Milton's) was not in question. In any event, he was able to help secure the safety of Milton. He served the crown in embassies abroad. He campaigned for religious toleration and became a satirist against the court party. He died in 1678 in London. His *Miscellaneous Poems,* including much of his best work, was not published until 1681, though the 'Ode' was cancelled from all but one copy and was first reprinted in 1776.

Aubrey, after commenting on his classical and political accomplishments, describes him in his later years: 'He was of middling stature, pretty strong set, roundish face, cherry-cheeked, hazel eye, brown hair. He was in conversation very modest, and of very few words ... [he] was wont to say *he would not play the good-fellow in any man's company in whose hands he would not trust his life.'* He had learned that caution. It is also recorded that he declared the 'cause too good to have been fought for', and that 'men should have trusted the King'.

Marvell was not a professional writer in the way Jonson or – in a sense – Donne had been. This accounts for the virtues and vices of the work. Most of the poems are in one way or another 'flawed'. The tetrameter couplets he favoured at times weary the reader: they can occasionally dictate rather than receive the poetry. The excessive use of 'do' and 'did' auxiliaries to plump out the metre mars the surface of many poems. Some of the conceits are absurd. Many of the poems, even 'The Bermudas', fail to establish a consistent perspective on a scene and visualization is therefore not always easy. Other poems are essentially static, an idea is stated and reiterated in various terms but not developed. This is the case even in 'The Definition of Love', which says memorably in eight ways that his love is impossible, but does not specify except in the most general terms why or how; or in 'A Dialogue between the Resolved Soul and Created Pleasure', which despite its dialogue form is no real dialogue: the figures merely bump against each other. The intellectual development is often, as in Donne, by sleight of hand, pseudo-logic, false syllogism. There are thematic inconsistencies. In 'Upon Appleton House' he suggests the superiority of natural over artificial order, then describes nature in terms of artifice. In stanza six he condemns Palladian architecture, and in stanza sixty-four evokes the woods, approvingly, in effectively Palladian imagery. The moral values are sometimes assigned to rather than discovered in his images. And Marvell is not usually, as Herbert and Donne are, dramatic in his presentation of incident.

Yet these 'flaws' are central to Marvell's art. It develops a seeming logic; but beneath that form of discourse the poetry follows its own rules of association and combination. There are two modes of discourse at work, a conscious mode and something unwilled yet compelling. One cannot decide how many of the poems' effects are deliberate and how many casual and accidental. They seem the products of a not altogether untroubled leisure at Nunappleton. T. S. Eliot contrasts Marvell and Donne. Donne would have been 'an indvidual at any time and place'; Marvell is 'the product of European, that is to say Latin, culture'. The difference is in the place and use of the 'I' in the verse. Donne's 'I' demands attention, Marvell's 'I' directs it. In Marvell the flaws do not disappear beneath gesture; the inconsistencies and uncertainties are aspects of a mind concerned with its subject, and that subject is not the self. However distinctively he appropriates a landscape or scene, it never becomes a *paysage intérieur*. The macrocosm overwhelms, is not displaced by, the microcosm.

Hence, in 'To his Coy Mistress', the poet begins with a cool and reasonable proposition; the poem gathers speed from that quiet beginning and rushes to the cruelly real resolution. Image follows image with precise brevity, each extending and enriching the idea. No element is distracting or tangential. The imaginative centre holds, and holds together, the diverse development. Marvell's wit does not always discriminate between the fresh and startling and the merely odd, yet what is odd is often delivered with such effective phrasing that it is memorable and charming in its absurdity. One instance is the salmon fishers who 'like Antipodes in shoes/Have shod their heads in their canoes'.

Marvell's verse holds so many surprises in part because of its quietness. The surprises emerge, are not insisted upon. He seems always to be recognizing significance in what he sees. His whole mind is engaged, along with his senses. He hasn't the specifically *poetic* approach which sees subjective intensity as the highest virtue and identifies intensity with a single-minded approach and a specific range of poetic effects. His brand of intensity would be best described as awareness, and even as he speaks he is aware of other things he might have said. His is a tough and intelligent imagination. The classics gave shape to his poems; the scriptures are never far from his thematic and linguistic processes.

He launches his poems quietly, he does not discharge them. They run smoothly like Herrick's but they run much more deep, and because of this with less absolute prosodic assurance and invention. If drama is generated, as in 'To his Coy Mistress', it is by control of pace and appositeness of imagery, not by situation or gesture. His poetry is urbane, to an extent detached, with recurrent motifs and words – 'green' is his favourite colour, and carries symbolic force when he uses it – and a marked tone which distinguishes it from the work of other Metaphysicals. He has his own themes, as well. Wise passivity marks some poems, a passivity which leads to close contact with the natural world as the individual mind relaxes and receives. Other poems strive for contact through passion or activity, the kind of contact in which individuality is lost in the teeming variousness of the world. Yet checking these themes is the theme of the impossibility – in love or action – of arresting time, achieving a permanence. It is not fanciful to suggest that the King's execution drove these themes deep in Marvell. It may even be felt in 'The Nymph Complaining for the Death of her Fawn', though not in any direct sense. For an intelligence such as Marvell's the lived experience of a crucial historical event was more powerful than any accident of private biography. Perhaps he is a poet of aftermath. Certainly, like Herrick, he came late in his 'literary period' and was overlooked by many of those who could have profited from reading him. Dryden took wit in a different direction, and it was already the age of Dryden.

The age of Dryden: an age in which writers wrote what they knew, not in order to explore the unfamiliar; an age of communication rather than discovery. Contrasting Marvell with Edmund Waller, his contemporary but more a man of what was to come than of what was, we perceive a radical difference. Waller – a cipher beside Marvell – delivers us finished ideas; Marvell discovers ideas. He has no settled opinions, except the fundamental ones. His poems balance particulars – of which he is certain – with conflicting generalities of which he is unsure, as in the line 'courteous briars nail me through', which dissolves the word 'courteous' on the cruel verb, and brings into its area of connotation the 'court' and the crucifixion. Such lines, quietly delivered, lead us not to an admiration of his wit but to an apprehension of his complex subject, whether in the 'Mower' poems, the dialogues, the 'Ode', the love poems or the great garden poems.

Henry Vaughan 1621?–1695

Look down great Master of the feast; O shine,
And turn once more our *Water* into *Wine*!

Henry Vaughan provides 'authentic tidings of invisible
things'. His chief collection of poems, *Silex Scintillans*
(1650, enlarged 1655), was the mature work of a man
whom bereavement, illness and the poems of George
Herbert had led to a passionate faith. The book's title
('sparking flint') he explains thus: 'Certain divine rays
break out of the soul in adversity, like sparks of fire out
of the afflicted flint.' Here is evidence of an hermetic
imagination, rarified in comparison with Herbert's. Comparison with Herbert is inevitable: as Vaughan said,
Herbert's 'holy life and verse gained many pious converts
(of whom I am the least).' His poems frequently echo in
phrase, syntax and development specific poems by Herbert. Edmund Blunden associated them in his poem 'The
Age of Herbert and Vaughan':

In close and pregnant symbol
  Each primrosed morning showed
The triune God patrol
  On every country road,
In bushy den and dimble.

The lines are truer of Vaughan than Herbert. Herbert
is aware of an immanent God while Vaughan's God is less
immediately present: the poet approaches him through

symbol but cannot readily perceive him in natural imagery:

> Some love a rose
> In hand, some in the skin;
> But cross to those,
> I would have mine within.

If Marvell is the poet of green, the 'green thought' in a 'green shade', his eye on the fruitful garden, Vaughan by contrast is the poet of white in its implications of purity and distance: 'a white, Celestial thought', the white light of stars, or in his translation of Boethius's 'Metrum 5', 'that first white age'. He is the most pure and rapt of the English devotional poets, the most spiritually attentive. His life is a spectrum of colour between the pure white of infancy and the pure white of eternity:

> I saw Eternity the other night
> Like a great ring of pure and endless light,
> All calm, as it was bright,
> And round beneath it, Time in hours, days, years
> Driv'n by the spheres
> Like a vast shadow mov'd.

This poem, 'The World', does not sustain such poetic intensity throughout; it dwindles to deliberate allegory. It examines the shadow, 'The fearful miser on a heap of rust', a vivid moment. The poem has the virtue of describing Vaughan's chosen territory for discovery: areas beyond any sense but intuition, 'invisible things', the things he evokes in 'Faith' ('Bright, and blest beam!'), 'The Passion' ('O my chief good!'), 'Peace' ('My Soul, there is a country') and others. His unique achievement is to bring the transcendent into the reach of the senses.

> There's not a wind can stir,
> Or beam pass by,
> But straight I think (though far),
> Thy hand is nigh;

Come, come!
Strike these lips dumb:
This restless breath
That soils thy name,
Will ne'er be tame
Until in death.

Such hermeticism does not obscure reality but casts illumination on what exists beyond it. Through human love it ascends to the divine, with the light of faith. The imagery of darkness belongs to the world and its works. Imagery of light – starlight and pure light – belongs to the fields of heaven and eternity.

'My brother and I,' wrote Henry Vaughan, 'were born at Newton in the parish of St Brigets in the year 1621.' Vaughan's father was a second son of a family in the old Anglo-Welsh gentry. Henry's twin brother Thomas became a famous hermetic philosopher (pseudonym 'Eugenius Philalethes') whose works were familiar in the next century even to Jonathan Swift. He was a priest ejected from his living at Llansantffraed after the royalist defeat in the Civil War. He died of mercury poisoning in an alchemical experiment.

More certain knowledge about Thomas than about Henry survives. Henry called himself the 'Silurist' because his native Breconshire had once been inhabited by the Silures. It was an acknowledgement of his roots. It is supposed that he went to Oxford around 1638, took no degree, and turned up in London to study law in 1640. He eventually became, we do not know by what steps, a doctor, and spent his later years practising medicine in his Welsh neighbourhood. In the Civil War he probably served with the royalist forces and tasted their defeat. Defeat coincided with personal bereavements. His first book, *Poems, with the Tenth Satire of Juvenal Englished* (1646), was generally an undistinguished work by one of the Sons of Ben. Many of the poems are addressed to a conventional 'Amoret'. His second book, *Olor Iscanus*

(1651, published after his third book) revealed a deepening seriousness. It begins in Wales, with the Usk, his true territory. London is remote. Almost best in the book are his translations of some of the verses from Boethius's *Consolation of Philosophy*, notably 'Metrum 5' with its rhythmic and thematic foretaste of two of his great poems, 'The Retreat' and 'Childhood':

Happy that first white age! when we
Lived by the earth's mere charity,
No soft luxurious diet then
Had effeminated men ...

This is more than a translation: it is the witness of a royalist who looks to a lost age. It *was* lost. He turned his attention elsewhere and suddenly found 'a country/Far beyond the stars'. The choice of the word 'country' is significant.

Silex Scintillans contains the best of his poetry. The debt to Herbert is great, but whenever an experience is sufficiently intense Vaughan's own idioms, rhythms and themes have an original command. His style is thick with Biblical echoes and allusions, so that each poem has for the Christian an immediate familiarity, a ready resonance much as we experience from Herbert's poems. Vaughan introduces many of the poems with Biblical epigraphs, to underline their source and their allegiance.

The book was the product of an abrupt conversion. The faith is fresh, notable for its lack of doubt. The drama of openings and developments, whether of simple allegory, allegorical journey, or emblem, at once relate it to and distinguish it from other Metaphysical work. His revelation is certain. There is no demand for proof beyond the proof he has received. The 'I' of the poems not only seeks, repents, and accepts the occasional scrap of comfort; it finds, almost effortlessly, in the innocence of a newly kindled faith.

After 1655 Vaughan composed little more verse. *Thalia Rediviva* (1678) adds poems, but they revisit the secular world of his first books and add little to Vaughan's credit. It is uncertain what happened to his assured genius. Faith may have cooled, conscience – endlessly pining over past sins and excesses – may have smothered the holy muse. His work as a doctor may have overtaxed him. And later in life he suffered litigation within the family, for he married twice, two sisters, and by each had four children who squabbled over property. It was not a quiet old age. When he died in 1695, he had written no verse of moment for forty years. His interesting if derivative prose book, *The Mount of Olives*, dates from 1652. His memorable prose and verse belong, at most, to a decade in a life of seventy-odd years. Even that work, by an obscure Welsh doctor buried near the river Usk, was forgotten until the nineteenth century when, first for his piety and then for his poetry, he was taken off the shelf, dusted off and re-edited. Since then his reputation has gradually grown secure.

Silex Scintillans, as C. H. Sisson points out, is best read as a whole book, to set the outstanding poems in the context of the imagination which produced them: 'the reader is in the presence of a mind of unusual integrity attempting to communicate experiences which are most often of an untraceable privacy. He did this in the language of Anglican Christianity because this was the natural language for him. It is not merely the ebullition of "I saw Eternity the other night" but the more permanent moods which underlie it and make the release possible: "For sin (like water) hourly glides/By each man's door". Or this: "My thoughts, like water which some stone doth start".' Along with the imagery of light comes that of water – baptism, cleansing, rejuvenation. If light is far and starry, water is close, physical and metaphysical or mystical. Vaughan brings us 'authentic tidings of invisible things' but also presents skilfully the created world in which he participated and lived a more full and difficult life than most men do.

John Dryden 1631–1700

Th' unhappy man, who once has trail'd a pen,
Lives not to please himself but other men:
Is always drudging, wastes his life and blood,
Yet only eats and drinks what you think good ...

In his Preface to *Fables Ancient and Modern*, Dryden
reflects on the permanence of Chaucer's characters: 'Mankind is ever the same, and nothing lost out of nature,
though every thing is altered.' This confident Augustan
sentiment – Dryden learned it from Lucretius – characterizes the father of the eighteenth century, a man whom
T. S. Eliot sees as dividing with Milton the rich heritage
of seventeenth-century poetry into two narrower traditions. 'In Dryden, wit becomes almost fun, and thereby
loses some contact with reality.' Dryden's mature language
is prodigiously efficient. It lacks the subtler registers of
more tentative poets; it lacks personal intimacy, doubt
and fear. It is a language suited to discourse and definition
more than to physical evocation or personal statement.
Ford Madox Ford is unsympathetic to Dryden's legacy:
'It is really to Dryden, writing wholly within the seventeenth century, that the eighteenth owes the peculiar
fadedness of all its adjectived nouns and latinized cliché
phrases.'

Critics define his qualities in other than poetic terms.
For Johnson he is the 'father of English criticism' and
speaks in a 'tone of adamantine confidence'. Matthew
Arnold characterizes him as 'a classic of our prose'. Eliot

takes a similar line: his 'lack of suggestiveness is compensated by his satisfying completeness of statement'.

The quality which has most drawn poets to him is what Hopkins calls his 'masculine' nature: 'his style and his rhythms lay the strongest stress of all our literature on the naked thew and sinew of the English language.' Wyndham Lewis pairs him with Defoe as a 'tongue that naked goes' – without fuss.

John Dryden was born in 1631 in Aldwinkle, Northamptonshire, of Puritan antecedents. He was educated at Westminster School, where he wrote and published at the age of eighteen his first notable poem, 'Upon the Death of Lord Hastings'. It is a deeply flawed work, combining memorable lines with strained – not to say mixed – metaphors and some ill-judged effects: the small-pox spots on the diseased lord are compared with 'rose-buds, stuck i' th' lily skin about./Each little pimple had a tear in it,/ To wail the fault its rising did commit'. The work suggests the manifold possibilities the boy had for development. A metaphysical impulse runs through the poem. There is a courtly instinct, too. But most effective are the moral conclusions, tightly drawn in efficient couplets.

He went up to Trinity College, Cambridge, taking his BA in 1654, and four years later his elegy on Cromwell's death appeared. Johnson notes in it the influence of Davenport. The poem is marred by the unrelatedness of the metaphors and the uncontrolled flow of matter which occasioned Johnson's just comment that Dryden had 'a mind better formed to reason than to feel'. With the Restoration, he was in the front line praising the King, in 'Astrea Redux', and Sir Robert Howard, whose daughter he was to marry in 1663. Charles II made him Poet Laureate in 1668. He brilliantly pilloried the King's foes in his plays – for he was an active dramatist from 1663 onward – and his satires. He was made Historiographer Royal in 1670, a reward for service and for his impressive but perhaps over-meticulous 'Annus Mirabilis', about the wonders of 1666. Dryden prided himself on getting the facts and terms right in his description of naval encounters, of the great fire, and of other specific incidents. It was Dryden's first major poem, possessing the authority of the mature style:

> Our dreaded Admiral from far they threat,
>   Whose batter'd rigging their whole war receives.
> All bare, like some old oak which tempests beat,
>   He stands, and sees below his scatter'd leaves.

His patriotism is of a novel, imperial stamp:

> Yet, like an English gen'ral will I die,
>   And all the ocean make my spacious grave.
> Women and cowards on the land may lie,
>   The sea's a tomb that's proper for the brave.

The satires and the King's favour won him the enmity of Rochester, who is said to have had him mugged one dark night.

In 1681 *Absalom and Achitophel*, a great political satire, appeared, with its attack on Shaftesbury and the party opposed to the court. A bald, less oblique attack on Shaftesbury, *The Medal*, followed in 1682. It was Dryden's most fruitful period, for the same year he published the Anglican *Religio Laici* ('A Layman's Faith'); and the allegorical *The Hind and the Panther* attempts to vindicate his later (1687) Roman Catholicism.

Much play has been made of Dryden's apparently opportunistic shifts of faith and political allegiance. Dr Johnson justifies the poet's religious sincerity as a Catholic by pointing to the letters and the life. Dryden's sons were all unquestionably devout Papists, two of whom served the church. As to his political opportunism, Ford Madox Ford makes the case for Dryden: 'it is difficult to see what other course a man writing on public matters could have taken if he set the peace of a sufficiently tormented country above all other matters.' When James II was dethroned Dryden was fifty-seven. He had found his faith, remained a Catholic, and lost both his royal appointments under William III. In bitter poems he satirized the new time-servers, especially Thomas Shadwell in *MacFlecknoe*.

He published two *Poetical Miscellanies* in 1684 and 1685. They included important poems. Johnson called 'On the Death of Mrs Killigrew' 'the noblest ode that our language has ever produced'. It is a masterly production, but must strike the modern reader as a coldly deliberate tribute:

> Art she had none, yet wanted none:
> For Nature did that want supply,
> So rich in treasures of her own,
> She might our boasted stores defy:
> Such noble vigour did her verse adorn,
> That it seem'd borrow'd, where 'twas only born.

The convention is refined but not animated.

Pope spent his early years in translation. Dryden turned to translations later on. With collaborators, he rendered Ovid's *Epistles*. In 1692 his outstanding *Satires of Juvenal and Persius* appeared. Three years before his death in 1700 *The Works of Virgil* were published. Some regard this translation as Dryden's masterpiece. Pope called it 'the most noble and spirited translation I know in any language'. His last major work, published in 1700, was *Fables Ancient and Modern*, an anthology of translations from Ovid, Boccaccio and Chaucer, including one of his most celebrated prose prefaces. Dryden's publisher, Tonson, ordered the verse by the yard, originally asking for 10,000 lines and receiving rather more than he bargained for. Dryden always wrote for money. As a freelance he was never very successful, but he survived comfortably. He was an occasional poet in a more thoroughgoing sense even than Jonson.

Dryden is one of those rare writers – with Milton, Wordsworth and Eliot – who by example and critical writing help to redirect the current of English literature. Without an understanding of Dryden's techniques and preoccupations, it is hard to understand the eighteenth century, on the eve of which he died, its achievements and *longueurs*, its stylizations, its manners and mannerisms. His importance is more than merely historical. He was the architect of that mansion in English literature which makes more demands on the modern reader than any other. One must adjust oneself to well-proportioned rooms in which familiar things are somehow unnatural in their definition and typicality; or to satirical quarters in which the familiar world is mercilessly turned topsy-turvy. Dryden affirms Augustan ideals. One critic called him 'a great representative poet' – representative of an age and a style – but not 'a great poet'. If we judge him by the effect he had, he is a great poet. If we judge the work itself, we cannot deny him the title, unless on the grounds of limited range of tone (on such grounds Milton himself would fail). Dryden's technical and formal range and assurance have few parallels. He is a civic, public, social poet. Our age may have a distaste for such work for its values, but it dismisses it at its peril. In dismissing Dryden one is dismissing the clearest of English poets, and the most accomplished of public poets.

Unlike Rochester, Dryden trusted reason as a means of exploration and of discourse. 'A man is to be cheated into passion, but reasoned into truth,' he writes in the preface to *The Hind and the Panther*. Reason has limits, and above reason stands faith, as he evokes it in *Religio Laici*:

Dim, as the borrow'd beams of moon and stars
To lonely, weary, wand'ring travellers,
Is Reason to the soul: and as on high,
Those rolling fires discover but the sky
Not light us here; so Reason's glimmering ray
Was lent, not to assure our doubtful way,
But guide us upward to a better day.
And as those nightly tapers disappear
When day's bright Lord ascends our hemisphere;

So pale grows Reason at Religion's sight;
So dies, and so disolves in supernatural Light.

Reason in the civic sphere leads to a perception of the need for order and authority. It is worth remembering that Dryden's three important early poems were in praise or in memory of figures of authority and power: Hastings, Cromwell and Charles II.

Reason is at the root of Dryden's aesthetic, with its formality of expression even when the tone is informal. He is seldom grandiloquent or assertive; the vein of wit runs through even his most sober work. He agrees with Hobbes about the place of Fancy and Judgement in the creative process. It is an aesthetic of balance: 'Time and education beget experience; experience begets memory; memory begets judgement and fancy, judgement begets the strength and structure, and fancy begets the ornaments of a poem.' Wit is in the interplay of judgement and fancy. Fancy perceives similitude in things dissimilar, judgement perceives distinctions in things similar. Rhyme, Dryden argues, helps to keep fancy under control.

Such a concepton of poetry compels the poet to be exact in his delineation of image and metaphor in order to illuminate and instruct. The truth of the figures – either literal, allegorical or satiric – must be retained. Implicit, too, is a propensity to work towards the general truth, and this produces an effect or tone of impersonality, so that one can hold Dryden responsible for the whole argument of a poem without always being certain of his personal attitude to the particulars.

The gap between Donne and Dryden, despite Dryden's early 'metaphysical' tendencies, could not be wider. Descartes and the new philosophy – and Thomas Hobbes – intervened. So did Cromwell and the Restoration, with its French habits picked up in exile. Poetry as a serious exercise had been called in question. Three modes, principally, appealed to Dryden and his age, all of them deliberate, public, and in one sense or another useful. First were the prologues and epilogues to poetic and dramatic works, comical, critical, expository or exhortatory. Dryden's comic epilogues are among his best. Mrs Ellen, 'when she was to be carried off dead by the bearers' at the end of *Tyrannick Love* (1670), exclaims, 'Hark, are you mad? you damn'd counfounded dog,/I am to rise, and speak the Epilogue.' She addressess the audience courteously as the ghost of the character she has played. She comes to berate the poet:

O Poet, damn'd dull Poet, who could prove
So senseless! to make Nelly die for Love,
Nay, what's yet worse, to kill me in the prime
Of Easter-term, in tart and cheese-cake time!
I'll fit the fop; for I'll not one word say
T'excuse his godly out of fashion play.
A play which if you dare but twice sit out,
You'll all be slander'd, and be thought devout.

The second acceptable mode was the self-consciously decorative and rhetorical occasional poem, usually occasional and celebratory. The 'Ode on St Cecilia's Day' and 'Alexander's Feast' reveal the full virtuosity of the poet in service of his occasion. And third came the heroic or religious epic, on a large scale, with ceremonious action, contemporary reference, and didactic intent. The obverse of this was the satiric mode which Dryden developed with a metrical smoothness and clarity of diction unlike Donne's, rejecting *asprezza* and the harsher tones. Thus in *Absalom and Achitophel*, the satire is cruel and direct, but the prosody impeccable: Achitophel's human deformity is not spared, but it does not deform the surface of the verse:

A daring pilot in extremity;
Pleas'd with the danger, when the waves went high
He sought the storms; but for a calm unfit,
Would steer too nigh the sands, to boast his wit.
Great wits are sure to madness near ally'd;

And thin partitions do their bounds divide:
Else, why should he, with wealth and honour blest,
Refuse his age the needful hours of rest?
Punish a body which he could not please;
Bankrupt of life, yet prodigal of ease?

Figurative langauge was not Dryden's *forte*. Often it is
not integrated into statement but runs alongside, deco-
rating and heightening but not always collaborating it
at a deeper level. Milton exemplifies another mode. In
'lik'ning spiritual to corporeal forms' he begins with
figure and metaphor and attempts a realization which
itself carries the moral significance, while Dryden teases
prose ideas into metaphor. In both cases a partial process
is enacted. Pope, by contrast, thinks in shapes and forms,
exploits reversals, contains his meanings in the figures
themselves but works as it were with atomized forms and
metaphors, divorced from the expected context and releasing new meanings in an original context. The poetry
tends to fragment. Milton's procedure comes closest to the
'organic' concept of poetic form enunciated by Coleridge
and exploited by the romantics. Dryden's procedure is
the most remote from this. He distrusts antithesis, paradox
and disjunction and he is wary of placing excessive confidence in plain narrative, at least for didactic purposes.
He plays off general meanings without committing himself to any but an intellectual organization.

His satires are conceived in a different way from Pope's.
For Pope the ideal order is no longer tangibly embodied:
his satiric exaggerations do not always suggest a verifiable
norm, his distortions have more malice than instructive
justness in their delineation. Dryden accepts the *status
quo* as the norm, accepts necessary authority, placing first
facts rather than values. This is his 'philosophical actual-
ism' learned from Hobbes. The fact has more authority
than traditional sanction, in politics as in literature: a
King's is a formal authority, not a sacred one; a poem to
be of value must be of use.

His tendency to stylize his material in order to draw its morals lucidly, the tendency in the plays of attitudes replacing passions and figures replacing characters, was due in part to Charles II's own taste. From his French exile he had brought a preference for rhymed, formalized dramas, for 'conscious genius' (as Johnson says) above all other. The monarch was a patron, and though he did not exactly call the tune, no doubt he tapped out a rhythm with his foot. Dryden was an obliging poet, to his King and later to his publisher. Flattery was his worst vice, yet he is so solid he somehow retains his integrity.

Dr Johnson's assessment of Dryden is still the most concise and judicious. Dryden rather than Sidney is 'the father of English criticism', especially on the strength of the *Essay on Dramatic Poesy* (1668). Dryden 'first taught us to determine upon principles the merit of composition.' Johnson criticizes the lack of an overall consistency of approach in Dryden's essays, the occasional marring casualness and partiality. But these faults do not endanger the broader achievement which (unlike Milton's or Cowley's) is at root not scholarly but critical. His art is to express clearly what he thinks with vigour. The kernel of Johnson's praise is this: 'he refined the language, improved the sentiments, and tuned the numbers of English poetry.' Before Dryden there was 'no poetical diction, no system of words at once refined from the grossness of domestic use, and free from the harshness of terms appropriated to particular arts.' The advent of such 'diction' was a mixed blessing. For Dryden himself, the refined diction sought to make language transparent to the thing expressed, capable of general statements of truth without obscurity or vulgarity: hence the excellence of his theory and practice of translation. To some of his followers, however, diction could mean refinement of manner, even affectation, rather than efficient, unencumbered expression. When Johnson claims that Dryden refined the sentiments of poetry, I believe he wishes to praise the public manner and the absence of individual quirkiness in the feelings expressed. Yet it is the element of individual tone, of apprehensible character, that we miss in Dryden. It is an overstatement to suggest that he 'tuned the numbers' of English poetry. He refined the heroic couplet and handed it as a vital instrument to his successors. His prosodic virtuosity in the songs from the plays, in the odes and elegies, is not in doubt: but he had equals among his predecessors, not least Ben Jonson. When Dryden 'refined' the language, he ridded it of much dross, it is true, but also of much of its expressive power. He tuned an instrument which could play certain tunes and harmonies but which was incapable of the older and some of the deeper music. The loss is felt not so much in his own work as in the work of his successors.

The efficiency of Dryden's verse, its chief virtue, was learned from his theatrical writing. What Homer was for Pope, the theatre was for Dryden. It gave him a sense of the public, and there he discovered and perfected his popular style. He was not 'much inclined' by his genius to write for the stage, but material necessity took him there and taught him. The plays contain little of his finest writing. Indeed, only one of his numerous plays, *All for Love*, based on Shakespeare's *Antony and Cleopatra*, retains theatrical appeal today. But the stage was his pacing-ground. Without that experience it is doubtful that he could have sustained *Absalom and Achitophel*, the best long political satire in the language, marred only by the inexactness of the allegory. The satires are full of the political and literary life of the time, but retain a wider reference. The prologues and epilogues contain much popular life of the time, and are not remote from common speech. The allegories, too, reflect his age's intellectual and spiritual life. Eliot's tribute to Dryden is partial and a little paradoxical: 'Dryden appeared to cleanse the language of verse and once more bring it back to prose order. For this reason he is a great poet.' It would be better to say that Dryden suggested a different order for poetic language than his predecessors had. What is prosaic in Dryden is his ideas, not his language. When Eliot suggests that he 'once more' brings the language of poetry back to prose order, we are inclined to ask, when in the history of English poetry up to Dryden's time had the language of poetry followed a strictly prose order? Dryden was not taking English poetry backwards but, inexorably, forward into a new territory which rejected as much as – perhaps more than – it discovered.

John Wilmot, Earl of Rochester
1647–1680

Nothing! thou elder brother even to Shade:
Thou had'st a being ere the world was made,
And well fixed, art alone of ending not afraid.

During his poetic apprenticeship, Pope wrote 'Upon
Silence', an imitation of Rochester's 'Upon Nothing':
'Silence! Coeval with Eternity;/Thou wert ere future's
self began to be.' His piece is just an exercise, while
Rochester's is one of the few necessary masterpieces that
poet wrote. Yet the young Pope took Rochester to heart,
as a master. Rochester attempted to think in verse, a feat
he performed with appalling lucidity in 'Upon Nothing',
in which he lays bare the philosophical basis for his
notorious conduct. That poem provides an explanation
for what most critics regard as the saddest squandering of
authentic genius in English poetry. When Pope, forty
years after his imitation of Rochester, came to sleep in the
bed Rochester had graced at Atterbury, he was 'With no
poetic ardours fir'd'. And no wonder, for Rochester has
left a very small *oeuvre* to hint his greatness; and the work
is formally conservative and eccentric in theme and subject. Pope came to see Rochester and the other poets of
Charles II's court, including Charles Sackville, Earl of
Dorset, Sir Charles Sedley, Sir George Etherege, William
Wycherley and Henry Savile, as a 'mob of gentlemen who
wrote verses'. Marvell called them a 'merry gang'.

The court of Charles II was congenial to wit and culture of a kind – an aristocratic kind. This was the Indian

summer of 'court culture'. F. R. Leavis finds the poets
lacking in 'positive fineness' and 'implicit subtlety'. The
country house is supplanted by the coffee house, the 'fine
old order' is gone.

A Restoration court laboured in the shadow of the
Commonwealth: a continuity had been broken, and with
that continuity perished the values of an old order. An
institution had been restored, but not its informing principles. A sense of vulnerability among court writers and
politicians shortened those perspectives which empower a
poet or statesman to take, naturally, the long view. Idealism of a powerful and defeated sort seemed concentrated
on the other side. Divine sanctions were gone, there was
less a sense of right than of tenuous success. Hobbes rather
than Filmer or Hooker was the philosopher of the day.
The influence of Hobbes on Rochester goes deep. As a
courtier, the poet's chief allegiance was to 'pleasure' conceived in a somewhat narrow range, and underlying this
allegiance was an irreligion, finally a virtually nihilistic
materialism. The old verities were undermined.

Charles II's court had more in common with the French
than with earlier English courts. The King had close connections with France, and the circumstances of his restoration added an alien element to his reign. Court writers
were self-absorbed and irresponsible in ways it had never
occurred to their predecessors to be. The lack of broad
civic courtesy, the absence of the imperatives of duty and
service, and the apparent liberty of the court *milieu* were
attractive to Voltaire.

And Voltaire found Rochester's work congenial. In
Lettres philosophiques he says, 'all the world knows Lord
Rochester's reputation'; he will introduce the other
Rochester, not just a well-placed libertine but a man of
genius, *'le grand poète'*, with his 'ardent' imagination.
Voltaire reserves special praise for the satires which,
whether the ideas expressed are true or false, reveal real
poetic energy. Marvell, too, saw Rochester as 'the best
English satirist', Aubrey tells us. Boileau was – with

Cowley – among the earl's favourite authors. It was to the contemporary European tradition that his satire belonged.

Rochester was of his age, experimenting with his life as his contemporaries experimented in science. It is fashionable nowadays to see him as 'essentially serious', a 'radical critic' of his time, even a moral visionary. On the evidence of the verse, apart from 'A Satire Against Mankind', he is neither socially radical nor penetratingly serious. His seriousness of theme emerges in only a few poems and there more as statement than exploration. He was hostile to reason, Dryden's tool, and thus denied himself the main avenue of philosophical exploration. Yet this hostility to reason is itself a theme, as in 'Tunbridge Wells':

Ourselves with noise of reason we do please
In vain; humanity's our worst disease.
Thrice happy beasts are, who, because they be
Of reason void, are so of foppery.

It is a crucial theme. Yet in accepting it, and in exploiting conventional poetic forms, Rochester cannot get far beyond – or, except on certain themes, in – satire and denies himself the scope of the long poem. It is hard to see what other strategy he could have worked out, given his temperament and his antecedents.

He was born in Ditchley, Oxfordshire, in 1647. His father, a royalist general, led an abortive rising in Yorkshire in 1655 and died in exile two or three years later. Rochester's mother was of a family with close Puritan connections. At the age of twelve Rochester went up to Wadham College, Oxford, a centre of the new scientific and intellectual developments that led to the foundation of the Royal Academy. In 1661 the precocious young noble was made an MA by Lord Clarendon himself. The restored King granted him a pension in 1660, in recognition of his father's service. Under such favourable stars, Rochester toured France and Italy and returned to England in 1664. He made himself visible at court. His feelings for Charles II were ambiguous, almost those of a young man for a forceful step-father. Some of his most scathing satires are directed against the monarch. In 1665 Rochester was confined to the Tower for attempting to abduct a Somerset heiress, whom he married two years later ('I'll hold you six to four I love you with all my heart', he wrote to her later, during one of his infidelities). Thanks to the plague, he was released from the Tower, joined the fleet, and gave intrepid service, though there is evidence that he was less stalwart ashore.

The remainder of his life, thirteen years, passed in a series of unsettled and rash acts with periods of study and work. If he wrote the notorious play *Sodom*, it was around 1670. Between 1673 and 1676 his best satires and 'Upon Nothing' were composed. He died, after a well-chronicled conversion, in 1680.

We can choose between two versions of Rochester. Etherege, in *The Man of Mode*, presents him as the charmingly inconstant and self-involved Dorimant. We can embellish this image with the story of the smashing of the sundials in the Priory Gardens and the murderous affray at Epsom. On the other hand we have the scholar (on the evidence of Anthony à Wood and of the fragments of his translation of Lucretius). Gilbert Burnet, who negotiated and chronicled his reconciliation with God, and was at best a Whig rascal, wrote of his good looks, his civility, and his intelligence: 'He loved to talk and write of speculative matters, and did so with so fine a thread, that even those who hated the subjects' were charmed by his treatment of them. But, Burnet adds, physical led to intellectual dissipation, 'which made him think nothing diverting which was not extravagant'.

The truth about Rochester is closer to Etherege's version. Dr Johnson praises the 'vigour of his colloquial wit', yet 'The glare of his general character diffused itself upon his writings.' The very shortness of his pieces reflects the shortness of his periods of sobriety and study: 'Everywhere may be found tokens of a mind which study might have carried to excellence.'

His work falls into four categories: extended satire, the libel or squib, the racy anecdote poem, and the love poem. Some of the love poems are spoken by women ('I could love thee till I die' and 'Ancient Person' are among the best). Love is of a resolutely physical nature, however wittily it comes masked. 'Leave this gaudy, gilded stage', ' 'Tis not that I am weary grown', 'Absent from thee I languish still' and 'The Mistress': these works rank high in English love poetry. They are forthright and have the air of sincerity. The anecdote poems, too, have power in their sometimes grotesque bawdiness and can be mildly erotic and startling. 'Fair Chloris in a pigsty lay' is the best-known of them. We might consider them down-market eclogues. The squibs and libels marry wit and malice and do some damage to their subjects, notably the King.

In his imitations of Ovid ('O Love! how cold and slow' and 'The Imperfect Enjoyment') he moves towards satire. It is useful to compare his imitations to Marlowe's (Elegia II, ix and III, vi). Less than a century separates them. Marlowe's versions are in a sense visualized and dominated by metaphor. They are vivid and undeflected by self-conscious wit. Rochester's versions have an intellectual clarity, but the idea is developed at the expense of metaphor. He argues rather than evokes. His language is more conventional and polite, his prosody smoother, than Marlowe's. In Marlowe there is a sultry, ambiguous sexuality, in Rochester a frank intellectual forthrightness, but without undertones – what Eliot, writing of Dryden, called 'lack of suggestiveness'. Compare Marlowe's:

Dost joy to have thy hookèd arrows shakèd
In naked bone? Love hath my bones left naked.
So many men and maidens without love!
Hence with great laud thou may'st a triumph move.

with Rochester's:

On men disarmed how can you gallant prove?
And I was long ago disarmed by love.
Millions of dull men live, and scornful maids:
We'll own love valiant when he these invades.

Rochester is the more correct; yet Marlowe, even in his awkwardness, is the more satisfying. The third line provides the clue to the radical changes in poetic procedure that have occurred.

Age, 'beauty's incurable disease', is the central apprehension of Rochester's harsh satirical vision. He satirizes affectation and the social forms which lead to a squandering of potential pleasure; and he satirizes those excesses which themselves foreshorten pleasure and which he, as much as the King, indulged. He cannot stop satirizing reason, that 'ignis fatuus', a contrived and misleading sixth sense: 'Huddled in dirt the reasoning engine lies,/ Who was so proud, so witty, and so wise.' This bleak apprehension of mortality is in the poetry unredeemed by religious certitude. The one virtue Rochester celebrates is love. In 'A Letter from Artemisia in Town to Chloe in the Country' he writes,

Love, the most generous passion of the mind,
The softest refuge innocence can find,
The safe director of unguided youth ...

It is 'That cordial drop heaven in our cup has thrown/ To make the nauseous draught of life go down'. Love a 'passion of the mind'? Marlowe would not have understood that. It would seem that Rochester's satire seeks to free this impulse of love from inhibition and convention. He is the apologist of what is now called 'sex' rather than love. Yet underlying even this theme is the pervasive truth stated in 'Upon Nothing':

Great Negative, how vainly would the wise
Inquire, define, distinguish, teach, devise,
Did'st thou not stand to point their blind philosophies.

Though his satire is directed at courtly society and society at large, much in the manner of Juvenal, the objective of his satire is hardly social. Unlike Pope's, Rochester's satire is informed by a metaphysical despair, not a social optimism. He had taken Hobbes to heart.

Jonathan Swift 1667–1745

If on Parnassus' top you sit,
You rarely bite, are always bit:
Each poet of inferior size
On you shall rail and criticize ...

Swift's reputation as a poet stands higher in this century
than it has done before. A number of modern poets have
looked to him, identifying particular and original virtues
in the verse which had long been regarded as peripheral
to his major prose work.

Born in Dublin in 1667, Jonathan Swift insisted on his
Englishness. He came of Yorkshire stock. His father died
before the boy was born. His education was paid for by an
uncle, first in Kilkenny and later at Trinity College,
Dublin, where he did not distinguish himself. He travelled
to England and became secretary to Sir William Temple
at Moor Park in Surrey. There, among other studies, he
laboured at verse, subjected his poems to endless revisions,
and fell under the influence of Cowley, whose Pindaric
odes appealed to many young poets. C. H. Sisson describes the Pindaric ode as practised by Cowley. It 'consisted in the irregular number of syllables in the lines,
producing, it may be supposed, the effect of surprise, if
not astonishment, and a certain wilful lunacy in the
sequence of thoughts.' The odes are negligible work.
Swift's first significant poem, 'Mrs Harris's Petition', was
not composed until he was thirty-four, by which time he
had put aside Cowley and opened his ears to the spoken

language of the day. The 'Petition' is thoroughly colloquial, in irregular long-lined couplets that take the tone of a woman speaking at great speed, making a deposition of sorts. It is undecorated and displays what De Quincey called Swift's 'vernacularity'.

By the time he composed the 'Petition' (1701) he had left Temple, giving up after real promise his secular ambitions, and taking holy orders (1694). He was to rub shoulders with men of power and with his prose writings to make a mark on English affairs. His first living, in Kilroot, Ireland, did not please him. He returned briefly to England but in 1699 was back in Ireland as chaplain to the Earl of Berkeley, a post from which he was ousted by private intrigue. He became vicar of Laracor. He grew deeply embroiled in religious and political affairs and eventually became Dean of St Patrick's, Dublin. With the death of Queen Anne the Whigs, his enemies, came to power. There was no further preferment for him.

He was in his later years a political enigma, 'with the Whigs of the State and the Tories of the Church,' Johnson said. His treatment by parties and patrons led him to a healthy distrust of men in power and intensified his sense of personal grievance and bitterness.

He considered life in Ireland to be exile. He did much for the Irish and earned their respect, if not their love. Through correspondence he maintained his friendship with Pope, Gay, Arbuthnot, Bolingbroke and a few others in England, but his mind ran on Irish affairs. He was aware of conditions at every social level, and his Toryism was of that particularist kind which will not tolerate exploitative corruption from any party.

His relations with women, especially 'Stella' and 'Vanessa', and his disgust with physical functions, have given much mileage to psychological critics. Disgust informs much of the prose and verse, but also a profound interest in common people, their language, actions and concerns. The verse provides a key to this aspect of his genius, and to his darker musings. It possesses some of the satirical virtues of the prose with an additional virtue: the 'I' speaks as itself with an uncompromised acerbity few poets have mastered. When he died in 1745, Ireland and England were in his debt. The topicality that has limited the appeal of some of his prose works is itself the appeal of the verse, which catches inflections and commemorates small actions now lost to us – the voices of gardeners, street vendors, labourers, which we hear a little too refined in Gay; and the voice of a cryptic man of conscience speaking of his world. He is commemorated by one of the great epitaphs: he lies *'ubi saeva indignatio ulterius cor lacerare nequit. Abi, viator, et imitare, si poteris, strenuum pro virili libertatis vindicatorem.'*

Boswell found Johnson's *Life of Swift* excessively hostile to its subject. In its thirty pages, the poems receive only three succinct paragraphs. They are just, as far as they go. In the poems 'there is not much upon which the critic can exercise his powers. They are often humorous, almost always light, and have the qualities which recommend such compositions, easiness and gaiety.' Their diction, prosody and rhyme are correct, conforming to Swift's own notion of good style, 'proper words in proper places'. Johnson's highest praise follows: 'perhaps no writer can be found who borrowed so little, or that in all his excellences and all his defects has so well maintained his claim to be considered as original.'

The originality is in part a function of the spareness of his mature style. As Johnson says, his thoughts were 'never subtilized by nice disquisitions, decorated by sparkling conceits, elevated by ambitious sentences, or variegated by far-sought learning'. In this he resembles Defoe, never shirking the difficult subject or elaborating for elaboration's sake. It is difficult to quote passages of Swift out of context. The poems are even and whole at their best.

Trifles and bagatelles, Johnson tells us, were necessary to Swift. Many of the poems are the product of a love of language as it is spoken and a fascination with people. The activities of humble folk provide much of the substance of the poems: to represent is at times a sufficient end. There are the 'Descriptions' of 'Morning', 'A City Shower' in particular, which seek only to realize a peopled scene with a slight satirical colouring:

Brisk Susan whips her linen from the rope
While the first drizzling show'r is borne aslope,
Such is that sprinkling which some careless quean
Flirts on you from her mop, but not so clean.

Bustling verbs animate scene and metaphor. Human actions rather than natural scenes or phenomena arrest Swift's attention. Ford Madox Ford comments on his 'most unusual power of conveying scenes vividly ... scenes rather of the sensibility than of material objects and land-scapes'.

In those pieces which go beyond the limited objectives the challenge of Swift is greatest. F. R. Leavis indicates the paradoxical nature of Swift's approach: 'Lacking the Augustan politeness, he seems with his dry force of pre-sentment, both to make the Augustan positives ... look like negatives, and to give the characteristic Augustan lacks and disabilities a positive presence.' Without 'Augustan urbanity', 'spiritual poverty' and 'hollowness' are emphasized.

Swift's irony is not normative, like Pope's, but radical: it is thematic rather than merely stylistic. This is why his poems, even those most topical, retain force today. 'I take it to be part of the honesty of poets,' he wrote, 'that they cannot write well except they think the subject deserves it.' The subjects he chose he approached as if for the first time, as if we stepped from a world of reason into a world of men. Bolingbroke was not quite fair to him when he suggested, 'If you despised the world as much as you pre-tend, and perhaps believe, you would not be so angry with it.' Swift was a vigorous hater, to be sure, but with a hatred rooted in disappointed expectation. He is merci-less not to the lower orders but to the superior, em-powered classes, and to the vain who persist in self-deception. Flattery is the greatest sin, fully chastised in the satirical 'On Poetry: A Rhapsody'.

Edgell Rickword and later C. H. Sisson took Swift's verse to heart. In an influential essay, 'The Re-Creation of Poetry' (1925), Rickword described a 'poetry of negative emotions, of those arising from disgust with the object'. 'Swift is a great master of this kind of poetry. His verse has no pleasure-value beyond that of its symmetry and concision, but it is the most intricate labyrinth of personality that any poet has built around himself, not excepting Donne.' Rickword is a great partisan of Donne, and this point cannot be taken lightly. Where Donne makes the labyrinth beguiling, Swift undecorates as he goes. The narrow, narrowing power of the verse is great. 'The Progress of Beauty' and 'The Furniture of a Woman's Mind' exemplify the voice of 'negative emotion'. So does 'The Progress of Marriage', where he directs the satire at himself, or 'Verses on the Death of Dr Swift', in which he becomes the subject. His imitation of Horace II.6, with wry self-knowledge and a canny understanding of the world, evokes the man and those who use him. Love is a spirit remote from this verse.

Swift is hard to recommend as a poet because he is so hard to display. There are no purple passages, no detachable maxims; the poetry is spread through the poem with an evenness that out-of-context quotation violates. The epitaphs, the spoofs, the eclogues, the anecdotes spoken by various voices, the ironic love poems, the first person poems, add to one another but will not be broken up into tags like the rich couplet bric-à-brac of Pope.

John Gay 1685–1732

Tell me, ye jovial sailors, tell me true,
If my sweet William sails among the crew.

Of the three poet-friends Swift, Pope and Gay, Gay was
the lightest and most cheerful. His epitaph reads, 'Life is
a jest; and all things show it,/I thought so once; but now
I know it.' It is as true to him as Swift's sober epitaph is
to that very different man. For Pope and his circle Gay
was a 'play-fellow' rather than a 'partner'. Pope reports
that he was treated 'with more fondness than respect ...
he was a natural man, without design, who spoke what he
thought and just as he thought it.'

This was not quite fair. Gay is one of the great paro-
dists. His satirical procedure is different in kind from
Pope's. Marcus Walsh, a recent editor of his work, prefers
to present him as 'ironist' rather that satirist, a sensible
strategy to distinguish him from his greater contemporaries. Gay lacks the certainty of moral orientation of Pope
and Swift: he cannot be tied to an opinion. He is amused
and alarmed by human fallibility, vanity and self-deceit,
but hasn't that rage which makes and mars the satires of
Pope and Swift. Evil is unclear to him, he avoids moral
absolutes.

He was born in Barnstaple, Devon, in 1685. His father,
who died when the boy was ten, was a Nonconformist man
of affairs from well-established Devonshire stock. The boy
was educated at the local grammar school and then apprenticed to a silk mercer in London. He disliked the job,

obtained his release, and returned to Devon, where he began writing verse.

In 1707 he went back to London to become a writer, and the next year published *Wine*. It celebrates wine in Miltonic parody: 'Of happiness terrestrial, and the source/Whence human pleasures flow, sing heavenly Muse.' Of a muse that failed another poet he writes as of the fallen angel Lucifer: 'Now in Ariconian bogs/She lies inglorious floundering, like her theme/Languid and faint.' He parodies the debate of the fallen angels. Closing time is like the departure of Adam and Eve from the garden. He parodies not only Milton's language and style, but also his plot and structure. A trivial subject is handled in the grand manner. It is clever and sustained but, as Dr Johnson says, inconsequential: an exercise that any versifier might perform. It lacks the underlying seriousness of his later parodic satires.

In 1711 he made the acquaintance of Pope. Gay found himself in the best possible literary *milieu*, with a friend and critic who, though his junior, could help and advise him, make suggestions, and exploit his talents in his own literary vendettas. If Pope did not fully appreciate Gay's benign genius, he valued his friendship and helped him in times of great need. Gay's nicest tribute to Pope, 'Mr Pope's Welcome from Greece', celebrates the translator of Homer as himself an Homeric hero.

Gay's talent for eccentric but accurate observation, and his sense of the vulnerability to real experience of the established literary modes and genres, inform all his verse. He could deflate the epic, the georgic, the eclogue, and the dramatic modes by literalizing rather than ridiculing them. As a result he laughed them back to life. He was able in his 'low style' to do things Swift might appreciate: write ballads and burlesques. In two of his several attempts he was a considerable dramatist. He had an instinctive, if not infallible, sense of his public.

Pope was the dedicatee of his first major poem, *Rural Sports*. The overall form is unsatisfying, but much of the detail is vivid. Johnson called it 'realistic pastoral'. It prepared the ground for *The Shepherd's Week* (1714), Gay's best 'pastoral'. *Rural Sports* exploits the pathetic fallacy to good effect. Fish and worms behave in such a way as to suggest the animal fable, a possibility he later developed. An uninsistent religious strain sounds through the poem. Country streams are 'Sweet composers of the pensive soul'.

The Shepherd's Week, a sort of truncated *Shepheards Calendar*, was part of Pope's campaign against Ambrose Philips, whose pastorals had been praised in preference to Pope's own. Gay imports into the polite, idealized world of swains and shepherdesses some of the Devonshire peasants of his youth. Spenser and Virgil, as well as Philips, are among his targets. Convention is invaded by flesh and blood. In 'Monday' he footnotes his own lines 83–88 and refers to their source in Virgil:

Populus Alcidae gratissima, vitis Iaccho,
Fermosae Myrtus Veneri, sua Laurea Phoebo.
Phillis amat Corylos. Illis dum Phillis amabit,
Nec Myrtus vincet Corylos nec Laurea Phoebi.

Johnson believed the pastoral mode could only be brought to life through burlesque. Gay adapts these lines as:

Leek to the Welsh, to Dutchmen butter's dear,
Of Irish swains potato is the cheer;
Oats for their feasts the Scottish shepherds grind,
Sweet turnips are the food of Blouzelind.
While she loves turnips, butter I'll despise,
Nor leeks nor oatmeal nor potato prize.

This kind of traduction into occasional common diction and common experience marks Gay's best work in parody, especially his dramatic masterpiece *The Beggar's Opera* (1728), a 'Newgate pastoral' composed at the suggestion of Swift. It sets out to discredit the Italian opera that had held the stage in London for ten years. This 'ballad opera', as Johnson called it, was an unparalleled success. The sequel, banned by Walpole, sold extremely well when

it was published (1729). Swift commented on the pre-
dominance of *humour* over *wit* in these works; the rules
are parodied and satirized – marriage and honour for
example – but finally upheld.

Having worked as secretary to the batty Duchess of
Monmouth, in 1714 he served under the Duke of Clarendon at Hanover. Queen Anne's death brought this brief
appointment to an end, and he experienced no courtly
preferment thereafter. Like Swift, he felt such disappoint-
ments deeply, and his sense of the social world clouded,
his poetry matured. In 1713 he had published *The Fan*;
but in 1716 he published *Trivia*. The change is remarkable.

The Fan follows rather too closely on the heels of
Pope's *The Rape of the Lock*. It is weak because it is un-
systematic and unsubtly overstated. It does not mytholo-
gize the real because it does not grasp it firmly enough. It
is literary, in the same spirit as *Wine*. But *Trivia: or the
Art of Walking the Streets of London* is the best evocation of London in verse. It originates in Juvenal's third
satire, as Johnson's 'London' does, but it is gentler and,
though less powerful, more complex than Juvenal's poem.
The parodic mainspring is Virgil's *Georgics* and the then
fashionable georgic tradition. The contrast between the
order of rural life which the form imposes, and the disorder of city life which is the subject, provides much of
the humour. The even georgic tone describes bizarre and
terrible incidents. The Great Frost, evoked in the second
section, includes an account of the death of an apple
vendor:

'Twas here the matron found a doleful fate:
Let elegiac lay the woe relate.
Soft as the breath of distant flutes, at hours
When silent evening closes up the flowers;
Lulling as falling water's hollow noise;
Indulging grief, like Philomela's voice ...

Doll, the pippin vendor, is decapitated as she falls through the ice, her voice dying in the 'pip-pip-pip' of her pippin cry. The incongruity between manner and matter is a measure of Gay's ironic power. Much of the effect is in the reader's uncertainty about the moral stance of the poet.

'Nothing about *Trivia* is straightforward,' writes Marcus Walsh, 'not even the title, which means primarily crossroads, but is also a Roman name for the goddess Hecate' – herself invoked at the beginning of the third book. The title 'points to the threefold structure of the poem, suggests the mediaeval *trivium* of studies in grammar, logic and rhetoric, and implies trivial in the modern sense'. Not only the title, but words, parodic passages and scenes bear equally concentrated sense. A bootblack is begotten by immaculate conception; Vulcan visits Patty and makes her patterns. We receive advice (as in a good Georgic) but here about our dress for walking the London streets: suitable shoes, coat, walking stick, hat; about the weather and the perils and the sights to see. We hear the creaking shop signs, the waggons and carriages, street cries. There is mud, a street fight, pick-pockets, whores, chairmen, vendors, watchmen, rakes. There is a fire. The values that inform georgic poetry are inverted even as the mode is parodied.

In 1720 Gay published his *Poems on Several Occasions* with great success. He lost money in the South Sea Bubble and was so disappointed that, without the help of Pope and his circle, he would have died. He survived, became Commissioner for the Public Lottery in 1722, and spent his later years at various houses, especially with the Duke and Duchess of Queensberry who took his chaotic affairs in hand. In 1725 he published 'To a Lady on her Passion for Old China', one of his most sustained polite moral satires: 'What rival's near? a China jar.' Two years later appeared *The Fables*, written for Prince William, later Duke of Cumberland. In 1738 sixteen posthumous *Fables* were published, more overtly moral and satiric than the earlier pieces, and in epistolary form after the manner of

Pope. Gay died in 1732 and was buried in Westminster Abbey.

The Fables proved his most popular poetic work, running through fifty editions, in various forms, before 1800. They were illustrated by Thomas Bewick and William Blake, among others. Gay uses his animals to illuminate human nature, either by contrast or caricature. The poems have variety of tone and approach. Some are serious, others simply comic. The moral, as Johnson said, cannot always be drawn. In adopting fable form, literary parody became more difficult for Gay, since fable itself is essentially parodic. One of Gay's characteristic processes is lacking, and modern readers may feel that lack. 'The Elephant and the Bookseller', 'The Butterfly and the Snail', 'The Two Monkeys', and the fox fables stand out from the rest. But beside *Trivia* the *Fables* offer a lesser form of entertainment. One need only compare them with Henryson's fables to see how limited they are. The sixteen published posthumously, in particular, despite their directness and the access of moral rigour, fall below the level of Gay's best writing.

Alexander Pope 1688–1744

Lo! thy dread empire, Chaos! is restor'd;
Light dies before thy uncreating word:
Thy hand, great Anarch! lets the curtain fall;
And universal Darkness buries all.

Using Dryden's measure, the heroic couplet, Pope re-
discovered many of the complexities of the poetic process
which Dryden had refined away. Pope thinks in metaphors, shapes and forms; he does not decorate a rational
line of thought with metaphor. Thought itself matters less
in his work than in Dryden's. There are none of those
spiritual crises which matured Dryden's ideas. For Pope
the crises were not religious or political but social and
literary. If as a man he was crudely ambitious, in some
respects dishonest, in love with his role as a poet and his
material profit as a writer above all else, he did manage
to command the friendship of such men as Swift, Gay,
Bolingbroke and Arbuthnot. If at the heart of his work
there is an unresolved philosophical contradiction, it is
this that provokes much of the best verse. He writes with
an assurance and authority which sets at nothing the ani-
mosity his character arouses. One tends to forget that he
was the sort of man who wrote his letters for publication.

Alexander Pope was born in Lombard Street, London,
in 1688. His father, a papist, was a merchant, and both his
parents were advanced in years when he was born. In the
year of Dryden's death, when the boy was twelve, his
family removed to Windsor Forest to join a Catholic

community. Soon the young Pope was writing imitations of the English poets – Waller, Cowley, Rochester, Chaucer, Spenser – and translating from various texts – Thomas à Kempis, Ovid, Statius and Homer among them.

At the age of twelve he contracted the first of a series of illnesses which, with his physical deformity, left him nearly an invalid for the rest of his life. He read eclectically and was encouraged in his writing. When he was nineteen, Dryden's publisher Tonson issued his *Pastorals* in the sixth volume of his *Miscellany*. The poems are of little interest today, but their promise attracted attention and Pope was auspiciously welcomed. In 1711 *An Essay on Criticism*, perhaps his best non-satirical composition, appeared and the *Spectator* and the *Guardian* took up the young prodigy.

Pope attributed the virtues of his *Pastorals* (which, he informs us with undue insistence, were written when he was sixteen) not to observation of nature but 'to some old authors, whose work as I had leisure to study, so I hope I have not wanted care to imitate.' His 'Discourse on Pastoral Poetry' (also, he insists, written when he was sixteen) is brilliant and lucid. Here is the literary – very literary – Georgic. In the first few lines, along with classical echoes, we hear Spenser, Milton and Waller. The syntax is arch, classicizing, and at times silly. 'Two swains, whom Love kept wakeful, and the Muse,/Poured o'er the whitening vale their fleecy care.' The muse appears to be wakeful and a shepherdess – until we realize she is a second cause for insomnia. Whatever the classical sanction for such figures of rhetoric, there is no native sanction. Lapses of syntactical clarity are common in Pope's work. De Quincey speaks of his problem as 'almost peculiar to himself. It lay in an inability, nursed doubtless by indolence, to carry out and perfect the expression of the thought he wishes to communicate. The language does not realize the idea: it simply suggests or hints it.' De Quincey chooses a couplet from the mature work which gives the impression of sense but under close scrutiny proves virtually meaningless. It is a false commonplace that Pope is a model of correctness.

And yet that couplet from the *Pastorals* includes characteristic virtues of Pope's writing: 'their fleecy care' is a round-about way of saying 'sheep', but it has the effect of stressing the shepherds' responsibility (an abstract meaning) and physically evoking the sheep. It combines a pictorial with a moral element, each rendered vivid by the epithet. This technique is most effectively developed in 'Eloisa to Abelard' (1716), a romantic 'heroic epistle' unique in Pope's work.

> In these deep solitudes and awful cells,
> Where heav'nly pensive, contemplation dwells,
> And ever-musing melancholy reigns;
> What means this tumult in a Vestal's veins?

'Deep' and 'cells' have physical connotations; 'solitudes' and 'awful' are abstract. The parallel construction mingles the four terms: a hermitage and a state of mind. Within the solitude is a rough hierarchy: melancholy reigns, contemplation dwells. It is a pensive, ever-musing kingdom, shaken by earthly desires. 'Vestal's veins' is almost oxymoronic in effect. Pope's thought attaches shapes and scenes, most vividly in the passage in which tears distort the visible world for Eloisa, the speaker:

> Can'st thou forget what tears that moment fell,
> When, warm in youth, I bade the world farewell?
> As with cold lips I kissed the sacred veil,
> The shrines all trembled, and the lamps grew pale.

In such passages there is a suggestion of the poet Pope might have become with different patrons, different admirers. 'Eloisa to Abelard' is a closely textured and thoroughly consistent evocation, with recurrent developing imagery of lips, eyes, tears, pallor, coldness and burning. The subject is human nature and human passion at their most paradoxical. Pope never tried the subject again, perhaps because it gave him only a limited scope for what De Quincey described as his 'talent for caustic effect'. Besides, the subject was 'unwholesome'.

'Windsor Forest' also suggests the 'lost Pope' – who might have been. The observations of nature seem to be not from 'old authors' but from the Forest itself. The evocation is vivid, if a little brittle, detail presented in terms of artifice, and each detail carrying a moral or interpretative weight. Transitive verbs animate the poem and assist in the fusion between concrete images and abstract qualities:

Oft, as in airy rings they skim the heath
The clam'rous lapwings feel the leaden death.
Oft, as the mounting larks their notes prepare,
They fall, and leave their little notes on air.

The phrase 'leaden death' for 'shot' or 'bullet' at once suggests the weight of ammunition and counteracts the movement of the previous line. The mounting larks are shot and fall, their music left suspended. A deft couplet completes a complex image which contains its own interpretation.

In 1712 *The Rape of the Lock* was first published, and in 1714 an extended version appeared. This masterpiece of English mock-heroic writing emerged from an actual event but pursued the social foible to absurd lengths. The poem does not cut deep satirically, but it amuses, and suggests the later themes. One reason for the ineffectualness of the poem as satire is that one senses the poet is at home in the world he describes, himself seduced by its opulence.

The next year Pope started to raise subscriptions for his translation of the *Iliad*. It appeared between 1715 and 1720 and profited him greatly. In 1725–6 the *Odyssey*, prepared with assistants, followed. In his work on Homer Pope fully mastered the couplet technique, with a finality that must at times seem glib, for the form forces false parallelisms, imposes a rigid pattern on the organization, and is suited more for aphoristic intellectual development than for narrative. Yet he mastered the style and made it flow. Johnson's estimate of the translation is as high as Pope's estimate of Dryden's Virgil: 'the noblest version of poetry which the world has ever seen.'

On the proceeds of his writing, he was able to settle at Twickenham, in a house with a famous grotto. There he lived until his death in 1744. He practised a frugality that rivalled Swift's, but without Swift's excuse. Success did not exactly spoil him, but the pleasures of prosperity induced him to undertake projects he should have left alone, especially in 1725 an edition of Shakespeare's works for which he had neither the scholarly acumen nor the editorial patience. He woke certain enemies, notably Theobald, who detailed his errors and earned himself a prominent place in the original *Dunciad*, from which he was ousted in later editions by Pope's foe Colley Cibber, a poet whose rising star Pope resented.

The substitution of Cibber for Theobald in the *Dunciad* – a poet for a scholar – is arbitrary. That it did little basic damage to the poem, and required little adjustment of the text, reveals how loose and, in a sense, unintegrated it is. Pope attended closely to the surface of the work, but the satire is only occasionally deep and telling. There is a progression through the four books, moving towards the triumph of Dullness, and exploiting different modes of humour from book to book. To begin with Pope develops literary satire and parody, passing on through coprological, sexual and even sadistic forms of humour. The fourth book remains most vital, with its scourging of customs and institutions of education. But the verve and power of the language are often in excess of the object satirized, a kind of overkill. One senses in all but the fourth book that the satire, unlike Dryden's, has little clear conception of a moral norm to which, by contrast, to refer us. It is hard to tell where Pope is firing from. He did not dislike the society in which he found himself. As De Quincey says, the rage is often merely 'histrionic', for its own effect. De Quincey goes further

and suggests that Pope was a hypocrite, and that his in-
sincerity spilled over into the non-satiric work as well.

Pope translated Horace's satires with his usual skill.
He was often at his best with borrowed anger. In 1735 he
wrote his 'Epistle to Dr Arbuthnot' (later called 'The
Prologue to the Satires') which survives as one of his
masterpieces, combining satire with personal statements
of great candour. It showed that his skill at composing
whole poems was still intact, even after the *Essay on Man*
(1733–4) which, despite memorable aphoristic phrases and
passages, is a failure both as didactic and philosophical
verse. It was attacked and defended for its morality; now
it is excerpted for its good passages but neglected as a
whole. Johnson's verdict is just: 'Never was penury of
knowledge and vulgarity of sentiment so happily dis-
guised.' It was technically a *tour de force*, but hollow at
the centre. De Quincey asks, which *should* have been
Pope's greatest poem? The *Essay on Man*. Which was in
fact his worst? The same. It 'sins chiefly by want of
central principle, and by want thereof of all coherency
amongst the separate thoughts'. Compared with the
Essay on Criticism, written twenty-two years before, the
later essay looks the more invertebrate and flimsy. Pope
had become a professional in the worst sense.

He had a style and technique which could deal with
almost any theme; but his sense of structure and his
ability to present consecutive and consistent thought were
limited. Johnson remarks on his 'poetical prudence': 'he
wrote in such a manner as might expose him to few
hazards. He used almost always the same fabric of verse;
and, indeed, by those few essays which he made of any
other, he did not enlarge his reputation ... By perpetual
practice, language had, in his mind, a systematic arrangement; having always the same use for words, he had words
so selected and combined as to be ready at his call.' It
was a dangerous form of facility: 'his effusions were always voluntary.' De Quincey stresses how his satiric rages
were similarly factitious.

He bit off in the *Essay on Man* not more than his style could chew, but more than his intellect could digest. It is hardly surprising that a number of the less ambitious poems such as 'Windsor Forest' retain a greater appeal than the large and amorphous 'major poem', the *Essay on Man*.

Some of the intellectual incompleteness of Pope can be blamed on his age, for he more even than Dryden was a man of his time. He has been called a 'cosmic Tory', a social optimist (though closer to Hobbes in his evaluation of the individual), believing 'whatever is, is right' and converting the *status quo* into a universal ethic. In such an approach there is a cool, impersonal arrogance, a quality he shares with some of his contemporaries who remained unable to choose between deism and Lockean psychology, but felt confident in rejecting traditional theology as outmoded. Pope is remarkably uncommitted intellectually. His distrust of empirical enquiry is as strong as Swift's, but without Swift's reasons. For such a mind the appeal of authority should be great, but Pope is wary even of authority.

The imagination 'gilds all objects, but alters none'. Such an aesthetic is remote from Sidney's as enunciated in the *Apology*. Pope seeks not to expand but to formulate and arrest thought and experience; not to particularize but to establish general truths. The belief that nature conceals, under its varied surface, a basic pattern or harmony, is a worked-up belief, as willed as the language itself. He was able in the *Essay on Man* to change the description of Nature as a 'mighty maze, and all without a plan' to a 'mighty maze but not without a plan'. So radical a change, so casually admitted, reveals how shallowly the current of his thought ran. Similarly, Cibber and Theobald, poet and scholar, were interchangeable in the *Dunciad*.

The best of Pope is excellent, but the excellences are to be found *in extenso* only in the earlier poems, the translations and the satires. Later excellences became local, and the admirable surface of his philosophical disquisitions yields like thin ice when we embark seriously upon it. The quality of his best writing depends upon the elusive way in which he can render concrete abstract or moral passages by combination of unexpected words, and by his rhymes which seal (in Coleridge's phrase) the 'conjunction disjunctive' of the couplets. Dryden's couplets tend to be self-contained; Pope's contain at their best a paradox, an irresolution, which compels one to read on. Pope makes whole poems only when he avoids the temptation to make a total statement.

As satirist and translator Pope is often unassailable. He had talents in other areas but limited their use. Arnold puzzled over the question: are Pope and Dryden classics? His famous answer was: 'We are to regard Dryden as the puissant and glorious founder, Pope as the splendid high priest, of our age of prose and reason, of our excellent and indispensable eighteenth century.' They are 'classics of our prose'. His assessment has had a strong influence on the fate of both writers among readers of poetry. Yet it underrates Dryden, and it makes of Pope a figure which his mature writings hardly corroborate.

James Thomson 1700–1748

What, what is virtue but repose of mind?
A pure ethereal calm that knows no storm,
Above the reach of wild ambition's wind,
Above those passions that this world deform,
And torture man, a proud malignant worm!

James Thomson's best-known poem is 'Rule Britannia',
though few would know to attribute it to him. In his own
day and for some decades after his death he was among
the most widely acclaimed British poets who inspired the
respect of men as different as Dr Johnson and Wordsworth. For modern readers his work is an acquired taste.
His chosen poetic antecedents – largely Miltonic – and his
intellectual procedures – in line with the fashionable
scientific and philosophical thought of his time – tend to
confine him to his period. His self-conscious modernity
soon dated. Miltonic blank verse did not so much liberate
as muffle his peculiar genius. His novelty is his subject-
matter: the literal seasons and the countryside. But how
suitable was Miltonic rhetoric to this subject? His contemporaries did not experience the disparity we tend to
feel between style and matter. Oliver Goldsmith reflects
on these lines:

O vale of bliss! O softly swelling hills!
On which the power of contemplation lies,
And joys to see the wonder of his toil.

'We cannot conceive a more beautiful image than that of the Genius of Agriculture, distinguished by the implements of his art, imbrowned with labour, glowing with health, crowned with a garland of foliage, flowers, and fruit, lying stretched at his ease on the brow of a gently swelling hill, and contemplating with pleasure the happy effects of his own industry.' Donald Davie suggests that Goldsmith was adding little to Thomson's intention, that it was natural for Thomson's readers to tease out the implicit meanings in this way, as they read, translating as it were out of code. The modern reader may have difficulty in identifying the happy peasant at all.

Thomson was born at Ednam, in the Borders, and reared in Southdean, a neighbouring parish to which his father, a minister, was translated. He was educated at Jedburgh and at Edinburgh University, where he studied Divinity. He published poems in Edinburgh journals, and when his prose was deemed 'too ornate' for the pulpit by his instructors, he left Edinburgh for London to become a writer (1725). He was tutor to the son of the Earl of Haddington and was introduced into Pope's circle. In 1726 he published a poem partly completed before he reached the capital. It was *Winter*, first of *The Seasons*, which were published together in 1730 and in various updated and revised forms between then and his death in 1748. The book was part of a programme he enunciated in 1726: poetry should free itself from social satire. To do this he abandoned the heroic couplet and looked for his subject-matter beyond the city gates.

Before 1730 he published shorter poems and an ill-fated tragedy, *Sophonisba*. In 1731 he travelled to the Continent and was given a sinecure on his return. In 1735 he published the poem *Liberty*, and thereafter composed more plays and collected a further sinecure and a pension from the Prince of Wales. A confirmed bachelor, he settled comfortably in Richmond. In 1745 he wrote his most succesful play, *Tancred and Sigismunda*. Three years later he composed *The Castle of Indolence*, regarded as his best poem after *The Seasons*. He died of a fever and was memorialized in William Collins's superb Ode:

In yonder grove a Druid lies,
  Where slowly winds the stealing wave!
The year's best sweets shall duteous rise
  To deck its poet's sylvan grave!

Johnson describes Thomson as of 'gross, unanimated, uninviting appearance'. He admired the work and gave Thomson the highest praise for his original 'mode of thinking, and of expressing his thoughts'. 'His blank verse is no more the blank verse of Milton, or of any other poet... His numbers, his pauses, his diction, are of his own growth, without transcription, without imitation. He thinks in a peculiar train, and he thinks always as a man of genius.' What is more, he possesses 'a mind that at once comprehends the vast and attends to the minute.'

Proximity to the subject and an excessive enthusiasm for the novelty of Thomson's subject-matter in an age poor in novelty lead Johnson to this – what must seem to us – overstatement. Thomson's language in *The Seasons* owes debts to Milton on almost every line. *The Castle of Indolence* is indebted to Milton and Spenser for its language and its manner. His originality of form consists of reviving the georgic – which had been done by several of his immediate predecessors. His poems include the new science and new attitudes, but they were not original to him. His poems reflect fashionable thought and spring from the discursive and experimental activity of his time. There is skill in handling of the blank verse, and there are notable passages, but as Johnson admitted, 'The great defect of *The Seasons* is want of method' – a failure of imagination.

The formal failure is concealed behind verbal exuberance. It is hard at times to see through the adjectival undergrowth to the subject. Thomson continually revised his poem, both to perfect it and to keep it abreast of new scientific findings. Johnson commends such revisions, lamenting only the loss of the earthiness of the 1730 version. To the original 4000 lines Thomson added roughly 1400 in successive revisions.

The Seasons is encyclopaedically comprehensive, with zoological, botanical, meteorological and geological information, political and moral reflections, and sentimental tales. It reflects perhaps a dissatisfaction with a poetry increasingly decorous and stylized, a form of reaction without the true radicalism of Smart, Blake or Wordsworth. It was acceptable music in a different key, with different themes, not *new* music.

Milton was responsible for the change of key. Thomson did not adopt the dynamics of Milton's language: he borrowed from the surface. He vulgarized Milton as he vulgarized the new science. It suited his ends. He blended the scientific discoveries of Newton with the optimistic deism of Lord Shaftesbury.

Coleridge disliked the style but saluted the poet. 'The love of nature seems to have led Thomson to a cheerful religion; and a gloomy religion to have led Cowper to a love of nature. The one would carry his fellow-men along with him into nature: the other flies to nature from his fellow-men. In chastity of diction, however, and the harmony of blank verse, Cowper leaves Thomson immeasurably below him; yet still I feel the latter to have been a born poet.'

His originality was to present nature itself as subject. Wordsworth owes him a verbal and thematic debt. He can be very convincing in his detailed writing. In *Winter* the birds in their motions foretell a storm:

Retiring from the downs, where all day long
They picked their scanty fare, a blackening train
Of clamorous rooks thick-urge their weary flight,
And seek the closing shelter of a grove.
Assiduous in his bower, the wailing owl
Plies his sad song. The cormorant on high
Wheels from the deep, and screams along the land.

Loud shrieks the soaring hern; and with wild wing
The circling sea-fowl cleave the flaky clouds.

There is also a delicious luxury in some of his *Summer*
effusions:

Bear me, Pomona! to thy citron groves;
To where the lemon and the piercing lime,
With the deep orange glowing through the green,
Their lighter glories blend. Lay me reclined
Beneath the spreading tamarind, that shakes
Fanned by the breeze, its fever-cooling fruit.

When he ascends from observation and sensation to generalization, he forfeits attention. In his optimism there
is a gloating aloofness which grates on the modern reader.
Unlike Swift, he is not eager to rouse others – the humble,
for example – to a sense of their potential. In *Summer* he
reflects: 'While thus laborious crowds/Ply the rough oar,
Philosophy directs/The ruling helm.' Here is a poet
whom Hobbes has left no mark on. He celebrates commerce, enterprise, ambition, in ways that would have
been impossible half a century later.

Thomson's poetry lives in its descriptions and in odd
lines, like the one describing the ancient Britons, 'Their
wealth the wild-deer bouncing through the glade'; a poet
then of fragments. His nature appears fragmentary because he celebrates a first cause through it, not – as Wordsworth does – a force latent in it. He lacks Wordsworth's
passionate engagement. His is an enthusiasm of the senses,
but the whole man is withheld. Wordsworth's imagination is continuous with the experienced world, Thomson's
tangential to it.

The attempt to find poetic epithets for scientific terms
mars some of the verse; and the obsolete science itself
mars certain passages. Even his most particular definitions
seem to answer no necessary poetic purpose. He screws his
language up by heightened diction and elaborated syntax
to produce the effect of poetry, but with a poetic cause

which is at best nebulous. Gilbert White's prose portrays a clearer nature than Thomson's verse can. White addresses himself to a subject, Thomson to an audience. Thomson's most useful contribution – to Cowper, Crabbe and Wordsworth among others – was to show how landscape might be used for emotional projection, for revealing the observer's mind as much as the thing observed.

In *The Castle of Indolence* Thomson undertook Spenserian form and diction and wrote what some regard as his finest poem. Formally it is more coherent than *The Seasons*. The old wizard indolence speaks lucidly and persuasively. The poem is a smoothly satirical record of temptation overcome, with knights and witty transformations. Each sense is tempted in turn. Thomson pillories various human types and espouses various causes. There are some memorable characters – for example, 'A little, round, fat, oily man of God' with 'a roguish twinkle in his eye', who is a bit of a lecher. We meet members of Thomson's circle which, in his later years, was distinguished chiefly for the presence of William Collins. The poem's Spenserian form imposes on Thomson a number of tautologies, ill-considered similes and solecisms, though they are not so numerous as to destroy altogether the effect of the piece. In the allegory, Art and Industry in knightly form destroy the castle and its wizard lord. As in *The Seasons*, here is the verse of whiggery which, set beside the work of Goldsmith or Johnson, reveals its rootedness in period, class and place. It is the sort of verse which *was* modern in its time.

Samuel Johnson 1709–1784

Let hist'ry tell where rival kings command,
And dubious title shakes the madded land,
When statutes glean the refuse of the sword,
How much more safe the vassal than the lord,
How sculks the kind beneath the rage of pow'r,
And leaves the wealthy traitor in the Tow'r,
Untouch'd his cottage, and his slumbers sound,
Though confiscation's vultures hover round.

Samuel Johnson: poet, novelist, lexicographer, biographer, critic, pamphleteer, editor, conversationalist. He is the moral and critical centre of his age, a point of reference and illumination for later ages, a man who represents, with broad wisdom and apparently effortless polish and authority of style, the radically English intelligence, with its power of generality and of particular discrimination.

Born in Lichfield in 1709, he was the son of a bookseller and early took an interest in his father's wares. He was educated at Lichfield Grammar School and later at Stourbridge Grammar School. When he was nineteen he went to Pembroke College, Oxford, where he suffered hardship and which he left in 1731 without taking a degree. He did not enjoy his year as a schoolmaster ('usher'). He was one of those lethargic men who, when they must, are capable of heroic labours and surprise even themselves with their powers. He undertook as his first literary job a hack translation of Father Lobo's *Voyage to Abyssinia* (published 1735), which was useful to him when he composed his novel *Rasselas* twenty-four years later, in the evenings of one week, to defray his mother's funeral expenses and to pay her debts. His memory was orderly and encyclopaedic, even if he tended to surround himself with disorder.

He married in 1735 and the next year opened a private school in Edial, Staffordshire, where he looked after six to eight pupils, among them his theatrical protégé, David Garrick. With Garrick he went to London in 1737, and thereafter put down roots in the metropolis. It was not an easy transition, for success came at its own pace. In 'London', an imitation of Juvenal's third satire, written the year after he arrived, he evoked a rough, unregenerate place: 'This mournful truth is everywhere confess'd/ *Slow rises worth, by poverty depressed.*' The poem is spoken by one preparing to leave the city. Johnson may have been tempted to do the same; but London was his destination.

He worked on his tragedy *Irene* and began writing pieces, and later reporting parliamentary debates, for the *Gentleman's Magazine*. His friendship with Richard Savage at this time led to the *Life of Savage*, the masterpiece among *The Lives of the Poets* (1779–81). In 1745 he published his plan for an edition of Shakespeare, and two years later his preliminary plan for the *Dictionary*. His poetic activity, always fitful, culminated in 1749 with 'The Vanity of Human Wishes', an imitation of Juvenal's tenth satire, and his first signed work. In the same year *Irene* was produced and published, without resounding success.

Independent periodical work on the *Rambler*, of whose 208 issues he wrote over 200, occupied him from 1750 to 1752, when his wife died. Despite this loss and his natural indolence, the projects he had initiated came to fruition, the *Dictionary* in 1755, the Shakespeare ten years later. He contributed to the *Idler* as well. In 1762 he was awarded a Royal Pension.

James Boswell arrived in his life in 1763, and thus

began the greatest literary biography in the language and much of the legend of Johnson. Boswell stands between the modern reader and Johnson. As Ford Madox Ford said, Johnson is destined to remain 'for ever a figure half of fun because of the leechlike adoration of the greatest and most ridiculous of all biographers'. Johnson presided over the Literary Club from 1764, and in his circle were Sir Joshua Reynolds (who left a striking portrait of the Doctor), Edmund Burke, Oliver Goldsmith, and others. In the same year he met Mrs Thrale, who tended him devotedly in his difficulties.

After his edition of Shakespeare was published, his literary activities diminished. In the nineteen years before his death in 1784 he published political pamphlets, *A Journey to the Western Islands of Scotland* (1775) where Boswell had conducted him two years earlier, and *The Lives of the Poets*, begun in 1777, which he struggled to complete for publication in 1779–81. He was awarded the degree of Doctor in Civil Law at Oxford in 1781, exactly half a century after he had left the place with no degree at all.

An account of his literary manner with its intellectual and stylistic evenness and balance does not reflect the underlying turbulence of mind which Johnson's prayers, letters and deeds suggest. For him, literary work was no place to explore subjective impulses and distresses. Rather, it was a place where fact, critical discrimination and imaginative and moral insight were called for. His temperament colours with its pessimism and acerbity much that he wrote and lends an intensity especially to his imaginative work. The observations on the poets and on Shakespeare are those of a man matured by extreme torments of mind, who understood motive and action, weakness and failure, because he could perceive in himself the human paradoxes. It is hard to understand why he should have remained hostile to Swift the man, for only Swift of his near contemporaries was his equal in imagination and inner dissatisfaction.

Johnson's severe Augustanism, when he came to judge works, must have appeared a little old fashioned even in his own day in its standards and expectations. But as Donald Davie writes, 'it is the mind which knows the power of its own potentially disruptive propensities that needs and demands to be disciplined.' Johnson's poetic forms are chosen for this reason. His couplets are unprecedented for their 'gravity, sheer weight', and if not 'personal' in the modern sense, are full of personal consequence.

His profoundly human sensibility leads him to stigmatize 'the cant of those who judge by principle rather than perception'. In his own case, 'principle' would seem to turn him away from Milton, and indeed he misreads 'Lycidas' for this reason. But perception, especially in his experience of *Paradise Lost*, overrides abstract principle. Reason is strong, but strong reason reveals the limits beyond which reason cannot be trusted. Beyond those limits one must make do with feeling or faith. His work on Shakespeare confirms the power of his perception, even in those passages where Shakespeare most violates Johnson's cherished principles.

This particularism is at the heart of Johnson's conservatism. His Toryism was more an orientation than a party affiliation: indeed he was a severe critic of parties. His antagonism to whiggery, however, was strong from his earliest years in London. In 'London', Thales cries as he leaves the city:

Here let those reign, whom pensions can incite
To vote a patriot black, a courtier white;
Explain their country's dear-bought rights away,
And plead for pirates in the light of day;
With slavish tenets taint our poison'd youth,
And lend a lie the confidence of truth.

A strong political scepticism guarantees the disinterestedness of his declarations.

His knowledge of past literature was comprehensive

and provided him with the means to measure present achievement. His 'imitations' of Juvenal and Horace take for their ground the work of earlier writers. But he follows Horace's advice and, in rendering an 'original', gives it to his own age. Hence he updates the references where he can, writes of London rather than Rome. At the age of fifteen he had translated Horace's *'Eheu fugaces'*, a suitable preliminary to 'London' and 'The Vanity of Human Wishes':

Your shady groves, your pleasing wife,
And fruitful fields, my dearest friend,
You'll leave together with your life,
Alone the cypress shall attend.

It is not literal translation, even here. In his *Life of Shenstone* he describes the nature and pleasure of 'imitation' as a creative mode: 'The adoption of a particular style, in light and short compositions, contributes much to the increase of pleasure: we are entertained at once with two imitations, of nature in the sentiments, of the original author in the style, and between them the mind is kept in perpetual employment.' The reader who knows no Juvenal, no Horace, no Latin, will be experiencing only half, or less than half, the poem, but will still find something of weight.

When he was seventeen he wrote 'Upon the Feast of St Simon and St Jude', a poem interesting chiefly for its skilful but hardly spirited use of the stanza form Smart was to develop in 'A Song to David'. Despite early evidence of prosodic precocity, Johnson relied most upon the heroic couplet. Among the ephemeral pieces certain poems stand out. 'An Ode on Friendship', in conventional quatrains and expressing conventional sentiment, has the authority of conviction. The 'Epitaph on Sir Thomas Hamner' is civic verse of a high order. His 'Prologue' composed for Garrick is a verse essay on the English stage with notable observations on Shakespeare, Jonson, the Restoration poets ('Intrigue was plot, obscenity was wit'), and the effect of excessive rule and refinement ('From bard to bard, the frigid caution crept,/Till declamation roar'd, while passion slept'). He conjures the 'vicissitudes of taste' from which he, having arrived in London a mature man of twenty-eight, always stood aloof. His was the perspective of a man whose sense of merit was one with his sense of cultural history. There was no compromising with tradition. Modern excellence had to measure itself against the known and proven excellences of the past.

As a critic, his is a sensual appreciation both of overall form and of the realized subject-matter. No critic before him had so often used the word 'image'. Donald Davie has pointed to the power of the *verbs* in the best Augustan writing, and the verbs provided perhaps Johnson's first point of access to a work. Certainly his own verbs are strong. For him wit (the 'constant presence of critical intelligence') is the fusion of idea and image to convey truth. Fusion: image and meaning do not run parallel; image contains and conveys idea. He condemns Pope for reducing strength of thought to felicity of language. Wit is, rather, seeing what is not obvious but what, when it is first produced, is seen to be just, and seen to be so in all its parts. He distinguishes intrinsic from external forms. It is the intrinsic form we perceive in the best works. In his *Life of Cowley* he writes, 'words being arbitrary must owe their power to association, and have the influence, and that only, which custom has given them. Language is the dress of thought.' The dress must fit not only the thought but the dignity of the speaker or the occasion. *Decorum* is therefore important in discrimination. The complex association of words with thought, image, speaker and prosody is what we can call form in the work.

Johnson as critic and poet seeks certain qualities. First is generality of reference. Natural detail should suit but not distort or displace the thought, should have 'a species of symbolic value', as W. J. Bate says. Johnson tends as a result to overuse the definite article in 'The Vanity of Human Wishes' in an attempt to impart universality which tends instead towards abstraction. Johnson also seeks to instruct. The poem should detect order and suggest moral direction, even if it reminds the reader of a truth rather than discovering a new truth. He also seeks to make the work pleasing, with the sensuous gratification of its sound, imagery and organization and the moral and intellectual pleasure of its novel rightness. Poetry is the 'art of uniting pleasure with truth'. Genius is 'a mind of large, general powers'. F. R. Leavis commends Johnson in Johnsonian terms: he convinces by 'focusing a wide range of profoundly representative experience'.

T. S. Eliot regarded 'The Vanity of Human Wishes' as the most accomplished satire in the language. Some readers see it as a work – like *Samson Agonistes* – in which the extremity of the moral is so intolerable as to outweigh the considerable aesthetic achievement. There is also a sense in which the almost epigrammatic completeness of many of the heroic couplets militates against the poem's overall integration. A continuity of argument, however, and the underlying imagery, create a unity. The imagery in particular is worth attention. Often it is not stated but sensed in allusive verbs or adjectives. Theatre, pageant (with fireworks) and performance are recurrent images. For example, in line 64 he mentions 'scene', and this is followed by 'solemn toys' and 'empty shows', 'robes and veils', until we come to the word 'farce' which draws together all the preceding allusions and moralizes them, connecting with the 'stage' imagery, an emblem of vanity. In line 74 he uses the word 'burning', then 'call', but not until line 76 do we surmise the fireworks, which we have sensed in advance. Even when we have surmised them, the image is not stated, only suggested. The evaporation of the 'call' connects with earlier images of mist, phantoms, the unreal masquerading as the solid. Johnson also qualifies concrete nouns with abstract adjectives. Such procedures coordinate the couplets and connect them.

Johnson's debt to Pope is – as Leavis says – considerable but selective. The moral and intellectual concentration of Johnson's couplets exceeds that of Pope. Johnson is altogether the more serious man; 'his warrant for public utterance,' as Leavis says, 'is a deep moral seriousness, a weight – a human centrality – of theme. It is a generalizing weight.' Johnson's abstractions are concentrations of meaning, not empty gestures at meaning. In his generalizing imagery, half the image remains static and located, the other half is in motion, transient: 'the *steady* Roman *shook* the world.' The connection between the mutable and the immutable (sometimes ironically reversed, as here) or between the placed and the evanescent, releases the general truth.

But there is more to Johnson even than the sum of all his writings. I value Ford Madox Ford's hyperbolic tribute: 'This was a man who loved truth and the expression of the truth with a passion that when he spoke resembled epilepsy and when he meditated was an agony. It does not need a Boswell to tell us that; the fact shines in every word he wrote, coming up through his Latinisms as swans emerge, slightly draped with weeds, from beneath the surface of a duck pond. His very intolerances are merely rougher truths; they render him the more human – and the more humane.'

Thomas Gray 1716–1771

In climes beyond the solar road,
Where shaggy forms o'er ice-built mountains roam,
The Muse has broke the twilight-gloom
To cheer the shivering native's dull abode.

Dr Johnson's best work is 'imitation' of Juvenal and
Horace, 'a reading of the originals so that they make sense
in our time,' as C. H. Sisson has written. The poet does
not pretend to radical originality. He prefers transposition
and a restatement in a new context of a proven work.
Other Augustan poets took 'imitation' differently, in the
spirit which led T. S. Eliot to weave into the texture of
his own work quotations and allusions to other poems and
literary works. Eliot's procedure, often ironic, borrowed
resonance to emphasize his own themes. Thomas Gray,
without so strong a sense of literary irony, 'imitated' in
this sense. Gray's critics and Gray himself chronicled and
annotated the 'sources' of many of his lines. His editor
Roger Lonsdale writes, 'one seems at times to be confront-
ing a kind of literary kleptomania, such is his dependence
on the phrasing and thoughts of other poets.' Gray's chief
originality is paradoxically the extent of his derivative-
ness, the tact of his borrowing, from Greek, Latin, English
and other writers. Collins runs him a close second.

Gray turns not to Pope or Dryden but, in his early
verse, to Shakespeare, Spenser and Milton for metaphor
and organization. His preference indicates a dissatisfaction with the narrow frontiers of Augustan verse.

But not to one in this benighted age
  Is that diviner inspiration given,
That burns in Shakespeare's or in Milton's page,
  The pomp and prodigality of heaven.

His enthusiasm for Thomson's *The Seasons*, for Macpherson's Ossianic forgeries, for the 'primitive' Celtic poets, his longing to infuse a primal energy into the increasingly effete literary customs of his day, his interest even in the Pindaric mode, all reflect a dissatisfaction, a casting about for alternatives. Some of his own poems, including 'The Fatal Sisters', 'The Descent of Odin' and 'The Bard', imitate Welsh and Norse poetry. He lacked however a radical originality. He sought to regenerate poetry from poetry. He never wrote, he said, 'without reading Spenser for a considerable time previously'. Ironically, his best poems are not those laboured 'original' compositions, but the thoroughly Augustan pieces, above all the elegies.

He was a *poeta doctus* with a vengeance. His debt to Dante, whom he imitated in the opening of the 'Elegy Written in a Country Churchyard', is great: he understood Dante better than any other Augustan and went so far as to translate the Ugolino passage into a blank verse that recalls Milton and Spenser. He translated passages of Statius and Propertius. He attempted in *Agrippina* a blank verse tragedy. For all his learnedness, he produced relatively little poetry, some of it in Latin and Greek.

Born in 1716 in Cornhill, he was the only survivor in a family of twelve children. His father was a scrivener, his mother and aunt kept a milliner's shop. He studied at Eton, where Horace Walpole, Richard West and Thomas Ashton became life-long friends. In 1734 he went up to Peterhouse, Cambridge, and wrote his first English poem, 'Lines Spoken by the Ghost of John Dennis', a vulgar and amusing piece in rough couplets. In 1735 he was admitted to the Inner Temple.

His intention was to pursue a legal career. In 1739 he

embarked on a tour of France and Italy with Walpole. An unfortunate falling-out with his friend hastened his return to England in 1741. Several deaths affected him deeply, and his father's death left him financially insecure. The law lost its attractions. He settled back at Cambridge, first at Peterhouse, later at Pembroke College, and apart from a few absences – in London for research, Stoke Poges for relaxation, York and the Lakes for rambles – he remained in Cambridge until his death in 1771. In 1768, after a long campaign, he was appointed Regius Professor of Modern History. He engaged in university politics and stooped to partisan satire in 'The Candidate', a poem which distressed his more matronly admirers by its vulgarity. He rhymed the word 'bitches' with 'stitches' ('a term for lying with a woman').

Shortly before his return to Cambridge his poetic energies were released, possibly by the tensions of bereavement. In 1742 he completed the 'Ode on the Spring', his first important composition, a mastery of pure convention. The verse, as Lonsdale says, is fully self-conscious, moralizing the subject and the moralizing convention as well, as it were undercutting itself. 'Ode on a Distant Prospect of Eton College' is a much finer poem, his first to appear in print. It is full of the depression induced by his personal losses. The intricate ten-line stanza form in tetrameters and trimeters is taut and understated. Generically, the ode is a 'topographical poem'. It may relate to an actual prospect in space, but the poetic prospect is across time, into the past. The view provokes an elegiac nostalgia, not without bitterness. Among Gray's poems it is the most subjective. The thoroughgoing pessimism of the worldly-wise man surveying innocent youth leads to the final stanza which Keats and Wilde were to echo. It has a terrible force:

Thought would destroy their paradise.
No more; where ignorance is bliss,
'Tis folly to be wise.

The 'Ode to Adversity' achieves a more positive formulation. Though it is a less compelling poem, perhaps for moral reasons Johnson preferred it to the Eton ode.

Walpole and Gray were reconciled in 1745 – fortunately, for Walpole was available for consultation over the 'Elegy' and superintended Gray's publications. Also, Walpole's cat drowned in a goldfish bowl, an accident which produces the best animal elegy in English, 'Ode on the Death of a Favourite Cat', with its satire on the character of woman.

'Elegy Written in a Country Churchyard' was completed in 1750 in Stoke Poges. The success of this, his great poem, became irksome to him. He was after another sort of originality, and yet his later work was criticized in the light of this great Augustan achievement. He had married in this poem – as Leavis says – two incongruous but mutually attractive styles, the sedate, tidy elegiac and a Miltonic rhetoric. 'Gray's great achievement was to crystallize into distinguished expression the conventional poeticizing of the meditative-melancholic line of versifiers who drew their inspiration so largely from the minor poems of Milton.' The 'Elegy' begins a sort of revolution, opening the way for less sophisticated and polite rural poetry.

We may balk at the excess of present participles – more than ten in the first twenty-one lines – or at Gray's tendency to define by negatives, but the participles suggest processes continuing in time and relate to the natural continuities; definition by negatives suggests what it specifically excludes, so that the poem evokes what is *not* even as it portrays what is. The quatrain works rather as an extended couplet: most of the quatrains possess the finality of epigrams.

The 'Elegy' animates with actual observations the convention, as it were wringing from it a bit of the world. If his success is, in Leavis's words, 'of taste, of literary sense' rather than 'of creative talent', what good sense, what good taste. It is invidious to suggest that taste and sense at such a level of achievement are not a form of 'creative talent'. Johnson's judgement, that the poem 'abounds with images which find a mirror in every mind, and with sentiments to which every bosom returns an echo', is borne out by the popularity of the work and the number of passages and lines which have entered common speech.

Elsewhere, Johnson says, Gray 'thought his language more poetical as it was more remote from common use'. The odes are vitiated by 'a kind of cumbrous splendour which we wish away ... glittering accumulations of ungraceful ornaments ... they strike, rather than please; the images are magnified by affectation; the language is laboured into harshness. The mind of the writer seems to work with unnatural violence.' This is the case with Gray's more experimental works and can be explained by his desire to suggest energy where he felt none, to drum up a passion but without motive force. Donald Davie identifies the fault: 'Gray seems to have been distinguished by low vitality.' He did not pour forth his verse vatically, even in his vatic poems. He laboured it line by line.

His 'low vitality' is reflected in the incompleteness of some of his major schemes, notably the projected *History of English Poetry*, for which he composed 'The Progress of Poesy', a work in the 'progress poem' tradition, a species of *translatio regni* of poetry from classical cultures to England, with due praise for English liberty, though not in the complacent tones of Thomson. Later he wrote 'The Bard', a poem whose lack of inner dynamic produces effects similar to those in Blake's most eloquent visions, where the *excessive* dynamic fragments the work and leads to ill-judged absurdities. It was inevitable that Gray should return to translation, to replenish his energies.

Just as Gray was indebted to earlier poets, so he is a creditor of a number of his successors. Wordsworth owes him occasional positive debts in phrasing, imagery and theme, especially in 'Hymn to Ignorance', and a paradoxical negative debt, for Gray was a poet against whom he could react in formulating his own practice and theory of poetic diction. Goldsmith owes Gray specific debts. 'The Alliance of Education and Government' is not generically remote from Goldsmith's much better poems, 'The Traveller' and 'The Deserted Village'. Goldsmith's verse is less preconceived than Gray's, less careful and more impassioned.

T. S. Eliot suggests that the second-rate among the eighteenth-century poets were those who, disaffected with conventional modes, 'were incompetent to find a style of writing for themselves'. Gray tried, but lack of matter and energy let him down. His formidable conventional skills do not suggest that he could have been other than he was. What he was – as a letter-writer as well as a poet – attests the positive, learned virtues of an age, and its limitations. But the 'Elegy' remains, a poem which anyone who cares for poetry at all can enjoy.

Christopher Smart 1722–1771

For the word of God is a sword on my side – no matter what
   other weapon a stick or a straw.
For I have adventured myself in the name of the Lord, and
   he hath marked me for his own.
For I bless God the Postmaster general & all conveyancers
   of letters under his care especially Allen & Shelvock.
For my grounds in New Canaan shall infinitely compensate
   for the flats & maynes of Staindrop Moor.
For the praise of God can give to a mute fish the notes of a
   nightingale.

'It is not impossible that when Smart is judged over the
whole range of his various productions – conventional
in form as well as unconventional, light and even ribald
as well as devotional, urbane or tender as well as sublime
– he will be thought of as the greatest English poet between Pope and Wordsworth.' It is hard to disagree with
Donald Davie's suggestion. Smart's genius and originality
are the product not of a candid, puzzled personality like
Cowper's, nor the lucid, nostalgic and humane sensibility
of a Goldsmith. They are rather the product of a distinctively *poetic* imagination. Smart seldom composes verse:
he is a poet rare in any age, most rare in the eighteenth
century, an enthusiast and a consummate verbal artist.
He might seem to resemble Blake, but he has greater
formal tact, a better ear and a better nature.

   With Cowper, a knowledge of the poet's biography
enhances our appreciation of the poems. With Smart the

case is different. Biography, as Davie points out, has obscured Smart's achievement. He is regarded for his madness (so much more colourful than Cowper's or Collins's) almost at the expense of the poems. It is too readily assumed that he wrote in madness, and that what he wrote in form and theme partakes of his derangement. But Smart's madness was not so much disorder as *alternative* order. His religious vision was not eccentric but direct and comprehensive. To say that an artist is 'mad' is to say very little. What matters is what he makes of his madness. Smart, of madness and sanity, made great poetry. Dr Johnson gives a memorable account of Smart's illness: 'I did not think he ought to be shut up. His infirmities were not noxious to society. He insisted on people praying with him; and I'd as lief pray with Kit Smart as anyone else. Another charge was that he did not love clean linen; and I have no passion for it.'

'A Song to David' was not, as far as we know, composed in madness. It is a poem structurally rigid, vital for stanzaic and prosodic, not conceptual, reasons. The *Jubilate Agno* (*Rejoice in the Lamb*) was a product of madness. Yet for all its apparent disjointedness, it has been found by recent critics and editors who follow Smart's own order for it, to be based on a clear scheme, the 'antiphonal structure of Hebrew poetry', as Davie says – with prosodic principles described by Robert Lowth. Lines beginning with 'Let' run parallel to lines beginning with 'For'. Despite the sense it gives of being extemporized and written at speed, it was in fact composed at a rate of one to three lines a day, almost as though it had been a devotional journal. It is, with most of Smart's work, profoundly erudite and allusive, and the psalmodic lines are deployed with considerable rhythmic versatility. Because Smart did not prepare the *Jubilate* for press, much of its obscurity and difficulty are due to the presentation by editors.

Christopher Smart was born in Shipbourne, Kent, in 1722. His father was steward of the Vane family's establishment. After his father's death he spent his youth in Durham under the supervision of the Barnard branch of the Vane family. He may have experienced a frustrated passion for a member of the Barnard family. They, in any event, helped him to Cambridge, where he was distinguished as a fine scholar and poet. In 1745 he was elected a fellow of Pembroke College. While at Cambridge he translated Pope's 'Ode for Music' into Latin, won Pope's approbation, and composed Tripos verses. He also wrote secular poems, amorous and otherwise.

Despite his academic virtues, he was not the ideal student or college fellow. He was overfond of drink, and he was something of a spendthrift. In 1747 he was arrested for debts to his tailor. In 1749 he went to London to try his hand as a freelance. He wrote ballads and, with remarkable success, fables for London periodicals. In 1752, the year before his marriage, *Poems on Several Occasions* was published. It included a georgic poem, 'The Hop-Garden', a tribute to hops and to his native Kent. Between 1750 and 1755 he won the Cambridge Seatonian Prize four times for religious verse, Miltonic in manner. 'On the Goodness of the Supreme Being' (1755) is the best of these, invoking David, 'Israel's sweet Psalmist', Smart's special muse:

> thy tuneful touch
> Drove trembling Satan from the heart of Saul,
> And quelled the evil Angel.

In 1755 he translated Horace into prose. Later he turned these versions into verse. Horace and David were his poetic mentors – an odd but, as it proved, a fruitful combination.

Between 1756 and 1763 he was confined for insanity, an illness brought on in part by his financial improvidence, which Dr Johnson helped to alleviate, and in part by religious fervour which was as much a manifestation as a cause of his disease. He worked hard after his release, but six years later was again imprisoned for debt.

He died, aged 49, in 1771, in King's Bench Prison. Most of his best religious poetry dates from 1759–63. The 'Song to David' was completed and published in the year of his release from asylum. The *Psalms* and *Hymns and Spiritual Songs*, published in 1765, date in conception and execution from this period. *Hymns for the Amusement of Children* appeared in 1770.

'Pope's "Messiah" is not musical, but Smart's "Song to David", with its pounding thematic words and the fortissimo explosion of its coda, is a musical *tour de force*,' wrote Northrop Frye. From the first stanza there is a driving quality, a regularity which is in no way monotonous, and a close sound organization, with strong alliteration and assonance, a deft deployment of monosyllabic and polysyllabic words almost as though they came from distinct language registers, and a concentration of climax in concise sequences of three words, usually expressing a progression to achievement in time, as in the final stanza, which picks up the word 'glorious' from the stanza before:

Glorious, more glorious is the crown
Of Him that brought salvation down
   By meekness, called the Son;
Thou at stupendous truth believed,
And now the matchless deed's atchieved,
   DETERMINED, DARED, and DONE.

Smart returned to this stanza form for some of his translations of the Psalms. It is a suitable, ecstatic form. The two lines of tetrameter tauten into trimeter, and the rhyme scheme (aabccb) is made the more rigorous by Smart's preference for assonance and approximation between the different rhymes. It is among the strictest forms a poet could use, especially over a span of eighty-six stanzas. Smart's versatility is great, from the opening invocation to David and Christ to the final stanza just quoted. The first three stanzas – the treble construction is especially meaningful for Smart – initiate the music and establish the themes:

O Thou, that sit'st upon a throne,
With harp of high majestic tone,
  To praise the King of kings;
And voice of heav'n ascending swell,
Which, while its deeper notes excell,
  Clear, as a clarion, rings:

To bless each valley, grove and coast,
And charm the cherubs to the post
  Of gratitude in throngs;
To *keep* the days on Zion's mount,
And send the year to his account,
  With dances and with songs:

O Servant of God's holiest charge,
The minister of praise at large,
  Which thou may'st now receive;
From thy blest mansion hail and hear,
From topmost eminence appear
  To this the wreath I weave.

Such verbal weaving combines with an overall structure
of schematic rigidity, as R. D. Havens pointed out in
1938. The stanzas are carefully bunched in 'threes, or
sevens or their multiples – the mystic numbers'. Davie
summarizes the structure: 'after three stanzas of invocation come two groups of seven describing David, then
three sets of three describing David's singing, and a further set of three describing the effects of his singing' and
so on. The alternation between the longer and shorter
runs of stanzas and the action of syntactical and rhythmic
parallelism and repetition within the 'bunches' creates a
varied and aurally beguiling progression.

It is the power of Smart's rhythms, combined with the
odd, inventive accuracy of his diction, that set him in a
class by himself. Early in his career he realized uncluttered
and unabstract poetic *impressions*, if not images; and in
his mature work even the obscure and recondite allusions

have a direct impact, not exactly visual but sensual. If David was the master of his rhythms, Horace taught him 'the curiosity of choice diction'. Marcus Walsh quotes Smart's preface to Horace: 'The beauty, force and vehemence of *Impression* ... by which a Genius is empowered to throw an emphasis upon a word or sentence in such a wise, that it cannot escape any reader of sheer good sense, and true critical sagacity.'

Behind the language and structure of the *Jubilate Agno* stand the examples of Old Testament language, the Prayer Book and, more remotely, Milton. Smart's imagination in this poem is allegorical in presenting detail if not overall form. Each line has a various significance revealed in punning and in contrived verbal parallelisms which Addison described as 'false wit', a wit aurally rather than analytically sensed to be right. 'Let Jotham praise with the Urchin, who took up his parable and provided himself for the adversary to kick against the pricks.' It is the old adversary, the Devil. The effect of rightness is sensed over long passages, cumulatively, as in the famous passage about the poet's cat Jeoffrey:

For he keeps the Lord's watch in the night against the
adversary.
For he counteracts the powers of darkness by his electrical skin
and glaring eyes.
For he counteracts the Devil, who is death, by brisking about
the life.
For in his morning orisons he loves the sun and the sun loves
him.
For he is of the tribe of Tiger.
For the Cherub Cat is a term of the Angel Tiger.

The Devil in the heart of Saul, the madness in the mind of Smart, provoke the Psalms of David and the *Jubilate*, exorcisms and charms against disruption, celebrations of the divine force. The works of nature and of art ('For flowers are peculiarly the poetry of Christ', 'For the TRUMPET of God is a blessed intelligence and so are all the instruments of HEAVEN') are aids against the adversary.

Smart achieves what Gray could not: his enthusiasm and his vaticism are genuine, the overflow of a full spirit, not contrived. He is not an imitator. He apprehends the force behind the poetry he most admires. His intuition is attuned to a broad tradition and not caught in the rut of convention. Marcus Walsh calls Smart's mature style 'mannered, religiose and self-conscious' – a 'homogeneous' style which 'unifies', the crucial word, 'a number of divergent influences'. It is the paradoxical combination of influences, and the disruption of his own mind, that make Smart so outstanding an eccentric poet. Scholarship and accidents of biography delivered him from the bondage of narrow convention into the sometimes anarchic freedom of the *Jubilate Agno* and the vivid originality of the 'Song to David', the outstanding works of a diverse genius.

Oliver Goldsmith 1730–1774

Yes! let the rich deride, the proud disdain,
These simple blessings of the lowly train;
To me more dear, congenial to my heart,
One native charm, than all the gloss of art ...

'All the motion of Goldsmith's nature,' wrote Thomas De Quincey, 'moved in the direction of the true, the natural, the sweet, the gentle.' He had an 'unpretending mind': a fair judgement. Johnson's epitaph for the poet witnesses to his literary achievement: *'Nullum fere scribendi genus non tetigit,/Nullum, quod tetigit, non ornavit'*. His literary activity was almost as varied as Johnson's: poet, novelist, dramatist, journalist, nature writer, essayist, correspondent. Like Johnson's, his reputation as a poet rests an a few very fine poems.

Oliver Goldsmith was one of those remarkable Anglo-Irishmen, like his friend Edmund Burke, whose roots remained deep in Ireland, yet who flourished in England. Goldsmith's 'Irishness' is as different from Burke's as their *milieux* and their destinies were. But their concerns and values are remarkably similar.

Probably in 1730, Oliver Goldsmith, fifth child of the Reverend Charles Goldsmith, was born in Westmeath. His father became curate of Kilkenny and moved to Lissoy where the boy spent his childhood. He went to Trinity College, Dublin, at the age of fifteen. Two years later his father died. The young Oliver, who had not distinguished himself academically, was publicly admonished for his part in a student riot. In 1750 he managed to take a degree. When he failed to get ordained, he became a tutor, perhaps toyed with emigration to America (as later he very nearly went to India), and at last in 1752 settled into medical studies, supported by relations, first at Edinburgh and later at Leyden. He travelled extensively in Europe, an experience which led to the conception and development of 'The Traveller, or a Prospect of Society' (1764), itself the germ of his poetic masterpiece, 'The Deserted Village' (1770).

In 1756 Goldsmith was in London, following his medical pursuits and perhaps serving as a proof-reader in Samuel Richardson's printing-house and as an under-schoolmaster. His literary aspirations grew, and journalistic and translation work began to find him. In 1759 *An Enquiry into the Present State of Learning in Europe* was published. Thereafter he was known as Dr Goldsmith and numbered among friends and associates Tobias Smollett, Edward Young, Edmund Burke and the other Doctor, Johnson.

His essays, 'letters' – satirical epistolary essays by fictitious foreign travellers – and his other writings found a market and a price. But Goldsmith was impecunious. He made the acquaintance of bailiffs. A new waistcoat would swallow up the money a wiser man might have saved. Goldsmith was too sociable for his pocket's good.

His *Essays* (1765) and *The Vicar of Wakefield* (1766) set him in the first rank among his contemporaries. But his immediate circle failed to take him very seriously. There was something like condescension in their banter, and in their criticism of his political analysis in 'The Deserted Village'. Johnson said bluntly, 'Goldsmith had no settled notions upon any subject; so he talked always at random. It seemed to be his intention to blurt out whatever was in his mind, to see what would become of it.' Goldsmith's incomplete 'Retaliation' (1774) is said to have been composed in response to Garrick's extempore, 'Epitaph': 'Here lies Nolly Goldsmith, for shortness call'd

Noll,/Who wrote like an angel, but talk'd like poor Poll.'
The 'Retaliation' savours just a little of resentment. We
would not surmise such a man from the tone of his plays
and lighter poems, notably 'The Haunch of Venison'
(1770), or from the sheer unpedantic readability of his
prose, which had not the gravity of Johnson's nor the
orotundity of Burke's, but is full of the virtues of character which De Quincey noted. It is no wonder he commanded an audience and had a market to feed with
prose and plays. Of the plays, *She Stoops to Conquer*
(1773) proved the most memorable. His poetic and prose
themes were serious: regret for the vanishing rural order
(which he tended to idealize), and a strong impatience
with the whiggery which was replacing the concept of
patrimony with the practice of investment and profit,
with appalling social consequences. He was the poet of
Burke's prose, catching the essence if not the logic of
Toryism. By the time he died in 1774, he had witnessed
poignantly to the end of an age.

Like Gray and Collins, Goldsmith as a poet was a great
borrower or 'imitator'; unlike them, his main source was
in his own prose works. There is remarkable continuity
between his prose and verse, rather as in the work of
Kipling. His poems – in common with many of the
eighteenth century – were pre-planned, pursuing a discursive rather than imaginative development. But as
Donald Davie writes of 'The Deserted Village' – and it
goes for 'The Traveller' as well – though it is 'an example
of poems consciously planned like essays', it appeals
'through a hidden imaginative continuity'. The poetic
process functions not in the argument but in the natural
imagery, presented as frail, subject to change and exploitation. 'The natural,' Davie says, 'which we think of
as robust, is thus associated with what is vulnerable and
fugitive.'

Most of Goldsmith's surviving verse is the work of his
maturity. The earliest work includes translations and
epigrams, proofs of wit and formal skill, and exercises

in social and literary irony. La Monnoye's 'Ménagiana' provided a model for his satirical elegies, where a fourth line in each quatrain undermines conventional sentiment with 'the truth'. Typical is a stanza from 'An Elegy on that Glory of her Sex, Mrs Mary Blaize':

She strove the neighourhood to please,
  With manners wondrous winning,
And never followed wicked ways,
  Unless when she was sinning.

'On the Death of the Right Honourable –' follows the same pattern. The satire is only accidentally social: its object is to ridicule a sentimental literary mode. Wittiest of his elegies is that 'On the Death of a Mad Dog'. Goldsmith could serve up poetry of the very sort he parodied, the sentimental mixture so favoured at the time, as in his touching romance 'Edwin and Angelina'. T. S. Eliot's general observation is fair: Goldsmith had 'the old and the new in such just proportion that there is no conflict; he is Augustan and also sentimental and rural without discordance'.

'The Double Transformation: A Tale', is the first largely original poem by Goldsmith. It has a debt to Swift, though it is more temperate than the Dean's writing, less socially scathing:

Jack sucked his pipe and often broke
A sigh in suffocating smoke;
While all their hours were passed between
Insulting repartee or spleen.

The moral of this tale is general, about the nature of beauty and of vanity, and what a wife owes a husband. By contrast, 'Description of an Author's Bedchamber' smacks painfully of autobiography: poverty was a condition well known to the poet.

'The Traveller' is indebted both to his prose and to Samuel Johnson, who contributed a number of lines, urged the poet to complete the work, and helped in other less tangible ways. Goldsmith drew on Montesquieu's *L'Esprit des Loix* in formulating the ideas: the poem was patiently conceived and exhaustively revised. He drafted it first with wide gaps between the lines, filling the gaps with his deliberations and deletions.

He exploited the then popular 'topographical' genre. The physical panorama suggests a moral panorama; natural detail acquires moral weight. The poem proceeds from Italy through Switzerland, France and Holland, to Britain. It originated in a letter Goldsmith wrote his brother, and perhaps for this reason there is great frankness and directness of address in its couplets, which have none of the remote formality of Johnson's or the brittleness of Pope's. The argument often stretches across the couplets, they are not emphatically end-stopped and can only be called 'heroic' in a very extended sense. The intellectual expansiveness which loosens the form reflects a quality of imagination concerned more with the process of thought than with the ripe, polished fruits of thought.

He treats justly the virtues and weaknesses of each nation his eye surveys. Particularly interesting is the way he evokes nations, their cultures and temperaments, through their landscape, stressing the continuity between man and his environment. Macaulay thought this work the noblest and most simply planned philosophical poem in the language. There is novelty in the way the poet introduces, as Roger Lonsdale points out, his own 'predicament and sensibility as matters of interest and importance' at the beginning and end. It is the eve of Romanticism.

Here, and more so in 'The Deserted Village', Goldsmith uses repeated words, not as Pope does to effect special emphasis, but throughout – words which are pivots of thought and mood, whose reiteration adds to the meditative tone.

The epistle dedicatory to his brother attacks blank verse, Pindaric odes and metrical experiments ('error is

ever talkative'), promising a wholesome formal conservatism. Worse than poetic is political partisanship: 'Party
entirely distorts the judgement and destroys the taste.
When the mind is once affected with this disease, it can
only find pleasure in what contributes to increase the
distemper.' For himself, 'Without espousing the cause of
any party, I have attempted to moderate the rage of all.'
Goldsmith is a moderator, but not a pragmatist. He has
his own orientation. 'At gold's superior charm all freedom
flies,/The needy sell it and the rich man buys.' His praise
for liberty puts Thomson's to shame. He argues against
party in the poem:

O then how blind to all that truth requires,
Who think it freedom when a part aspires!
Calm is my soul nor apt to rise in arms,
Except when fast approaching danger warms:
But when contending chiefs blockade the throne,
Contracting royal power to stretch their own;
When I behold a fractious band agree
To call it freedom, when themselves are free;
Each wanton judge new penal statutes draw,
Laws grind the poor and rich men rule with laws;
The wealth of climes, where savage nations roam,
Pillaged from slaves to purchase slaves at home;
Fear, pity, justice, indignation start,
Tear off reserve and bare my swelling heart;
Till half a patriot, half a coward grown,
I fly from petty tyrants to the throne.

The lament for rural depopulation, the new enclosures,
the decay of the countryside, he fully articulates. It was
thus that the Industrial Revolution -- as Davie points out
-- was recorded in poetry. Few poets had experience of
the new industrial cities. They witnessed the change
almost entirely in terms of its effects on rural England.
Cowper, Crabbe, and even Hardy, observe the decay of
the established order, but only from a distance perceive
the new order and its vicissitudes.

'The Deserted Village' focuses initially on one 'place', Auburn, which Goldsmith idealizes and generalizes, making it representative. The poem was drafted first in prose, then corseted into couplets which disciplined and condensed the expression, but always with reference to the main design. The idealization of Auburn, possibly the Lissoy of his childhood, is not excessive. If it is sentimental, it is not falsely so; it serves as the ground against which he develops an essentially meditative poem, not an argument as he had in 'The Traveller'. Place and thought are to an extent secondary to the elegiac emotion, the sense (not just an idea) of the irrevocable loss of organic, traditional communities sacrificed to the whims of commerce, enclosure, exploitation. For Goldsmith the social process represents a loss of personal roots, and yet his lament is comprehensive because his own is by extension a general experience. The blisses of village life – 'charm', 'sweet' and 'there' recur too frequently in his evocation – are so generalized as to be almost abstract. But the effects of loss, like the causes, are vividly particularized before the general judgement which is appealingly simple and just:

> Ill fares the land, to hastening ills a prey,
> Where wealth accumulates and men decay:
> Princes and lords may flourish or may fade;
> A breath can make them, as a breath has made;
> But a bold peasantry, their country's pride,
> When once destroyed, can never be supplied.

Times are altered from 'When every rood of ground maintained its man'. Trade is the instrument of change. Before, the peasant crowned 'A youth of labour with an age of ease'. The lines about the man who 'Bends to the grave with unperceived decay,/While resignation gently slopes the way', have often been cited for the complete appositeness of their verbs, the exact marriage of language with image and with moral content. Such usage gives the lie to those critics who accuse Goldsmith of having an 'essentially prosaic' imagination. This is the author of *The Vicar of Wakefield*, to be sure – the Vicar himself is invoked in lines 133–192. But the imaginative procedures of the poet and the novelist are inevitably distinct.

Satire is too weak a word for Goldsmith's passionate sorrow at the predatory effects of those who would replace modest happiness with egotistical splendour, displace the organic and vital with the formal, monumental and ornamental ('The country blooms – a garden and a grave'), force common men to leave their native land and emigrate to unknown places, for they have no power against the power of money. The concluding passages, with Johnson's final quatrain, are too familiar to require quotation.

William Cowper 1731–1800

Your sea of troubles you have past,
  And found the peaceful shore;
I, tempest-tossed, and wrecked at last,
  Come home to port no more.

Critics tend to damn Cowper with faint praise. In one
anthology the headnote reads, 'Of all the poets in this
selection, Cowper is perhaps the smallest in poetical
stature. He would probably have counted himself lucky
to figure in such grand company' (James Sutherland).
D. J. Enright strangles his enthusiasm on a short lead:
'uneven as his poetry is, Cowper speaks with an individual, if quiet, voice, and ... although he is unlikely to
enjoy any future vogue, he has something to offer which
will never fall entirely out of fashion or out of date.' The
'if quiet' and 'entirely' dissuade the would-be reader.

In important ways Cowper is an original writer, and the
emotional and intellectual range of his poems is wide.
The 'milder muse' dominates, but there are reasons for
that. Acquaintance with his darker verses makes the
'milder muse' a formidable and healing figure. Donald
Davie is right to suggest that Cowper's work gains clearer
definition when we understand his motive in writing.
His Augustanism is illuminated when we realize that the
poems 'were written under the shadow of psychosis'.

Coleridge's original lectures on English poetry defined
three periods, the third running from Cowper to 'the
present day'. For him, something important *began* with

Cowper, a poet who read Herbert with delight, knew Milton's work as few before him had, and developed a personal discursive blank verse style that in directness and variety of tone foreshadowed Wordsworth's. Thomas De Quincey often joins Cowper's name with Edward Young's and Wordsworth's as meditative poets of a kind, always allowing to Wordsworth the chief laurel.

William Cowper was born in 1731 at Great Berkhamstead where his father, a grand-nephew of the first Earl Cowper and one-time royal chaplain, was rector. On his mother's side he could claim kinship with John Donne. His first great trauma was his mother's death when he was six, a loss consolingly weighed in the remarkable poem, 'On the Receipt of my Mother's Picture Out of Norfolk', written after his earliest experience of madness. At his first school he was bullied. He went on to Westminster School where he was happier and could excel. Among his classmates was the satirist Charles Churchill. He read most deeply in Homer, Milton and Cowley. He translated Homer and the Latin poems of Milton.

At the age of eighteen he entered the Middle Temple and in 1754 he was called to the bar. He fell in love with his cousin Theodora whose father, sensing Cowper's instability and poor prospects, opposed the match. It was another blow to Cowper. His 'Delia' poems, addressed to Theodora, though not his best work, attest to a genuine devotion. He came to expect failure, even to court it. He began to withdraw from the world, and his father's death, leaving him only a modest inheritance, precipitated his decline. He was a Commissioner of Bankrupts (1759–65). His family exerted itself to secure him a better post, but he was incapable of accepting it. He attempted suicide and was confined to an asylum.

His recovery coincided with a sudden evangelical conversion. Later he could write, 'The path of sorrow, and that path alone,/Leads to the land where sorrow is unknown.' He was raised up by reading a text in Romans. Tenuously 'cured', he went to live in Huntingdon with the Reverend and Mrs ('My Mary') Unwin (1765–7). The Unwins, Anglican evangelicals, supported him, and after her husband's death Mrs Unwin tended Cowper in his illnesses. His love for her was the subject of several poems more mature and memorable than the 'Delia' poems:

Thy indistinct expressions seem
Like language uttered in a dream;
Yet me they charm, whate'er the theme.
　　　My Mary!

They almost married, but desisted at a recurrence of Cowper's malady. She fell ill in 1791 and he helped look after her until her death in 1796. He died, miserable and ill, in 1800, having composed his tragic poem 'The Castaway' in 1798:

No voice divine the storm allayed,
　No light propitious shone;
When, snatched from all effectual aid,
　We perished, each alone:
But I beneath a rougher sea
And whelmed in deeper gulfs than he.

The 'he' is one who was mercifully drowned. The 'I' survived to suffer. Images of storm, shipwreck, drowning and isolation are a *leitmotif* through the poetry, even in unexpected humorous contexts. Shipwreck and drowning symbolize human vulnerability. A theological and a psychological element coexist in the image: it comes at points when Cowper is peculiarly, darkly himself. 'Alexander Selkirk', ostensibly about the human prototype for Robinson Crusoe, is a personal vision. 'The Loss of the Royal George', a superb dirge, seems fraught with personal consequence.

Happy times preceded his miserable end. With Mrs Unwin he moved to Olney. There they encountered the Calvinistic Reverend John Newton. He prompted from the poet the *Olney Hymns* at a time when Cowper was again suffering mental torments. His faith had been awakened, but he doubted his own election for salvation. He dreamed that God had damned him.

Davie suggests that Cowper's depressive madness was connected with the extreme Calvinism of the evangelicals. He recovered from the dream of damnation into a resignation of worldly ambitions, an acceptance of his fall from grace. In nature he discovered an objective, external consolation. In tending leverets and birds he gave purpose to his retirement. The nature he described in his verse with minute and loving particularity appealed to those caught up in the vogue for the Picturesque. Unlike them, he came to nature directly, not through art.

His earliest attempt at extended verse was the eight *Moral Satires*, suggested to him by Mary. He seems to have worked best when someone ordered poems from him. Newton suggested the hymns, Lady Austen provoked *The Task*, 'John Gilpin' and other poems. In a sense the occasions for his poems were offered by those solicitous for his health and keen to distract him from reflection on his condition. The verse is, however, much more than therapy. It has the mild urgency of a man intent to look abroad, away from himself. Nature at least cannot rebuff him. His verse is strenuously normative and moralized. Its care is the product of self-doubt in quest of certitude. The tenuous overall structure of the long poems reveals the tenuousness of Cowper's control. The surface is hard to fault, however. Coleridge above all praises the 'clarity of diction' and 'harmony' of the blank verse.

Cowper translated extensively. His blank verse Homer is not a masterpiece. But his versions of Horace, Virgil and Ovid are variously good. He translated from French and from the Greek Anthology, revealing a technical omnicompetence in his epigrams, hymns, anthems, elegies, lyrics, pastorals, discursive poems and epistles (in verse and prose, for he is among the best letter-writers in the language).

Norman Nicholson concentrates on the paradoxical nature of the poet: 'a recluse who became the spokesman of a great popular religious and democratic movement; and an oddity, an eccentric, a refugee from society, who, perhaps more than any other English poet, expressed the aspirations of the average man of his time.' The poems have 'the merit of good conversation', in other words, a sense of audience. Normative verse is powerful when it is won through to, when the poet wishes to achieve normality himself.

The 'merit of good conversation' was not common in verse in an age still overshadowed by Pope, whom Cowper admired with cool reservations. In poets who laboured under the spell of Milton, too, conversational qualities were rare. Cowper's Milton was not monitored through Thomson: it was Milton himself, whom he set out to edit in 1791. He eludes sub-Miltonic grandiloquence because of his constant awareness of a particular audience, his concern with specific issues, and because of his choice in *The Task* of a loose associative form in preference to a narrative structure. His debt to Milton was not, like Gray's and Collins's, to the shorter poems, but to the mature idiom of the great religious poems. His other master was Homer; he doubted only the morality of devoting so much time to an unredeemed poet.

D. J. Enright compare's Cowper's with Herbert's religious content. Cowper requires our assent to his presentation of faith, while Herbert's representations are of faith as experience. Cowper teases out his morals, Herbert as often as not leaves the moral implicit. Cowper is didactic, where Herbert is devotional, with the immediacy of prayer and not the remove of sermonizing. Coleridge admires in *The Task* the 'vein of satire which runs through that excellent poem, together with the sombre hue of its religious opinions'. 'Opinions' is the right word, opinions affirmed rather than conveyed onto the pulse. Yet the opinions must have been widely held, for between its publication in 1782 and 1800 eleven editions of *The Task* appeared.

In 'Table Talk', first of the *Moral Satires*, Cowper

presents his claims as a poet modestly. 'I play with syllables, and sport in song.' The understatement goes too far. This poem begins with philosophy and politics and, like good table talk, takes much else in its stride, most memorably the halcyon poetic Genius. His literary firmament includes Homer, Virgil and Milton. The absence of Shakespeare is evidence of how essentially literary a poet Cowper was in his earlier work.

In 1783, the year of Crabbe's *The Village* and Blake's *Poetical Sketches*, Cowper began *The Task*. Lady Austen had commanded an epic about the sofa. 'I sing the Sofa. I, who lately sang/Truth, Hope, and Charity.' Soon he is back to Truth, Hope and Charity. After a history of seats, a comment on the suitability of sofas for sufferers from gout, he expresses a desire that he may never experience that illness. Why?

For I have loved the rural walk through lanes
Of grassy swarth, close cropped by nibbling sheep,
And skirted close with intertexture firm
Of thorny boughs ...

The sofa serves to establish tone: the drawing room, comfort, conversation. It also inaugurates what is virtually a theme: the rich texture of things in the world, physical sensations; and the theme of illness and enforced repose or retirement.

The poem is connected not by argument or narrative but by tone. The development is by association, a continual interchange between particular observation and moral generalization which images provoke or illuminate. Cowper frequently suggests in his blank verse the tone and subject of Wordsworth:

Nor rural sights alone, but rural sounds,
Exhilarate the spirit, and restore
The tone of languid nature ...

'Languid' is not Wordsworthian, but more than a common debt to Milton associates the poets in our minds.

They partly share a vision of nature. Of the cacophonous birds, Cowper writes that they

> have charms for me,
> Sounds inharmonious in themselves and harsh,
> Yet heard in scenes where peace for ever reigns,
> And only there, please highly for their sake.

Cowper is less elemental, more comforting than Wordsworth.

Abstracted from the poetry, the thought of *The Task* is undistinguished, but in context it is often realized. Only the positive moral exhortations, against slavery and blood sports for example, or in favour of certain religious views, weary the reader. In promoting reform Cowper prefers exhortation to satire. Poetically, satire is the more effective.

The finest moment in the poem comes in the third book, 'I was the stricken deer', an evocation of the function of Christ and the true nature of redemption which for a moment sets Cowper on a par with Herbert. The vivid descriptive passages, about cucumbers, greenhouses, animals, the winter landscape, the hearth, add a documentary interest to the poem. One need only compare *The Task* with Thomson's *The Seasons* to see how the Augustan imperatives were being radically questioned and eroded.

In 'John Gilpin', 'Epitaph on a Hare' with its accuracy and gentle elegiac humour, 'The Poplar-Field' which meant a great deal to Coleridge and to Hopkins, and 'Yardley Oak' – that majestic unfinished moral poem – readers find the readiest access to Cowper. They first hear him in church when they sing his *Olney Hymns*, 'Oh! for a closer walk with God' and 'God moves in a mysterious way'.

Thomas Chatterton 1752–1770

Begin, my Muse, the imitative lay,
Aonian doxies sound the thrumming string;
Attempt no number of the plaintive Gray,
Let me like midnight cats, or Collins sing.

Thomas Chatterton is remembered more for what he meant to the Romantics than for anything he wrote. A little of his work is outstanding, all of it provides evidence of a genius that did not have time to mature. The work fills three volumes, and there are *longueurs*. He was no Rimbaud. To the Romantics he symbolized genius untutored, misunderstood and misprized by 'the ingrate world' (Keats). Keats used often to intone the magnificent lines from the Minstrels' song in the play *Aella*:

Comme, wythe acorne-coppe and thorne,
Drayne mie hartys blodde awaie;
Lyfe and all yttes goode I scorne,
Daunce bie nete, or feaste by daie.
   My love ys dedde,
    Gon to hys death-bedde,
     Al under a wyllowe tree.

To Chatterton's memory Keats dedicated an indifferent sonnet and *Endymion*, the poem he described as 'a feverish attempt, rather than a deed accomplished'. Keats, who was in almost as great a hurry as Chatterton, sets his hero 'among the stars/Of highest Heaven'. In a letter to

Reynolds he confides, 'I always somehow associate Chatterton with autumn. He is the purest writer in the English Language. He has no French idioms, or particles like Chaucer – 'tis genuine English idiom in English words.' In a letter to his brother he adds, 'Chatterton's language is entirely northern. I prefer the native music of it to Milton's cut by feet.' Chatterton's 'pure' English was useful to Keats in his emancipation from Milton. His enthusiasm was for the 'Rowley poems', in pseudo-dialect, not for the very precocious but otherwise unexceptional English poems.

Wordsworth's reference to Chatterton in 'Resolution and Independence' carried the poet's name further in time and space than any other tribute did: 'I thought of Chatterton, the marvellous Boy,/The sleepless Soul that perished in his pride.' Coleridge was not behindhand in his tribute. For over thirty years he tinkered with his 'Monody on the Death of Chatterton', spoken figuratively at the poet's grave (as a pauper suicide, his grave was unmarked). The life and death of the poet most detain him. The poems he praises in passing are the 'Rowley poems'. Coleridge's significant poetic debt to Chatterton is in the metrical organization of 'Christabel'.

What, apart from the life, was the appeal of Chatterton? Why do some claim him as 'the first Romantic'? There are undeniably fine poems and stanzas, especially among the 'Rowley poems'. Best are certain passages of *Aella*, 'An Excelente Balade of Charitie (As wroten bie the goode Prieste Thomas Rowley 1464)', and 'Eclogue the Third'. The authority of his 'language' is felt in the amusing and, in tone at least, plausibly mediaeval quatrain 'There was a Broder of Orderys Blacke':

There was a Broder of Orderys Blacke
    In mynster of Brystowe Cittie:
He layd a Demoisell onne her Backe
    So guess yee the Taile of mie Dittie.

Such verse is as remarkable for its oddity as for its quality, and the oddity and quality are separable. The best passages in *Aella* lose something, but not their imaginative force, when translated back into English (for Chatterton drafted them in English and then mediaevalized the language).

Chatterton was popular until about the middle of the nineteenth century, then his neglect began. His popularity was in large part a result of the fact that he was the first Romantic *legend*, a lesson in resistance to the death against literary and social conventions.

He was born in Bristol in 1752. His father, a schoolmaster and sub-chanter at the Church of St Mary Redcliffe, died before the boy was born. Chatterton's mother supported him, working as a seamstress and running a 'dame school'. It was she who, one day disposing of some antique documents, aroused in the hitherto listless child an enthusiasm, first for the illuminated letters, then for the old words. She taught him to read. Later he busied himself studying at St Mary's and at home.

When he was eight he was sent to a remarkably grim school in Bristol. He kept to himself there. At the age of ten he began to write poems. 'On the First Epiphany', written when he was eleven, was published. He composed satirical as well as religious verse, revealing an informed scepticism about matters of public morality. In 1764 he presented a pupil-teacher with a forged mediaeval poem. His victim was duped.

In 1767 the poet was apprenticed to an attorney. He wrote more forgeries. Most of the 'Rowley poems' were completed in 1768-9. He duped several Bristol burghers, some of his friends, and he almost succeeded with Horace Walpole. Ambition to be a writer took him to London. Pride forbade him to return home a failure and so, in 1770, in his eighteenth year, starving and in despair, he poisoned himself with arsenic in a rented room in Holborn.

His life of ambition, talent and pride was frustrated at each endeavour. Chatterton could find no equal to converse with in Bristol. His forgeries were admired as antique manuscripts, not as poems. He could find no patron. Grub Street exploited his energy but not his genius. And yet he achieved the 'Rowley poems'. Was he a 'native' or 'born' poet? Romantic poets believed in such creatures. But as Coleridge pointed out in a note on 'Resolution and Independence', Wordsworth could name only two: Chatterton and Burns.

Chatterton's invention of Sir Thomas Rowley, fifteenth-century 'Secular Priest of St John', was not perverse. His perverse forgery work consisted in providing 'authentic' pedigrees for drab notables or convenient documents for local historians. Thomas Rowley by contrast was a serious enterprise. He has a character and tone. He lives in an idealized mediaeval Bristol. Rowley's rank, religious vocation ('The Church of Rome [some Tricks of Priestcraft excepted] is certainly the true Church,' Chatterton wrote in his 'Articles of Belief'), his erudition, all extended Chatterton beyond the cramped, commercially developing Bristol in which he had no wealth, status or prospect, and was compelled to observe a faith which he found colourless and hypocritical. Rowley was necessary to him, and his best poems partake of that necessity.

'Forgery' was a relatively common device for escaping from conventions at the time. Macpherson's famous Ossianic forgeries, and Walpole's own *The Castle of Otranto* which pretended to be translated from an Italian original, were two of the best-known. A harking back to pre-Renaissance culture, a hankering after 'native' roots and styles kept writers such as Gray and Warton active. There was a growing interest in philology and earlier versions of the language.

Chatterton's dramatic instinct allowed him not only to describe but to enter the world of Rowley. He owes major debts to Shakespeare, and his most sustained long work is the play *Aella*, which, though unstageable, is dramatic. His language derives most from Chaucer's, but his imagination is at home in the fifteenth and sixteenth centuries. His forgeries were not mosaics of philological plagiarisms, any more than Gray's poems were mosaics of poetic plagiarisms. They made a solid structure of old- and new-baked bricks.

Behind Chatterton's English poems stand Pope, Gay and Swift. Without Rowley he would have remained a minor Augustan. With Rowley he became an original poet, a proto-Romantic, using the past as a way of apprehending a world and of rejecting the conventions of a narrowing culture.

Keats, in the preface to *Endymion*, speaks of himself and of adolescence in terms directly applicable to Chatterton. 'The imagination of a boy is healthy, and the mature imagination of a man is healthy; but there is a space of life between, in which the soul is in ferment, the character undecided, the way of life uncertain, the ambition thick-sighted.' It was in this space that Chatterton perished.

George Crabbe 1754-1832

Lo! the gay lights of Youth are past – are dead,
But what still deepening clouds of Care survive!

George Crabbe arrived late on the Augustan scene. He
commanded a large audience, but many poets and critics
found him dry and remote. Byron was an exception:
'Though nature's sternest painter yet the best', he called
him. Wordsworth imitated him in *The Excursion*. And
Crabbe lived long enough to learn from Wordsworth, attempting blank verse and exploring his childhood (*Infancy, A Fragment*, 1816), but by then his best work had
been done.

'Pope in worsted stockings' or 'a provincial Pope' were
the accepted versions which roused F. R. Leavis to his
extravagant defence of a writer who combined some of
the virtues of a novelist with those of an eighteenth-
century poet. He praises Crabbe's use of couplets in
dialogue. They are not evidence of 'awkward elegance
clothing an incongruous matter'. The couplet 'represents,
one might say, "reason's self" '. Leavis goes much further:
'in the use of description, of nature, and the environment
generally, for emotional purposes he surpasses any
Romantic.' Here Leavis goes too far. Crabbe is, however,
a master story-teller, and it is more useful to see him in
the poetic narrative tradition of Chaucer than in the
novel tradition of the eighteenth century. In 'Peter
Grimes', 'Procrastination', 'The Frank Courtship', 'The
Lover's Journey' and elsewhere, the verse establishes a

continuity between individual and communal experience, between the weather of the heart and that of the world, mental and physical landscapes. There is also humour in some of the portrayals. Crabbe's originality is dramatic and psychological; it is not accompanied by formal or stylistic inventiveness, but by conventional skills.

He was born in Aldeburgh, Suffolk, in 1755, the son of a collector of salt-duties. This background was hardly privileged. When he was twenty-six, Edmund Burke patronized him and attempted to 'civilize' or 'Londonize' the young poet. But he affected only the surface, for Crabbe was not the sort of man to change his nature upon command.

For his early schooling he went to Bungay and Stowmarket, Suffolk. When he was thirteen he was apprenticed to a surgeon-apothecary. He started writing poems. When he was seventeen he became engaged, but was not married until eleven years later. At the age of twenty he set up practice as a surgeon in Aldeburgh. *Inebriety*, a moral poem, was his anonymous début.

Soon he was in London, ostensibly to pursue surgical studies, perhaps also to seek patronage as a poet. In 1780, with £5 in his pocket, he returned to London to become a full-time writer. Burke took him up. *The Library*, a dull long poem in the manner of Pope, appeared. Burke introduced him to some of the great men of the day. He was ordained deacon and returned to Aldeburgh as curate in 1782. Shortly thereafter he was ordained a priest and appointed chaplain to the Duke of Rutland at Belvoir Castle.

The Village, his first major work, was published in 1783. Dr Johnson read, corrected and praised it. It reveals a skilled poet with broadly social concerns and a richly documentary technique. It is not surprising to learn that Henry Fielding was Crabbe's favourite novelist – a moralist who teaches through laughter and whose moral categories correspond to psychological realities. Crabbe is a literalist in expressed intent, a portrayer and interpreter rather than a visionary. He does not conceal rural ills 'in tinsel trappings of poetic pride'. His poetry is richer than Cowper's because his range of experience and human involvement was greater. His temperament was conservative in face of needless change, and his radicalism consisted in this: he showed what was, before suggesting what ought to be. He sensed that what was being destroyed – by individuals in their own lives and by political and commercial interests in the life of the community – was more valuable than what was replacing it. Social issues interested him less than social verities:

> ... cast by fortune on a frowning coast,
> Which neither groves nor happy valleys boast;
> Where other cares than those the Muse relates,
> And other shepherds dwell with other mates;
> By such example taught, I paint the cot
> As Truth will paint it, and as Bards will not ...

Of the poor he asks, 'Can poets soothe you, when you pine for bread,/By winding myrtles round your ruined shed?' In the first book of *The Village* he expresses firmly, if a bit repetitiously, a poetic commitment to which he remained true, by and large, in his later work.

His craft improved, his concerns became more profound as they became more particular, but his orientation did not change. C. H. Sisson writes, 'Crabbe started from what was in front of him, and particularly from what had been in front of him in his early years.' He is often 'old-fashioned' but seldom nostalgic.

In 1785 he became curate of Strathern, Leicestershire, was doctor to the poor of the parish, and he studied botany and entomology, work useful in his later poetry and which he published separately in 1795. In 1789 he moved to the living of Muston, Leicestershire, where he stayed for three years before moving back to Suffolk, and which he kept until 1814, returning in 1805 when laws against absentee clergy were passed. About 1790 he began taking opium on doctor's orders and continued the practice for the rest of his life. His wife's manic-depressive illness, the death of his third son, and other troubles deeply afflicted him. He went through a period of abortive activity. He wrote and destroyed three novels, began work on *The Parish Register* (1807) and *The Borough* (1810). In *The Parish Register* he first found the voice that was to distinguish his best work. In *The Borough* he went further, writing twenty-four 'letter' poems about the life of a country town. The twenty-two year gap in poetic publication was not time wasted. After so many false starts, he had found his pace and his manner, and *Tales* (1812) is his masterpiece, including twenty-one stories in various tones, on various subjects.

After the death of his wife (1813) and with the success of his books, Crabbe's remaining years were active but not very fruitful. He met many writers, including Wordsworth, Southey and Scott. He travelled, he wrote further poems and tales but even the once popular *Tales of the Hall* (1819) is inferior to *Tales* (1812). In 1832 he died in Trowbridge. His son was his excellent biographer.

Crabbe's declining years passed in an age increasingly alien from that which had shaped his imagination. F. R. Leavis wrote that he was 'hardly at the fine point of consciousness in his time'. C. H. Sisson replies, 'What an excellent thing not to have been! How many false hopes did this solid and pertinacious observer decline to share!' His provincial conservatism no longer requires apology. The ills he sensed afoot have now worked themselves out into those human consequences which writers 'at the fine point of consciousness' of the time failed to foresee. Crabbe was no prophet, but he saw in Suffolk depopulation, enclosure, grinding poverty, corruption among the gentry and by the gentry of the poor, psychological illness, breakdown in community, the triumphs of Methodism (which ate into his own congregation). It was a world John Clare, at a different level, had to contend with. Crabbe was a witness, one of the most honest and uncompromised in English poetry.

As Sisson points out, Crabbe was born in the same decade as Blake and Burns; his first writings appeared five years after the publication of Goldsmith's 'The Deserted Village'; he was read and blotted by Johnson; he met, influenced, and was influenced by Wordsworth; he survived Keats's death by eleven years. The only other English poet who provides so impressive a bridge is Michael Drayton (1563-1631). Unlike Drayton, Crabbe did not remake his art with each change of fashion. His work reveals an integrity different in kind from Drayton's.

Novelists have admired Crabbe. Jane Austen and E. M. Forster were among his champions. But the analogy between his and the novelist's art is tenuous. The scope of the *Tales* is novelistic, but the individual scope of each tale is not. They are different in manner and intention, and though they share a landscape, the landscape alters its character from tale to tale. In the mature tales, the morality is contained in the action, and in a number of them it is not so much morality as psychology that interests the poet. The consequences of action are social or personal, tending to a particular rather than a general resolution. It is in the condensed nature of the style, its power of suggestion, that Crabbe's affinity with Chaucer and his distinctness from the novelists of his time are most apparent. Lovers pass through a landscape which smiles, each detail illuminating an aspect of their happiness; but when love has foundered, they return through the same landscape as though through another world, altered, frowning. Crabbe's connotative precision in creating such correspondences is the essence of his originality. In 'Procrastination', for example, the physical objects with which people surround themselves define character; moral abstractions acquire a physical weight:

Within that fair apartment, guests might see
The comforts culled for wealth by vanity:
Around the room an Indian paper blazed,
With lively tint and figures boldly raised;

Silky and soft upon the floor below,
Th' elastic carpet rose with crimson glow ...

The objects blaze, rise, glow, as if animated, while the
human inhabitants, surrounded by the spoils of empire,
are almost inanimate. Most vivid is the time-piece above
the heiress's head:

A stag's-head crest adorned the pictured case,
Through the pure crystal shone th' enamelled face;
And while on brilliants moved the hands of steel,
It click'd from prayer to prayer, from meal to meal.

Though the device in the final line recalls Pope, the effect
is purely Crabbe's. Elsewhere a hostess of the new breed
(though 'a pale old hag' – Crabbe does not mince words)
'carves the meat, as if the flesh could feel'. Such accuracy
lays character bare. In 'Peter Grimes', the best poem in
The Borough, the changing seascapes figure the change in
the protagonist's troubled mind, without ever ceasing to
correspond to the actual world. In a tale such as this, motive is always clear Peter Grimes's cruelty to the boys he
kills is his attempt vicariously to punish the waywardness
of his own youth. His actions are not abstract sadism:
they have a psychological source. Crabbe's is a poetry of
consequences.

The best tales were not easily achieved. Crabbe moved
from an early Popean rigidity of narrative and descriptive structure to a more relaxed and comprehensive manner. His concerns, first documentary, became social and
then individual – a movement inwards towards character,
but always from a firm apprehension of the given, common world. The moralizer became a moralist as the tales
became able to contain, in a single statement, morality
and psychology. Sequence was replaced by close parallelism, and within a single tale subtle verbal, syntactical and
rhythmic repetitions prepared the way for climaxes, reversals and conclusions, as in 'Peter Grimes': 'And hoped
to find in some propitious hour/A feeling creature

subject to his power'; 'He'd now the power he ever loved
to show,/A feeling creature subject to his blow.'

The triumph of Crabbe's *Tales*, that 'mixture of iner-
tia and originality', as Howard Mills described it, is the
presentation of stories 'intensely personal and dramatic,
yet socially representative'. The language may at times
be hackneyed, uninventive. We do not look for purple
passages or finely honed couplets. We look through, rather
than at, the style, which is efficient and not flashy. We see
through its transparency the Suffolk world.

William Blake 1757–1827

For Mercy has a human heart,
Pity a human face,
And Love, the human form divine,
And Peace, the human dress.

William Blake spent all but three years of his life in London. He was born there in 1757, and there seventy years later he died. His father was a haberdasher. What formal education Blake received was in art: he became an engraver's apprentice and studied at the Royal Academy of Art. His graphic work became an integral part of his literary activity.

Even in his childhood he had visions: 'Ezekiel sitting under a green bough' and – in Peckham – 'a tree full of angels'. These figures stayed with him for life. T. S. Eliot praises the sort of imaginative independence he had: a manual trade (engraving, etching) freed him from a literary 'career'. He could follow his own desires in reading, and he was not instructed in the Augustan imperatives of taste. Lack of formal education was an advantage to his natural temperament.

When he was twenty-four he married the illiterate Catherine Boucher, daughter of a market gardener. He taught her to read and she became his assistant in etching and binding. His first book was *Poetical Sketches* (1788). He etched, watercoloured and bound most of his other books: *Songs of Innocence* and *The Book of Thel* (1789),

The Marriage of Heaven and Hell and *The Gates of Paradise* (1793), *Visions of the Daughters of Albion, Europe, Songs of Experience,* and *The Book of Urizen* (1794), *The Book of Los* and *The Book of Ahania* (1795) and others. Later large ventures were *Milton* (1804–8) and *Jerusalem* (1804–20).

In 1800, patronized by William Hayley, Blake moved to Felpham on the Sussex coast. Hayley employed him as an illustrator for three years – an arrangement neither man in the end enjoyed. Hayley, at the suggestion of Blake's friend, the painter Flaxman, had chosen a man of more imaginative integrity than he had intended. He tried various ways of taming the artist. He wanted from Blake a sort of work he could not provide for long. Mr and Mrs Blake, whatever their eventual reservations about Hayley, enjoyed Felpham, nature, the sea: it was their first extended stay outside the metropolis. In 1803 the notorious soldier turned up in the Felpham garden and sealed their fate. The gardener asked the soldier to cut the grass. Blake, who didn't like soldiers, ordered him off. The soldier demurred, and Blake threw him out, cursing (among others) the King, and saying uncritical things about Napoleon. When he was tried on a charge of high treason at Chichester (1804), Blake was acquitted thanks to Hayley's testimony, and thus ended the not altogether happy idyll by the seaside.

As illustrator and poet Blake was so startlingly original that he won few admirers. He had, as T. S. Eliot says, 'a peculiar honesty, which, in a world too frightened to be honest, is peculiarly terrifying. It is an honesty against which the whole world conspires, because it is unpleasant. Blake's poetry has the unpleasantness of great poetry.' The neglect of his poetry became virtual oblivion after his death in 1827, and it was only with Gilchrist's *Life* (1863) that interest in him was renewed. Since then it has grown to enormous proportions.

Lack of audience distorted the development of Blake's writing. F. R. Leavis observes, 'he had no public: he very early gave up publishing in any serious sense. One obvious consequence, or aspect, of this knowledge is the carelessness that is so apparent in the later prophetic books. Blake had ceased to be capable of taking enough trouble.' This is not quite right. Judging from the manuscripts, Blake took considerable trouble; but it may have been the wrong sort of trouble, and Leavis rightly points to 'the absence ... of adequate social collaboration' in his work. He is also right to suggest that Blake's 'symbolic philosophy is one thing, his poetry another'. The more pronounced the philosophy becomes, especially in the prophetic books, the more opaque and poetically inert the symbolism. Blake's best poems exist independently of his symbolic philosophy.

Yet the poet's genius produced that curious philosophy, which hates the word 'philosophy', and which helped to generate what Leavis calls 'a completely and uncompromisingly individual idiom and technique', rendering the poet 'individual, original, and isolated enough to be without influence' – in his own age, in any event. It was this genius which also limited his large work. For any but the absolute *aficionado* of Blake, Eliot's words about the prophetic books ring true: 'You cannot create a very large poem without introducing a more impersonal point of view, or splitting it up into various personalities. But the weakness of the long poems is certainly not that they are too visionary, too remote from the world. It is that Blake did not see enough, became too much occupied with ideas.' Eliot perceives in Blake a failure of cultural and philosophical bearings, an eccentricity that tends towards solipsism. By contrast Crabbe, a lesser poet, may be a better teacher, at least about the world we actually inhabit.

Blake's prophetic and biblical pretensions are clear from the poems' titles: 'The Book of', and even the 'Songs', suggest Old Testament prophets and King David. Biblical reference, allusion and cadence inform his work even where he tilts at conventional religion. Disillusion was his chief instructor. Like Wordsworth, he lamented

the direction taken by the French Revolution. Between
the *Songs of Innocence* (1789) and the *Songs of Experience*
(1794) his social optimism faltered. Innocence speaks with
a voice which is all transcendence, Experience with a voice
incapable of transcendence. Behind Blake's poems there
is always an apprehended social reality, a consciousness
of particular evils and injustices in the ways of man to
man. When he approaches such apprehensions directly,
as in 'London', he is among the first and finest poets of
the modern city with its human consequences. In his
prophetic books he has translated the perceived reality
away from direct perception, into a symbolism which can
effect, on a grand scale, a process of regeneration. But the
regeneration is symbolic, and the actual world it hovers
above is perplexed but untouched by it. Blake, when he
is 'timeless', tends to become oblique, obscure, a poet who
demands exegesis. His earlier work has an immediacy
which the older Blake forfeited, draping perception with
a symbolic veil.

From his earliest *Sketches*, Blake has his own tone and
method. In rejecting 'imitation', both formal and perceptual, he established his originality. 'An Imitation of
Spenser' is remarkably un-Spenserian. He was experimenting with an archaic mode, looking for a route away from
the eighteenth century: 'That wisdom may descend in
faery dreams.' The imitation fails because the mythology
and the archaized language do not answer his needs. Eliot
overstates the affinity between Blake and his eighteenth-
century predecessors and contemporaries. There are obvious common epithets and strategies, but what is striking
is Blake's radically original formal imagination and his
freedom from the constraints of conventional diction.

Imitation is the shadow of a shadow; art for Blake is
creation. What the eye sees as real *is* real, whether it is a
simple raincloud or the weeping child within the cloud.
Blake's poetry is a seeing and seeing into, with unconventional eyes. He does not describe, but projects. Man's divine part is his ability to create, a faculty Blake exercised

for over half a century. He sees what is and what is implicit. His rejection of prescribed forms is part and parcel of his rejection of social institutions. In *The Book of Thel* he makes it clear that wisdom cannot be contained or simplified in 'a silver rod' nor Love in 'a golden bowl', both probably ecclesiastical or sacramental references. The lines from *Thel* were originally included in *Tiriel*, itself a cry against the limiting tyranny man imposes on man.

Most remarkable of the *Sketches* is 'To Autumn', written in his 'teens. In it he suggests a collaborative relationship with Nature:

> O autumn, laden with fruit, and stained
> With the blood of the grape, pass not, but sit
> Beneath my shady roof; then thou may'st rest,
> And tune thy jolly voice to my fresh pipe;
> And all the daughters of the year shall dance!
> Sing now the lusty song of fruits and flowers.

This conventional pastoralism of a city boy becomes original poetry in the second line. Autumn evolves into a figure, walking, stained with autumnal juice. Is it sacrificial or Dionysian? The fifth line suggests the latter. The poem continues:

> 'The narrow bud opens her beauties to
> The sun, and love runs in her thrilling veins;
> Blossoms hang round the brows of morning, and
> Flourish down the bright cheek of modest eve,
> Till clustering Summer breaks forth into singing,
> And feathered clouds strew flowers round her head.

> The spirits of the air live on the smells
> Of fruit; and joy, with pinions light, roves round
> The gardens, or sits singing in the trees.'
> Thus sang the jolly Autumn as he sat;
> Then rose, girded himself, and o'er the bleak
> Hills fled from our sight; but left his golden load.

Autumn sings through the poet's lips. Love, a substance

flowing through the veins of flowers, is contained in them, not abstracted from them. Nature has an aspect: 'brow', 'cheek'. The clouds are 'feathered' and active, strewing not rain but (the effect of the rain on plants displaces the rain itself) flowers, and the 'singing' of the line before turns the clouds into birds. No simile is used: Blake suggests equivalences, connections, evoking a natural wholeness. What in another poet would be abstraction in Blake breathes the air, though it would be impossible to paraphrase or draw a diagram of the scene. The images are transparent, it is a vision and not a scene.

Conceptually the poem is impressive; prosodically it could hardly be more interesting. The enjambements throughout, but especially in the first line of the second stanza, are dramatically effective, enhancing the surprise of the vision. In other *Sketches* there is an excess of adjectives, in this poem the adjectives pull their weight. The syntactical and rhythmic parallelism from stanza to stanza produces the effect of rhyme, though the poem is unrhymed. There is a strong continuous rhythm but no metrical regularity.

Soon after completing the *Sketches*, Blake annotated Swedenborg's *Divine Love*. We love what contains most of us, what is most human, a dog more than a wolf. The poet leads the reader to love, the end of the golden chain that leads to Eden. 'Think,' Blake writes, 'of a white cloud as being holy, you cannot love it, but think of a holy man within the cloud, love springs up in your thoughts, for to think of holiness distinct from man is impossible to the affections. Thought alone can make monsters, but the affections cannot.' Around this time he put a child in a cloud in the introduction to the *Songs of Innocence*, a poem which recalls the procedure of 'To Autumn'. When the child in the cloud weeps, with pity rather than sorrow, we are a little disconcerted by such rain; and the cutting of the reed or pipe and the making of a pen are equally perplexing. The poet forfeits a measure of independence when he consents (it is consent, unlike the introduction to the *Songs of Experience* with its imperative 'Hear the voice of the Bard!') to write. In *The Marriage of Heaven and Hell* Blake says, 'the Poet is Independent and Wicked; the Philosopher Dependent and Good.' The poet should be his own law, creating the world in which he walks. For such a poet the world is an extension of the senses, he proceeds from sense to vision. The grandest poetry, according to Blake, is immoral, as are the greatest heroes: Iago, Satan, Christ 'the wine bibber', and others. When he set Milton in the devil's camp he was praising the poet who outshone the philosopher, Milton's Satan over Milton's God.

In annotating Wordsworth Blake gives further evidence of the process of his imagination. Physical objects, he says, are at variance with the imagination: objects do not exist apart from perception. When we adapt this statement to Blake's own imagery, we resolve a problem. Many of his images are deflected from definitive particularity into abstraction. In the opening of *The Marriage of Heaven and Hell*, however, his imaginative process is vividly revealed:

Once meek, and in a perilous path,
The just man kept his course along
The vale of death.
Roses are planted where thorns grow,
And on the barren heath
Sing the honey bees.

The first three lines are figurative, moral language; the three that follow are images. The figurative and the particular correspond rhythmically; rhyme connects 'vale of death' with 'barren heath'; and parallelism connects the rose and the meek man, the honey bees and the just man. The images are equivalents for the figurative language, body it forth. Here Blake does not deflect the image into abstraction: he segregates two distinct modes, as it were two registers of language, bodiless and embodying. Language enacts the division between heaven (the word) and hell (the substance). Over the following three stanzas Blake mingles and re-segregates these registers in service of the theme.

In his best work Blake avoids simile unless its point of reference is contained in the poem. For example, in 'The Echoing Green' he writes in line 26, 'like birds in their nests', thus recalling 'skylark and the thrush' earlier in the poem. He distrusts similes because they tend to abstract qualities – moral or otherwise – from the subject and the thing to which it is compared. Simile disembodies qualities and is therefore at variance with Blake's vision. Thus 'The Sunflower' and 'The Rose' are not referred to human experience, though they include it. The Lamb and the Tiger are not equated with Christ, though they partly include or embody him.

Blake's allegiance to the plain language of the King James Bible, his elected innocence of eighteenth-century diction and convention, and his social vision made it possible for him to write balladic lyrics ('The Little Black Boy', 'The Chimney Sweeper', and many others) in a language more direct than Wordsworth's in his sometimes studied ballads. The miraculous effortlessness of the *Songs of Innocence* and *Experience* proceeds from a sensibility untroubled by decorum, and from a verbal tact that takes his poems, with unparaphrasable directness, onto the pulse, affecting the reader's imagination without stumbling at the threshold of his intelligence. The poems work at that deep level where we are touched by 'Lycidas', 'The Song to David', 'Kubla Khan', and a very few other poems in the language.

In both sequences the subject-matter is similar. Tone, emphasis and conclusions differ. Innocence does not comprehend beyond its Innocence (though what is beyond Innocence hovers disturbingly near the poems, as in 'A Blossom', 'The Echoing Green', 'The Chimney Sweeper' and others); Experience is the more melancholy because it remembers but no longer possesses Innocence. Yet in the Experience poems we sense occasionally positive powers at work in the gloom, as in 'Holy Thursday' and 'The Lily'.

Auguries of Innocence carries the aphoristic statement of Blake's themes to extremes, a couplet monotony unrelieved by effective enjambement. The couplets, taken separately, contain effective paradox; but taken together they detract from one another. The poem asks to be read as a polemical creed, with all that this implies of wilful devising. There is none of the transparence of the *Songs*: *Auguries* taxes thought, prejudice and belief.

Among the prophetic books, *The Book of Thel* stands out as the most poetically lucid. It too considers the theme of innocence and experience, employing an original perspective. The unborn soul foresees her life and finally looks back from her grave. She travels through various states of creative innocence, revealed successively by lily, cloud, worm and clod. Each, with its limits, terrifies the free and unborn Thel. She rejects such life, unable to comprehend the 'curb upon the youthful burning boy' and the 'little curtain of flesh on the bed of our desire'.

But *The Book of Thel* is not entirely satisfactory. It demands exegesis in terms of Blake's symbolic philosophy. So, too, does *Urizen*. That poem enacts a process of reduction, from unlimited potential to human and natural bondage. 'Like a human heart, struggling and beating,/ The vast world of Urizen appeared' – but that world is by stages constrained, dwindling to the one-dimensional world of Ulro. Part of the concluding section is powerful and succinct:

They lived a period of years;
Then left a noisome body
To the jaws of devouring darkness.

The giants themselves are reduced and their progeny are pygmies: in short, philosophers:

And their children wept, and built
Tombs in the desolate places,

And found laws of prudence and called them
The eternal laws of God.

These become creatures of 'non-entity', frequently alluded
to particularly in *Los*.

Liberty for Blake is pre-eminently a state of mind and
spirit and entails the ability to create. His philosophy is
connected with this belief. There are four states of perception, the highest with four dimensions: in descending
order, Eden, Beulah, Generation and Ulro. Four anti-
theses rule the development of the prophetic books:
imagination and memory; innocence and experience in
religion; liberty and tyranny in society; outline and imitation in art – all four pairs, as Northrop Frye says, variations on the antithesis of life and death. Yet knowledge
of Blake's scheme, or the elaborate explication of figures,
does not make the *poetry* better. If the poetry exists on a
primary level, knowledge and explication perfect understanding. But without that primary level of communication to the mind or to the senses, a poem becomes a game
for exegetes.

Like the philosophies Blake rejects, his too can traduce
imaginative originality, can obscure what was visible before, can distort the real. *Milton* opens with four of his
best and best-known quatrains, 'And did those feet in
ancient times.' He urges 'Mental Fight'. Yet the prophetic
chapters that follow are a poetic disappointment, quite
apart from the merits or otherwise of their philosophy.
The same disappointment is experienced in *Jerusalem*,
despite occasional electrifying lines – for example,
'Trembling she wept over the space and closed it with a
tender moon.' The later prophetic books are scattered
with such moments limited to a rhetorical and philosophical scheme that corresponds only remotely to the
world it would illuminate. There is a failure of clarity
and a failure of thought. It may be that Blake had despaired of an audience and wrote to entertain and expand
his own consciousness, or that of angels. These works have,

of course, served many critics and scholars in their careers. They have answered to a number of modern 'causes' because they accept indiscriminately a number of interpretations. 'Thought alone can make monsters.' Blake forgot that early wisdom.

Robert Burns 1759–1796

O wert thou in the cauld blast,
  On yonder lea, on yonder lea,
My plaidie to the angry airt
  I'd shelter thee, I'd shelter thee.

There are several versions of Robert Burns. Wordsworth, in 'Resolution and Independence', evokes 'him that walked in glory and in joy/Behind his plough, along the mountain side.' This idealized Burns was common early in the nineteeth century. For Keats he was more complex. In 'On Visiting the Tomb of Burns' he writes:

All is cold Beauty; pain is never done:
For who has mind to relish, Minos-wise,
  The Real of Beauty, free from that dead hue
    Sickly imagination and sick pride
  Cast wan upon it! Burns! With honour due
    I oft have honour'd thee. Great shadow, hide
Thy face; I sin against thy native skies.

Writing to Reynolds from Scotland Keats says, 'One song of Burns is of more worth to you than all I could think of for a whole year in his native country. His Misery is a dead weight on the nimbleness of one's quill ... he talked with Bitches – he drank with blackguards, he was miserable. We can see horribly clear in the works of such a Man his whole life, as if we were God's spies.' And yet neither misery nor joy characterizes Burns's work. He is sufficiently of the eighteenth century to find more interest in man, his foibles, his institutions, his ballads, than in agonized personal revelation or in natural description. Byron, less drawn to the accidents of his biography, valued the lucid pathos of the poet. Matthew Arnold in 1880 wrote a warm appreciation of Burns's comic and satirical work, criticizing the sentimental poems. His assessment was crucial in the re-appraisal of Burns's merits.

There is too the political version of Burns. Radicals – English, Scottish and European – have set up their image, stressing the anticlerical satires, the tilting against hypocrisy and rank, the 'egalitarianism'. Burns's life attracts them too: it does little credit to the Scottish bourgeoisie and the gentry. His declared sympathy for the American and French revolutions adds to his usefulness from this point of view. His enormous appeal in the Soviet Union is partly explained by this. In 'Scots wha hae' he wrote:

By Oppression's woes and pains,
By your sons in servile chains,
We will drain our dearest veins,
  But they shall be free!

In more familiar manner he wrote 'Is there, for honest poverty' ('For a' that').

The version which most irked Hugh MacDiarmid, who loved Burns's poems but led the Scottish 'renaissance' with the cry, 'Not Burns – Dunbar!', was the one which adapted the poet to narrowly chauvinistic ends. The Scottish expatriates and the nostalgic Scots at home championed him with what Arnold called 'national partiality'. Further, Burns's rural and ballad poetry in Scottish dialect had – in MacDiarmid's view – set a disastrous example for a century of dialect poets who imitated what had become an outmoded idiom and subject-matter, producing a kind of linguistic and cultural caricature.

Robert Burns answers to all these partial descriptions and includes rather more than their sum. He wrote over six hundred poems, and his formal, tonal and thematic range is greater than that of his Scottish predecessors and most of his English contemporaries.

He was born in Alloway, Ayrshire, in 1759, into the family of a tenant farmer, an event the poet later commemorated in 'There was a lad was born in Kyle'. The gossip in the poem predicts, 'He'll be a credit till us a'': and also that he will have an active future among the ladies. Burns's father and neighbours, though poor, hired a well-educated tutor to see to their children's education. Later, the father himself undertook to teach them.

At the age of fifteen, while working on his father's farm, he wrote his first verses. It was not woodnotes wild he warbled. Though his Latin was indifferent, he was well-read in the English poets and understood French well enough to read Racine. The Scots poetry of Allan Ramsay first suggested to him the potential of his dialect. Robert Fergusson's Scots verse acted as the eventual catalyst: having read it, Burns began his remarkable 'demotic' career. He had a native tradition and a native tongue. To Fergusson he addressed three poems, largely about that poet's (and perhaps his own) hardships and neglect: 'Curse on ungrateful man, that can be pleas'd,/And yet can starve the author of the pleasure.' Burns's English poems have considerable merit, but they are pale beside the Scots work. He realized this himself: 'These English songs gravel me to death,' he wrote. 'I have not the command of the language that I have of my native tongue. In fact, I think that my ideas are more barren in English than in Scotch.' His attempts to 'translate' his poems were fruitless.

Bibliographically, the most important year in Burns's life was 1786, when the Kilmarnock edition of *Poems Chiefly in the Scottish Dialect* was published. In the years between the poet had witnessed his father's death in 1784, a year after his bankruptcy. Burns was now provider and head of the family. His first child out of wedlock was delivered by his mother's servant Betty Paton in 1785. It was a daughter.

Tho' now they ca' me, Fornicator,
And tease my name in kintra clatter,
The mair they talk, I'm kend the better;
    E'en let them clash!
An auld wife's tongue's a feckless matter
    To gie ane fash.

He also composed 'The Fornicator. A New Song'. 'The rantin dog the Daddie o't' is a song put in the mouth of Betty. Throughout Burns's work we find songs of a sexual frankness and jollity as outspoken as some of the poems of the Restoration, and yet a good deal more wholesome than those.

In 1785 Burns met Jean Armour, whom he married in 1788 after she had borne him two sets of twins. His brilliant satirical attacks on Calvinism seem to have begun more or less with her pregnancy. In the same month in which *Poems* was published the Calvinists took their revenge and exacted from the poet a public penance for fornication with Jean. He had been tempted to emigrate with another girl, composing poems about his intended departure. The gossip had been right; he had a complicated and thorough love-life.

Poems proved a success and the next year a second, enlarged edition was published. Both editions omitted the church satires and included instead more general satirical pieces. But with the church satires, the *Poems* contain the core of Burns's original work. Most of it had been composed in 1785 and early 1786 – a remarkable production, including 'To a Mountain Daisy', 'Halloween', 'The Address to the Deil', 'To a Mouse', 'To a Louse', 'The Cottar's Saturday Night', the best epistles, 'The Twa Dogs' and others: satires, pious pieces, dramatic monologues, mock-elegies, songs, lyrics and flytings. The poet was twenty-six. Four years later he wrote 'Tam O'Shanter', completing his important original work. He wrote more poems but his chief literary labours thereafter related to the collection and publication of Scottish songs.

Literary Edinburgh took him up – no doubt as one who 'walked in glory and in joy/Behind his plough', a role he found it hard to sustain without considerable alcoholic ingestion and the camaraderie of low types. As a result, literary Edinburgh in general put him down again. Sir Walter Scott as a boy of fifteen saw the poet and recalled his 'manners rustic, not clownish', his 'massive' countenance, his shrewd look: 'The eye alone indicated the poetical character and temperament. It was large, and of a dark cast, and literally glowed when he spoke with feeling and interest.' Lord Glencairn and Mrs Dunlop became the poet's patrons and friends. His admirers secured him a post in the Excise Division in Dumfries, and rented a farm for him. He worked hard, putting his imaginative energy into collecting and revising songs for *The Scots Musical Museum* (1787-1803) and the *Select Collection of Original Scottish Airs* (1793-1818). He travelled widely, gave up farming, was promoted in the Excise. His work took him out in all weathers. He caught rheumatic fever and died in 1796, at the age of thirty-seven, leaving his wife with a large progeny. Jean was not his only love. There had been Betty, and Mary Campbell, and Mrs McLehose ('Clarinda'), and others.

Burns probably died a bitter man. Certainly he had been ill-used. He had foibles, and his opinions were firm and outspoken. But he did not deserve the hardships that were his lot, or the hostility he aroused. Carlyle in his essay gets the proportions right: 'Granted the ship comes into harbour with shrouds and tackle damaged, the pilot is blameworthy ... but to know *how* blameworthy, tell us first whether his voyage has been round the globe or only to Ramsgate and the Isle of Dogs.'

Burns's importance must first be assessed in the Scottish cultural context. His debts to the Augustans are few. It is a common error to use him in connection with English romanticism, but this is misleading. As Donald Davie says, he was 'adopted posthumously'. Nor, in reading Wordsworth's and Keats's tributes to him, do we recognize any but a shadow of him. Only Byron – of course, another Scot – heard him more or less clearly. Leavis goes too far when he suggests Burns 'counts for much in the emancipation represented by the *Lyrical Ballads*'. He counts for *something*, but a comparison between Burns's and Wordsworth's ballads reveals how little. Arnold makes the same error as Leavis when he writes, 'Wordsworth owed much to Burns, relying for effect solely on the weight and force of that which with entire fidelity he utters, Burns could show him.' Wordsworth's 'At the Grave of Burns' and other poems written on Burns and about his neighbourhood, borrow one of the Scottish poet's forms, but not his inventive energy. He records a debt:

> He has gone
> Whose light I hailed when first it shone,
>   And showed my youth
> How verse may build a princely throne
>   On humble truth.

It was a moral even more than a poetic lesson he learned.

Arnold stripped away much of the sentimental gloss that had been applied to Burns. 'Let us coldly say that of much of this poetry, a poetry dealing perpetually with Scotch drink, Scotch religion, and Scotch manners, a Scotchman's estimate is bound to be personal.' Burns's world is 'often a harsh, a sordid, a repulsive world' – part of its attraction and also its limitation. Much of the bacchanalian verse is 'poetically unsound', vitiated by a factitious bravado, written in reaction, to shock and amuse, but not to extend or interpret experience. He often lacks 'the high seriousness which comes from absolute sincerity'. One feels this in the poems about fornication as well as in the poems about drink. Defiance in poetry is rare, especially difficult to achieve when the poet defies an audience without questioning his own position. And yet there is an undeniable and great poet in Burns whom Arnold compares with Chaucer: 'Of life and the world,

as they came before him, his view is large, free, shrewd,
benignant – truly poetic, therefore; and his manner of
rendering what he sees is to match.' Unlike Chaucer, he
has 'a fiery, reckless energy' and 'an overwhelming sense
of the pathos of things'. After all, his best poems were
written when he was a young man.

Arnold directs attention to a poem central to Burns's
oeuvre, but until then generally neglected, 'The Jolly
Beggars'. It has 'hideousness', 'squalor', 'bestiality', 'yet the
piece is a superb poetic success. It has a breadth, truth,
and power which ... are only matched by Shakespeare and
Aristophanes.' Other good poems possess 'archness and
wit' as well as 'shrewdness'. These include 'Duncan Grey',
'Tam Glen', 'Whistle, and I'll come to you my lad', 'Auld
Lang Syne' – and, no doubt, 'A Red, Red Rose', 'Green
Grow the Rushes', 'The Banks o' Doon', and a score of
others.

After reading extensively in Burns, one tends reluctantly to agree with Hopkins who wrote in a letter to
Bridges of ' a great want' in Burns's utterance. Hopkins
defined the want a little imprecisely: 'he had no eye for
pure beauty.' It may rather be a quality he shares with
another poet equally versatile: Dunbar. There is little
repose in Burns. The closest he comes to repose is in a
few lyrics and the epistles, where he particularizes his address to one or two and speaks with that candour Arnold
commented on in his essay. 'Epistle to Davie, a Brother
Poet' confesses his sourness at his own wants, at the unequal distribution of wealth, but finds consolation in the
open air:

What tho', like Commoners of air,
We wander out, we know not where,
  But either house or hal'?
Yet *Nature*'s charms, the hills and woods,
The sweeping vales, the foaming floods,
  Are free alike to all.
In days when Daisies deck the ground,

And blackbirds whistle clear,
With honest joy, our hearts will bound,
    To see the *coming* year:
        On braes when we please then,
            We'll sit and *sowth* a tune;
        Syne *rhyme* till 't, we'll time till 't,
            And sing 't when we hae done.

William Wordsworth 1770–1850

The deeper malady is better hid,
The world is poisoned at the heart.

The last four decades of Wordsworth's life were a sort of
aftermath: he wrote copiously and competently, but in
general dully. When he was seventy-three he became Poet
Laureate. 'Daddy Wordsworth', Fitzgerald called him.
Rossetti's supercilious quip was, 'good, you know, but
unbearable'. For Tennyson he was (metaphorically) 'thick-
ankled'. The poetry which radically challenged the prejudices of his age and challenges, even as it provides, some
of the prejudices of ours, was for the most part written
before 1807.

Wordsworth was born in 1770 (the year of Chatterton's
death) at Cockermouth in Cumberland. His sister Dorothy
was born the next year. By the time he was thirteen he
was an orphan. His sense of isolation stemmed in part
from the loss of his parents: the family is for him a recurring image of informing stability, security and continuity.

He was educated at Hawkshead Grammar School, where
he began writing verses in the manner of Pope. At the age
of sixteen he composed the lines,

Calm is all nature as a resting wheel.
The kine are couched upon the dewy grass;
The horse alone, seen dimly as I pass,
Is cropping audibly his later meal.

The first two lines are literary, the latter two literal. Already, underlying a conventional apprentice-piece, the original mind of Wordsworth is at work on perceived nature. The poem, about memory and the image of home, isolation, and resentment at the officious care some people lavished on him, suggests in faint outline themes of moment to the mature poet.

At St John's College, Cambridge, he failed to distinguish himself. In 1790 he went to France and Italy, crossing the Alps on foot. The next year he returned to France and became involved with the revolutionary movement and with Annette Vallon, a Frenchwoman who bore him a daughter. He did not marry her and a complex remorse followed from this and from the failure of his political idealism.

In 1793 his first interesting published poems appeared. 'An Evening Walk' and 'Descriptive Sketches' relate to some of his experiences on the continent. The first is an assured piece in couplet form, full of Augustan abstractions and physical detail, but without continuity between the two levels of perception: sights and thoughts rather than imaginative vision. The 'Descriptive Sketches' included excellent writing and was useful to the poet when he came to write 'Cambridge and the Alps' in *The Prelude*. The poet's politics are eloquent but insubstantial, the fruit of thought rather than observation:

Once, Man entirely free, alone and wild,
Was blest as free – for he was Nature's child,
He, all superior but his God disdained,
Walked none restraining, and by none restrained:
Confessed no law but what his reason taught,
Did all he wished, and wished but what he ought.

Such was the optimistic ideology of the time: the reasonable savage, the natural man. As the French Revolution declined into the Terror and its aftermath, Wordsworth's enthusiasm faded. He wrote *The Borderers* (1795-6), an unperformable tragedy instinct with Godwinism, and the poem 'The Convict', in anapaestic measure, in which he examined closely the physical and emotional nature of a man isolated and in fear.

Wordsworth met Coleridge in 1795. They became neighbours in Somerset, where they collaborated on *Lyrical Ballads* (1798). They travelled to the Continent; and Wordsworth and his sister Dorothy spent the winter together in Goslar, Germany. The poems written in Goslar are among Wordsworth's best. The winter landscape, the stimulating presence of his beloved sister, and the recent memory of his conversations with Coleridge which had helped to clarify his own poetic processes: these factors brought him to his mature manner. The poems are largely personal and include the first book and other outstanding parts of *The Prelude* (written at Coleridge's suggestion), 'Nutting', the 'Lucy' poems, and others. The poems he had composed in Somerset still bore – apart from 'Lines written above Tintern Abbey' – strong eighteenth-century affinities. The Goslar poems belong to the nineteenth century, to Wordsworth's personal voice. In the 'Lucy' poems he struck briefly upon a tone and manner which he never repeated and which none of his imitators, not even Arnold, managed to approach, try as they might. It is impossible to relate the poems to specific incidents or a specific person, though there is an abundance of theories. The loved and lamented child may be emblematic. The physicality of the devotion and of the sense of loss, the mysterious courtship and the suggested characterization, and most poignantly the vision of death itself, bring these poems closer to ballads than the deliberate literary ballads Wordsworth had composed before.

In 1799 he moved with Dorothy to Grasmere, where he spent most of his remaining years. He wrote 'Michael' in 1800. A new, enlarged edition of *Lyrical Ballads* including his controversial 'Observations' appeared in 1800. Later he added his note on 'Poetic Diction'. From this period date some of the best sonnets. Like Milton, whom he invokes in 'Milton! thou should'st be living at this hour', he used the form most effectively for civic subjects: a call to arms, a brief exhortation, a concise statement of principle, or a broad observation. His best-known sonnet, 'Upon Westminster Bridge', is a love-sonnet addressed to a city.

He married Mary Hutchinson in 1802. Losses – his brother's death, Coleridge's physical decline, Dorothy's troubles, the political developments in France – sobered him. *The Prelude* was completed in its first version in 1805. It was not published in his lifetime but in 1850, the year of his death, by which time he had altered it significantly, and not always for the better. The year 1807 marks – with the publication of 'Intimations of Immortality', 'Miscellaneous Sonnets' and 'Sonnets dedicated to Liberty' – the end of Wordsworth's major period.

He continued to write, however, freed by a sinecure of £400 per annum, and to travel. In 1814 *The Excursion* appeared. It incorporated 'The Story of Margaret' ('The Ruined Cottage'), Wordsworth's first major attempt at blank verse, which had so impressed Coleridge in 1797. *The Excursion* is a poem in nine books. *The Prelude* was to lead into it; and it was to be succeeded by a third extended poem, the three under the general title *The Recluse*. Coleridge helped Wordsworth to map it out as a great philosophical poem about man, nature and society. But Wordsworth was not that *kind* of philosopher, and Coleridge – who helped his friend in so many ways towards his best poetry – must bear some responsiblity for having given Wordsworth a distorted view of the nature of his own gifts. *The Recluse* was to have 'for its principle subject the sensations and opinions of a poet living in retirement'. The sensations were in the range of Wordsworth's style; but the opinions were less distinguished and less readily accommodated. In *The Prelude*, ideas rise out of experience; in *The Excursion* they are imposed upon it. *The Excursion* depends on a flimsy narrative. It includes extended debates on religious faith. A Pastor illustrates the effects of faith by examples from the lives of people lodged in his churchyard. General conclusions are drawn, and the final books reflect on social themes, particularly the Industrial Revolution, its effect on the poorer classes, and the need for proper educational institutions for the children of the poor.

Other poems took their plots from legends and classical mythology. A few early poems appeared in later years – 'Peter Bell' (1798) and 'The Waggoner' (1805) as late as 1817. Of the later work, 'Yarrow Revisited' is among the best, an occasional poem which draws on the experience of two earlier poems. But it is slight when compared with what had come before.

Wordsworth's conversion in his later years was complete. The young radical became a vociferous opponent of liberalism. Burke was a hero to him. The author of *The Prelude* composed *Ecclesiastical Sonnets*, the pensive solitary became a talker.

Coleridge remained faithful to the Wordsworth he most valued, the pre-*Excursion* poet. The earlier poems reveal, he says, a 'union of deep feeling with profound thought, the fine balance of truth in observing, with the imaginative faculty in modifying, the objects observed; and above all the original gift' – which he shares with Spenser and Milton, incidentally – 'of spreading the tone, the atmosphere, and with it the depth and height of the ideal world around forms, incidents, and situations, of which, for the common view, custom had bedimmed all the lustre, had dried up the sparkle and the dew drops.' We might quarrel with the word 'ideal', which introduces a Coleridgean distortion; but otherwise the account is hard to better.

Wordsworth's concerns follow a clear development. Nature was his first passion. With the French Revolution he became an enthusiast with a social vision for mankind which, as it happened, history betrayed. From mankind he turned to particular man, to solitary figures in known landscapes, to the expression of nature in relationship with man, the correspondence between the given world and the inner life. It was a synthesis between his earlier concerns, and his development through the three phases occurred in about ten years. Beyond this, after 1807, came religious faith, either the cause or effect of his loss of imaginative certainty. He was reduced to adjusting reality to an orthodox interpretation – no longer a discoverer.

Poems such as 'Resolution and Independence', in their very titles, record a debt to the eighteenth century, to the age of Johnson with its moral and psychological categories. Throughout, his poetry is normative, integrating, not aberrant or extreme. He portrays extremity only to celebrate survival and endurance. Even the relative lack of 'poetic diction' in *Lyrical Ballads* is a radical response to conventions of the eighteenth century, deliberate poetic strategy and not originality in the spirit of Burns, Blake or Smart. The title *Lyrical Ballads* itself was polemical, addressing readers with eighteenth-century expectations, announcing that two distinct genre – lyric and ballad – were to be mingled, against the rules.

The word 'ballad' has misled readers in the matter of Wordsworth's attitude to the language of poetry. 'Ballad' must suggest 'popular' song in a popular idiom. But 'We Are Seven' was the only one of the *Lyrical Ballads* to have been published as a broadsheet. None of them has a compelling narrative line. Narrative of action was never one of Wordsworth's notable talents. His language avoids some of the snares of hackneyed poetic diction, but it is a language men might *speak*: they would hardly be likely to sing it. The poems are addressed not to the broad audience to which Burns appealed but to the audience that read Crabbe and Cowper, the audience whose language Wordsworth, with a Cumberland accent, actually spoke. It is only Coleridge, in 'The Ancient Mariner', who achieves consistent balladic effect.

Wordsworth made his intentions clear in the famous preface to the 1805 edition. He declared himself against the 'gaudiness and inane phraseology of many modern writers'. He proposed 'to choose incidents and situations from common life, and to relate or describe them throughout, as far as was possible, in a selection of language really used by men.' He does not mean rustic language, but natural language without 'gaudiness or inane phraseology'. 'A selection of language' is the perfect definition of a diction. He is choosing an alternative diction, but a diction nonetheless. It may approximate at times to the language of unaffected rustic men, 'because such men hourly communicate with the best objects from which the best part of language is originally derived', but he 'purified' it of defects repugnant to reason. Arnold called it writing without style.

Beyond this was a philosophical and psychological purpose: to trace through his incidents and situations, 'the primary laws of our nature: chiefly as far as regards the manner in which we associate ideas in a state of excitement'. The formulation derives from Wordsworth's close reading of Hartley, a profound influence on him as on Coleridge. He followed this purpose in *The Prelude* as well, taking for subject the development of his own mind.

Wordsworth speaks to and of men. His survivors achieve dignity despite suffering and loss, especially in 'Michael', the masterpiece in this mode, and in 'The Old Cumberland Beggar'. Their suffering is part of them much as they are part of the landscape through which they move. His best delineations of character are those in which he records aftermath. If he seems to relish the suffering of others at times, he is drawn to it as a purifying force, a force which isolates and defines essential integrity.

In the Preface, Wordsworth formulates his view of the poetic process. 'I have said that poetry is the spontaneous overflow of powerful feelings; it takes its origin from emotion recollected in tranquillity; the emotion is contemplated till by a species of reaction the tranquillity gradually disappears, and an emotion, kindred to that which was before the subject of contemplation, is gradually produced and does itself actually exist in the mind. In this mood successful composition generally begins.' It is the least understood of Wordsworth's statements. He does not say that poetry is 'emotion recollected in tranquillity': that is the point of departure. Poetry is in effect re-creation of primary experience. 'I wandered lonely as a cloud' (1804) seems to have been written almost as an illustration of this belief.

The Prelude is Wordsworth's most remarkable work. The two versions (1805, 1850) differ radically. The old poet strengthened weak phrases, drew the texture in more tightly, omitted some of the interjections, changed to transitive verbs many of the 'to be' constructions. He made the poem more literary and subtly altered emphases. There are thematic changes as well. He played down the early radicalism and antagonism to Cambridge; he blamed himself for his French enthusiasms; he added some fine passages, among them a tribute to Edmund Burke. Nature he regarded more meekly, God became an orthodox figure. The 'feeling' – essential in the early version – becomes contemplative, 'observing', 'pondering'. For all the 'literary' gains, there is a loss of immediacy.

The thirteen books (fourteen in 1850) of *The Prelude* trace the 'Growth of a Poet's Mind' from his first consciousness to his disappointment with the French Revolution and his return to nature in a different mind. The poem is dedicated to Coleridge and in its direct address has at times the candid tone of a verse epistle, directed to a single person rather than to a wider audience. The blank verse is deployed with such freedom and spoken assurance that it is hard to decide whether to call it iambic pentameter or quantitative verse.

The poem is philosophical rather than visionary. His literal imagination required that he establish scene or incident before it would release a meaning. Blake is consistently visionary, while for Wordsworth there are

        spots of time
Which with distinct pre-eminence retain
A vivifying virtue.

He requires a 'real solid world/Of images'. His imagination was

> for the most
> Subservient strictly to the external things
> With which it communed.

Nature, as we learn from the Tintern Abbey poem, he went to first

> more like a man
> Flying from something that he dreads than one
> Who sought the thing he loved.

The first books of *The Prelude* provide a fuller account. Nature becomes in them a force with which the isolated imagination is attuned:

> For I, methought, while the sweet breath of Heaven
> Was blowing on my body, felt within
> A corresponding mild creative breeze,
> A vital breeze which travelled gently on
> O'er things which it had made, and is become
> A tempest, a redundant energy
> Vexing its own creation.

Such energy must issue in creation.

Fear (danger) and Beauty (desire) were the fundamental emotions. He shows their relation in various incidents: when he waits for the horses; the gibbet; on Windermere lake; in the destruction of the copse. When he responds to nature destructively he feels footsteps following, or the mountain in pursuit. This too is part of the reciprocity with nature which formed his imagination, and the loss of which depleted his poetry. In book three the dissociation from nature begins. Cambridge, that *multum in parvo* of so much that repelled him, quickened his temporary alienation. But in book four, above Hawkshead, his consecration to poetry occurs: he triumphantly regains his sense of nature. 'I made no vows, but vows/

Were then made for me.' He begins to observe the inhabitants of the landscape, the old soldier for example: 'a
desolation, a simplicity.'

In the fifth book he considers liberalism and education.
Formal teaching renders youth intellectually precocious
but unfeeling. He recalls himself as a boy hooting on the
banks of Windermere lake and being answered by the
terrifying silence. It is in book six that the Winander boy,
now an adult, crosses the Alps on foot and experiences
most clearly the permanent forms and the transitory content of nature. It is the core of his imaginative perception:

> The immeasurable height
> Of woods decaying, never to be decay'd,
> The stationary blasts of waterfalls,
> And every where along the hollow rent
> Winds thwarting winds, bewilder'd and forlorn,
> The torrents shooting from the clear blue sky,
> The rocks that mutter'd close upon our ears,
> Black drizzling crags that spake by the way-side
> As if a voice were in them, the sick sight
> And giddy prospect of the raving stream,
> The unfettered clouds, and region of the Heavens,
> Tumult and peace, the darkness and the light
> Were all like workings of one mind, the features
> Of the same face, blossoms upon one tree,
> Characters of the great Apocalypse,
> The types and symbols of Eternity,
> Of first and last, and midst, and without end.

Against such a realization, the writing of the seventh book,
with its external portrayals of the city and its corrupting
powers, seems thin, the conventional contrast between
city and country life is unmemorable. Wordsworth is seldom poetically comfortable when he goes to town. After
the 'Retrospect' in book eight, books nine and ten take us
to France, and books eleven and twelve describe how Reason impaired his natural sympathies and instincts. He had

become in his French enthusiasms more a foe of false-
hood than a friend of truth. But on his return those 'spots
of time' from the past renewed their 'vivifying virtue'. His
imagination was restored. In the moonlit landscape, the
last book confirms this recovery:

A meditation rose in me that night
Upon the lonely Mountain when the scene
Had pass'd away, and it appear'd to me
The perfect image of a mighty Mind,
Of one that feeds upon infinity,
That is exalted by an underpresence,
The sense of God, or whatsoe'er is dim
Or vast in its own being ...

Often Wordsworth's finest moments occur when, from a
great height, he surveys what is before him, and from
what he sees or surmises flows the meaning which he feels:
in the Alps, above Tintern Abbey, and here, too.

'Lines Composed a few miles above Tintern Abbey' preceded the completion of the 1805 *Prelude*. In the 'Lines'
he insists on natural 'connection', recurrence ('again' is
used several times in the first verse paragraph), and on
presence ('this' and 'here'). He experiences the force of
memory and of what is to come, stationed firmly himself
in the present and among particulars. In condensed form
this poem contains much of the substance of *The Prelude*.
As William Empson demonstrates, the poet gives and explains the experience at the same time, choosing his words
so that they present scene and meaning together.

The most memorable of Wordsworth's great poems is
the 'Intimations of Immortality' ode, written between
1802 or 1803 and 1806. Technically it is a *tour de force*. A
very few readings and it is fixed in the reader's mind,
though not as argument, rather as a developing mood or
attitude, an apprehension, distilling as experience the
wisdom of *The Prelude*. It is a less positive formulation
and less lucid intellectually in its attempt to find 'strength
in what remains behind', as though the 'real world/Of

images' and those 'spots of time' were already losing their force. And so they were, the sense of that 'mighty Mind' was overcoming the sense of the particulars of its creation. But not before, by a radical questioning of poetic convention, a powerful and original vision of nature, and by the development of a comprehensive personal style, Wordsworth – with Coleridge – had extended the language and thematic range of English poetry.

Samuel Taylor Coleridge
1772–1834

O happy living things! no tongue
Their beauty might declare:
A spring of love gushed from my heart,
And I blessed them unaware ...

With Dr Johnson, Samuel Taylor Coleridge is the greatest
critical intelligence among the English poets. His interest
extended beyond poetry to society, philosophy and religion. Poetry was at the heart of a wider concern with
language and the power of imagination and ideas. He was
a creature of his time. Unlike Johnson, he had no settled
opinions; he was a man in search of truth and perplexed
by indecisions, personal, philosophical, political and aesthetic. In his writing we sense consistency of principle but
uncertainty of application. His mature political thought
is lucid; but he cannot – for example in *On the Constitu-
tion of Church and State* – bridge the gap between idea
and the embodiment of idea in practical, institutional
forms. His integrity is such that he will not indulge in
casuistry to escape from intellectual corners.

Uncertainty had its aesthetic consequences. Unlike the
other great Romantics, Coleridge never established a
dominant personal voice or mode. He wrote Augustan
verse of little distinction, some discursive poems, and then
the handful of nature poems and meditations in which
he was most himself, and finally the three great poems
which defy classification and achieve remarkable imper-

sonality: 'Christabel', 'Kubla Khan' and 'The Rime of the Ancient Mariner'. Of the three great poems, two are ostensibly unfinished. Throughout his poetry there are fragments, including 'The Destiny of Nations'. Other poems he worked on for many years but remained dissatisfied with them. His 'Dejection: An Ode' makes a virtue of necessity and adopts a fragmentary form, juxtaposing verse paragraphs which are thematically but not logically sequential. The formal fragmentation is an aspect of the theme. He never completed his vast projected philosophical work. His attempt to schematize a philosophy transcendental by nature distorted ideas accessible only to imaginative approach, not to analysis.

One can trace his self-doubt and indecision to his earliest years. Born in 1772 in Ottery St Mary, Devon, he was the youngest son of the local vicar. His father, who understood and indulged him, died when the boy was nine years old. No one could replace this benign figure of authority. Coleridge's mother did not understand him; and when he came to marry in 1795 he chose a woman too like his mother, thus preparing the difficulties of his later years.

He attended Christ's Hospital School in London, where Charles Lamb was a junior classmate. There he had excellent masters, read the classics and modern literature, and grew interested in the literature of travel. In 1791 he went to Jesus College, Cambridge. He was too well-prepared for that university. The curriculum bored him, he was idle, got into debt, and suddenly on impulse enlisted in the 15th Dragoons, from which his family rescued him. He returned to Cambridge but did not finish the degree.

He met Robert Southey in 1794. Their shared enthusiasm for the French Revolution and Coleridge's admiration for Southey's poems made them fast friends. They planned to found a 'Pantisocracy', as Coleridge christened it, indulging his love of abstraction, a commune in America on the banks of the Susquehanna river. The project proved a pipe-dream, but it led directly to Coleridge's marriage to Southey's sister-in-law. Already Coleridge was taking opium.

He first published poems in 1793 in the *Morning Chronicle*. In 1796 he started his own newspaper, politically and religiously non-conformist: the *Watchman*, which ran for only ten issues. Thus by the age of twenty-four he had failed to complete his Cambridge course, contracted a disastrous marriage, and seen two cherished projects run aground. He had also written without success for the theatre. But he had a new enthusiasm: Wordsworth.

He first met him in 1795 and was immediately impressed with his work. In 1797, when Wordsworth settled near Coleridge in Somerset, the two collaborated in *Lyrical Ballads* (1798). Coleridge contributed 'The Rime of the Ancient Mariner', and his poetry developed rapidly – as did Wordsworth's – as a result of their friendship. Between 1795 and 1802 Coleridge composed his best work, starting with 'The Aeolian Harp' (1795) and including the flawed but interesting poems 'Reflections on Having Left a Place of Retirement' (1795) and 'The Destiny of Nations' (1796). There followed 'This Lime Tree Bower My Prison' and 'The Ancient Mariner' (1797); 'Christabel' (1797, part two 1800); 'Frost at Midnight', 'Kubla Khan', 'Fears in Solitude' and his recantation 'France: An Ode' (1798); the fragmentary 'Hexameters' to Dorothy and William Wordsworth (1798-9); 'The Keepsake' (1800) and – the falling off was noticeable in those two poems – his final masterpiece, 'Dejection: An Ode' (1802). Thereafter the muse was fitful in her attentions. Coleridge's major poetic achievement was complete: he was thirty years old.

His interest in German transcendentalist philosophy – he did much to advance the ideas of Kant and Schelling in England – was an outgrowth of his early neo-platonist studies. In 1796 in 'The Destiny of Nations' he had expressed his essential vision:

For all that meets the bodily sense I deem
Symbolical, one mighty alphabet
For infant minds ...

The use of the singular 'sense' suggests at an early stage
his view of the interdependence of the senses, the fusing
perception we meet elsewhere in the 'swimming sense' before the manifold spectacle of nature; or in the line describing synaesthesia, 'A light in sound, a sound-like
power in light'; or 'to see is only a language'. In the 1796
poem we also visit Plato's cave:

Placed with our backs to bright Reality,
That we may learn with young, unwounded ken
The substance from the shadow ...

After visiting Germany in 1798-9, he returned to
England and settled near Wordsworth in Cumberland to
continue his studies. He fell hopelessly in love with
Wordsworth's sister-in-law. He wrote journalism, lectured
and travelled, suffered further financial hardships and
grew increasingly dependent on opium. In 1810 he
quarrelled with Wordsworth. It was one of the greatest
losses of his life, and though they were reconciled, they
never re-established the original friendship. Coleridge's
reputation grew as his powers declined. In 1817 the prose
masterpiece, *Biographia Literaria*, was published. His
mature political writing is the quintessence of that English Toryism rooted in Filmer and Hooker, adhered to by
Swift, Johnson and Goldsmith, and richly proclaimed in
public by Edmund Burke. It has no connection with the
modern Tory party. Coleridge died in 1834.

It was largely after the composition of his major poems
that he set down his poetics in prose. Intellectual energy
and creative power he had seen as wrestlers locked in com-
bat. Intellectual energy had won, he was a critic, and he
took issue with Wordsworth. Wordsworth had declared
that there was no essential difference between the language of prose and the language of verse. The inessential

difference was metre, which in verse bridled the emotions and created associations, balancing the 'commonplace' with intense emotion. It protected the reader from too direct an assault from the poet's emotions. Coleridge argued that there *was* an essential difference between prose and verse: they are languages distinct in construction and in effect. Metre is not a negative force, a bridle, but part and parcel of the statement, the vehicle for emotion itself, a positive power. Each passion dictates a pulse and form of expression. Metre provides overall harmony by unifying the parts. Instinct or imagination elects and judges metre: 'could a rule be given from without, poetry would cease to be poetry, and sink into a mechanical art.' The instinctive and the involuntary play a greater part in Coleridge's conception of poetry (and in the best of his poems) than in the case of most of his predecessors. In this conception Romanticism has its first clear articulation: the notion of organic form and intuitive formulation. From these follows the famous 'suspension of disbelief': we judge a work first on its own terms, and only then do we judge the terms. Coleridge evolved as well his much-debated theory of Imagination, secondary Imagination and Fancy. The first he describes as the 'living Power, Prime Agent of all human Perception'; the second as an 'echo of the primary, coexisting with the conscious will, yet still identical with the primary in the *kind* of its agency, differing only in *degree* and *mode* of operation'; and the third as 'a mode of memory emancipated from the order of time and place, blended with and modified by that empirical phenomenon of the will, which we express by the word "choice"'.

Coleridge's mind, unlike Wordsworth's, was never fully possessed by the power of physical objects. His early work is full of transitive verbs, while Wordsworth employs the verb 'to be' more than most great poets, as it were assuring himself of the otherness and presence of objects. Coleridge is interested in connection, and for him the life of imagination can be more vivid than the life of the senses themselves. 'This Lime Tree Bower My Prison' illustrates this. The poem has the colloquial directness of a blank-verse epistle. In it, the poet has suffered an injury and is unable to accompany his friends – notably Lamb, just down from the city – on a walk. He gives them directions, then relaxes in his lime tree bower. There in imagination he sees what they will see in reality, and his perception is heightened by the fact that he sees through the eyes of Lamb, released into nature from a city existence. Coleridge imagines his friend's response. The extended syntax of the long sentence describing the friends' descent is mimetic language at its best. They see particulars and then the wider panorama. Passive in his bower Coleridge experiences the immediate sensuous pleasure of his place, the memory of the route his friends have taken, their own pleasure as he imagines it, and an additional, integrating sense of wholeness and well-being, despite his injury. He draws a moral:

> Henceforth I shall know
> That Nature ne'er deserts the wise and pure;
> No plot so narrow, be but Nature there,
> No waste so vacant, but may well employ
> Each faculty of sense, and keep the heart
> Awake to Love and Beauty! and sometimes
> 'Tis well to be bereft of promis'd good,
> That we may lift the soul, and contemplate
> With lively joy the joys we cannot share.

He concludes, 'No sound is dissonant that tells of Life.' This poem, written in the same year as 'The Ancient Mariner', develops in such lines the themes of that greater poem. Nature, even in desolate places or circumstances, provides qualities to waken the heart. The Mariner's perception of this fact prepares the way for his redemption.

For Coleridge, perception is a vital, active faculty: it detects a large continuity, and then assimilates the various data of perception into that continuity or organism. 'I regulated my creeds by my *conception*, not by my *sight*,' he says. Images are the materials of which conception builds its edifice: he is after unity, not causal process.

'The Aeolian Harp' was his first remarkable poem. Milton, Gray and Cowper, prime mentors of his early work, stand a little off and let the young poet speak. He begins with great particularity, addressing his new wife, who leans against his arm. His senses move from the cottage to the vines that cover it, then outward to the clouds; the scent of the beanfields reaches him, and the 'stilly murmur of the distant sea/Tells us of silence'. Thus all the senses are involved. Then the Aeolian Harp – an instrument placed on a casement where the breeze can draw sounds from it – sounds. Its strain draws the poet's mind away from the actual world to a world of imaginative suggestion and romance, until his wife's rebuke draws him back. The poem is moralistic, in a conversational blank verse at once gentle and joyful. With 'This Lime Tree Bower My Prison' it is one of Coleridge's most positive statements.

The stringed musical instrument is for Coleridge an important image for releasing imaginative energy through its harmonies. Its use here foreshadows the 'dulcimer' in 'Kubla Khan'. In form and tone the poem prepares the way for 'Frost at Midnight' and, more remotely, for 'Dejection: An Ode'.

'The Frost performs its secret ministry,/Unhelped by any wind': thus 'Frost at Midnight' opens. It is a powerful poem, with the conflicting emotions of paternity, solitude and unfulfilment. The experience is vividly evoked: 'the owlet's cry/Came loud – and hark, again! Loud as before.' He is agitated by the stillness: the fluttering 'film' on the grate suggests a stranger may come. The place in which he sits musing becomes an extension of the poet's mind, the frost is itself an agent, like the poet's imagination, performing its secret ministry on Nature as his imagination does on memory. He returns to his own childhood, and then turns to his child, contrasting his past with her present. The poem ends with a benediction for his daughter.

The earlier discursive nature poems were concerned with existence in space, with landscape and panorama. 'Frost at Midnight' and 'Dejection: An Ode', concern themselves with time. They are nocturnal, reflective, and profoundly personal rather than expansive across an observed scene and generalizing in tendency.

In 'Dejection: An Ode', Coleridge confronts the failure of his imaginative vision. His marriage was decaying, he was hopelessly in love, and he was unwell. The wry opening soon gives way to nocturnal despair. We hear the Aeolian harp and tones of 'Christabel' and 'The Ancient Mariner'. A storm rages but does not now, as it would have done before, rouse his imagination: 'A grief without a pang.' Stars and moon: 'I see, not feel, how beautiful they are!' He echoes Wordsworth, Milton and his own earlier verse. This poem ends too with a benediction – for his beloved. He himself is beyond such grace. One great poem could be made of his failure of vision.

The discursive poems illuminate the great unparaphrasable poems which are his main poetic achievement. The least of the three is 'Christabel', his longest poem, and an incomplete ghostly romance which by a technique of rapt questioning and breathlessly stated images establishes dramatic tension: 'Is the night chilly and dark?/ The night is chilly but not dark', 'Is it the wind that moaneth bleak?' These passages foreshadow Christabel's interrogation of the mysterious Geraldine. Nothing is defined. We know it is 'a month before the month of May', and May is the month of romance. Poor Christabel will not savour the fruits of May. An eerie, gothic atmosphere is established and sustained. The unaffected simplicity of the novel stressed-verse form, with its variable rhyme-scheme, gives pleasure for almost seven hundred lines. Geraldine is a supernatural creature who, by a spell, silences Christabel. The protagonist, thus rendered mute, observes and suffers the beginning of Geraldine's evil designs. *Desunt nonulla*.

'The Rime of the Ancient Mariner' achieves what no

other literary ballad of the period had done: the tone of genuine folk-ballad. Despite the impersonality of the ballad-singer's voice, Coleridge explores in dramatic ways one of his favourite themes, developed earlier in the discursive poems. The ancient mariner chooses one of three young men bound for a wedding feast and tells him his story: his ship ice-bound near the pole, the albatross of good omen, his gratuitous act of slaying the bird, the punishment wrought on the whole ship; his penance and regeneration when in his heart he blessed the creatures he saw around the becalmed ship. Thereafter he must travel the world teaching from his experience reverence and love of God and his creatures. In 625 lines Coleridge, with continuous dramatic and intellectual tension, touches upon our deepest consciousness. The poem works upon the reader like a dream: there is no question of belief or disbelief: we merely attend. Passages of the poem have entered the common language; its images have drawn back to the surface important elements of folk culture and of hermetic symbolism.

Rudyard Kipling quoted two lines of Keats and three of Coleridge from 'Kubla Khan':

A savage place! as holy and enchanted
As e'er beneath a waning moon was haunted
By woman wailing for her demon lover!

'These are the pure Magic. These are the clear vision. The rest is only poetry.' It is a sacrilege of sorts to 'interpret' the magic. Like 'Christabel', 'Kubla Khan' is, some still believe, a fragment, a poem that emerged from a dream and was interrupted in composition by the person from Porlock. Many interpretations have been offered, but each seems partial and distorting. More valuable are formal studies, the close consideration of imagery and its relatedness. Interesting but not very useful are the elaborate searches for sources. What the poem means is strictly inseparable from the actual words and rhythms it uses. Paraphrase can hardly get a toe-hold.

It is not until the second half of the poem that the 'I'
appears:

A damsel with a dulcimer
In a vision once I saw ...
Could I revive within me
Her symphony and song,
To such a deep delight 'twould win me,
That with music loud and long,
I would build that dome in air ...

The first half of the poem evokes the pleasure dome. In
the second half the 'I' wishes to retrieve it. Could he hear
the music he once heard in a vision, he could re-create in
air 'That sunny dome! those caves of ice!' He would be
like Kubla Khan, himself sacred and exalted. The dulcimer relates to those harps met elsewhere in Coleridge's
work, instruments which harmonize the world of ideas
and the world of the senses, which liberate the imagination from the constraints of literal vision. But in 'Kubla
Khan' the poetry achieves an intensity unprecedented in
the discursive poems. The dulcimer's sound would re-
create not things perceived but things imagined. Contemplation authenticates, but can even transform and
generate objects of contemplation, as in 'Frost at Midnight'. 'Could I revive within me': it is a conditional
clause, and the fact is he cannot. He cannot even 'complete' the poem. His vision is interrupted. If he could
complete it he could complete himself, become one with
'flashing eye' and 'floating hair'. The poem is about the
desire, not the failure of the desire, and in this impossible
hope resides its power. It belongs near the end of Coleridge's greatest creative period. His next – and last –
major poem *is* about the failure: 'Dejection: An Ode'.

Walter Savage Landor
1775–1864

Manners have changed, but hearts are yet
The same, and will be while they beat.

Walter Savage Landor is best known today for two or
three lyrics and for Dickens's genial caricature of him as
Boythorn in *Bleak House*. His large production of *Imaginary Conversations* (1824, 1828, 1829) is now not much
read. His long poems, despite the enthusiasm they aroused
in Southey, De Quincey, Shelley and others, have been
forgotten. Posterity has not much attended to him, except
for a few of the best poets of that posterity; Yeats, Pound,
Frost and others. It is no wonder that he appealed to
them. He is one of the most civilized voices of his day,
a man who found the past serviceable in the present. His
radicalism had to do with roots, primarily classical ones.

He was born at Ipsley Court, Warwickshire, in 1775. His
mother was of an old family, his father a successful doctor.
The fractious boy was withdrawn before being expelled
from Rugby, where he had excelled in Classics and written
fine Latin poems. He was then rusticated from Trinity
College, Oxford, where he had the reputation of a wild
Jacobin. His active romantic life soon got under way, and
it provided him with some of his best pretexts for poems.

His first book, *Poems* (1795), he suppressed in part for
its simplistic political enthusiasms. The first poem in the
collection declares his settled literary passion for Sappho,
Anacreon, Ovid and Catullus. They remained his guiding
lights. *Gebir: A Poem in Seven Books* (1798, Latin trans-

lation 1803) and *Poetry by the Author of Gebir* (1802) gained him the admiration of a few of his contemporaries. In 1805 his father died and he came into the family estates. He made Southey's acquaintance in Bristol in 1808. Though later in life he met the leading writers of the day, Southey remained his closest literary friend.

He married in 1811 and spent much of the rest of his life in flight from this unfortunate match. *Count Julian*, a non-dramatic tragedy, appeared in 1812. In 1814 he left England, not to return for eighteen years. Much of the time he spent in Italy. The historical trilogy *Andrea of Hungary, Giovana of Naples* and *Fra Rupert*, occupied him until 1839–40. Publication of the two volumes of *Hellenics* (1846, 1847), *The Italics* (1848), *The Last Fruit off an Old Tree* (1853) – perhaps his best book – and his *Heroic Idyls* (1863), including Latin poems, complete the main bulk of his large, uneven output. A few fine poems appeared in his last book, notably 'Ye who have toil'd' which proves that his senility was not so complete as some critics have suggested. He died in Florence in 1864. His long life may or may not have been happy, but there was an unusual intellectual and temperamental consistency about it, from his early troubles at Rugby through his polemical activities on the larger social stage.

His poetry, too, has consistency and continuity. When he is described as a neo-classical poet, it does not associate him with the Augustans but distinguishes him – or some essential part of him – from the Romantics. His intense, unquestioning commitment to poetry, his belief that the poet is by nature more responsive than other men, his sometimes careless and insensitive enthusiasms, associate him with his Romantic contemporaries. So does his occasional sentimentality, his emotional ends. Yet his programme was distinct from their diverse programmes, from the outset.

Gebir is an heroic poem and a political allegory in blank verse. It tells the story of two brothers. Gebir is a prince and conqueror, his conquests stayed by love and his life destroyed by treachery. Tamar is a pastoral figure who wins the love of a sea-nymph and is transported beyond the world of mortals. *Gebir* was not a poem in search of an audience. It challenged rather than invited readers, and the challenge will probably be accepted by few today. It is superbly crafted but deliberate and cold in execution. The action is slow, Miltonic, as of large-scale figures in a remote land. Anthologists have rescued choice passages, but not the poem itself. Landor addressed to reluctant readers his late and excellent 'Apology for *Gebir*'.

Throughout his career he produced poems formally and thematically related to this one, among them 'Crysaor' and 'The Phocaeans'. The plays and 'scenes' and his historical trilogy share the general faults and local virtues of *Gebir*. Landor's penchant for historically remote events to illuminate present social and political problems was an artistic error, imposing on him anachronism, distortion both of subject-matter and subject. His command of extended forms is intellectual rather than imaginative. Landor the poet is visible in certain passages only. It is best to turn to the shorter poems and lyrics. They too are remote, but in a different sense.

His most characteristic work is to be found in the *Hellenics*. Landor's classical imagination was Greek, not Latin, despite his excellence in Latin versification and his debts to Ovid and Catullus. In 'On Classick and Romantick' he wrote,

Abstemious were the Greeks; they never strove
To look so fierce; their muses were sedate,
Never obstreperous: you heard no breath
Outside the flute; each sound ran clear within.

His lyric art achieves a distillation. He seeks to contain and generalize his subject, whether landscapes or images of human perfection or relationship. Measure, balance, fidelity and form are classical qualities he pursues. This is 'Dirce':

Stand close around, ye Stygian set,
  With Dirce in one boat conveyed!
Or Charon, seeing, may forget
  That he is old and she a shade.

This, by the author of *Gebir*: the contrast exemplifies
the larger paradox of Landor's imagination. The Romantic and classical, the radical and conservative, coexist in
tension, producing two voices.

One should not overlook the quality of poems such as
'Fiesolan Idyl', in which Landor writes with an emancipated, guiltless sensuality, even sexuality. His style may
refine, but it also intensifies, and he is among the most
quietly sensuous of English poets. Unlike Burns, Landor
never seems to explore the senses merely for effect.

In *Hellenics* the verse has some of the plainness of
Catullus. Those poems to Ianthe and Rose Aylmer are
among the finest lyrics in the language. Landor was sensitive to diction, if not register, in his language. The short
poems plainly conform to a single plan and tone. It may
not be a language men speak, but we instantly recognize
it. Landor's language does not date: it is secure within
tradition,

The Greek Anthology, with its recurring themes of love
and the erosions of time, spoke intimately to him. The
thrift of his verse relates to the short Greek poems, and it
can be devastating in epigrammatic lampoon as in the
longer lyrics. How can so few words carry so large a
weight, like an ant shouldering a boulder? His much-
anthologized 'I strove with none' is a fine example: a
biography in four lines, with a moral severity which a
lesser author would require several stanzas to convey. The
fact that Landor's themes are age-old commonplaces does
not render them the less useful. His forms, too, are
traditional. His originality is in the fact that he used
them, and used them so well, in the nineteenth century.
One can be an 'innovator', as Robert Pinsky points out
in his excellent study of Landor's poetry, by reviving,

adapting and developing traditional forms. Such a commitment is a guarantee against excess, untruth, perilous invention: 'Thoughts when they're weakest take the longest flights,/And tempt the wintry seas in darkest nights.'

Not least among Landor's poems are those addressed to members of his family (for example the excellent 'To My Child Carlino') and to his friends (Wordsworth, Browning, Dickens and others) and poets whom he admired but never met (Keats, Burns). They convey judicious observations on life and literature, praise, celebration, advice. To Browning he writes, as of himself:

There is delight in singing, though none hear
Beside the singer: and there is delight
In praising, though the praiser sit alone
And see the prais'd far off him, far above.

'Landor,' says Pinsky, 'not only wrote well, but he also had a peculiar, extreme concern for the idea of writing well, and this concern modified every subject he touched.' Pinsky places Landor exactly: 'Landor's career seems especially pertinent to the definition of two kinds of poetry: poetry which emphasizes the discovery of content' – as Wordsworth's does – 'and poetry which emphasizes the discovery of tone.' If we analyse a lyric by Landor, we are apt to find that its effect is well in excess of its 'content', that the experience of it vanishes before analysis. It is not that the poems lack meaning, but that the meaning is largely the effect, itself a product of the tone.

Landor left his mark largely on other poets. Later in the century Swinburne and Hopkins read him attentively. Ezra Pound is his most eloquent modern champion. If Pound makes excessive claims for him, these claims have at least helped to generate new interest in a writer who in his best work brought into English poetry qualities which were tonic in his time – in any time.

George Gordon, Lord Byron
1788–1824

Thou shalt believe in Milton, Dryden, Pope;
   Thou shalt not set up Wordsworth, Coleridge, Southey . . .

Byron, with Burns and Sir Walter Scott, is probably the best-known British Romantic on the Continent. With Scott he shares narrative skills and a strong sense of audience and how best to exploit it. With Burns he shares verbal directness in poems such as 'To Thomas More' and 'So, we'll go no more a'roving', and certain political sympathies: peer and ploughman were both in different centuries radicals. All three were sons of Scotland, though Byron's roots in that nation did not go very deep.

Byron still divides poetry audiences into partisans and opponents. W. H. Auden, after describing just how peculiar and extraordinary the poet's life was, assures us that 'He had no unusual emotional or intellectual vision, and his distinctive contribution to English poetry was to be, not the defiant thunder of a rebel angel, but the speaking voice of the tolerant man-about-town.' Of course, Byron did not have emotional or intellectual vision. Ford Madox Ford doubted whether he had an intellect at all, and was confident that he had no heart (a point on which Auden seems agreed). The word 'tolerant' is at least debatable. Auden urges Byron as a model for those young poets, presumably without vision, who wish to write with 'speed, wit, and moral seriousness combined with lack of pulpit pomposity'. Ford disagrees: 'To an Anglo-Saxon concerned for his poetry and his language, both verse and language of Byron are odious.' Ford despises Byron's speech and his posturing. In him he identifies a vulgarity – not the honest vulgarity of a writer like Burns, but a profound vulgarity of sensibility, a moral dishonesty which is part and parcel of his heartlessness. Byron is, certainly, undiscriminating. His attacks on Southey, Wordsworth, Coleridge and Keats are the effusions of prejudice rather than the fruits of judgement. Byron hated Southey's conversion from radicalism to Toryism: this condemned the older poet *tout court*. But Byron had not lived through the trauma of the French Revolution. His politics were not *lived* until he courageously went to Greece to put them to the test. He was a Whig aristocrat whose politics were more the product of certain social aversions and personal pique than of pondered experience. It is significant that Greece was the theatre he chose to act in. His conscience was more energetic abroad than in England.

Unfortunately, biography is a necessary critical tool when we approach Byron's verse. His most original invention was the Byronic Hero, and one must determine the degree to which this creature, his attitudes and gestures, correspond with Byron, and to what degree they amount to a *persona*, a consistent mask through which he projects his views.

He was born with an ill-formed foot in London in 1788, son of a profligate Scottish aristocrat and officer and an emotionally volatile and unstable heiress. His parents separated in 1790 when Byron's father had spent most of his wife's fortune. The son idealized his absent father, a violent and egotistical man. He also suffered from a Calvinist nurse who filled him with forebodings about damnation.

He came into the title in 1798, went to Harrow and then in 1805 to Trinity College, Cambridge. His physical disability made him aggressively eager to excel in anything that tested courage and prowess. He was a man of enormous energy in love and other activities. At Cambridge he published his first book, *Fugitive Pieces* (1806) and then republished it the next year in two revised, enlarged and retitled versions. It was hardly a remarkable début, but it did not perhaps merit the contempt it received in 1808 in the *Edinburgh Review*. The attack was productive: in 1809 appeared Byron's first important poem, his satire *English Bards and Scots Reviewers*, over a thousand lines of invective and justification, in which the poet assumes an aloof and superior tone belied by the length and obvious rancour of his piece. He connects his name with those of Pope, his chief idol, and Dryden. In defending himself he attacks everyone else in sight, including Southey, Wordsworth and Coleridge. The poem is an essay of considerable skill but it evinces little judgement either of the poet's own work or of that of his contemporaries.

He left England in 1809 and spent two years abroad in Portugal, Spain, Greece and the Levant. He swam the Hellespont and addressed some amusing verses to Leander. And he started the composition of *Childe Harold's Pilgrimage*, a fictionalized account of his travels. The narrator is not the ebullient Byron known to his foes and friends, but morose, enigmatically bitter, good-looking, intelligent, cultured, with certain social ideals and an eye for the picturesque. If he were less nebulous he would be fascinating. As he travels he reflects on what he experiences. More interesting than these reflections is the question: why is he so *gloomy*? Byron was not quick to deny that Childe Harold and George Gordon were the same person. Was this his darker side? Inspired by his nurse's Calvinism, perhaps, or his love for his sister? In fact the narrator isn't quite Byron. He is the beginning of the Byronic Hero. The poem is struggling towards dramatic monologue form. The lack of overall design, the chronicle progression, and the unifying force residing entirely with the narrator, point towards the picaresque mode of *Don Juan*, Byron's masterpiece.

He returned to England in 1811 to find his finances in

disrepair. So he wrote. Books one and two of *Childe Harold's Pilgrimage* appeared in 1812. Byron was 'famous overnight'. He soon began to capitalize on his success, writing a series of verse narratives, popular adventure novellas as it were. *The Giaour* (1813) went into eight editions in one year. There were *The Bride of Abydos, The Corsair, The Prisoner of Chillon,* and others. These works are poems by virtue of the fact that they are in efficient verse. They offer no interpretation of experience but rather escape into adventure, with bold characterization – the heroes usually have a secret and undergo hardship – and some violence and romance.

Such works earned him money and fame. The skills they display are considerable. As well as his picaresque epics and satires, his narratives and squibs, he wrote lyrics, the visionary 'The Dream', elegies and plays. The best of his dramas – which are not the best of his work – are *Cain* (in particular), *Manfred* and *Sardanapalus.*

Following in his father's footsteps, he married an heiress in 1815 and left her in 1816, for reasons never satisfactorily explained, after the birth of a daughter. There was a scandal and the poet rounded on what he took to be social hypocrisy. He left England for Italy and never returned home.

His books continued to appear. The third and fourth books of *Childe Harold's Pilgrimage* (1816, 1818) were successful. *The Lament of Tasso* was a dramatic monologue spoken by Tasso to his beloved in prison. In a similar spirit he later put words about Italian independence into the mouth of Dante. In 1818 he began the first five of the sixteen books of the unfinished *Don Juan* and, as it were to warm up for that task, composed *Beppo.* He became friendly with the Shelleys and in 1822 joined with Leigh Hunt to produce the *Liberal,* a periodical which ran for four issues and carried his most famous attack on Southey and his most effective personal satire, *The Vision of Judgement.* In 1824 he joined the Greek army in the struggle for independence from the Turks. He died of a fever in Missolonghi in 1824.

Byron's hatred for 'sentimental and sensibilitous' people, reflected in his dismissal of Keats, became an aggressive virility in his work and masked his own sexual ambivalence. Everywhere in his work one senses his impetuous, unresting nature, and personal amorality of a sort which was to become more common later in the century: 'the great object of life is sensation – to feel that we exist, even though in pain.' One cannot help thinking of Rochester in connection with Byron, not only in terms of their moral views but also of their stress on 'Nothing', and the formulation of the preacher in Ecclesiastes, 'Vanity of Vanities'. The most illuminating difference between them is intellectual. Rochester had and developed ideas, while Byron had opinions and prejudices which, as Auden suggests, were commonplace, certainly not 'unusual'.

Among the shorter poems, some of the passionate 'Hebrew Melodies' stand out as fine lyrics with, at times, balladic power. There are passages in *Childe Harold's Pilgrimage* which anthologists can never resist – for example 'Roll on, thou deep and dark blue ocean' from Canto IV. Those entrusted with making selections from Byron are faced with a difficult choice. Swinburne's selection includes large chunks, Arnold's includes principally purple passages. Swinburne chose for sonority and extension, Arnold for shape and content. Swinburne was right: Byron's effects are cumulative. The local felicities are less happy when they are divorced from context.

Byron conceived both *Beppo* and *Don Juan* after reading a poem by John Hookham Frere. From him he borrowed the *ottava rima* form – he had used it before, but never in satirical spirit – and a poetic plan, which was to have no plan, to write a picaresque work, open-ended, reminiscent of Laurence Sterne's narrative in *Tristram Shandy*. In *Beppo* Byron mastered the measure; in *Don*

Juan he mastered the digressive manner. He chose for his scene nothing less than the whole world.

Don Juan which, as Eugenio Montale says, is Byron's only *readable* poem, records six major and several lesser adventures of the hero, a passive man whom circumstances and women draw into action. The adventures begin in the boudoir of Donna Julia in Spain, include cannibalism in an open boat, and the famous love affair with Haidée, the high-point of Byron's art. The amusing scenes in Turkey, where Juan is sold into slavery and encounters the Sultana Gulbayez ('Christian, canst thou love?') give way to the Russian court and Catherine II's inclinations. The poem ends, or is discontinued, in the midst of Juan's diplomatic mission to England, where three ladies court him. Amongst the light satire and frivolity there are passages of impassioned writing, especially in the third canto, when Byron writes 'The isles of Greece', a superb statement of commitment to a cause.

The mountains look on Marathon –
  And Marathon looks on the sea;
And musing there an hour alone,
  I dream'd that Greece might still be free;
For standing on the Persians' grave,
I could not deem myself a slave.

It rises to suasive passion: but it ends with a vision, not of popular freedom, but of a hero.

Byron's creation of the *Don Juan* narrator is his artistic triumph. The voice, urbane and amusing, is that of a droll cynic who can speak with great tact and delicacy, as in the Haidée episode, but is also capable of virulence, good-humour, mischief and bathos. Byron deflates many portentous stanzas with an absurd rhyme, the silliest being 'Euxine' and 'pukes in'. The narrator can talk on any subject, loves digressions more and more as the poem proceeds, and responds in whatever way the subject requires. He is responsible for the poem's limitations as well. What Landor wrote of Byron's work as a whole has particular force with reference to *Don Juan*. Byron, he says, 'possesses the soul of poetry, which is energy; but he wants that ideal beauty which is the sublimer emanation, I will not say of the real, for this is the more real of the two, but of that which is ordinarily subject to the senses.' In short, there is progression without unity. In the narrative each incident is isolated from the one before. There are some parallelisms and contrasts, but as often as not they are accidental. It is the vice of picaresque writing that it has no memory, it forgets its adventures as soon as they are done.

From the outset the tone presents a problem. 'And if I laugh at any mortal thing,/'Tis that I may not weep': yet there is little in the poem for tears. The serious subjects are seriously treated – for example the question of Greek freedom. Byron calls the poem an 'Epic Satire'. But there is more comedy than satire in it. That is to say, there is no consistent satirical perspective and no consistent target. Wellington and the court come in for effective direct assault at various points, and critics find other correspondences. But satire in the poem is switched on and off at will. The poet laughs at his own language more often than he chastises any particular evil. In scope, the poem is epic, including Europe, Africa and Asia Minor in the action. But it is an epic without gods.

The *theme* of *Don Juan* is reversal in language and action, a movement from what seems to what is. At the outset, Juan's parents are presented as paragons of beauty and virtue. Each is then undermined with small telling details, until we know Doña Inez to be a doting hypocrite (based on Byron's own mother). Each possible relationship is thwarted, each outlandish fear is actualized. The morality of the poem, if it has one, seems to be the breaking down of self-deception, and we too are betrayed time and again by Byron, as by Sterne, in what we expect and desire from the narrative.

We lose interest in the story after the first five books and concentrate on the sexual, alimentary and travel imagery, on incident and digression, and finally on the narrator himself. He takes over from his hero, reminisces, cajoles, jests. The poem becomes more a journal than a narrative, and the increasing casualness of the author after the relative narrative completeness of the early books proves the lack of overall conception. The poem loses momentum and interest in proportion as the narrator plays with our expectations. His cleverness becomes a wearisome mannerism, repetitious and wilful. 'My tendency is to philosophize/On most things, from a tyrant to a tree.'

Byron's creative life divides into two periods: 1805–1817 (before *Beppo*) and 1817–1824 (after *Beppo*). The discovery of a new use for *ottava rima* provided him with the ideal vehicle for his expression. He could write a 'moral satire' without any specific morality of his own. He was a judge working, as it were, without laws, attacking hypocrisy but not from a perspective of self-knowledge. The knowing tone which gains the reader's complicity stands in for any deeper integrity. The language is efficient without delicacy or 'effeminacy'. In *Don Juan* the narrator at times becomes indistinguishable from Byron himself.

Percy Bysshe Shelley 1792–1822

Walk upon the winds with lightness,
Till they fail, as I am failing,
Dizzy, lost, yet unbewailing.

'Wordsworth, Scott, and Keats,' wrote Matthew Arnold, 'have left admirable works; far more solid and complete works than those which Byron and Shelley have left. But their works have this defect – they do not belong to that which is the main current of the literature of modern epochs, they do not apply modern ideas to life.' So much the better, we might be tempted to think. But Arnold continues, 'They constitute, therefore, *minor currents*,' and so, he claims, does the work of their followers. By contrast, Shelley and Byron will be remembered 'long after the inadequacy of their actual work is clearly recognized, for their passionate, their Titanic effort to flow in the main stream of modern literature; their names will be greater than their writings.' The last part of Arnold's prophecy has come true to some extent. If Shelley is not quite so effective a name to conjure with as Byron, if his biography and beliefs – in free love, revolution and so on – are less celebrated, it is because Shelley had a far better mind, with ideas as well as opinions. He did not court an audience. He was a poet first and last, a man of vision. What clouds his work is in fact the very 'modern ideas' Arnold attributes to him, ideas which have no practical application and are no longer modern; and a conscious distance from what Arnold means by 'life'. His roots in a particular landscape and community were quite as shallow as Byron's; or perhaps one should say that the aristocratic *milieu* into which he was born was too shallow to detain him. It did provide him with the voice of a gentleman, but at heart he was cosmopolitan, a European, a disciple of Goethe. The Mediterranean held an irresistible attraction for him. He learned lessons from classical philosophy and literature, Italian and Spanish culture. Dante was among his masters and he translated some of the *Divine Comedy*. He also translated passages of Homer, Euripides, Virgil, Cavalcanti, Calderón and Goethe.

In a sense Byron and Shelley are part of the dynamic surface of English poetry, the 'major current' which has more or less flowed away; their language and sentiments have been so successful as to have been trivialized. To read them today, one must break down the trivializing barriers. Inevitably one recognizes in Shelley the greater poet of the two.

Both poets – who became friends – had in common, as well as class and opinions, certain formative experiences. But there were radical differences in their poetic programmes. Shelley's political and philosophical formulations were the product of positive thought and desire rather than reaction. In aesthetic terms Byron was old-fashioned in comparison with Shelley, for Shelley advanced the art of English poetry by an original approach to language and an original – if fanciful – view of the poetic vocation and character.

Percy Bysshe Shelley was born in 1792 at Field Place, Horsham, Sussex, the family seat. His father was a baronet. He attended Eton, where he concentrated on scientific studies. He was already writing, and reading the fashionable literature of the time. In 1810 he went up to University College, Oxford. There he read Godwin's *Political Justice*, which fired his imagination. The next year he was sent down for allegedly writing a pamphlet entitled *The Necessity of Atheism*. In the same year he married the sixteen-year-old Harriet Westbrook whom he left after three years. She drowned herself in the Serpentine in 1816.

He entered upon a correspondence with Godwin and carried his radicalism into a wider arena in 1811. Robert Southey influenced the verse of his *Queen Mab*, but when he met Southey, the older poet's political views repelled him. He admired Leigh Hunt for his liberal outspokenness, however, and became friendly with him. More fruitful was his friendship with Thomas Love Peacock, the novelist. In 1821 Shelley answered Peacock's *Four Ages of Poetry* with his well-known *Defense of Poetry*.

In 1814 he called at Godwin's house and met Mary – Godwin's daughter by Mary Wollstonecraft – with whom he eloped to the Continent. In 1816 they were married. *Alastor: or The Spirit of Solitude* was composed in 1815–16. Shelley describes this Miltonic poem 'as allegorical of one of the most interesting situations of the human mind', namely, 'a youth of uncorrupted feelings and adventurous genius' (a projection of Shelley himself) 'led forth by an imagination inflamed and purified through familiarity with all that is excellent and majestic, to the contemplation of the universe.' The 'Preface' is a catalogue of abstractions. The poem is better than the description. It ends when Alastor, frustrated in his search for the embodiment of the ideal, 'descends to an untimely grave'. It is a sort of Platonist's *Prelude*, floating free of the informing world and existing in an eloquent void. To this period also belongs the 'Hymn to Intellectual Beauty'.

In 1816 the Shelleys were with Byron on the Continent, and returning made the acquaintance of Keats. Keats and Shelley became amicable rivals. Shelley wrote *The Revolt of Islam* (1817) in 'competition' with *Endymion*. He left England again in 1818, disaffected with a social world he saw through the eyes of the embittered Byron. He translated Plato's *Symposium* and steeped himself in Greek literature. In 1819 he wrote *Prometheus Unbound*, one of his masterpieces in terms of prosody and construction. He allegorizes his sense of the modern state of liberty of imagination in the central metaphor, and he develops his philosophy of endurance and creation:

To suffer woes which Hope thinks infinite;
To forgive wrongs darker than death or night;
    To defy power, which seems omnipotent;
To love, and bear; to hope till Hope creates
From its own wreck the thing it contemplates;
    Neither to change, nor falter, nor repent;
This, like thy glory, Titan, is to be
Good, great and joyous, beautiful and free;
This is alone Life, Joy, Empire, and Victory.

The Cenci was composed around the same time. It is more dramatically successful than the Romantic plays written by his contemporaries, but the high claims some critics make for it are doubtful.

1819 was his first year of sustained creation. In response to the Peterloo Massacre he composed the impassioned *The Mask of Anarchy*. He wrote for an imagined audience and adopted a plain form of address. The usually soaring poet hovers near to the actual earth and delivers himself of a direct and extremely suasive statement about political fear and violence:

I met murder on the way –
He had a mask like Castlereagh –
Very smooth he looked, yet grim;
Seven blood-hounds followed him.

The corrupt oppressors are simply and vividly drawn, as in a cruel caricature. Hope addresses the oppressed in lines which float free of context with the power of slogans:

'Rise like Lions after slumber
In unvanquishable number –
Shake your chains to earth like dew
Which in sleep had fallen on you –
Ye are many – they are few!'

Yet it is not the popular language of ballad. Such language was beyond the range of this aristocratic populist. He can write directly, but only in his own manner. The poem is an allegorized narrative, not a documentary account. Abstractions moralize an abstract action. In this case the allegory is clear because specific incidents provoked it: and even if we did not know the cause for the poem, it would still be effective.

'Ode to the West Wind' was prompted by a sense of personal loss. Both his children by Mary had died, he was homesick and politically disappointed. 'To a Skylark' and 'The Cloud' belong to this important period, and 'The Sensitive Plant' and 'Letter to Maria Gisborne' followed. Towards the end of 1819 Shelley met Sophia Stacey, for whom he wrote 'The Indian Serenade' ('I arise from dreams of thee'), 'To Sophia' ('Thou art fair, and few are fairer') and other poems. To a later love, Emilia Viviana, he wrote *Epipsychidion* (1821).

Unlike Byron, Shelley valued Keats highly ('a rival who will far surpass me') and invited him to Italy. Keats declined, though he made his final journey later in the year. Upon his death Shelley composed 'Adonais', his best elegy – some say it is more about Shelley himself than about Keats – and perhaps his best poem. Shelley referred to it as 'the least imperfect of my compositions'. It is one of the clearest expressions of his Platonic philosophy, outshining *The Witch of Atlas* with its lucidity.

When the Greek war of independence began Shelley wrote *Hellas* (1821). His later poems were increasingly occasional in character. He satirized Wordsworth in 'Peter Bell the Third', a long and eventually doleful jest against Wordsworth's subject-matter and manner. In 1822 some of his finest lyrics, including 'O, world! O, life! O, time!' and 'When the Lamp is Shattered', appeared. He worked on the unfinished *Triumph of Life* and joined Byron and Hunt in planning the magazine the *Liberal*. In July, sailing to Lerici, Shelley was drowned when his boat, the *Don Juan*, foundered in bad weather. Had he not died, what direction would his work have taken? There was evidence that he was developing towards clearer outline in his poems, a more direct relationship between his imagination and the world it was compelled to occupy. The power of specific impulses was already a chief motive in the mature poems; the specific image might have followed.

The most memorable characterization of Shelley's work is Arnold's: 'a beautiful and ineffectual angel, beating his wings in a luminous void in vain.' George Santayana defended him ambiguously: 'Shelley really has a great subject matter: what ought to be; and ... he has a real humanity – though it is a humanity in the seed, humanity in its internal principle, rather than in those deformed expressions of it which can flourish in the world.' This is as much as to say, with Arnold, that the angel beats its wings not in the world but in a void. It sees 'what ought to be' but has no strategy for bringing the ideal into being. Leavis writes that, 'Shelley, at his best and worst, offers the emotion in itself, unattached, in the void.' T. S. Eliot found he could read Shelley when he was fifteen, but not later on, for Shelley's ideas required assent or dissent, belief or disbelief. 'I can only regret that Shelley did not live to put his poetic gifts, which were certainly of the first order, at the service of more tenable beliefs – which need not have been, for my purpose, beliefs more acceptable to me.'

Some of Shelley's figures are drawn from his early scientific studies. Edmund Blunden tells us that 'many of the poet's strangest and most seemingly superficial figures are his presentations of scientific fact as it was accepted in his day.' This is interesting, but not very helpful to the modern reader. More to the point, Blunden shows how recurring figures in the long poems – few are without eagles, serpents, sunrises, storms – do not possess a consistent value. Now a specific man is an eagle, now the eagle embodies a vision or idea. One thing is certain, however. Shelley's eagle is never an eagle. As well as the variable figures, Shelley uses certain adjectives time after time not to clarify the sense but to impart a tone, a colouring.

Shelley has, if not two voices, two processes. The one urges into the void, with large statements whose actual applicability eludes us. These are statements by the poet as 'unacknowledged legislator of mankind' – also unelected and without constituency. The other process tends to particularize emotion: the love poems, elegies, statements of disappointment or resignation. Often the same abstracting technique is at work, but the poems have a determined effect, as in 'Stanzas written in Dejection near Naples' or 'Lines written among the Euganean Hills'. Between these two processes there is a crucial difference: the first constructs experience, the second interprets it. Shelley's most popular poems are in the latter category. He sees himself as a moral but not a didactic writer: he seeks to 'awaken' and 'enlarge' the mind, and this he does most effectively through experience, not through projection.

F. R. Leavis mounts an attack on Shelley. He argues that the poet requires a suspension of the critical intelligence. Shelley's figurative language is at fault, there is 'a general tendency of the images to forget the status of the metaphor or simile that introduced them and to assume an autonomy and a right to propagate, so that we lose in confused generations and perspectives the perception or thought that was the ostensible *raison d'être* of imagery'. Leavis goes on to speak of Shelley's 'weak grasp upon the actual', and we demur. A number of poems come to mind in which the actual is recognizably rendered: 'Music, when soft voices die', 'Ozymandias', 'Sonnet: England in 1819', 'Lines to an Indian Air', passages in *Prometheus Unbound*, 'Song to the Men of England':

Wherefore feed, and clothe, and save,
From the cradle to the grave,

Those ungrateful drones who would
Drain your sweat – nay, drink your blood?

Perhaps it depends upon what one means by actual. Shelley proves that an idea *can* be as actual and poetically viable as an image: it depends, of course, upon the realization of that idea. Certainly metaphor generates metaphor in Shelley, and the poems often tend away from their point of departure. Much of the time this is a consistent technique, an attempt at creative disorientation in order to release ideas from the trammels of what *is*. Static imagery acts against this process; hence imagery and metaphorical language are set in process, are interrelated but not related outwards to specific points in the world, which would distort the Platonic realism of his ideas. The language contains its meanings, emancipated from the actual, as a self-referring structure. Swinburne, without Shelley's serious philosophical sanction, carried this strategy to extremes.

Implicit in Shelley's work is a radical questioning of the rationalist tradition, of normative and conventional art. His emphasis on emotional fluency, on the mystical source of poetry (the dying coal), his belief in the centrality of the poet, are well enough known, and certainly not popular in England today. That poetry is 'not subject to the control of the active powers of the mind', that there is no 'necessary connection' between it and 'consciousness or will' – such a view is almost offensive. One does well to distrust Shelley. But within the vast range of his poetry, plays and prose there are, apart from masterpieces to be valued, lessons to be learned, even if only by reaction. His imaginative strategies cannot be borrowed, any more than Milton's can, but they are in a deeper sense exemplary. The unoriginal young poet can turn to Byron for simple lessons, but the serious and questing poet will recognize in Shelley a more valuable mentor.

John Clare 1793–1864

No, not a friend on earth had I
But my own kin and poesy.

'The golden furze-blooms burnt the wind', 'hollow trees like pulpits', 'the velvet of the pale hedge-rose': John Clare has a distinctive vision of natural detail. In poem after poem he effaces himself in loving contemplation of his subject. His distinctive pathos, not heard elsewhere in English poetry, consists in his perception of the vulnerability of natural things, and of his own vulnerability reflected in them. But in the nature poems he is reluctant to speak of himself. As Edmund Blunden wrote, 'In spite of his individual manner, there is no poet who in his nature poetry so completely subdues self and mood and deals with the topic for its own sake.' He expresses himself in the choice of flora and fauna and in the words he applies to them, but such 'self-expression' is only obliquely an objective of the poet. The weather in his poems is seldom stormy, there is little heightening of natural processes. The external world remains external. He chooses insects for their distinct otherness:

These tiny loiterers in the barley's beard,
And happy units of a numerous herd
Of playfellows ...

or birds, flowers, streams, fields, meadows. 'Fairy Things' is a characteristically particularizing poem. Most of his work is in the present tense, precisely focused: 'He gives no broad impressions – he saw the kite but not the kite's landscape,' wrote Edward Thomas. Yet taken together the poems reveal in rich detail the Northamptonshire countryside that was his world.

Born in Helpstone in 1793, he was ill-placed for poetry from the outset. His father, the illegitimate son of a wandering fiddler-schoolmaster and the parish clerk's daughter, was a farm labourer who, though poor, did his best to educate the boy. Clare interspersed farm work and studies. At the age of seven he was tending the geese; before his teens he was helping at the plough.

Clare fell in love with Mary Joyce, whose father eventually forbade their friendship. He came in his madness to regard her as his first wife, to whom he addressed poems, and with whom he held conversations in his mind long after she died a spinster.

The poet farmed, gardened, became a soldier, even spent some time among gipsies. He read what he could: Thomson's *The Seasons* first helped him define his own direction. He was 'itching at rhymes' (an expression he uses several times). When he was twenty-seven his first book, *Poems Descriptive of Rural Life and Scenery*, appeared. It was a success, running through four editions in one year.

In the same year he married, and within a month the first of his children was born. He visited London and was exhibited to literary and aristocratic circles. He had been classified a 'peasant poet', a character which limited his scope and which he came to regret. Success raised great expectations and distanced him from his rural community. It was little short of disastrous for him, for the fame proved short-lived. He had hoped for financial security, but that goal he was never to achieve.

The Village Minstrel appeared with rather less success the next year. Clare visited London again, met Lamb, Hood and others, and began contributing verse and prose to periodicals on a regular basis. His prose articles and letters have a character all their own, homespun and frank. But verse was his natural medium.

In 1823 he began to suffer periodic illnesses not unconnected with his later mental troubles. In 1824 he spent more than two months in London, meeting Coleridge and De Quincey. De Quincey held him up as an example: here was a man who, without advantages, rose on genuine merit to literary achievement. 'His poems were not the mere reflexes of his reading. He had studied for himself in the fields, and in the woods, and by the side of brooks.' His chief defect as a poet was his assiduous accuracy, which De Quincey felt tended to displace emotion. He recalls how in the metropolis the rural poet was drawn not so much by 'the gorgeous display of English beauty, but the French style of beauty, as he saw it amongst the French actresses in Tottenham Court Road'. De Quincey also chronicles Clare's 'rapturous' enthusiasm for Wordsworth which 'depressed his self-confidence'.

The Shepherd's Calendar appeared belatedly in 1827, and failed. In seven years Clare had seen himself famous and forgotten. He was breadwinner for nine dependents, including his parents. The strain told on him. The years 1828 and 1829 were perhaps his best. In 1830 illness returned, he grew haggard and weak. Lord Milton provided him with a new cottage three miles from Helpstone, and he moved to it reluctantly. His madness began in earnest in 1833. *The Rural Muse* (1835) – his best book, though it appeared in a form very different from that he intended – failed despite good notices. It was the last book published in his lifetime. *The Midsummer Cushion* – a vast and uneven collection of his later work – was not published until 1979.

He was committed to an asylum in Epping Forest in 1837. Four years later he ran away home, making the four-day journey on foot and with considerable hardship. Soon he was shut up in the Northampton asylum, where he spent his remaining twenty-three years. He died in 1864.

Edward Thomas contrasts Clare with Burns: 'Unlike Burns, he had practically no help from the poetry and music of his class. He was a peasant writing poetry, yet cannot be called a peasant poet, because he had behind him no tradition of peasant literature, but had to do what he could with the current forms of polite literature.' The work has few of the characteristics of his class, though scansion and pronunciation sometimes reflect his North-amptonshire accent. Clare's sense of social issues – unlike Barnes's – is narrow and local: he apprehends them only as they affect him. He is harsh on those better-placed than he who misunderstand and misprize poetry and poets. 'An Effusion on Poesy' addresses a 'genteel opinionist in poetry':

Labour! 'cause thou'rt mean and poor,
Learning spurns thee from her door;
But despise me as she will,
Poesy! I love thee still.

In 'Impromptu on Winter' he identifies the 'petty gentry' with the chilling weather.

Close to his heart was the issue of enclosure. It distressed him for personal rather than social reasons. The plight of the peasants is not directly included in poems such as his lament for the loss of Swordy Well, where he had played and tended cows. 'The Fallen Elm', on the same theme, is one of his best poems; and 'Remembrance', written during his illness, returns to it again:

Enclosure like a Buonaparte let not a thing remain,
It levelled every bush and tree and levelled every hill
And hung the moles for traitors, though the brook is
    running still
It runs a naked stream cold and chill.

Such poems can be seen to include, in Clare's representative lament, the general loss. But his work is generally free of people, apart from those intimately associated with him. Poetry, like nature, is a place away from men:

'Thou light of the world's hermitage', an art that illuminates solitary devotion.

His poetic models were literary: his muse homely, but still a muse:

> who sits her down
> Upon the mole hill's little lap,
> Who feels no fear to stain her gown,
> And pauses by the hedgerow gap.

This precious lady is out of place in Clare's literal world. She is one of a number of conventional blemishes, which include borrowings in diction from Thomson, an excess of epithets and superfluous adjectives, a tendency to overwrite, all faults which became less numerous in his later work, and which the sympathetic reader learns to overlook. They hardly mar the excellence of visualization and presentation in such poems as 'Evening Schoolboys', 'Hares at Play', 'Rural Scenes', 'The Shepherd's Tree', 'My Schoolboy Days' or the autobiographical nightmare 'The Return' (1841): 'So on he lives in glooms and living death,/A shade like night, forgetting and forgot.' In diffuse form this poem expresses the same anguish as 'I Am', his best and best-known personal poem, in which his isolation is heightened by tempest and sea imagery, until he witnesses 'the vast shipwreck of my life's esteems'. The poem stands without apology beside Cowper's bleakest statements.

Clare's greatest poetic foe was his facility. He could write poem after poem without blotting a line. Sometimes they came merely from a joy at utterance. Facility and a reluctance to revise mean that many of the poems are effusions, go on too long, have no shape or cogent development. Some have arresting opening lines:

> Leaves from eternity are simple things
> To the world's gaze – whereto a spirit clings
> Sublime and lasting. Trampled underfoot,
> The daisy lives, and strikes its little root
> Into the lap of time ...

Such excellence is marred by prolixity as the poem unfolds. Facility admitted readily the conventional phrase; and Clare repeats images and whole lines from time to time.

The poet often begins his poem with 'I love' – the leaves, the gusts; or to walk, to hide, to hear. He describes what he loves, and that act of loving description is the poem. If the poem succeeds, we know *why* he loves. It is in the nature poetry that Clare's chief claim lies. The poems that show the tensions of his mental illness are more popular today, but for other than poetic reasons in most cases. The accomplishment of the poet who wrote, 'The fish were playing in the pool/And turned their milk-white bellies up', is visual and verbal. Clare may have come to imitate his earlier in his later work. His range of statement is not wide, and he was so prolific as almost to exhaust his rich subject matter. He is not, as some have claimed in recent years, a 'great poet'. But his best writing – I hesitate to say his best poems, for the best writing is often contained in weak poems – his best writing is in a class of its own. Only Edward Thomas, of later poets, learned its abiding lessons.

John Keats 1795–1821

And still they were the same bright, patient stars ...

'Milton had an exquisite passion for what is properly, in the sense of ease and pleasure, poetical luxury,' wrote John Keats, 'and with that, it appears to me, he would fair have been content, if he could, so doing, preserve his self-respect and feeling of duty performed.' But Milton had other passions, religious and social, and therefore 'devoted himself rather to the ardours than the pleasures of song'. Keats, unlike Milton, was almost content in his passion for poetical luxury. As Arnold said, 'Keats as a poet is abundantly and enchantingly sensuous; the question with some people will be, whether he is anything else.' Arnold sets out to prove that Keats, though he lacked fixed purpose, was in his pursuit of Beauty on his way towards something moral and wholesome, towards the 'ardours' of song. He quotes from Keats's 'Epistle to Reynolds':

> But my flag is not unfurl'd
> On the Admiral-staff, and to philosophize
> I dare not yet.

The virtue of Keats's poetry is precisely that he does not 'philosophize'. Unlike some of his Romantic contemporaries, he escaped the imposed distortion of a world view which, when it recognizes itself, adjusts the world to suit it.

Louis MacNeice is fanciful when he defines Keats as a 'sensuous mystic'. Such a category blurs into impressionism. Arnold is closer to the truth in suggesting that Keats's 'yearning passion for the Beautiful' (Keats's own expression) 'is not a passion of the sensuous or sentimental poet. It is an intellectual and spiritual passion.' Keats claimed that, had he been strong enough, he would have lived alone and pursued his quest for Beauty through particular experiments: 'I have loved the principle of beauty in all things.' 'I am certain of nothing but the holiness of the Heart's affections and the truth of the imagination.'

He was born in London in 1795, son of a livery stable manager who died when the boy was nine, leaving Keats, his brothers Tom and George, and his sister Fanny to the care of their mother. She remarried and sent the children to live with her mother at Edmonton. Mrs Keats died six years later of consumption, the illness which killed Tom in 1818 and Keats himself in 1821. The estate of his father was left in charge of managers of doubtful integrity, and when Keats most needed money none was to be had.

He attended school at Enfield from 1803 to 1811 and studied Latin, French and history. He translated the *Aeneid*, but only started his 'serious' reading after he had left school. He was apprenticed to a surgeon (1811) and when he was twenty entered Guy's Hospital as a student and dresser. His poems began to appear in print. Around his twenty-first birthday he composed his first great sonnet, 'On First Looking into Chapman's Homer'. The plan for *Endymion* (1818) took shape. He met Leigh Hunt who introduced him to artists and writers and shaped his early taste. Hunt, despite the aestheticizing influence he had on Keats's poetry at the time, convinced his young protégé of the connection between poetry and the other arts. Keats's best work often finds its pretext and inspiration in art rather than in nature. Hunt introduced him to Hazlitt and Haydon, two complementary intelligences, one acerbic and strict, the other expansive and enthusiastic. He was to meet Shelley (who elegized him in 'Adonais') and – in 1818 – Wordsworth.

With Shelley's help he published his first book of poems in 1817 and followed it with *Endymion* the next year. *Endymion* elicited savage reviews from *Blackwood's Magazine* and the *Quarterly Review*. Keats came to accept some of the justice of his reviewers' censure. But their hostility, it is now known, was a product of their ill-will towards the liberal Hunt: Keats was caught in the cross-fire. Certain poets were quite as hostile as the reviewers, however. Byron at a later date described Keats as 'this miserable self-polluter of the human mind'. Byron despised what he took to be the poet's effeminacy, passivity and nostalgia.

1818 was the beginning of Keats's majority. He composed 'Isabella, or the Pot of Basil', and in an eventful year saw his brother George off to America, nursed his brother Tom through his final illness, travelled to Scotland and Ireland, contracted his own consumption on the Isle of Mull in July, and met Fanny Brawne, with whom he fell precipitately in love and to whom he wrote those love-letters which Arnold described as 'underbred and ignoble'. They are not Keats's best letters. He also began the composition of *Hyperion*.

In 1819 he composed the main body of work for which he is remembered: 'The Eve of St Agnes', 'La Belle Dame Sans Merci', the great Odes, 'Lamia', and other work. He completed *Hyperion*. At the beginning of 1820 his fatal illness took hold. In September he sailed to Italy with his friend Severn. On board ship he wrote the final version of the sonnet 'Bright Star'. In November, from Rome, he wrote the last of his famous letters. In February 1821 he was buried in Rome. On his grave appears the epitaph, 'Here lies one whose name was writ in water.'

The last five years are remarkable for the wealth of Keats's human experience after he had decided to abandon medicine for poetry, and for the rapidity with which his writing matured. His earliest surviving work reveals his skill as a phrase-maker: he had an uncanny ability to catch an image in a memorable phrase or line. 'I look upon fine phrases as a lover,' he wrote. 'I stood tip-toe upon a little hill' reveals his early power and his faults. The volleys of adjectives and the occasional mixed metaphors make way for memorable visualizations. The clouds are 'pure and white as flocks new shorn' sleeping 'On the blue fields of heaven'; we hear 'A little noiseless noise among the leaves,/Born of the very sigh that silence heaves.' He decrees himself a poet of praise, who watches 'intently Nature's gentle doings'; and if, as Edward Thomas believes, we are given no sense of actual setting, we do experience a number of particular natural phenomena: the minnows, the flowers, the breezes. We meet with Apollo, a presiding spirit in his work; with the image of ascent, looking upward, and final soaring, which are important in several of his poems. In 'I stood on tiptoe' the emotion spills over images clearly described but does not fuse with those images. In his mature work, Keats contains emotion in the particulars evoked: indeed it is the emotion which unifies them. He had some way to go. The father of poets was still the 'dear delight/Of this fair world'. Nature he apprehended as isolated phenomena; the countryside was like a vast natural gallery; its underlying processes, which Wordsworth witnessed, were invisible to the casual walker.

In the 1817 volume, 'On First Looking into Chapman's Homer' is the only great poem. It defines a response: how he felt upon reading the book. He responds like an astronomer looking up at a new planet or like a Conquistador (a modern Odysseus, a warrior hero) looking down on a new sea. Planet and sea are actually old, but are seen for the first time.

'Sleep and Poetry', also in the 1817 collection, is over four hundred lines in length. It defines his 'poetics', such as they were at the time. Apollo glows in his firmament, and there is much concrete imagery. In rather unruly couplets the poet severely rejects Augustan conventions: 'musty laws lined out with wretched rules', the tendency to 'inlay, and clip, and fit' till 'the verses tallied'. Certainly these verses, with many feminine rhymes, a fulsome enthusiasm, and lack of clear progression, owe a very limited debt to the eighteenth century. 'A drainless shower / Of light is poesy,' he declares.

In *Endymion* Keats's rapid development began. The poem was written in a short time, and the poet admits it is 'a feverish attempt' and not 'a deed accomplished'. He asks at one point, 'Muse of my native land, am I inspired?' Probably not: but what is interesting in the poem, apart from the anthologized passages which are remarkable, is the evidence of a transition from the poet who praises to the poet who feels; from the poet who describes from without to the one who employs 'negative capability', abandons his own identity and writes as it were from within his images, 'becoming' the sparrow on the gravel. The poem develops the theme that beautiful forms and figures, myths richly told, clarify and strengthen the minds of men, not merely for a moment, but for ever. Poetry expands and permanently deepens the reader's awareness:

> Nor do we merely feel these essences
> For one short hour; no, even as the trees
> That whisper round a temple become soon
> Dear as the temple's self, so does the moon,
> The passion poesy, glories infinite
> Haunt us till they become a cheering light
> Unto our souls, and bound to us so fast,
> That, whether there be shine, or gloom o'ercast,
> They always must be with us, or we die.

Endymion's faults are structural. The verse is so delighted with the details of its setting, with nuances of look and movement, with its theme and its own self-intoxicating cadences, that the narrative is slow and nothing draws the local felicities into a satisfying whole. Some of the blame

for this failure belongs to Spenser, though many of the
virtues are Spenserian as well. The chief weakness is in
the mode itself which also condemned *Hyperion* and *The
Fall of Hyperion* to survive as unsatisfactory contexts for
some of Keats's most brilliant passages.

The poems composed in late 1818 and in 1819 move
beyond such criticism. The narratives 'Lamia', 'The Eve
of St Agnes' and 'Isabella, or the Pot of Basil' are compact
and dramatic and, though they have gothic and magical
elements, they enact human dramas, romantic in nature
and comprehensive in emotional range. The gods move
off. Keats ceases to moralize the poem as it progresses,
becomes the implicit interpreter.

In 'Lamia' he develops a story borrowed from Burton's
The Anatomy of Melancholy, one of his favourite books.
Lamia, a sorceress, loves Lycius. She is transformed into
a beautiful girl whom he courts and wins. At the wedding,
the sage Apollonius, Lycius's old tutor, recognizes Lamia
and names her. She vanishes, and with her all Lycius's
expectations and dreams. Lycius was deceived, but he
was joyful. The sage, representing truth, rescues him
from deceit and kills him.

Philosophy will clip an Angel's wings.
Conquer all mysteries by rule and line,
Empty the haunted air, and gnomed mine –
Unweave a rainbow, as it erewhile made
The tender-person'd Lamia melt into a shade.

The relation between feeling and fact fascinated Keats.
The poem enacts without resolving the theme. It is the
metaphor of an emotion, like most of the poems of his
maturity. 'Lamia' explores dream in the context of fact;
'The Eve of St Agnes' sets passion in the context of time,
a theme of great moment for a poet already aware of his
illness; and 'Isabella, or the Pot of Basil' portrays love
thwarted by social circumstances.

'The Eve of St Agnes' and 'Ode on a Grecian Urn'
approach Keats's main themes from different, not to say

opposite, angles. At the opening of 'The Eve of St Agnes' Keats distances us from the narrative, giving us a long view. We approach, the story is enacted and realized, and then, in a Chaucerian manner, it is thrown back into the long view. The lovers escape in time, but not from it. Madeline finds reality inferior to her dream: 'And those sad eyes were spiritual and clear: /How changed thou art! how pallid, chill and drear!' By contrast, in the 'Ode on a Grecian Urn', we are brought close to the object of contemplation from the first line, in which it is personified. The poet would animate the marble figures. But they have escaped from time and they can expect no fulfilment, they are eternally arrested. The poet leaves us in the presence of the urn: it is not distanced or placed in context but is its own context, fills our perception.

'The Eve of St Agnes' stresses the vulnerability of the lovers' relationship. Outside forces continually penetrate into the rooms. The storm is audible against the inner warmth, moonlight illuminates the inner scene; the wind agitates the inner furnishings. The elements intensify passion, and then absorb it when the lovers step into the night and cold reality. Age is the backdrop of their drama. Old Angela and the beadsman figure the future of youth. Through the poem we follow the contours of unresolved emotion, not the progression of a thought. Porphyro, the lover, knows without realizing the truth of passion, for he sings to Madeline 'an ancient ditty, long since mute' from Provence: 'La belle dame sans mercy'. Keats's poem of that title relates closely to his narratives, though it is more condensed and mysterious than they.

The three great verse narratives, with their rich detail, idealized characterization, and the gothic and magical elements, were of considerable importance to poets and painters later in the century. The Pre-Raphaelites in particular drew sustenance from them. 'The Eve of St Agnes', the best of the narratives, owes Chaucer a debt for its richness and tone, and Shakespeare a debt for its characterization. *Romeo and Juliet* cannot have been far from Keats's mind when he composed the poem. To Shakespeare there is a further debt for the phrasing of descriptions. *Cymbeline* may figure specifically in the evocation of Madeline's bedchamber. But Keats's poem is not imitative. He had by 1819 assimilated and appropriated the work of those poets who meant most to him, including Spenser and Milton as well.

The Odes – 'To a Nightingale', 'On a Grecian Urn', 'To Autumn', and the lesser 'To Psyche' and 'On Melancholy' – are Keats's finest works. He perfected in them his sense of form and coupled it with his proven tact in phrasing. One cannot complain of the poet's lack of experience nor can one say he reveals a merely sensuous imagination. The Odes are the final step beyond moral romance to the romance of feeling itself, feeling as subject, the 'true voice'.

In 'Ode to a Nightingale', the image of intoxication precedes the bird, which is not recognized until the fifth line and is never seen. Its effect announces it, and it remains a pure effect, a Dryad of the trees and not a literal creature. The first stanza introduces all the thematic ingredients of the poem: joy, sorrow, music, death, and the rapture which frees the poet into the world of sense. A conflict of desires develops in the poem: first a desire to become an equal of the Dryad, and second a desire to die at the height of the ecstasy its song inspires.

Perception is by senses other than sight, for in the darkness there is no light 'Save what from heaven is with the breezes blown/Through verdurous glooms and winding mossy ways'. Yet none of Keats's poems equals this one for vividness of evocation. All his senses are involved, drawn by the bird's song and the night away from the sordid world the bird has never known:

The weariness, the fever, and the fret
   Here, where men sit and hear each other groan;
Where palsy shakes a few, sad, last gray hairs,
   Where youth grows pale, and spectre-thin, and dies ...

Age and death: the death of his brother informs that last line. Recollection of the actual world breaks his reverie. How is he to escape – through poetry? His mind holds back, though his imagination is 'already with thee' in the light of heaven. Twice his emotion rises to the bird, twice it is recalled, first by the reality of the human condition and then by a sense of his own inadequacy. He contemplates death, but that thought corrects itself with the reflection that in death he would be deaf to the bird's 'high requiem'. The word 'forlorn' – like a bell, contrasting with the bird's song – calls him back again to the world. The bird flies as at the word's tolling, a sort of knell to the feeling and its cause. 'Fled is that music: Do I wake or sleep?' Keats's deepest feelings have woven themselves into the texture of the poem, itself elicited by an actual nightingale the poet heard in a garden. 'O for a life of Sensations rather than Thoughts!' he had written. The Odes achieve such a life. Thoughts are subservient to the tone of feeling, remain unresolved and potent.

'Ode on a Grecian Urn' remains Keats's most debated poem. It is well to remember that the urn, not Keats, declares 'Beauty is truth, truth beauty'. Keats adds, 'that is all/Ye know on earth, and all ye need to know.' Is it a statement of faith? Or is the 'ye' the urn, and is he reflecting on its knowledge rather than ours? The presentation of imagery, the repetitions of 'happy' and 'ever' and 'forever', with their intensely mournful effect, and the tone of the poem balance, if not contradict, the categorical closing statement. Can we assume the poem is different in kind from the other Odes and the narratives? In fact the conclusion cannot be usefully abstracted from the context of the poem itself.

Each stanza depends upon a contrast between the static portrayal and the activity portrayed. Opening with the 'still unravished bride of quietness', child of 'silence' and 'slow time', Keats moves on to examine the images on the urn: 'maidens loth', 'mad pursuit', 'struggle to escape', 'pipes and timbrels', 'wild ecstasy'. The serenity of the object gives way to the violence and passion of its decoration. The sexual element is strong throughout the first three stanzas, beginning with 'Thou *still* unravished bride', 'panting', fear and desire. Yet all are arrested at the height of passion. The actions that find fulfilment only in time are translated into a timeless context.

In the fourth stanza Keats passes on to the procession to sacrifice and the village which, emptied of its populace, will 'evermore' be silent and empty, and never know why it is 'desolate', only that it is so. In the last stanza the urn becomes a 'Cold Pastoral': the expression verges on oxymoron. Having brought the urn to life, revealing through the play of his imagination on it his own intense ambivalence about time and the nature of beauty, he delivers the final lines with an air of finality which only has a significance in the qualifying experience of the poem itself.

'Poetry should surprise by a fine excess, and not by singularity.' In the Odes what is dazzling is the fine excess, the wealth of entirely apposite imagery which, in stanzas of impeccable prosodic development, answers to the poet's deepest concerns. If Keats lacked the intellectual resources of Coleridge or Shelley, he came close all the same to solving problems of poetic form that they had puzzled over. The Odes indeed appear to the reader as the wording of his own highest thoughts, 'almost a remembrance'.

William Barnes 1801–1886

Come, Fanny, come! put on thy white,
'Tis Woodcom' feäst, good now! to-night.

William Barnes wrote his best poems in the Dorset dialect
for much the same reason that Burns wrote his in Scots.
'To write in what some may deem a fast out-wearing
speech-form may seem as idle as the writing of one's name
in snow on a spring day,' Barnes said. 'I cannot help it.
It is my mother tongue, and it is to my mind the only
true speech of the life that I draw.' There is no other
point of comparison between Barnes and Burns. If Burns
lacks repose, Barnes lacks driving energy, extremes of
feeling, flights of rhetoric, social and sexual urgency,
satiric sting. Burns was a Scots poet in the tradition of
Dunbar and Henryson. Barnes was an English dialect
poet. He tends a narrower field and ponders it at his
leisure. He is a wise poet, and a poet almost by chance.
He wrote his poems, 'as if I could not help it, the writing
of them was not work but like the playing of music.'
    Few poets are as inextricably part of their place as
Barnes. Hopkins wrote to Bridges, 'Barnes is a perfect
artist. It is as if Dorset life and Dorset landscape had
taken flesh and blood in the man.' This is as true of the
eclogues as of the lyrics and elegies. Hardy commented on
the same quality, the 'closeness of phrase to vision'.
Barnes's stated aim was 'to purify our tongue and enrich
it from its own resources'. This he did in 'Linden Lea',
'The Wold Well', 'Lullaby', 'The Clote', 'Woodcom'

Feäst' and many other poems which are spoken, naturally and natively.

He was born in Bagber, Sturminster Newton, Dorset, in 1801. His father was a farmer, and not very prosperous. When Barnes was five his mother died, and he was raised largely by aunts. The rural life he evokes in his poems was a lived, not an artificial experience. A poem in 'common' or 'national' English tells of his early years:

We spent in woodland shades our day
In cheerful work or happy play,
And slept at night where rustling leaves
Threw moonlight shadows o'er our eaves.
   I knew you young, and love you now,
   O shining grass, and shady bough.

The nostalgic conventionality of this language is seldom heard in the dialect poems. In 'The Leäne' – one of his best poems – he contrasts was and is:

Years ago the leäne-zides did bear grass,
   Vor to pull wi' the geeses' red bills,
That did hiss at the vo'k that did pass,
   Or the bwoys that pick'd up their white quills.
But shortly, if vower or vive
   Ov our goslens do creep vrom the agg,
They must mwope in the geärden, mwore dead than alive,
   In a coop, or a-tied by the lag.

The poem reflects on the consequences of enclosure.

The parish vicar and the schoolmaster took a close interest in the young Barnes. He learned Greek and Latin. At the age of thirteen he became a solicitor's clerk, and the solicitor furthered his education. When he was eighteen he became a clerk in Dorchester. His progress was gradual. He met Julia Miles, decided to marry her, and did so – nine years later. At the age of twenty-two he printed his first poems. One was a translation of Bion. He became an engraver, started a school, then another in Dorchester. He was a fine school-master, original and erudite. His chief learning was in languages. His poems attest to a knowledge of forms classical, Persian ('Woak Hill') and Welsh, among others. His *Philological Grammar* reveals him on at least nodding terms with the more than sixty languages which suggested his 'principles and forms'. *The Glossary of the Dorset Dialect* (1844, 1863, 1886) was his most valuable contribution to philology and lexicography.

His first collection, *Poems of Rural Life, in the Dorset Dialect*, appeared in 1844. Further collections followed in 1846 and 1868. As well as poetry, he wrote books on mathematics, currency, social questions and archaeology. E. M. Forster criticized his prose intelligence as 'provincial'. He might as well have said deeply rooted in a living community and language, and profoundly learned. 'Provincial', in Barnes's case, is not a pejorative term. Perhaps he pursues his desire to purge English of its Latinisms and to Saxonize it rather too far. But that was one of only a few intellectual excesses and did not mar the verse.

He became a Bachelor of Divinity (Cambridge) and was given his first church in 1847. His wife's death five years later provoked some of his finest poems and led to a decade of difficulty. Beyond the emotional was the practical bereavement: Julia had managed his affairs, a task for which he had no talent. In 1862 he was given his first and only living of Winterbourne Came, he was again secure and remained so until his death in 1886. For twenty-four years he was an exemplary parson. Thomas Hardy knew him at this time as the 'aged clergyman, quaintly attired in caped cloak, knee-breeches, and buckled shoes' – the shoes are on display in the Dorchester museum – 'with a leather satchel slung over his shoulders, and a stout staff in his hand'. A 'little grey dog' followed at his heels. Hardy memorialized Barnes in his fine poem 'The Last Signal' and later prepared a selection of his verse.

Barnes loved the lives around him. His concern at the enclosure of common land and its consequences for the poor farmers (his own uncle had been bankrupted) informs many poems. 'The Common A-Took In' is an eclogue on the subject. Thomas and John exchange views on the value of common land. Thomas comments,

'Tis handy to live near a common;
But I've a-zeed, an I've a-zaid,
That if a poor man got a bit o' land,
They'll try to teäke it vrom en.

He suggests that 'they' might rent out 'bits o' groun' which by rights belong to the poor in any case: a further indignity.

The eclogue form appealed to Barnes because, as C. H. Sisson writes, 'it suited his sense of the plurality of lives about him'. His poetry catches variety of inflection, tone and character. He took as his model the *Idyllia* of Theocritus in preference to Latin or English versions of the mode. 'The dialogue,' Sisson writes, 'is remarkable for being so ordinary. What other poet of mid-Victorian times has presented us with speakers of such solid actuality?' Metre and speech are perfectly wedded. And, Sisson adds, 'The resonances of the ancient speech carry with them more of the physical presence of the speaker, of the gestures and facial expressions and turns of mind and emotion. Speech is a physical thing, and poetry draws deeply upon the physical personality.' Among the best eclogues are 'A Ghost', 'The Veäiries', 'The Lotments' and 'The Heäre'.

The dialect elegies for Julia speak of a particular grief but generalize the griever into a representative rural figure. To have spoken otherwise would have been, for Barnes, self-pitying and bad taste. There are related poems of resignation which at once celebrate and lament things lost. 'The Happy Days when I were Young' and his last outstanding poem, 'The Geäte a-vallen to' are in this category. There are elegies in common English, too.

In praising the dialect poems, one should not overlook the English poems. There are moments in them of fine visualization: the rider recording 'My mare's two ears' white tips'; the 'ribby bark' of trees; nightfall when 'The mill stands dark beside the flouncing foam'. 'A Winter Night' is the sort of poem which may have sparked off some of Hardy's *Satires of Circumstance*. Of the English poems, 'Black and White' is perhaps the best. Its metrical dexterity, internal rhymes and alliteration 'in the Welsh manner', and the modulated refrain (Barnes's use of refrains is always masterly) place it on a par with some of Hardy's best work and with the best of Barnes's dialect poetry, too. It is a report on experience and a celebration:

At the end of the barton the granary stood,
Of black wood, with white geese at its side,
And the white-winged swans glided over the waves
By the cave's darksome shadows in pride:
Oh! the black and the white! Which was fairest to view?
Why the white became fairest on you.

Alfred, Lord Tennyson
1809–1892

Lo! in the middle of the wood,
The folded leaf is woo'd from out the bud
With winds upon the branch ...

'Do you know, a horrible thing has happened to me. I have begun to *doubt* Tennyson,' Hopkins wrote to a friend in 1864. His doubt began after reading *Enoch Arden* (1864). There he found competent, interesting verse, but without the continual excitement of Tennyson's earlier work. Hopkins chose the right time to record a doubt. Much of Tennyson's weakest work dates from the last thirty years of his life; and most of his best was written between 1830 and 1835.

Few poets have enjoyed a longer working life than he did. His first poems appeared in book form when he was eighteen, his last in the year of his death: sixty-five years of writing, and perhaps fifty of those with only Browning as a serious rival, and that only in the 1860s. Tennyson built his huge poetic edifice on a narrow base. A master wordsmith, he was unable to sustain extended form; he was no master of narrative; and he could not easily brook criticism, except from his brilliant friend Arthur Hallam (1811–1833), whose early death affected the course of Tennyson's life and poetry.

Alfred Tennyson, first Baron Tennyson, was born in Somersby, Lincolnshire, in 1809, son of an aggressively melancholy country rector from whom he inherited a temperamental gloominess, and from whom he received his early education in a well-provided rectory library. It was there that at the age of eight the poet began to write. In 1827 he and his elder brother, Charles Tennyson Turner, issued *Poems by Two Brothers*. In 1828 Tennyson went to Trinity College, Cambridge, where he met Hallam. Tennyson paid attention to Hallam, clarifying in discussion his ideas about the nature of poetic language. In 1830 *Poems Chiefly Lyrical* was published and received some hostile attention. Another book, *Poems*, followed in 1833. Hallam sent the first of these books to Leigh Hunt, who – having backed Keats, Shelley and Byron – set about 'discovering' Tennyson as well: 'We have seen no such poetical writing since the last volume of Mr Keats,' wrote Hunt. There was a flavour of Keats in the volumes that included 'Mariana', 'Claribel', 'The Lotus Eaters', 'The Palace of Art', 'The May Queen', 'Oenone' and 'The Two Voices', a debate on suicide. 'Tithonus', one of Tennyson's best poems, dates from this period, though it was not published until 1860.

Hallam died in Vienna in 1833. The loss was not only of an intimate friend and collaborator: Hallam was to have married Tennyson's sister, and it must have seemed to the poet like the loss of a brother. For nine years he published very little. He may have been distressed by a savage notice in the *Quarterly Review* which had trodden heavily on Keats and Shelley before him. But he was writing *In Memoriam*, the best of his long works; and he was courting his future wife and making heavy weather of his finances. *Poems* (1842) brought him back into the public eye. It included early work but also 'Locksley Hall', 'Ulysses', 'Morte d'Arthur' – the prototype for *Idylls of the King* – and other important work. In 1847 *The Princess: A Medley* appeared, memorable for its great lyrics which include 'The splendour falls', 'Tears, idle tears' and 'Now sleeps the crimson petal'. The blank verse narrative tide advances on these islands of lyric poetry, and they can be rescued from their context without damage to their integrity as poems.

In 1850 Tennyson received his public laurels and ful-
filled a private desire. He was married after a courtship
whose length reflected not reluctance but lack of money.
He published *In Memoriam*, and he became Poet Laureate in succession to Wordsworth. The 'Ode on Wellington' and 'The Charge of the Light Brigade' are masterpieces of Laureate art. Few Laureates have been so
apparently sincere and so prosodically competent in the
execution of their duties. 'The Charge of the Light
Brigade' entered and remained in the common memory.

Fame came to weigh heavily on him. He moved to
Farringford, Isle of Wight. *Maud: A Monodrama* (1855)
and the first four *Idylls of the King* (1859) confirmed his
hold on the English poetry of the day. *Enoch Arden*
registers the effect upon the poet of too strong a sense of
audience. Hopkins speaks of it as Tennysonian rather
than Tennyson, self-imitation. The Representative Voice
of Tennyson sounded, and some of his readers recoiled.
The sentimental rendering of a tale with great dramatic
potential – a tale like one of Crabbe's – and a failure of
subtlety were patent. The volume included 'The Northern Farmer, Old Style', a dialect poem which, beside
Barnes's, hardly merits attention. In 1869 *The Holy
Grail* appeared, and the Arthurian romance grew.

Over two decades remained to him. He had made a
second residence near Haslemere, and from there he
issued his verse plays. Shakespeare provided his model, but
Tennyson was a poet of lyrical reflection, and just as his
narrative skill was slight, so too his dramatic talents were
unsure. Nowhere are his narrative and dramatic limitations clearer than in *Maud*. Maud's madness is mere
ranting in comparison with Lear's madness. Lear's language breaks and resolves in purely connotative and
accidental combinations (controlled by the wider imaginative logic of the play). Lear's madness is dramatically
integrated by being syntactically and semantically dis-
integrated. Maud, for his part, raves in long lines which
are dramatically unconvincing because so lucid: not a

condition of mind but a state of feeling, or a statement about feelings, a passion against social and other ills. It is not the character who speaks – or if he speaks it is not in character. This is not to condemn the poetry, which is powerful, but the monologue mode that here fails the poet.

During Tennyson's years of dramatic enterprise he published *Ballads and Other Poems* (1880). *Tiresias, and Other Poems* (1885) salvaged some old and added new work. *Demeter, and Other Poems* (1889) included 'Crossing the Bar'. The appearance of his last book, *The Death of Oenone*, coincided with his own death in 1892.

Even excluding the plays, it is a vast *oeuvre*. In it we distinguish between poems of feeling and poems of sentiment, poems of thought and poems of received opinion. When Browning acquired an audience, he became garrulous. When Tennyson acquired an audience, he sometimes became sententious. And yet the Representative Voice doubts, and Tennyson's politics, like his religion, seem rooted in memory of the past and fear of the future. He is a liberal who distrusts progressivism even as he acknowledges the injustices and evils that fuel progressivism. In every respect Tennyson was intellectually an enigma, which is why he was, for many, a philosopher, a spokesman for their own indecisions and doubts.

Arnold wrote to his mother in 1860: 'The real truth is that Tennyson, with all his temperament and artistic skill, is deficient in intellectual power; and no modern poet can make very much of his business unless he is pre-eminently strong in this.' Arnold is right in his analysis but wrong in his conclusion. Had Tennyson possessed 'intellectual power' or genuine 'philosophy', it would hardly have improved his best lyrics, though he might have avoided some of his fatuities. His *poetic* weakness is not intellectual: it is a narrowness of register. He tried every genre he could find, he mastered any number of verse forms; but whole registers of language were inaccessible to him. When he tried consciously to elude his refining style, he turned out poems such as 'Dora', arch and affected, a talking down, quite unlike Wordsworth's voice in similar circumstances. Or he adopted dialect, without conviction or real authority.

Tennyson had poetic vices. They stemmed from his ignorance of the limits of his talent and led him to undertake enormous poetical expeditions kitted out with the wrong equipment. Yet his virtues too are great. He consistently maintains, even in dull poems, prosodic interest. His instinct for the appropriate rhythm in verse is unmatched among the Victorians. Its virtue is that it *is* an instinct. His passion for open vowels is sometimes monotonous, because it was part of his mimetic theory of language. He believed sound and syntax could create equivalents to motion and image. In 'The Palace of Art' he draws syntactical portraits. 'The Lotus Eaters' is a mimetic exercise. He is said to have regarded 'The mellow lin-lan-lun of evening bells' as his best line. To begin with he was more interested in shaping a language adequate for experience and image than in creating a suitable vehicle for ideas. He would often salvage old lines from forgotten poems and plug them into suitable new contexts.

Such lines came from the past and had a special virtue. The past was a place of certitude for the poet. Early in his career he began building Camelot and never substantially improved – in the whole of the *Idylls* – on 'The Lady of Shalott' and 'Morte d'Arthur', despite the slow eloquence of 'The Passing of Arthur. His Arthurian world is a dream place which nurtures lyrics, and where 'The Lady of Shalott' loses romantic innocence. As a background for action and heroic narrative it is too brittle and brightly painted to contain large figures without a degree of ironic adjustment and lightness, and Tennyson was not a poet who ironized.

He has another past to call on, and another stratum of myth and legend of more intimate concern to him. From there he retrieved two of his finest poems, 'Ulysses' and

'Tithonus'. Out of these characters he coaxes his most complete monologues: they answer to his need. 'Ulysses' was composed shortly after Hallam's death. Tennyson readily assumes the mask of age. He is in basic sympathy with his character and that character's inaction.

Ulysses's landscape illuminates his mind. Details are imbued with symbolic significance. It is remarkable how the speaker forces value from the very sense of partiality: the past is indeterminate and lost, recalled in fragments; the future is unclear. This condition usually led Tennyson to compose lyrics of despair. But here Ulysses pilots him towards an unsurrendering hope. Ulysses is totally isolated, separated from the islanders (hoarders, feeders, sleepers) who 'know not me', from his old comrades, from his own youth. 'I am become a name.' Tennyson achieves psychological plausibility by presenting the inconsistencies in Ulysses's reflections, his eager glossing over of motive. His son Telemachus will

> make mild
> A rugged people, and through soft degrees
> Subdue them to the useful and the good.

He thus ennobles and passes on to his son a responsibility he does not want for himself. His passion is to seek knowledge and adventure elsewhere, not in the present but *through* the past, to re-meet his peers. The mask of age is animated by the force of youth, the drive towards an ever-receding horizon. It is an emblem for the quest of the artist.

Arthur Hallam inspired the indirectness and the condensed evocative style of 'Ulysses' and of 'Tithonus'. One is tempted to call it 'symbolist' writing. Hallam's death inspired *In Memoriam*, a series of elegies in a taut quatrain form with a cyclic abba rhyme scheme which is simple and expressive in its redistribution of conventional rhyme emphases. The classical debts of the elegies to the Greek poets, to Horace and others, are clear in imagery and in conventions such as the garden of Adonis. There are direct phrasal echoes as well. It may have been these models which helped him to develop a private experience with wide general reference. In the sixth elegy he writes, 'Never morning wore/To evening but some heart did break.' Such passages invite the reader to attach his own grief to Tennyson's. With Virgilian tact he touches the deepest sentiments of the age, the sense of loss and the fear of the future, the generalized guilt and the religious doubt. The poem enacts a 'ritual of recovery' – moving from emotional despair through various stages not to happiness, but to a sort of wisdom, a metaphysical rebirth, a meeting beyond the grave, 'soul in soul'. The only plot or chronology is the cycle of the seasons which at first counterpoint and later corroborate the feelings of the poem. Easter and Christmas have a special, changing significance as the poems develop. Dream, memory and desire are qualified and at last controlled by duty, dogma and moral steadfastness. Tennyson called *In Memoriam*, with its steady ascent from the depths, a 'Divine Comedy'. The poet emerges from grief first by the agency of personification. 'Sorrow' becomes a figure, then 'Love' and 'Faith' move free. Thus the ideas are teased out of the feelings, gain force and at last ascendancy, until Tennyson can write, ' 'Tis better to have loved and lost/Than never to have loved at all.' Religion finds a foothold and helps in the recovery. But as T. S. Eliot pointed out, 'It is not religious because of the quality of its faith, but because of the quality of its doubt.' Tennyson acknowledges as much: 'There lives more faith in honest doubt,/ Believe me, than in half the creeds.' He illustrates it, too:

> but what am I?
> An infant crying in the night;
> An infant crying for the light:
> And with no language but the cry.

Or, more haunting, 'What hope of answer or redress?/ Behind the veil, behind the veil'. There is the plain language of despair as well: 'On the bald street breaks the blank day'; and 'A weight of nerves without a mind'. The use of religious imagery may be distasteful in 'They call me in the public squares/The fool that wears a crown of thorns', or in the identification of Hallam with Christ, his exaltation to the status of Victorian *hero* (the parallel between Carlyle's and Tennyson's thought has often been commented on), but this religious metamorphosis is necessary to the theme.

Tennyson spoke directly to his age in this very personal sequence. The success of *In Memoriam* as a long poem depends on its fragmentariness. The sections are, as it were, elegiac idylls, assembled into a progressing sequence. Like *Maud*, it is held together by what Eliot called 'the greatest lyrical resourcefulness that a poet has ever shown'. Elegies and poems of aftermath were Tennyson's particular *forte*.

The idyll, a brief poem that describes an idealized incident or scene, suited Tennyson in 'Ulysses' and 'Tithonus'. The *Idylls of the King*, despite – or because of – the labours Tennyson expended on them, fail. They are not idylls in the generic sense at all. They are chunks of Arthurian epic, large and a little vulgar, like those Victorian paintings that glitter with thick paint and seem to reflect rather than reveal themselves to the light. The poetry is written at low pressure, with none of the urgency that lends *Maud* and *In Memoriam* their compelling readability, their sense of discovery.

Among Tennyson's juvenilia is a poem called 'Song' ('A spirit haunts') which contains in small many of the qualities Tennyson later developed. Keats may have affected the early poem, but it is in Tennyson's distinctive style: formally complex, vivid in image and mimetic in language, answering at once to an actual scene and a subjective mood. The words evoke and enact in a single process:

The air is damp, and hush'd, and close
As a sick man's room when he taketh repose
    An hour before death;
My very heart faints and my whole soul grieves
At the moist rich smell of the rotting leaves,
    And the breath
  Of the fading edges of box beneath,
And the year's last rose.
    Heavily hangs the broad sunflower
      Over its grave i' the earth so chilly;
    Heavily hangs the hollyhock,
      Heavily hangs the tiger-lily.

Robert Browning 1812–1889

Grow old along with me!
The best is yet to be,
The last of life, for which the first was made.

The Ring and the Book (1868–9) is variously claimed as
Browning's masterpiece; as a splendid failure; and as an
enormous, and enormously tedious, poem marking the
transition between the poet's good work and the garrulous
and unsatisfactory verse of his last twenty years. It is certainly a *long* poem, recounting a seventeenth-century
Roman murder from various points of view and in various
voices that fill twelve books. Browning described it as
'truth broken into prismatic lines'. He got the facts
from a 'square old yellow book' picked up for eight pence,
and he swears he never deviated from those facts.

Before his critics, Browning himself becomes like that
'square old yellow book'. There are as many views of him
as there were versions of the murder story. Some portray
him as a sublimated anal-erotic, others as an ordinary
entertaining fellow. Some find deep philosophy in him
and others see only sham. Such variety of approach proves
Browning's contention that individual imaginations deal
variously with a given reality. It was this individuality
and human diversity he explored – or so some contend.
Others affirm that his dramatic monologues were all
Robert Browning trying on a succession of masks, so he
could not be pinned down. In either case, Browning's
words have a validity: 'art remains the one way possible/

Of speaking truth, to mouths like mine at least.' What
was that mouth like? What truths does it tell?

Robert Browning was born in London in 1812, son of
a well-to-do bank employee who provided his son with an
education and, eventually, a private income. Father and
mother – she a sensitive, devout lady – encouraged the
boy's writing. In 1833 he published *Pauline* – anonymously, which was fortunate, because it was not well
received. Some suggest that because of its reception
Browning preferred afterwards to wear a mask rather
than expose himself. *Pauline*, written when he had gradu-
ated out of an early enthusiasm for Byron into a passion
for Shelley, was vulnerable verse.

He visited Italy in 1834, and published his second
ambitious poem, *Paracelsus*, in 1835. Carlyle, Wordsworth and others were generous to it, but it was not a
success. Nor was *Sordello* (1840), a poem that baffled his
readers. It is a poem about a young poet who fails to discover his art when he withdraws from the world. One
thinks of *Alastor* as its generic cousin, but Shelley's was
the better poem.

Before he married Elizabeth Barrett in 1846 and eloped
to Italy, he wrote eight plays. Only one of them is remembered, *Pippa Passes*. He claimed to hate the 'perfect
gallows' of theatre production. Certainly his talents did
not lie in that direction. His drama is not a mirror held
up to nature but a projection of the spirit: characters
rather got in the way or suffered from garrulity.

The *Dramatic Lyrics* (1842) and *Dramatic Romances*
(1845) showed him the way to his best work. In Italy with
his wife between 1846 and her death in 1861, he wrote
Men and Women (1853) and *Dramatis Personae* (1864),
published after his return to England as a widower. *The
Ring and the Book* followed. Thereafter he produced a
great deal of work: *Balaustion's Adventures* and *Prince
Hohenstiel-Schwangau* (1871), *Fifine at the Fair* (1872),
Dramatic Idyls (1879–80) and *Jocoseria* which includes the
engaging 'Cristina and Monaldeschi' (1873). There were

other works. He died in 1889. Ten years later his correspondence with Elizabeth Barrett Browning was published with great success.

His work was slow to find an English audience. America was more permeable. His fame – based eventually on poems written between 1842 and 1864 – increased at home as his writing became more wordy and diffuse. A life that had been a solitary quest, undisturbed by excessive attention, changed into a life of celebrity. His fame rivalled that of Tennyson. Were greatness measured by influence, he would be held the greatest of Victorian poets. His effect is discernible in Pound, Eliot, Auden and many writers of our own day. His development of the dramatic monologue, the 'persona' poem, his insistence on something like a speaking voice in poems of great physical particularity, and his lack of an articulate philosophy or world-view, made him a suggestively incomplete figure, at once sufficiently original to instruct and not so uniquely original as to intimidate.

Browning developed his dramatic monologue form from various sources. His own writing for the stage must have suggested the possibility to him. He had also Byron's personae poems, Shelley's veiled personal statements, Landor's *Imaginary Conversations* and other work to draw on. His originality was in making the form his primary instrument for exploring the world – or rather, a past world, Italian, Provençal, English and so on. His work has little commerce with the present.

He felt a need to detect form, order and design within the variousness of reality, without diminishing a sense of that variousness. The important thing, he felt, was to avoid imposing *a priori* values and forms on experience. He aims to detect, and to a limited extent he succeeds. But as Arnold wrote to Clough in 1848–9, 'Browning is a man with a moderate gift passionately desiring movement and fulness, and obtaining but a confused multitudinousness.' Had Arnold written that after reading *The Ring and the Book*, his judgement would have been even harsher. In that work it is possible to prove that there is a comprehensive organization, but it is an organization of artifice, not of imagination, a conscious patterning not detected but imposed, not thematic but mechanical. George Santayana – a little brutally, perhaps, but the Browning bandwagon was rolling very fast in 1910 – pointed to the inconclusiveness of Browning's poetry, its gesturing at wholeness, and the limited scope of Browning's comprehension. He spoke of his 'truncated imagination', described his art as 'inchoate and ill-digested', the personae 'always displaying traits of character and never attaining character as a whole'. It is hard to disagree with Santayana's analysis; nor is it necessary to do so. There is much to admire in Browning, without demanding wholeness of vision or even of conception. Detail, felicities of rhythm, the occasional masterly vignette are what one values. Nine tenths of the poetry can be read once and not read again.

From Byron Browning picked up a certain touristical vulgarity. The materialism of his 'historical' characters, the concerns they express at moments of crisis, are curiously Victorian and English concerns. His sentiments, too, can be cloyingly Victorian. He often selects the eccentric, the morally deformed, the man with a grudge, a guilt, a secret or a crime to his credit. He chooses them for effect. His vulgarity is a kind of journalistic prurience and a love of opulence of detail: he is wide-eyed. The Italy he evokes is not that of Dante or Michelangelo, as Santayana says. One learns more from the poems about Browning's own prejudices and tastes than about his ostensible subjects. His dramatic monologues are not so much self-explorations by characters as stories obliquely told. Soliloquies lay bare a mind or conscience; but Browning's monologues inform and entertain, turned outwards towards an audience.

'Though lyric in expression,' he writes of his 1863 poems, they are 'always Dramatic in principle.' They are 'utterances of so many imaginary persons, not mine'. This is disingenuous: the imagination is his, after all, and they emanate from there. Though his 'persons' have 'pasts' and individuating gestures, they are not clearly distinguished by diction. They speak in a remarkably similar language, choosing only different forms and faces.

The shorter poems are generally what he called 'lyric in expression'. Their dramatic nature is evident if we consult the index of first lines. Like Donne, whom he admired, Browning plucks at our sleeve with a startling phrase, plunges us in *in medias res*, ignites our curiosity time after time. And it is our curiosity that he satisfies. His syntax can be effectively mimetic, scurrying in breathless clauses to its climaxes, or pacing with dignity, or deliberating ponderously, as the action, not the character, requires.

Many of the monologues are addressed to an assumed interlocutor. They are confessions ('The Confessional' tells of an evil confessor and the girl who speaks reproves us with, 'You think Priests just and holy men!' but they're not). In 'The Laboratory' the speaker gleefully chuckles, 'To carry pure death in an earring, a casket,/ A signet, a fan-mount, a filigree-basket.' Women tell secret acts, men secret desires. Some speakers frankly address an audience ('How They Brought the Good News from Ghent to Aix'); some, apparently mumbling into a beard, are overheard. 'Soliloquy in a Spanish Cloister' has a jealous monk railing against Father Laurence. It is a little masterpiece of malice, uncannily complete in its delineation of the monk's own deadly vices:

Saint, forsooth! While brown Dolores
  Squats outside the Convent bank,
With Sanchicha, telling stories,
  Steeping tresses in the tank,
Blue-black, lustrous, thick like horse-hairs,
  – Can't you see his dead eye glow,
Bright as 'twere a Barbary corsair's?
  (That is, if he'd let it show!)

The actual pronunciation of lines three, four and five causes salivation in the reader. The poem has a wide range of malicious expression. There are other poems which incorporate dialogue. Best of all is that pair of poems 'Meeting at Night' and 'Parting at Morning', in the first of which the man arrives (an evocation of great thrift and speed), and in the second of which the woman experiences his departure.

Such examples clarify Browning's themes: Love, Religion, and Time. Love is largely a matter of the lower passions: it does not exalt but taxes its partisans. Religion is a world of colour, ceremony and dark desires, hardly a place for transcendence of the physical world but rather a heightening of its qualities. His treatment of Time and the isolation of the individual provides his most memorable statements.

'Never the time and the place / And the loved one all together,' he begins a late poem. It is the theme of unfulfilment so lucidly explored by Hardy, who himself owes a debt to Browning. The right moment passes, the chance of happiness is lost, in lover or in action. Loss produces isolation. Many of Browning's couples are separated by incompatibility, by a third party's jealousy, or by death. 'My Last Duchess' portrays a character's desire for isolation and objectification and its cruel consequence: a woman is murdered and retained as an artefact. Isolation and individuation are explored through the presentation of characters on the point of death, where they become luminously single and particular as their lives, lusts or worries pass before them in review. Few are noble in thought, sentiment or deed: we are dealing with the vast middle-range of mankind, each unique and none transcendent. When Browning speaks, or seems to speak, for himself, a more tempered and credible voice sounds, as in 'By the Fire-side'.

The technical delight and brilliance of imagery of poems such as 'A Toccata of Galuppi's' and 'Two in the Campagna' draw the reader back to Browning. The poems that merely tell a story can be exhausted in a couple of readings; those that have more than a conventional sentiment superadded ('Infinite passion, and the pain/Of finite hearts that yearn') or brilliance of conception and execution are less readily exhausted. One of Browning's best poems is 'Childe Roland to the Dark Tower Came', a dark quest, an allegory without any but a vague reference to the common world, a nightmare (indeed, it is based upon a dream) in which action alone seems to save the knightly protagonist. From the opening lines, 'My first thought was, he lied in every word,/That hoary cripple, with malignant eye' to the last stanza:

There they stood, ranged along the hill-sides, met
   To view the last of me, a living frame
   For one more picture! in a sheet of flame
I saw them and I knew them all. And yet
Dauntless the slug-horn to my lips I set,
   And blew, '*Childe Roland to the Dark Tower came.*'

the spell is maintained, even over patches of weak writing. The theme is that of unspecified triumph in the face of the defeat of others. It is this nebulous, not quite discovered theme that draws from Browning his best poems: something not deliberate but sought for in a deep region of his mind. We look behind the mask, so much is concentrated in the language and the urgent rhythms. His purpose may have been, as a character says in 'Old Pictures in Florence', 'To bring the invisible full into play.' Such an aim is achieved not when the invisible is rendered visible, but when it deepens the visible, giving psychological verity to a vivid surface. Browning is no more or less a realist than Dickens: 'realists' can, at their best, be 'fantasists'.

Matthew Arnold 1822–1888

And we shall sink in the impossible strife,
And be astray for ever.

Swinburne, though he later changed his mind about
Arnold, wrote of *New Poems* (1867), 'The majesty and
composure of thought and verse, the perfect clearness and
competence of the words, distinguish this from other
poetry of the intellect now more approved and ap-
plauded.' He had in mind Tennyson and Browning –
crude instruments beside Arnold's antique lyre. Swinburne's large, rhetorical words are not altogether im-
precise, for *New Poems* included 'Thyrsis', 'Heine's Grave'
and 'Rugby Chapel'. The best poems show a resolute
composure, if not 'majesty', a dignity suited to Arnold's
moral seriousness. They also accommodate feeling to
thought – there is no feeling in excess of thought. Arnold
has the seriousness, if not the certainty, of Johnson. He
wrote that Virgil's *Aeneid* is pervaded by a brooding
melancholy, 'the haunting self-dissatisfaction' of the poet's
heart. Arnold, in his lyrics, elegies and poems of action is
similarly self-dissatisfied: with his poetry, his life, his
society, and his apprehension of time. There is a generalized pathos in his best work, a vision of the human condition in the nineteenth century which combines the
uncompromising negative clarity of an Old Testament
prophet with the manners of a classical patrician: resignation tempers his vehemence. He sees things as they are
and will be. This is most amply stated in the finest poem

of the Victorian period, 'Dover Beach'. A moment of happiness regards itself in the context of history. Gazing at the sea, the poet calls his beloved to watch and listen with him. He hears the tide on the shingle. Sophocles had heard in that sound 'the turbid ebb and flow/Of human misery'. He too finds thought there. The Sea of Faith is ebbing, and with it the certainties of faith. He listens to:

Its melancholy, long, withdrawing roar,
Retreating, to the breath
Of the night-wind, down the vast edges drear
And naked shingle of the world.

Ah, love, let us be true
To one another! for the world which seems
To lie before us like a land of dreams,
So various, so beautiful, so new,
Hath really neither joy, nor love, nor light,
Nor certitude, nor peace, nor help for pain;
And we are here as on a darkling plain
Swept with confused alarms of struggle and fight,
Where ignorant armies clash by night.

The clarity of negative vision emerges naturally from a particularized situation: 'Come to the window, sweet is the night air.' Beside Browning's 'dramatic' monologues this monologue grows even taller, for both its technical and intellectual accomplishment. The lines contract and expand tidally; the rhythms have the variety and hesitancy of a speaking voice; the enjambements point the tone and the rhythm.

Arnold was not invariably so severe a writer, nor so good a one. Some of his poems are sententious and drab. If his best poems were sober in tone and elegiac in manner, there were reasons, and not all of them personal. The society he moved through as a schools inspector was hard to square with the rich cultural world he possessed. His social criticism and his poetry flow from a sense of this disparity between the real and the potential. While his criticism suggests that change is possible, his poetry acknowledges – in the choice of classical and heroic subjects and the elegiac mode – that there was a steady declension from the past to the materialist, philistine Victorian present he lived in. In his own life, there was an undeniable declension as well.

Tennyson and Browning enjoyed considerable financial independence. Arnold, son of the famous educationalist Thomas Arnold, headmaster of Rugby, was condemned to work he did not relish and which took him away from writing. He never achieved his great poem. He was born in Laleham, Surrey, in 1822. His father moved to Rugby in 1828. Arnold's early education was at Rugby and Winchester. Fox How, near Grasmere, was a holiday retreat. There, one of his neighbours was Wordsworth; and there much later (1850) he met Charlotte Brontë.

He went to Balliol College, Oxford, where he wrote poems and won prizes for his work. In 1845 he was elected Fellow of Oriel College. His friends and family considered him a dilettante at the time and were not prepared for the deep seriousness of his poems published anonymously in 1849, *The Strayed Reveller, and Other Poems*. It contained 'The Forsaken Merman' and the famous sonnet to Shakespeare.

In 1851 he married and was appointed Inspector of Schools. The next year, again anonymously, *Empedocles on Etna, and Other Poems* appeared. Among the 'other poems' was 'Tristram and Iseult'. In 1853 *Poems, A New Edition* (this time with his name on it) was published, with a selection from the earlier books and 'Sohrab and Rustum', 'The Scholar-Gipsy' and 'Memorial Verses to Wordsworth', one of the best elegies in the language. *Poems: Second Series* (1855) included the disappointing poem of action, 'Balder Dead'. *Merope: A Tragedy* (1858) was unsuccessful. His final collection, *New Poems* (1867), was hardly new. Apart from 'Thyrsis', devoted to the memory of Arthur Hugh Clough and composed in 1864–5, most of the work dated back to his best years as a poet, between 1847 and 1857, but particularly 1848 and 1852. In this sense he is like the great Romantics, essentially a *young* poet, composing his best work in his late twenties and early thirties, and then losing the main force of his gift.

Arnold became Oxford Professor of Poetry in 1857. He was re-elected and served until 1867, and his critical activity may have helped to curb his poetic impulse, though *Merope* proves the impulse was already declining. He had the will, but no longer the integrating imagination. His great prose works followed. He was promoted to Senior and later Chief Inspector of Schools. He engaged in educational campaigns and the range of his prose criticism is wide. He made a lecture tour of the United States. He retired from the inspectorate in 1886 and died in 1888. The last thirty years of his life he was pre-eminently critic and public man, and he did not like the role. The bitterness of 'Growing Old' is perhaps an oblique reply to Browning's sentimental 'Rabbi Ben Ezra'. 'What is it to grow old?' Arnold asks. He lists the answers, the last containing that 'self-dissatisfaction' turned on the world:

It is – last stage of all –
When we are frozen up within, and quite
The phantom of ourselves,
To hear the world applaud the hollow ghost
Which blamed the living man.

The poem 'The Last Word' is equally uncompromising. The terrible disparity between youth, youthful hope, and age, recurs. It provides the dramatic tension in *Empedocles on Etna*. The young poet Callicles confronts Empedocles who *has been* young. In 'Youth and Age' the theme is again enacted: age acquires calm as its crown: that is not the crown youth was after.

Arnold evolved a theory of poetry so exacting that he could not – except in 'Sohrab and Rustum' – live up to it. He plays down lyric and elegy, modes in which he was most eloquent. He stresses the importance of a suitable, large subject, preferably heroic. 'Action' is the goal he strives for: excellent actions appeal 'to the great primary human affections' which do not change. Classical and legendary subjects speak to the constant elements in the mind. He comments, 'it is a pity ... that the poet should be compelled to impart interest and force to his subject, instead of receiving them from it.' There were few common subjects to turn to, in an age whose art wanted sanity. The classics taught balance and proportion, and sanity was the great virtue of the ancient writers, the lack of it the great vice of the moderns. Arnold's is a normative, civilizing aesthetic, at a time when the wasting modern 'dialogue of the mind with itself has commenced'.

Except in 'Sohrab and Rustum', Arnold is not a successful poet of action. Even 'Sohrab and Rustum' is 'action' in a sense very different from Homer's poems. The unwitting father slays his son: but the choice and dramatic isolation of this theme and its slow, considering treatment, are distinctively Victorian. The theme of youth and age (and age defeating youth) is here again.

Preference for classical literature was preference for formal perfection. With the Greeks, Arnold says, action took precedence over expression: 'They regarded the whole; we regard the parts.' Expression should, ideally, be subordinate to action. In Arnold's poems action is subordinate to the meditated theme. Arnold defines through the Greeks 'the necessity of accurate construction'. This suggests an external and deliberate form, but the best of Arnold's poems do not conform to arbitrary laws: they follow the progression of the poet's mind through his subject. 'Heine's Grave', 'Memorial Verses', 'Thyrsis' and 'The Scholar Gipsy' have natural movement which we can trace, but which it is hard to believe was *pre*determined.

Arnold's elegies and memorial sonnets, his 'Requiescat', which shows too close a dependence on Wordsworth's 'Lucy' poems, and even 'Dover Beach' celebrate figures or moments as they lament their passing. 'Thyrsis' and 'The Scholar Gipsy' celebrate as well. They choose characters who have withdrawn from the social world to criticize and to reject it. Both poems are full of place-names which lend a tone of intimate address, giving the reader a sense of familiarity with the landscape. We are never far from a hamlet or rural habitation. The landscape is cultivated, without wilderness, almost a large untidy garden. There is no more, Edward Thomas says, than 'a graceful wildness and the idea of escape'. We do not credit the action but the experience, particularized in the spirit of Keats (who perhaps suggested the verse form) and not that of Theocritus, to whom Arnold points us. Though thirteen years separate the two works, they are companion pieces – so much so that one can confuse passages from one with the other.

There are other poems less well-known than these which share with them an intimate tone and a wealth of detail, but are more dramatic and bold in tracing. 'A Dream', with hesitant syntax and rhythm and repetitions, creates a mood of difficult remembering:

Was it a dream? We sail'd, I thought we sail'd,
Martin and I, down a green Alpine stream,
Border'd, each bank, with pines ...

In many of the poems the garden and associated imagery figure vividly: not only the garden of Greek idylls or of childhood, it has a Biblical source as well, a dimension of Eden, his own and our shared past. Regret, not remorse, informs such evocations. Arnold is too far removed from the firm faith which perceived the flaming sword and the angel at the gate. Gate and sword exist in memory. The sea of faith recedes, as time claims the past. 'In the two Hinkseys nothing keeps the same.' There is a goal, a light, at the end of 'Thyrsis', but it is dim. 'To Marguerite', from the 'Switzerland' sequence, answers Donne: each man is an island, and love itself cannot change that condition:

Who order'd that their longing's fire
Should be, as soon as kindled, cool'd?
Who renders vain their deep desire? –
A God, a God their severance rul'd!
And bade betwixt their shores to be
The unplumb'd, salt, estranging sea.

This is spoken not from behind a mask, not by a persona,
but by the poet's own voice. He does not contrive a metaphysical apotheosis, the way Tennyson does in *In Memoriam*. He does nothing to deflect the apprehension. It is
a bold, severe and uncompromising poetry, the truest
written in the Victorian period.

Algernon Charles Swinburne
1837–1909

Look, you, I speak not as one light of wit,
But as a queen speaks, being heart-vexed ...

There is something absurd about the image of Algernon
Charles Swinburne, aged thirty, kneeling before the
Italian leader Mazzini and reading him 'A Song of Italy'.
There is much that is absurd about Swinburne: his en-
thusiasms, his life, his poems.

Swallow, my sister, O sister swallow,
　How can thy heart be full of the spring?
　　A thousand summers are over and dead.

That first line is one of the most curious errors of taste in
English poetry. In the Mazzini episode, so like a painting
by one of his Pre-Raphaelite friends, we can read a great
deal about the man: his passion for liberty and his desire
for subjection; his ostentation; his naïve political and
poetic romanticism. There is another Swinburne, the
lover of the Elizabethans, of Landor, of the severe intellect
and language of Johnson, of Blake (whom he did much to
restore to favour), Whitman, Baudelaire, the Marquis de
Sade. He stands opposite to Hopkins. Hopkins was all
decision and the consequences of decision, Swinburne all
indecision and its consequences. Each poet developed a
distinctive language which represents two extremes of
approach to syntax, diction, rhythm and form. Their
failures are complementary.

Swinburne had every social advantage: education,

access to the notables of his day, money, devoted friends. What did he make of them? There were compensating disadvantages, psychological and social, for it was late in the day to be a Romantic; the *fin de siècle* began well before the *fin*; to make a gesture had become for the poet what to act had been for poets of earlier times. Vagueness of thought and sentiment were confused with profound sensibility. Swinburne reacted against a rigorous public code of morality. His visit to Mazzini was one aspect of this reaction. His prostration before hired flagellants was another. He was piqued when critics questioned the morality of his verse.

He was born in London in 1837. His father was an admiral, his mother a cultured and titled lady. There were ancestral estates, holidays on the Isle of Wight, and in general a spoilt childhood. He was presented to Wordsworth when he was twelve, and by his late adolescence he could take great poets in his stride. He remained spoilt. His emotional development was arrested in adolescence. The poetry can hardly be said to have developed thematically after 1866. Once it got in gear it stayed in that gear for forty-four years. There is good writing and bad writing, but the rhythms and the approach remain roughly constant, apart from increasing fluency and facility and a gradual decrease in tension with the years. In this earliest work we have much of the best poetry. His description of love from *Atalanta* is a good example:

Thou art swift and subtle and blind as a flame of fire;
Before thee the laughter, behind thee the tears of desire;
And twain go forth beside thee, a man with a maid;
Her eyes are the eyes of a bride whom delight makes afraid;
As the breath in the buds that stir is her bridal breath:
But fate is the name of her; and his name is Death.

Here, too, are the main themes: love, death, fate, fear, pain; and the incantatory rhetoric, the evanescent image. We seem to see, but it is the passage of ghosts.

He went to Eton where he read the Elizabethans and

wrote a sado-masochistic drama. He fell in love with Sappho, Victor Hugo, Walter Savage Landor and Mary Queen of Scots. Later he wrote three plays about Mary Queen of Scots. He left Eton for unspecified reasons and went on to Balliol College, Oxford, where he met the Pre-Raphaelites and fell under the spell of Rossetti and William Morris. He left Oxford without a degree and, in London, met among others Ruskin, Browning and Arnold. In 1864 he met Landor in Florence.

His first book, *Atalanta in Calydon* (1863) is in classical tragic form. The choruses include many of his best-known poems. Ruskin called the whole effort, 'The grandest thing ever done by a youth, though he is a demonic youth.' Ruskin was forgetting recent history. There was, after all, Keats.

In 1866 *Poems and Ballads*, probably Swinburne's best collection, was published. Its prosodic range is formidable. The book was severely criticized on moral grounds and occasioned from the author the slightly pompous and inconclusive 'Notes on Poems and Reviews', in which he characterized his book as 'dramatic, many-faced, multifarious', and stressed the overall unity of organization, refusing personal responsibility for any single statement wrenched from context. Most passionately he defends 'Anactoria', his adaptation of Sappho's ode, 'the supreme success, the final achievement, of the poetic art'. He sought to 'express and represent' the poet herself, not translate the poem. He played variations upon the sapphic theme, and the musical analogy is in place, for the poem follows the logic of the ear, as it were, not the logic of thought.

Still, the moral objection to Swinburne retains some force. Poems such as 'Laus Veneris' cannot but raise certain qualms, and later work too must be looked at in a moral light: not because it is immoral in subject-matter, but because in aestheticizing experience it impoverishes judgement.

In 1871 appeared *Songs Before Sunrise*, poems about

Liberty, which share a dullness with *Songs of Two Nations* (1875). There was another collection of moment still to come, *Poems and Ballads: Second Series* (1878). His life was increasingly disorganized and libidinous. His friend Theodore Watts-Dunton took him under his wing in 1879. They moved to Putney and there lived until the poet's death in 1909. There were several later collections of poems, notably the third series of *Poems and Ballads* (1889). Swinburne wrote verse up to his death, but like other Romantics he died young: the later work – including novels, plays and fine criticism – came from a different part of his mind from the early poetry.

Swinburne's originality of taste must be acknowledged. To have read and appreciated Whitman in England in the 1860s was remarkable. To have admired and imitated Baudelaire during the poet's own lifetime was even more remarkable:

I know not how this last month leaves your hair
Less full of purple colours and hid spice,
And that luxurious trouble of closed eyes
Is mixed with meaner shadow and waste care ...

His enthusiasm for Blake, and early on for Matthew Arnold's poems, bespeaks a discriminating modern sensibility. He was an excellent advocate. From this we turn to his poems.

Ezra Pound valued most his translations of Villon. Whatever their merits as translations, they were among the best verse Swinburne wrote. He had a substantial text to work from. In his original poems, he is a poet of natural and unnatural forces, not of nature. His specifically musical rhythms attempt to cast a spell with their hypnotic repetitiveness and exaggerated cadences. We attend to the flow of words, not to the articulation of thought or the evocation of imagery. There is seldom specific content: it is emotion diffused over a wide area. Quotation is difficult because the effect depends upon taking large doses, rhythmic chunks.

Edmund Wilson was severe about the language. It is monotonous, often preponderately monosyllabic. It has none of the vigour of speech. Eliot was of the same mind. Swinburne's is a language of disorientation. Words float free of their expected sense, serve an attitude or sentiment, lose particular reference. The nouns have no gravity, the adjectives relate not so much to the nouns as to the pervasive tone. 'Sweet' and 'light' and other words do overtime, but do little work. The very smoothness of the rhythm neutralizes the normal force of language. Mixed metaphor, the heaping up of lush verbiage point to an alternative poetic order. Eliot indicated how intellectually loose and metaphorically unconsidered the verse was. It is able – the moral question again – to make a corpse momentarily attractive in 'The Leper'. A scribe's necrophiliac passion impels him to fondle, kiss, and otherwise molest a body, reflecting (it is a monologue in Browning's manner):

Nothing is better, I well know,
Than love; no amber in cold sea
Or gathered berries under snow:
That is well seen of her and me.

Something must be wrong with a style which can aestheticize and morally neutralize such a scene.

Six months, and I sit still and hold
In two cold palms her two cold feet.
Her hair, half grey half rusted gold,
Thrills me and burns me in kissing it.

In so far as the poems have conflict, it is between simple polarities: pain and pleasure, life and death, love and death, love and time, youth and time. The enactment of such conflicts could hardly be called a poetry of ideas. It is a poetry of moods. The synaesthesia or mixing of the senses – audible sights, visible sounds and so on – is part of this reductive process, owing a very superficial debt to the profound art of Baudelaire. Fingers, lips, the 'pores of sense', do the work eyes do in other verses. In a sense we *ingest* Swinburne, rather as the sea, a favourite image of his, ingests as it were maternally the swimmer.

Swinburne's poems raise fundamental questions about the nature of poetic language, the limits to which schemes of rhythm can be usefully carried, the ultimate effectiveness of sound-patterning when intellectual control is in abeyance. What value has a poetry without ideas and without specific content beyond mood and feeling – even when the subjects are ostensibly intellectual, like 'liberty', and the content almost perceptible? Can poetry hope in any valid sense to approach the condition of music *in the terms* of music? Was Swinburne a poet, at another pole from Hopkins but like him, struggling at the end of an exhausted tradition, seeking energy in technical facility? The choruses from *Atalanta* and poems such as 'Tristram of Lyonesse', 'Dolores', 'A Forsaken Garden', 'The Triumph of Time', 'Laus Veneris' and 'A Nympholept' raise these questions, and the moral question. They do not answer them very conclusively. Perhaps the power of the choruses from *Atalanta* is that they have a context and touch a specific theme at a specific season:

> winter's rains and ruins are over,
> And all the season of snows and sins;
> The days dividing lover and lover,
> The light that loses, the light that wins;
> And time remembered is grief forgotten,
> And frosts are slain and flowers begotten,
> And in green underwood and cover
> Blossom by blossom the spring begins.

Yet even here we meet the all-purpose 'all', meaning nothing, the over-taxed 'and', the facile word-spinning in lines four and five behind which we grope for meaning. Either the reader has a taste for this sort of 'magic', or he stands back in mute astonishment.

Gerard Manley Hopkins
1844–1889

> I say that we are wound
> With mercy round and round
> As if with air ...

The poetry of Gerard Manley Hopkins did not reach the reading public until 1918, in an edition prepared by his friend Robert Bridges. His is a small body of poetry: a handful of juvenilia which escaped the fire, forty-eight mature and more or less finished poems, and a number of fragments. Letters, notebooks and other prose complete the *oeuvre*.

Hopkins was born in Stratford, Essex, in 1844, into a well-to-do family. His mother was pious, his father wrote verses and encouraged his children to draw and play music. Hopkins never gave up these pursuits. His first ambition was to be an artist. Ruskin and the Pre-Raphaelites prescribed his early world. In his verse he never completely outgrew an adolescent sensualism. He wrote 'The Bugler's First Communion' when he was in his thirties, and there he evokes a communicant who seems to step out of one of the more sentimental canvases of the time, charged with an energy quite alien to a priest and slightly indecent when *he* utters it at such an occasion: the 'Breathing beauty of chastity in mansex fine', 'limber-liquid youth, that to all I teach/Yields tender as a pushed peach', and so on.

From a brilliant performance at Highgate School, Hopkins went to Balliol College, Oxford, in 1863, where he secured a first class degree in Greats four years later. It was a time of intellectual activity and crisis for him. He struck up his life-long friendship with Robert Bridges. He ruminated upon language, setting down in a note-book that 'the onomatopoeic theory' of language 'has not had a fair chance. Cf. Crack, creak, croak, crake, graculus, crackle.' The concerns of the mature poet can be identi-fied here. He was making his way in a healthily assertive if naïve fashion towards the mimetic theory of language which he developed in his mature poems. He asks not only what language means but how it means to the senses, how it contains what it signifies.

He was led by a dissatisfied faith and by his love for ceremony, in an Oxford where the Oxford Movement was in some disarray, to the ceremonialism of the Anglo-Catholics. He succumbed to the Roman Catholics in 1866 and was received into the church by John Henry Newman. In his years at Oxford he was influenced as well by Walter Pater, who tutored him, and by Matthew Arnold, then Professor of Poetry. Pater and Arnold spoke languages so different in form and seriousness as to be virtually anti-thetical.

At University began what might be called Hopkins's vision of discipline. He describes the effect of religious faith on the imagination in an image. Imagine the world reflected in a water-drop: a small, precise reflection. Then imagine it reflected in a drop of Christ's blood: the same reflection, but suffused with the hue of love, sacrifice and redemption. Religious faith discovers for the imagination this underlying truth. In the light of the suffusing truth of love, sacrifice and redemption, Hopkins began to relish the uniqueness of things, what made them 'indi-vidually distinctive'. This he called 'inscape' – an artist's term. 'Instress', another bit of jargon, refers to the power or force maintaining the inscape. Inscape is manifest, instress is divine, the immanent presence in the object of the divine.

In his later studies the work of Duns Scotus appealed
to him, as it were against the grain of Aquinas and orthodox Jesuit discipline. Scotus confirmed his version of
particularism in his 'principle of Individuation' or *haec-
ceitas* ('thisness'). Scotus licensed him to assert his own
individuality and gave him confidence for a number of
poems, one of them addressed to Scotus himself. The stress
falls on the 'I', which Scotus (the 'he') had empowered
him to use in this way:

But ah! this air I gather and I release
He lived in; these weeds and waters, these walls are what
He haunted who of all men most sways my spirits to peace;
Of realty the rarest-veined unraveller; a not
Rivalled insight . . .

Veins – the unseen lines of inscape – Scotus unravelled,
approaching 'realty', not 'reality'. The old abstraction is
elided into a new, unique term.

Taken together, his suffusing faith and his particularism emancipated Hopkins from the panoramic and from
the intellectualizing Romantics. Objects do not evoke
nebulous sentiments. They point in one direction, elicit-
ing feeling not for themselves but for God. It is a vertical
vision: things relate not among themselves but through
God. The sonnets which express concern for social ills –
'God's Grandeur' and 'The Sea and the Skylark' – propose no political solution but see through or beyond industrial landscapes to nature, and through nature to God.
'God's Grandeur' makes original use of imagery of in-
dustrialism to magnify, by contrast, nature which 'is
never spent' despite environmental depredations. In his
prose these experiences brought him near to utopian
socialism; in his poems they bring him close to God:

And for all this, nature is never spent;
  There lives the dearest freshness deep down things;
And though the last lights off the black West went

Oh, morning, at the brown brink eastward, springs –
Because the Holy Ghost over the bent
World broods with warm breast and with ah! bright wings.

The adjective 'bent' relates back to the octave of the sonnet, with its metallic imagery and the contrasting imagery of the natural and human worlds.

After Oxford and some travelling, Hopkins became a Jesuit novice (1868). He burned the verse he could find, though from his time at Oxford three poems of interest survive: 'Let me be to thee as the circling bird', 'The Habit of Perfection' and 'Heaven-Haven'. Such poems had accepted the Ignatian discipline before the poet curbed himself to it. They are remarkably clear in comparison to some of Hopkins's later work.

Seven years passed before he wrote another poem. He mastered Welsh and Welsh prosody in that time, but he had vowed not to write original verse unless his superiors asked him to. In 1875 they consented to his memorializing a shipwreck in which a number of nuns had perished. 'The Wreck of the Deutschland' is packed with seven years' concentration of religious experience and the inevitable ruminations on language and poetic form. The poem is dense, complex and forbidding. Bridges could not stomach it. He suggested that poetry requiring a 'conscious effort of interpretation' was bad if that conscious effort was expended on unravelling, not complexity of image, idea or metaphor, but *syntax*, syntax arranged in such a way as to distract from, rather than lead through, the poem. Bridges was not far wrong, though it is fashionable among critics to sneer at him (a critic whose word Hopkins valued and took to heart) for his strictures.

Syntax may be the line or vein of the poem's inscape, making it a unique object. But is anything gained by calling Christ, 'Mid-numbered He mid three of the thunder throne'? Is it not an intolerable circumlocution? When the poem ends with a line containing six genitive cases, unpronounceably expressing dependent relations and coming perilously near mixed metaphor ('Our hearts' charity's hearth's fire, our thoughts' chivalry's throng's Lord'), the effort required of the reader is analytic, not imaginative.

The poem is in two sections, the first largely personal, the second dealing with the wreck and allowing digressions. The singer in the first section reflects on the nature of God and his relation with Him, on faith and on nature. The fourth stanza is richly achieved:

> I am soft sift
> In an hourglass – at the wall
> Fast, but mined with a motion, a drift,
> And it crowds and it combs to the fall ...

God punishes and gives grace, the storm at sea and the salvation. Man – the poet, the ship battered by the storm – learns through suffering to recognize grace. The first ten stanzas (the first section) possess remarkable unity of imagery. The ship hurries to Christ the Host for succour. The force of individuation comes from Christ, God as man, and not from God Himself. Christ is 'lightning and love' – lightning first.

The second section recounts the events of the shipwreck in a verse full of sound and fury. There are digressions on Luther, on the poet's stay in Wales. The initial conflict of sea and ship is narrowed to Gertrude, the nuns, the sailors. But the force and concentration of the first part are dissipated.

In his poems Hopkins uses or mingles two basic verse-forms. The first is accentual-syllabic or, as he calls it, running rhythm: a strict number of syllables and of regularly placed stresses, allowing some stress but not syllabic variation. The other is what he calls 'sprung rhythm', in which the number of syllables varies but the number of stresses in each line remains constant. 'Sprung Rhythm,' he writes, 'is measured by feet of from one to four syllables, regularly, and for particular effects any number of weak or slack syllables may be used.' He develops the definition at length and applies the form with great variety of effect.

The influence of Welsh poetry on his alliterative and assonantal writing cannot be denied. He develops in some poems an English *cynghanned* – the patterned repetition of consonants. They provide another vein holding the poem together, and usefully, for the poems often draw or compel into relation remote images, harmonizing them through the expedient of sound organization. The best example of this is 'Pied Beauty'. 'The Starlight Night', too, with its nativity, depends on close sound organization. Only controlled cadence resolves the difficult and perhaps inaccurate syntax of the famous 'Windhover'. Some poems, notably the unspectacular but very good sonnet 'The Valley of the Elwy', have more conventional virtues, the syntax flowing smoothly, the tension existing between the sonnet form and the spoken rhythm of the statement. It was a necessary step towards the dark sonnets to ungarble his style. As he wrote to Bridges, 'No doubt my poetry errs on the side of oddness ... I hope in time to have a more balanced and Miltonic style.' The triumphs of the odd style at its oddest are 'Peace', 'The Leaden Echo and the Golden Echo' and 'Spring and Fall' ('Márgarét, are you grieving'), one of those poems which stays in the mind after two or three readings.

Neglect preceded the dark sonnets. 'The Wreck of the Deutschland' was not printed. Nor, in 1877, was 'The Loss of the Eurydice' which, though a lesser work, is much clearer than the earlier memorial poem. 'And you were a liar, o blue March day', and the last line, 'Prayer shall fetch pity eternal', show positive development towards a clearer individuality. There were poetic aberrations, like the sonnet to Purcell. Still he was unpublished. It is hard to determine the effect this neglect had on his poetry. It deeply unsettled the poet. His nervous and physical illness which began in 1874 and never left him was no doubt aggravated by it. He prepared a preface for his poems. He wanted and needed an audience for the clarification of his verse. It was not to be. In 1884 he was appointed Professor of Greek at University College, Dublin. In 1885–6 he wrote the dark sonnets. In 1889 he died.

The dark sonnets are his finest work, for here the ruptured syntax, the inversions and the sound patterning answer a violence of spiritual experience as intense as any in English poetry. In the work of George Herbert, which Hopkins admired, Christ is the wooer, the soul is the wooed. In Hopkins, the soul, painfully aware of its own fallen nature, desperately woos Christ. There is almost despair, for Christ has withdrawn, grace is denied.

Pervading one of the sonnets, 'Carrion Comfort', is the metaphor of eating; 'No worst' is pervaded by the language of storm; 'I wake to feel the fell of dark' dwells on the disgusting nature of the body, its taste and smell. Whatever the psychological motive of the poems, they are powerful statements of love and loss, of a desire which grace has not satisfied, of unfulfilment. The poet who step by step 'individuated' himself here at last stands apart even from his God. To have become a Catholic against the wishes of his family; a Jesuit against the advice of his friends; and a disciple of Scotus against the orthodoxy of his order: he had made himself alone. In his poetry, too, he had developed a solitary, inimitable idiom. He aimed to create phrases from which the meaning would 'explode' on the reader, and in the dark sonnets he achieves such phrases. His crisis came, by transposition, to mean a great deal to the audience he acquired thirty years after his death:

I wake to feel the fell of dark, not day.
What hours, O what black hoùrs we have spent
This night! what sights you, heart, saw; ways you went!
And more must, in yet longer light's delay.
    With witness I speak this. But where I say
Hours I mean years, mean life. And my lament
Is cries countless, cries like dead letters sent
To dearest him that lives alas! away.

Bibliography

The bibliographies provided here are rudimentary. In general, they direct the reader to accessible editions and inexpensive selections of the poets' work (primarily books in print, the editions as recorded in *British Books in Print*), to a few critical books and studies, and to those of the poets' prose books which cast light on the poetry or the period. Under 'Editions' are included selections, prose writings, letters (the standard editions listed first, selections alphabetically by editor afterwards); and under 'Criticism' are included studies, critical symposia and bibliographies.

Because of the scope of this volume, a detailed biography of anthologies and criticism would be almost as long as the book itself. One can, in the available space, do little more than direct the reader to some of the major anthology series.

Oxford University Press anthologies are remarkably comprehensive in their coverage and reasonable in price. There are, to supplement the Oxford Books which, in general, anthologize periods, the Penguin anthologies which include both Oxford style books and anthologies with generic or thematic orientation, such as the *Penguin Book of Everyday Verse*, edited by D. Wright, or the *Penguin Book of Pastoral Verse*, edited by J. Barrell and J. Bull. Both Oxford and Penguin series are extensive, and the reader can acquaint himself with the work of some of the less-known writers discussed here by turning to those anthologies. Some of them – Dame Helen Gardner's Penguin *Metaphysical Poets*, for example – are particularly valuable.

Of great value is the Heinemann Educational Books 'Poetry Bookshelf' series, with introductory selection and notes for many of the fifty poets included here. 'Poetry Bookshelf' includes some anthologies as well, notably J. Dalglish's *Eight Metaphysical Poets*,

V. de S. Pinto's *Poetry of the Restoration*, D. Davie's *The Late Augustans* and D. Wright's *Seven Victorian Poets*. Carcanet's 'Fyfield Books' series provides similar useful introductions to individual poets. Faber's 'Choice of Verse' series, too, includes a number of selections of this sort. One should not overlook the attractive Muses' Library series, or Penguin's two series – the collected editions and the 'Poet to Poet' series. These volumes are mentioned in the bibliographies.

Critical series are numerous and, in general, I have not detailed them in the selective bibliographies. The Macmillan Casebooks Series are anthologies of essays about specific writers and works, providing useful distillations of critical thought from all periods on many of the fifty poets considered here. Hutchinson Educational published a valuable three volume series, *The Poets and their Critics*, edited by H. S. Davies (I, II) and J. Reeves (III). The British Council issue 'Writers and their Work', introductory booklets on most of the authors in this volume. Evans produce a 'Literature in Perspective' series and Prentice-Hall publish a 'Twentieth Century Views' series of critical anthologies on individual writers. There is, too, the 'Critical Heritage' series. These are a few of the sometimes useful critical resources available.

For general background and history the choice is again wide. The seven volume *Penguin Guide to English Literature*, like the seven volume Sphere Library *History of Literature in the English Language*, is an inexpensive and approachable series of critical anthologies. There is the Oxford *History of English Literature* in twelve volumes and a similar Cambridge history. Among the most readable and engaging series by a single author is Basil Willey's excellent 'Background' books (*The Seventeenth-Century Background*, *The Eighteenth-Century Background*, etc.).

These are merely introductory suggestions. It is a curious fact that in a few cases there are critical books in print about authors whose poems are no longer available. Criticism develops, it sometimes seems, in disregard of its pretext.

The critical writing most valuable to the reader seeking orientation will often be that of other poets or of critics with clear vision. Johnson, Coleridge and Arnold are essential reading not only as poets but as critics of poetry. In this century, the essays of T. S. Eliot continue to live, as do some of those of Ezra Pound and Ford Madox Ford. The serious reader will not neglect the criticism of William Empson or of F. R. Leavis. Edgell

Rickword's essays, and the criticism of Donald Davie, C. H. Sisson and Yvor Winters are all worth close attention. One could extend the list; but for the reader who has tried some of these suggestions, the list will extend itself.

Matthew Arnold

Editions:
Tinker, C. B. and H. F. Lowry, *Poetical Works*, Oxford
Allott, K., *Poems*, London, 1974
Thompson, D., *Selected Poems and Prose*, London, 1971
Ricks, C., *Selected Criticism*, London, 1972
Lowry, H. F., *Letters to Arthur Hugh Clough*, Oxford, 1968

Criticism:
Allott, K., *Matthew Arnold*, London, 1960
Rowse, A. L., *Matthew Arnold: Poet & Prophet*, London, 1976
Trilling, L., *Matthew Arnold*, London, 1975

William Barnes

Editions:
Jones, B., *Poems*, London, 1962
Nye, R., *Selected Poems*, Manchester, 1972
Forster, E. M. (introduction), *100 Poems*, Dorchester, 1971

Criticism:
Davies, A. T., *William Barnes, Friend of Thomas Hardy*, London, 1967

William Blake

Editions:
Keynes, Sir G., *Complete Writings*, Oxford, 1969
Bateson, F. W., *Selected Poems*, London, 1967
Bronowski, J., *Selected Poems*, London, 1975
Crehan, A. S., *Selected Poetry and Letters*, London, 1976
Erdman, D. V., *The Illuminated Blake*, Oxford, 1975
Gardner, S., *Selected Poems*, London, 1962
Keynes, Sir G., *Poetry and Prose*, London, 1961
Keynes, Sir G., *Songs of Innocence and Experience*, Oxford, 1970
Raine, K., *Choice of Verse*, London, 1970

408 Bibliography

Criticism:
Clark, Sir K., *Blake and Visionary Art*, Glasgow, 1973
Frye, N., *Fearful Symmetry: a study of William Blake*, Boston, 1967
Keynes, Sir G., *William Blake: Poet, Printer and Prophet*, London, 1965
Raine, K., *William Blake*, London, 1970
Wilson, M., *The Life of William Blake*, Oxford, 1971

Robert Browning

Editions:
Jack, I., *Poetical Works 1833–1864*, Oxford, 1976
Milford, Sir H., *Poems*, Oxford, 1949
Allott, K., *Selected Poems*, Oxford, 1967
Harper, J. W., *Men and Women and Other Poems*, London, 1975
Lucie-Smith, E., *Choice of Verse*, London, 1967
Reeves, James, *Selected Poems*, London, 1967
Williams, W. F., *Selected Poems*, Harmondsworth, 1971

Criticism:
Jack, I., *Browning's Major Poetry*, Oxford, 1973

Robert Burns

Editions:
Kinsley, J., *Poems and Songs*, Oxford, 1971
Beattie, W., *Poetry*, London, 1972
Fraser, G. S., *Selected Poems*, London, 1968

Criticism:
Douglas, H., *Robert Burns: A Life*, London, 1976

George Gordon, Lord Byron

Editions:
Page, F. and J. D. Jump, *Poetical Works*, Oxford, 1970
Auden, W. H., *Selected Poetry*, New York, 1967
Dunn, D., *Choice of Verse*, London, 1974
Jump, J. D., *Childe Harold's Pilgrimage and other Romantic Poems*, London, 1975
Marchland, L. A., *Don Juan*, Boston, 1958
Skelton, R., *Selected Poems*, London, 1967

Criticism:
Jump, J. D., *Byron: A Symposium*, London, 1975

Thomas Campion

Editions:
Davis, W. R., *Works*, London, 1970
Davis, W. R., *Observations on the Art of English Poesie*, London, 1969
Davis, W. R., *English Lute Songs*, London, 1967
Hart, J., *Ayres & Observations: Selected Poems and Prose of T.C.*, Manchester, 1976

George Chapman

Editions:
Wain, E., *Selected Poems*, Manchester, 1978
Criticism:
Swinburne, A. C., *George Chapman: A Critical Essay*, New York, 1977

Thomas Chatterton

Editions:
Taylor, D. S., and B. B. Hoover, *Complete Works*, Oxford, 1971
Lindop, G., *Selected Works*, Manchester, 1972
Criticism:
Meyerstein, E. H. W., *Life of Thomas Chatterton*, London, 1930

Geoffrey Chaucer

Editions:
Fisher, J., *Complete Poetry and Prose*, London, 1977
Robinson, F. N., *Works*, Cambridge, Mass., 1974
Skeat, W. W., *Complete Works*, Oxford
Coghill, N., *Choice of Verse* (modern English), London, 1972
Coghill, N., *The Canterbury Tales* (modern English), London, 1972
Wright, D., *The Canterbury Tales*, London, 1969

Criticism:

Brewer, D., *Geoffrey Chaucer*, London, 1974
Bronson, B. H., *In Search of Chaucer*, Toronto, 1967
Coghill, N., *The Poet Chaucer*, Cambridge, 1967
Hussey, M., *Introduction to Chaucer*, Cambridge, 1965
Hussey, M. (ed), *Chaucer's World*, Cambridge, 1967
Robinson, I., *Chaucer and the English Tradition*, Cambridge, 1974

John Clare

Editions:

Tibble, A., *The Midsummer Cushion*, Manchester, 1979
Robinson, E., and G. Summerfield, *The Shepherd's Calendar*, Oxford, 1973
Tibble, J. W., and A. Tibble, *Letters*, London, 1970
Tibble, J. W. and A. Tibble, *Prose*, London, 1970
Reeves, J., *Selected Poems*, London, 1968
Robinson, E. and G. Summerfield, *Selected Poems and Prose*, Oxford, 1967
Tibble, J. W. and A. Tibble, *Selected Poems*, London, 1974

Criticism:

Martin, F., *The Life of John Clare*, London, 1964
Storey, N., *The Poetry of John Clare: A Critical Introduction*, London, 1974

Samuel Taylor Coleridge

Editions:

Coleridge, E. H., *Poetical Works*, Oxford, 1969
Coleridge, S. T., *Biographia Literaria*, London, 1975
Griggs, E. L., *Collected Letters*, Oxford, 1971
Beer, J. B., *Poems*, London, 1970
Empson, W., and D. Pirie, *Verse, a Selection*, London, 1972
Reeves, J., *Selected Poems*, London, 1967
Roper, D., *Lyrical Ballads*, London, 1968

Criticism:

Richards, I. A., *Coleridge on Imagination*, London, 1962
Walsh, W., *Coleridge: The Work and the Relevance*, London, 1967
Watson, G., *Coleridge the Poet*, London, 1966
Watters, R., *Coleridge*, London, 1971

William Cowper

Editions:
Inglesfield, R., *Poems* (facsimile of the 1782 edition), London, 1973
Nicholson, N., *Choice of Verse*, London, 1975

George Crabbe

Editions:
Mills, H., *Tales, 1812 and Other Selected Poems*, Cambridge, 1967
Day-Lewis, C., *Selected Poetry*, London, 1973
Lucas, J., *A Selection of Crabbe's Verse*, London, 1968
Criticism:
New, P., *George Crabbe's Poetry*, London, 1976

John Donne

Editions:
Grierson. Sir H., *Poetical Works* (3 vols); Oxford, 1971
Smith, A. J., *The Complete English Poems*, Harmondsworth, 1971
Hayward, J., *Selected Poetry*, London, 1970
Milgate, W., *Satires, Epigrams and Verse Letters*, London, 1967
Redpath, R. T. H., *Songs and Sonnets*, London, 1967
Criticism:
Bennett, J., *Five Metaphysical Poets*, Cambridge, 1966
Leishman, J. B., *John Donne, The Monarch of Wit*, London, 1967
Smith, A. J., *John Donne, the Songs and Sonnets*, London, 1966

John Dryden

Editions:
Kinsley, J., *Poetical Works*, Oxford, 1967
Kinsley, J., *Poems and Fables*, Oxford, 1970
Kinsley, J., *The Works of Virgil, translated by J. D.*, Oxford, 1961
Dobrée, B., *Dryden's Poems*, London, 1964
Watson, G., *Of Dramatic Poesy and Other Critical Essays* (2 vols), London, 1971
Kinsley, J., and G. A. E. Parfitt, *Selected Criticism*, Oxford, 1970
Auden, W. H., *Choice of Verse*, London, 1973

Roberts, P., *Absalom & Achitophel and Other Poems*, London, 1975

Criticism:

Bredvold, L. I., *The Intellectual Milieu of John Dryden*, Ann Arbor, 1966

Wykes, D., *A Preface to Dryden*, London, 1977

George Gascoigne

Editions:

Miller, R. L., *A Hundred Sundry Flowers* (from the 1573 ed), Kennikat Press, 1976

Wells, R., *Selected Poems*, Manchester, to be published in 1980

John Gay

Editions:

Dearing, V. A. and C. E. Beckwith, *Poetry and Prose*, Oxford, 1975

Dearing, V. A. and C. E. Beckwith, *Fables*, London, 1969

Dearing, V. A. and C. E. Beckwith, *The Beggar's Opera*, London, 1962

Oliver Goldsmith

Editions:

Davis, T., *Poems and Plays*, London, 1977

Lonsdale, R., *The Poems of Gray, Collins and Goldsmith*, London, 1976

Egan, D., *The Deserted Village*, London, 1978

Garnett, R., *Selected Works*, London, 1967

Jeffares, A. N., *Selections*, London, 1963

Rudrum, A. and P. Dixon, *Selected Poems of Johnson and Goldsmith*, London, 1965

John Gower

Editions:

Macaulay, G. C., *English Works*, Oxford, 1957

Peck, R. A., *Confessio Amantis*, London, 1968

Criticism:
Thomas, W. V., *Portrait of Gower*, London, 1976

Thomas Gray

Editions:
Starr, H. W. and J. R. Hendrickson, *Complete Poems*, Oxford, 1966
Lonsdale, R., *The Poems of Gray, Collins and Goldsmith*, London, 1976
Johnston, A., *Selected Poems of Gray and Collins*, London, 1967
Criticism:
Harris, C. E., *Thomas Gray, Poet 1716–71*, London, 1971

Robert Henryson (William Dunbar and Gavin Douglas)

Editions:
Elliott, C., *Poems*, Oxford, 1975
Wood, H. H., *Poems and Fables*, London, 1958
Kinsley, J., *William Dunbar: Poems*, Oxford, 1970
Coldwell, D. F. C., *Selections from Gavin Douglas*, Oxford, 1964

George Herbert

Editions:
Gardner, Dame H., *Poems* (2 vols), Oxford, 1961
Patrides, C. A., *English Poems*, London, 1974
Auden, W. H., *Selected Poetry*, London, 1973
Reeves, G. E., *Selected Poems*, London, 1971
Thomas, R. S., *Choice of Verse*, London, 1967
Criticism:
Bennett, J., *Five Metaphysical Poets*, Cambridge, 1966

Robert Herrick

Editions:
Martin, L. C., *Poetical Works*, Oxford, 1956
Clayton, T., *Cavalier Poets: Selected Poems* (including Suckling, Carew, Lovelace), Oxford, 1978

Gerard Manley Hopkins

Editions:
Gardner, W. H., *Poems and Prose*, London, 1970
Abbott, C. C., *Letters to Robert Bridges* (and correspondence
with R. W. Dixon), Oxford, 1955
Gardner, W. H. and N. H. Mackenzie, *Poems*, Oxford, 1970
Reeves, J., *Selected Poems*, London, 1967

Criticism:
Bergonzi, B., *Gerard Manley Hopkins*, London, 1977
Gardner, W. H., *Gerard Manley Hopkins*, Oxford, 1958

Samuel Johnson

Editions:
Fleeman, J. D., *Complete English Poems*, Harmondsworth, 1971
Smith, D. N. and E. L. MacAdam, *Poems*, Oxford, 1974
Archer-Hind, L., *Lives of the Poets* (2 vols), London, 1975
Bronson, B. H., *Rasselas, Poems and Selected Prose*, London, 1971
Rudrum, A. W. and P. Dixon, *Selected Poems of Johnson and
Goldsmith*, London, 1965
Wilson, M., *Prose and Poetry*, London, 1967

Criticism:
Bate, W. J., *The Achievement of Samuel Johnson*, New York, 1961
Wain, J., *Samuel Johnson*, London, 1974

Ben Jonson

Editions:
Donaldson, I., *Poems*, Oxford, 1975
Gunn, T., *Selected Poems*, Harmondsworth, 1974
Johnston, G. B., *Poems*, London, 1968
Parfitt, G. A. E., *Poems*, London, 1975

Criticism:
Nichols, J. G., *The Poetry of Ben Jonson*, London, 1969
Parfitt, G., *Ben Jonson: Public Poet and Private Man*, London, 1976

John Keats

Editions:
Garrod, H. W., *Poetical Works*, Oxford, 1973
Allott, M., *Poems* (annotated), London, 1972
Barnard, J., *Complete Poems*, Harmondsworth, 1973
Day-Lewis, C., *A Choice of Verse*, London, 1971
Gittings, R., *Selected Poems and Letters*, London, 1967
Gittings, R., *Odes*, London, 1970

Criticism:
Bate, W. J., *John Keats*, Cambridge, Mass., 1963
Dickstein, M., *Keats and his Poetry: A Study in Development*,
Chicago, 1974
Gittings, R., *John Keats: The Living Year*, London, 1962
Jones, J., *The Dream of Truth*, London, 1969
Ricks, C., *Keats and Embarrassment*, Oxford, 1974

Walter Savage Landor

Editions:
Grigson, G., *Poems*, London, 1971

Criticism:
Forster, J., *Walter Savage Landor, A Biography* (reprint), London,
1972
Pinsky, R., *Landor's Poetry*, Chicago, 1968

William Langland

Editions:
Kane, G. and E. T. Donaldson, *Piers Plowman: 'B' Version*, London,
1975
Bennett, J. A. W., *Piers Plowman*, Oxford, 1972
Brook, S., *Piers Plowman: Selections from the 'B' Text*,
Manchester, 1975
Goodridge, J. T., *Piers Plowman* (in modern English),
Harmondsworth, 1970

Criticism:
Coghill., N., *Langland. Piers Plowman*, London, 1964
Salter, E., *Piers Plowman: An Introduction*, Oxford, 1963

416   Bibliography

Richard Lovelace

Editions:
Wilkinson, C. H., *Poems*, Oxford, 1930
Clayton, T., *Cavalier Poets: Selected Poems* (including Herrick, Carew and Suckling), Oxford, 1978

Christopher Marlowe

Editions:
Bowers, F., *Complete Works* (2 vols), Cambridge, 1973
Pendry, E. D., *Complete Plays and Poems*, London, 1976
Orgel, S., *The Complete Poems and Translations*, Harmondsworth, 1971
Millar, M., *Poems*, Manchester, 1968

Criticism:
Levin, H., *Christopher Marlowe: The Overreacher*, London, 1965
Steane, J. B., *Christopher Marlowe: A Critical Study*, Cambridge, 1970

Andrew Marvell

Editions:
Donno, E. S., *Complete Poems*, Harmondsworth, 1972
MacDonald, H., *Poems*, London, 1966
Hutchings, W., *Selected Poems*, Manchester, 1978
Kermode, F., *Selected Poetry*, New York, 1962
Legouis, P., *Poems and Letters*, Oxford, 1972
Reeves, J. and M. Seymour-Smith, *Poems*, London, 1971

Criticism:
Bennett, J., *Five Metaphysical Poets*, Cambridge, 1966
Legouis, P., *Andrew Marvell: Poet, Puritan, Patriot*, Oxford, 1968
Leishman, J. B., *The Art of Marvell's Poetry*, London, 1968

John Milton

Editions:
Bush, D., *Poetical Works*, Oxford, 1966
Beeching, H. C. (with Skeat and Williams), *The English Poems of John Milton*, Oxford, 1965

Burden, D. H., *Shorter Poems*, London, 1970
Carey, J., *Complete Shorter Poems*, London, 1971
Carey, J. and A. Fowler, *Poems*, London, 1968
Darbishire, H., *Poems*, Oxford, 1961
Enright, D. J., *Choice of Verse*, London, 1975
Patrides, C. A., *Selected Prose*, Harmondsworth, 1974
Tillyard, E. M. W. and P. B. Tillyard, *Comus and some Shorter Poems*

Criticism:
Broadbent, M., *John Milton, an Introduction*, Cambridge, 1973
Empson, W., *Milton's God*, London, 1961
Frye, N., *Five Essays on Milton's Epics*, London, 1976
Kermode, F. (ed), *Living Milton*, London, 1960
Parker, W. R., *John Milton: A Biography*, Oxford, 1968
Patrides, C. A. (ed), *Essays on Milton's Epic Poetry*,
Harmondsworth, 1967
Peter, J., *A Critique of Paradise Lost*, London, 1968
Prince, F. T., *The Italian Element in Milton's Verse*, Oxford, 1962
Ricks, C., *Milton's Grand Style*, Oxford, 1965
Waldock, A. J. A., *Paradise Lost and its Critics*, Cambridge, 1966

Alexander Pope

Editions:
Davis, H., *Poetical Works*, Oxford, 1966
Butt, J., *The Poems of A.P.*, London, 1965
Bateson, F. W., *Epistles to Several Persons*, London, 1961
Dobrée, B., *Collected Poems*, London, 1975
Heath-Stubbs, J., *Selected Poems*, London, 1964
Levi, P., *Selected Poems*, Harmondsworth, 1974
Porter, P., *A Choice of Verse*, London, 1971
Sutherland, J., *The Dunciad*, London, 1963

Criticism:
Knight, G. W., *The Poetry of Alexander Pope, Laureate of Peace*,
London, 1965
Reeves, J., *Reputation and Writings of Alexander Pope*, London,
1976
Russo, J. P., *Alexander Pope: Tradition and Identity*, Cambridge,
Mass., 1973
Tillotson, G., *On the Poetry of Pope*, Oxford, 1950

Sir Walter Raleigh

Editions:
Nye, R., *Choice of Verse*, London, 1972
Bullett, G., *Silver Poets of Sixteenth Century* (anthology),
London, 1967

Criticism:
Greenblatt, S. J., *Sir Walter Raleigh: The Renaissance Man and his Roles*, New Haven, Conn., 1973
Stebbing, W., *Sir Walter Raleigh: A Biography* (facsimile of 1899 edition), n.p., 1977

John Wilmot, Earl of Rochester

Editions:
Vieth, D. M., *Complete Poems*, New Haven, Conn. 1975
Adlard, J., *The Debt to Pleasure*, Manchester, 1974
Pinto, V. de S., *Poems*, London, 1963

Criticism:
Greene, G., *Lord Rochester's Monkey*, London, 1974

Percy Bysshe Shelley

Editions:
Hutchinson, T., *Poetical Works*, Oxford, 1970
Rogers, N., *Complete Poetical Works*, Oxford, 1972
Blunden, E., *Selected Poems*, London, 1973
Holloway, J., *Selected Poems*, London, 1960
Raine, K., *Selected Poems*, Harmondsworth, 1974
Spender, S., *Choice of Verse*, London, 1971
Webb, T., *Selected Poems*, London, 1977

Criticism:
Holmes, R., *Shelley: The Pursuit*, London, 1974

Sir Philip Sidney

Editions:
Ringler, W. A., *Poems*, Oxford, 1962
Bullett, G., *Silver Poets of the Sixteenth Century* (anthology),
London, 1967

Dorsten, J. A. van, *A Defence of Poetry*, Oxford, 1966
Evans, M., *Arcadia*, Harmondsworth, 1977
Jones, K. D., *Selected Poems*, Oxford, 1973
Shepherd, G., *An Apology for Poetry*, Manchester, 1964

Criticism:
Hamilton, A. C., *Sir Philip Sidney: A Study of his Life and Works*,
Cambridge, 1977

John Skelton

Editions:
Kinsman, R. S., *Poems*, Oxford, 1969
Henderson, P., *Complete Poems*, London, 1949

Criticism:
Pollet, M., *John Skelton: Poet of Tudor England*, London, 1971

Christopher Smart

Editions:
Callan, N., *Collected Poems* (2 vols) London, 1949
Walsh, M., *Selected Poems*, Manchester, 1972

Edmund Spenser

Editions:
Smith, J. C. and E. de Selincourt, *Poetical Works*, Oxford, 1970
Hamilton, A. C., *Selected Poetry*, New York, 1966
Hales, J. W., *The Faerie Queene* (2 vols), London, 1966
Henderson, P., *The Shepherd's Calendar and Other Poems*,
London, 1965

Criticism:
Renwick, E. S., *Edmund Spenser*, London, 1964

Henry Howard, Earl of Surrey

Editions:
Jones, E., *Poems*, Oxford, 1964
Bullett, G., *Silver Poets of the Sixteenth Century* (anthology),
London, 1967

Jonathan Swift

Editions:
Davis, H., *Poetical Works*, Oxford, 1967
Horrell, J., *Collected Poems* (2 vols), London, 1958
Williams, Sir H., *Poems* (3 vols), Oxford, 1958
Doren, C. van, *The Portable Jonathan Swift*, London, 1948
Sisson, C. H., *Selected Poems*, Manchester, 1977

Criticism:
Donoghue, D., *Jonathan Swift: A Critical Introduction*,
Cambridge, 1969
Quintana, R., *Swift: An Introduction*, London, 1966

Algernon Charles Swinburne

Editions:
Rosenberg. J. D., *Selected Poetry and Prose*, New York, 1968
Nye, R., *Choice of Verse*, London, 1973
Lang, C., *Letters* (6 vols), New Haven, 1959–1962

Criticism:
Henderson, P., *Swinburne: The Portrait of a Poet*, London, 1974

Alfred, Lord Tennyson

Editions:
——, *Complete Works*, Oxford, n. d.
Ricks, C., *Poems*, London, 1969
Blunden, E., *Selected Poems*, London, 1960
Cecil, Lord D., *Choice of Verse*, London, 1971
Jump, J. D., *In Memoriam, Maud and Other Poems*, London, 1975
Criticism:
Henderson, P., *Tennyson: Poet and Prophet*, London, 1978
Palmer, D., *Tennyson*, London, 1973
Ricks, C., *Tennyson*, London, 1972

James Thomson

Editions:
Robertson, J. L., *Poetical Works*, Oxford, n.d.
Ridler, A., *Poems and Some Letters*, London, 1963

Sambrook, J., *The Seasons and The Castle of Indolence*, Oxford, 1972

Henry Vaughan

Editions:
Rudrum, A., *Complete Poems*, Harmondsworth, 1976
Shaw, R. B., *Selected Poems*, Manchester, 1976

Criticism:
Bennett, J., *Five Metaphysical Poets*, Cambridge, 1966

William Wordsworth

Editions:
Hutchinson, T. (revised E. de Selincourt), *Poetical Works*, Oxford, 1969
Smith, D. N., *Poetry and Prose*, Oxford, 1973
Brett, R. L. and A. R. Jones, *W. W. and Coleridge: Lyrical Ballads*, London, 1968
Butt, J., *Selected Poetry and Prose*, Oxford, 1971
Maxwell, J. C., *The Prelude: A Parallel Text*, Harmondsworth, 1971
Roper, D., *W. W. and Coleridge: Lyrical Ballads*, London, 1968
Selincourt, E. de, *The Prelude*, Oxford, 1966
Sharrock, R., *Selected Poems*, London, 1968
Thomas, R. S., *A Choice of Verse*, London, 1971

Criticism:
Bateson, F. W., *Wordsworth, A Re-Interpretation*, London, 1968
Danby, J. F., *Simple Wordsworth*, London, 1960
Jones, J., *The Egotistical Sublime*, London, 1964

Sir Thomas Wyatt

Editions:
Muir, K., *Collected Poems*, London, 1963
Rebholz, R. A., *The Complete Poems*, Harmondsworth, 1978
Bullett, G., *Silver Poets of the Sixteenth Century* (anthology), London, 1967

Criticism:
Muir, K., *Sir Thomas Wyatt: Life and Letters*, Liverpool, 1963

Index